*International Congress of the P.E.N. Clubs,
34th, New York, 1966*

THE WRITER AS

INDEPENDENT SPIRIT,

Proceedings of the
XXXIV International P.E.N. Congress
June 12–June 18, 1966

New York City

PUBLISHER'S NOTE

This volume is composed of two identical texts, each presented under a separate title page. The first is a summary in English of the tape-recorded discussions which were held in P.E.N.'s two official languages, English and French. The second is a translation into French of the first.

NOTE DE L'EDITEUR

Ce volume est composé de deux textes identiques, chacun étant présenté sous un titre séparé. Le premier est un résumé en anglais des débats, en français et en anglais, les deux langues officialles du P.E.N., enregistrés sur bande magnétique. Le texte français se trouve à partir de la page 131.

Contents

Foreword

1. A WORD ON INTERNATIONAL P.E.N.

In the expectation that this book will come into the hands of readers unfamiliar with P.E.N., the following introductory remarks are offered.

The letters P.E.N. stand for *P*oets and playwrights, *E*ssayists and editors, and *N*ovelists. Today the essay is a dying art; half a century ago, when P.E.N. was founded, "essayists" seemed a convenient category under which to gather writers of every form of prose not narrowly subsumed under *belles lettres*. The fact is that the creative intellect and the creative imagination have joined in the greatest talents to produce works that are received and read as literature, however librarians may classify them. The philosopher Croce, in his day an international president of P.E.N., was as much a man of letters as his predecessor, the novelist Galsworthy. Today an important part of P.E.N.'s "essayist" membership is made up of admirable writers who devote their gifts to satisfying the world's insatiable thirst for information and enlightenment about the glories and miseries of our times. The short answer to the question "Who belongs to P.E.N.?" is in the P.E.N. Charter printed on a later page: ". . . all qualified writers, editors and translators" who subscribe to the aims defined in the Charter, "without regard to nationality, race, color or religion."

Some 8,000 writers make up the underlying membership of International P.E.N. They are grouped in 79 centers in 58 countries; more centers than countries, primarily because the world contains more cultures, more languages in which living literatures flourish, than states— even today. Thus we have three centers in Switzerland, four in the Yugoslav Federation, three in South Africa, a French Center and a Flemish Center in Belgium, an English and a French Center in Canada. We have a Yiddish Center, and we have a Writers-in-Exile Center; two centers on the vast Australian continent, and two in the United States. P.E.N. is represented in seven East European lands, in Africa, Latin America, and Asia. To name islands only—there are centers in New Zealand, Ceylon, Indonesia, Iceland, Ireland (Dublin and Belfast), Cuba, Jamaica, Puerto Rico. P.E.N. congresses have been held throughout Western Europe and twice in Yugoslavia; in Tokyo, Rio de Janeiro, and in New York. The 1967 congress will be held at Abidjan, in Ivory Coast.

P.E.N. was an idea born in the generous mind of an English novelist, Mrs. Catherine Dawson Scott, in 1921. It is not much remembered that the First World War, too, had its horrors and bred its hatreds, and that they, too, sobered men's minds—for a time. Mrs. Dawson Scott's idea was that the writers of the world should join together to further the efforts then being made to build an international order on a foundation of justice and with permanent peace as its objective. She took her idea to John Galsworthy, then at the height of his fame and powers. He saw its merit, and with the support of H. G. Wells and George Bernard Shaw among others, founded the English P.E.N. Center. Galsworthy persuaded Anatole France to accept the presidency of the French Center. Maurice Maeterlinck became an international vice-president. Thomas Mann presided over the German Center when it was formed. An International Secretariat was established in London (still its seat). Already in 1923 membership was wide enough to prompt the holding of the first international congress in London. When, the following year, the second congress was held in New York, twenty centers were represented. Forty-two years later, at the congress here reported, more than six hundred writers assembled from fifty-nine countries.

Mrs. Dawson Scott's objective was very much that of other great-hearted men and women of those postwar years—remote and abstract. But in the decade that followed, P.E.N. moved towards more concrete goals under both external and internal pressures. The first came from the suppression of freedom of expression, the burning of books, and the imprisonment and even "liquidation" of writers by increasingly savage totalitarian regimes. The second was the natural inclination of P.E.N. members, when they came together, to talk shop.

At the Dubrovnik Congress, in 1933, the delegates rejected a demand by the then Nazified German Center that anti-Nazi German members be not seated at the congress. The Nazis responded by withdrawing from International P.E.N. It was then that P.E.N. first organized the assistance it has continued to render refugee writers from many lands, the last great wave extending from the institution of Communist regimes in Eastern Europe in 1945–1948 through the aftermath of the Hungarian uprising of October-November 1956.

With this went continual intervention by P.E.N. in defense of writers imprisoned on trumped-up charges of "offenses against the state"— the modern form of *lèse majesté* or *Majestätsbeleidigung*—against which P.E.N. protests or, when the chances of obtaining results seem to recommend an alternative, intercedes on behalf of the accused. Czechoslovakia, East Germany, Hungary, Indonesia, Portugal, South Korea, the Soviet Union, Spain and Yugoslavia are among the countries whose authorities have been thus addressed, either through the respective P.E.N. centers or, where no center exists (as in Madrid and Moscow), through the national writers' union. This is a continuing function carried on by the association's Writers-in-Prison Committee, of which Miss Rosamond Lehmann is chairman.

As for P.E.N.'s professional concerns, it is understandable that meetings of individual centers should be devoted mainly to matters of special interest to the local literary community while International P.E.N. deals with problems of universal literary interest. Here are some "themes" put before international meetings:

The Art of Prose	The Theatre in Our Time
Criticism	The Author and the Public
Translation	Literature in the Age of Science
The Writer and Semantics	The Writer and the Cinema
Tradition and Innovation	Intellectuals in the Contemporary World
Youth and Literature	The Writer and Society

Among its other activities, the International Secretariat publishes *Arena,* a magazine devoted to translations into English of current writing in languages of limited diffusion, and an annual anthology of P.E.N. poets; it recommends every year to UNESCO works in languages with a limited reading public for translation into French and English; its International Writers Fund awards annual prizes for writing in those languages, the translation of which into English it assures.

Finally, it should be said that P.E.N. is the only worldwide association of writers that exists. Governments, UNESCO, and the press recognize it as the spokesman for the universal literary community.

2. THE NEW YORK CONGRESS

At the closing session M. Roger Caillois, director of the Literature Section of UNESCO, remarked with satisfaction on the "ecumenism" of a congress which, including observers from eleven countries still without P.E.N. centers, embraced sixty writers from fifteen Asian lands (four delegates from Israel), twenty-three from seven Latin-American republics, and nine from five of the sub-Saharan states of Africa. Twenty-six delegates were present from the seven East-Central European centers, among them four from the P.E.N. *Zentrum Ost und West,* in East

Berlin. We record with regret that the passports of three Czechoslovak delegates were recalled, and the visit of six observers from the Soviet Writers' Union was abruptly canceled, on the eve of the congress; equally disappointing was the failure of the Cuban P.E.N. Center to acknowledge the host center's two successive invitations. The *Zentrum Ost und West* having offered a resolution intended to forbid the holding of a P.E.N. congress in any country to which P.E.N. members were denied entry, the American Center obtained its assent to the following substitute motion which was passed unanimously by the International Executive Commitee:

International P.E.N. deplores measures taken by any government which have the effect of preventing P.E.N. members from leaving their own country or entering a foreign country in response to an invitation to attend a P.E.N. congress, a meeting of the International Executive Committee, or any other meeting called under the auspices of P.E.N.

For P.E.N. to "deplore" is to recognize that it cannot impose its will on sovereign governments. But the resolution serves notice that P.E.N. will not meet in countries where these conditions are not satisfied. It is worthy of note that they were fully satisfied by the Johnson Administration.

The keynote of the congress was struck by Arthur Miller in these words excerpted from his presidential address:

None of us comes here as a representative of his government. None of us is obliged to speak as an apologist for his culture or his political system. In this congress, as in previous ones, the devout Communist, the militant anti-Communist, the apolitical, the anarchist, the Catholic, the Jew, the Protestant, Buddhist or Mohammedan, the realist, the surrealist, the drunk and the sober leave behind the categories and turn their attention to the one problem which all of us share as human beings—the nurturing of culture. And I mean by culture the faithful and profound rendering of the writer's awareness of his reality. Deprived of this kind of accounting, men lose their past, cannot deal with the present, and betray their future.

P.E.N. is resolutely apolitical. It is not to be inferred from this, however, that political views are not intruded into its debates. In 1965 for example, at the Bled Congress, a resolution pleading for a cessation of hostilities in Vietnam was offered by the Japanese delegation. Although the overwhelming majority of delegates present were individually favorable to the substance of the resolution, it was ruled out of order on the grounds that this political motion had no place in the deliberations of a literary body. In New York, a resolution against nuclear armament was moved by the distinguished President of the Greek

Center and not found receivable; the decision was protested by the Bulgarian and Yugoslav delegations.

At the New York congress, in the give-and-take of discussion during the working sessions, delegates found themselves moved by their sentiments to make political points. Our colleagues from Vietnam, from the Taipei Center, from South Korea, from Thailand, speaking out of full hearts and with entire dignity, referred to matters understandably near to them. The well-loved Ignazio Silone, a lifelong fighter against injustice and inhumanity, made an impeccably argued statement in which his political position was not disguised. Pablo Neruda, equally a lover of justice and humanity, retorted with perfect courtesy and firmness. The talented Valery Tarsis, new to P.E.N. and perhaps unaware of its traditions, chose to exceed the bounds of propriety by personal references and by calling for a resumption of hot war against the Soviet Union ("against ideology" he later explained). It did not please the assembled delegates and drew from the anti-Communist Writers-in-Exile Center the following statement:

The Center of the Writers-in-Exile is composed of members of various political and philosophical beliefs. The views of Valery Tarsis, who is a member of the center's London branch, expressed after the Round Table IV meeting on Friday, June 17, do not necessarily agree with those of other members. After Mr. Tarsis' public pronouncements, which do not correspond with the best interests of our organization, contradict its basic objectives, and do harm to the cause it is fighting for, his membership has been strongly questioned by other members of our organization.

Those who may have feared that intrusion into the field of politics would come from the Communist delegations will be interested to observe that they were initiated from the anti-Communist side, Pablo Neruda and Dr. Kamnitzer responding.

This volume takes its title from the overall theme of the congress— *The Writer as Independent Spirit.* A P.E.N. congress theme requires the approval of the International Executive Committee. It is to the honor of International P.E.N. that in its governing body, where writers from nearly threescore states of varying social systems sit side by side, no voice was raised to express doubt of the *bona fides* of the host center in proposing a theme that might at first blush seem to some provocative. The Program Note on the theme, printed on pages xxv-xxvii hereof, displays clearly enough that the congress was asked to deal with certain new technological, economic and social phenomena and to consider to what extent these insistent forces contained potential threats to the writer's independence.

If this theme was at no time challenged during the congress, the reason was that it was responsive to the innate impulse in every true writer to be free to express his own experience of life and response to that experience. P.E.N. members, meanwhile, hold that diversity of philosophical beliefs and social aims is a concomitant of the individual writer's freedom to write and to publish.

Readers will observe in perusing the program annexed to the Proceedings that the organizers made room for only two set speeches. One was Arthur Miller's presidential address. The other was Saul Bellow's brilliant and unreserved assault on what he saw as the efforts of the literature faculties of the American and British universities to capture and make their own—where once they had repulsed and anathematized—living literature. Those speeches apart, the congress took the form of Round Tables at each of which ten participants discussed a given sub-theme, their discussions being followed by interpellations from the floor. In all, our Index of (identifiable) speakers indicates that 116 delegates and guests were able to make their views known.

This format (as we say in the United States) was adopted in order to avoid the inspissated boredom that tends to result from the reading of a merciless succession of papers, day after day, while the power of attention of the audience grows every day more feeble. To this extent it was undoubtedly a success. It was also adopted in the reasonable expectation that the sessions would be enlivened by a running debate between the participants. Here the results varied from table to table.

Round Table I, with Professor Marshall McLuhan in the chair, had for its subject *The Writer in the Electronic Age.* Mr. McLuhan succeeded with his usual debating skill in stirring up his fellow "discussants" (to use a cant term of our universities); and if he talked rather more than a chairman is expected to do, the fault was not his. With few exceptions, his fellows at the table saw in him what he certainly professed not to be—the enemy of the book; some even of the free spirit; and the debate that ensued went on almost altogether with him on one side and them on the other.

Many delegates were stung by the subject and it was repeatedly referred to at other sessions. Writers from the newly industrialized states, where literacy remains limited and book publishing may be said to be in its infancy, thought it peculiarly "Western" and of no concern to them. Europeans found the American writers excessively frightened of this ogre, though only Miss Nott appeared to have studied the subject seriously and only M. Gandon to have written about it satirically. (Buckminster Fuller, who really knew the subject as engineer and seer, sat aloof from a discussion which to him may have seemed beside the point.) M. Caillois, speaking at the closing session of the congress, corrected a misapprehension: he had heard almost superstitious fears of electronic deviltry expressed by Europeans at a colloquium of Les Rencontres Internationales in Geneva. It did on the whole seem clear, however, that Mr. McLuhan was taken less seriously by the Europeans than by the American and British participants.

M. Louis Martin-Chauffier presided over the second Round Table. Here the question was— Were or were not the "human sciences" threatening to oust literature from its immemorial role as the supreme delineator of the spiritual nature of man? Was literature becoming a "secondary source" of our knowledge of man's soul? More than once, the distinguished chairman found himself begging his colleagues to carry on a dialogue and cease from pronouncing monologues. M. Ellison early furnished them a chance to do so in a challenging statement in which he declared roundly that the new sociology and the new psychology were offering themselves as a "substitute for art"; that the sociologist had become the "manipulator" of a "mythology" of his own creation; and that, instead of looking within themselves, and looking to the insights of the accumulated body of literature to learn what man was, writers themselves were "abandoning belief in art" and taking their notions of man from these scientists.

Dr. Parres, a psychiatrist, admitted that Dostoevsky had "written more memorably about aggression" than any scientist had done. M. Nadeau, the historian of Surrealism, said that Shakespeare in one age and Balzac in another were "practising psychology before the science of psychology existed." There was wide agreement on the paramountcy of art; but Mme. Mileva appeared to put society ahead of the person as the writer's subject, Dr. Kamnitzer pointed to "the human species" as today's Hamlet, the majority were clearly against withdrawal into the "ivory tower," clearly of opinion that writers had much to learn from the sciences, though agreeing with Mr. Petroveanu's view that when literature made use of scientific concepts its "human implications" outlived whatever scientific theories it employed. There was no mention of the contemporary scientists whose theories have of late strongly influenced writing in its formal as well as social aspects— the philologists Jakobson and Saussure, the anthropologist Levi-Strauss, the Marxist sociologist Althusser, for example.

M. Robert Goffin's table had before it a theme that was not instantly self-explanatory—*The Writer as Collaborator in Other Men's Purposes*. Three clarifying questions were asked. Was it true that the publisher, the magazine editor, the producer (cinema, television, the theatre) were imposing degrees of conformity which require a surrender of the writer's independence? That as a consequence bad writing was driving out good? That the insatiable demand for information about our times was drawing creative talents into writing that called upon their skill rather than their insight and imagination? The poet-chairman began by inquiring prudently what his colleagues thought this added up to, and got a variety of answers.

But if the theme was ill-phrased, the discussions generated heat and the participants knew what they were talking about. The notion that the immense growth in "informational" writing had lured authors away from the production of works of the imagination did not win general assent.* Mr. Jovanovich observed that "the disappearance of literary forms was not a new thing" and that if the novel were to disappear "it would not be because other men than writers had driven it out." Miss Lehmann did not believe that writers had to write in response to public demand. Creative writers wrote under "some imaginative compulsion"; they had to do what they were doing, and did it without thought of the reader. Mr. Lasky found himself recalling a word learnt in Heidelberg: *Janein*, "yesno." Dostoevsky may have been inspired by a newspaper cutting to write *Crime and Punishment,* as Capote had been to write *In Cold Blood;* even so, what Capote wrote was "high journalism" (which Lasky preferred to "low art"); it was not what Saul Bellow had called for in his address—"an imaginative response to a problem of life."

Did publishers and editors assume extraordinary prerogatives? When he recalled that writers and publishers had always had their differences, Mr. Lasky was tempted to say no. But this question could not be answered without relating it to the third question: was bad writing driving out good? Good writing had always been uncommon; one might again answer no. Yet it was a fact that editors were "tampering" with copy; and that they did so implied "a lack of respect for words and for the writer's independence." In America, magazine English had become "stupefying and degenerate" to the point where thinking and deciding about serious problems had become literally impossible (he quoted examples). The chairman had been present when, in

---

* At the "electronic" table Mr. Podhoretz had referred with approval to the suggestion of the essayist, Paul Goodman, that if television took over information altogether it would relieve literature of a burden.

New York a quarter of a century ago, Maeterlinck had been asked to revise his text because, "Though you know what you want to say, we know what our readers want to read." Mr. Hope-Wallace confirmed that, in London, editing in the interest of "house style" was widely practiced; the bad writing that resulted was a product of "bad thinking and untruthfulness." Digging deeper, Mr. Lucie-Smith said (like Confucius before him) that a sick language meant a sick society. On the other hand, Mr. Jovanovich declared that writing in America had never been so good as now; Mme. de Sainte-Soline asserted that the modern French novel was written with a meticulousness not to be found in the hastily scribbled, incident-filled old-fashioned novels of the last century. Publishers, she said, did commission books; and writers were happy enough to accept their proposals.

For Mr. Jovanovich, the implication in the words "other men's purposes" was that the writer was being "sentimental about himself." M. Bloch-Michel and Mme. de Sainte-Soline agreed. The cinema and television, said M. Bloch-Michel, were art forms which inescapably influenced those who chose (they were not forced) to write for them; indeed, they were forms which, paradoxically, we had seen influencing the writing of literature itself. Television, said Mme. de Sainte-Soline, did a better job depicting the Paris Markets than Zola in *Le ventre de Paris;* and when novels were no longer a source of information about society, their scene shrunken to a single room, or a bed, their characters restricted to one or two or three people, television was left to fill the vacuum. Mr. Sternberger pointed out that there were other kinds of masters than the employer of a writer. There was government, doctrine, commitment. In West Germany, Socialist members of the celebrated Gruppe 47 had voluntarily written for their party during the last elections. John Locke had served a cause of his own volition; Milton, too. Dante had sought to help the Emperor Henry VII unify the Holy Roman Empire against the Papacy. Meanwhile, in the media mentioned, the rule was teamwork, the essence of which is collaboration. Mr. Hope-Wallace put it that curtailment of the writer's role was a condition of the art of television; he was "writing for people who were not reading." This, with M. Bloch-Michel's exposition, appeared to answer decisively in the negative Mr. Milano's shrewd question—whether there was anything *inherent* in the mass medium that hampered the writer's freedom.

Mr. Herzfelde believed that collaboration was honorable where there was a "common conviction" between those who collaborated. Mr. Keene pointed to willing collaborators: Auden and Stravinsky, Queneau and Butor with their book designers, translators of poetry with those who "possess" the languages (he did not refer specifically to the common practice of the finest American poets who translate Russian poetry with the aid of intermediaries who coach them in Russian metaphors, symbols, intonation, metric conventions, breaches of convention).

Before the participants rose they heard from Mr. Florentino, of the Philippine Republic, of a world in which the writer's problem bore no relation to what they had been discussing; it was the problem of literacy, of an electric lamp to read under, a market for the publisher. And from their chairman they heard a plea for translation of works from the "less favored languages"—a "salutary reminder" as Mr. Lucie-Smith emphasized.

It was at Professor Douglas Young's table on *The Writer as Public Figure* that the controversial political views reported on an earlier page had been aired. Those views will be read in the text and require no restatement here, though it may be noted that, speaking in rebuttal, Mr. Silone said that his concern had been to oppose "the theory of the intellectual as the servant of a higher power." Far from seeking to revive the cold war, he favored the entry of Soviet and Chinese writers into this free association where the life of literature was frankly discussed without mental reservation and with mutual respect.

Only Miss Lehmann was at pains to speak directly to the theme before the table from the point of view of the writer's function and career. Quoting W. H. Auden's lines, "Private faces in public places are nicer than public faces in private places," she said that privacy, not publicity, was her preference. For a writer to be interviewed on his opinion of public events, and to appear on lecture tours and the television screen, seemed to her to risk encouragement of the belief that one's views were important. "Great writers had often had foolish opinions." A writer's *raison d'être* was to write; his time should preferably be spent "absorbing without having to give out," using what Keats had called his "negative capability." One proper theme for a P.E.N. round table might be "the writer as silent figure": twenty minutes of absolute silence, each writer at the table being limited to a single sentence. She was persuaded that very good ideas might come out of that.

Miss Lehmann had obviously not been offended by the question whether militant advocacy of an ideology might endow the writer with a public *persona* which would tempt him to act a part. Others who spoke on this formulation were quick to reject it, though particular instances were condemned, as when M. Follain severely arraigned

Maurice Barrès' sadistic exaltation of evisceration by bayonet as appropriate treatment of the German enemy in the war of 1914–1918.

Concerning the question, does the "ideology" of a classic writer play a part in the value we now lend his work—the anti-papal Dante, the humanitarian Hugo, the elitist Stefan George—only M. Caillois, speaking at the closing session of the congress, found it worthy of examination. The preferred subject round the table was "commitment": What did it signify? Was it an absolute danger? A danger at all for the writer (by which was generally meant the poet, playwright or novelist)?

A broad definition was furnished by Mr. Lovinescu who described as committed every writer who had not lost his faith in man, and as uncommitted those who refused to believe in the possibility of a human order. He stressed that commitment did not mean for him a "beatific and grandiloquent optimism" but rather a severe, sometimes despairing, and noble discipline. This was not to say that truth was not to be found in the works of uncommitted writers. Though himself "structurally a committed writer" he had to recognize that in our times some of the most anguishing cries and most authentic portrayals of human frailty had come from writers who had lost all faith, even in art.

On the whole, it may be inferred from what went on that Mr. Lovinescu's definition was found acceptable. With one exception, all participants were "believers," and even Mr. Bell appeared to believe in philosophic doubt. Mr. Bell was alone in condemning public commitment as commonly conceived in the great debates on current questions. Nobody quoted Luther ("God help me, I can do no other") and Mr. Bell did not quote that greatly committed dictator, Cromwell ("I beseech ye, gentlemen, by the bowels of Christ, bethink ye that ye may be mistaken"). Mr. Bell began by saying that since the time when man's experience was substituted for revelation and tradition as the source of his explanation of himself and his world, man had been living in a state of tension between self and society. In the modern world his "I" or ego had been subjected to various lures—power, ideology, self-righteous moralizing—which he had rationalized by the idea of commitment. It was important that a writer should say, "I feel the truth, I see it, I must speak it." But when he spoke in this way he was not only expressing a thought, he was pronouncing an affirmation. He was like a man running down the street shouting, "I've got an answer, who's got a question?" If his answer was not the product of a necessary degree of knowledge, judgment, and attitude of mind then the risk was that his commitment was no more than a belief. Beliefs were not to be disdained, but they were not necessarily truths. In Mr. Bell's view, the writer's role as public figure was essentially to test faith, test commitment; and remain in a state of doubt.

Mr. Bell was heard with respect, but he seems to have won no converts. Mr. den Doolaard, who had begun by saying that "commitment and writing are frequently two facets of the same personality" and that he did not like the implication he saw in the Program Note that commitment might be undesirable, did not contradict himself when he later said, "Let the writer commit himself to writing; thereafter he can support causes." Mr. Datta (who had reminded Mr. Bell that a man who had no beliefs was not a man at all), spoke his own mind when he said that "one should write the best poem possible and hope for an audience." His impression was that he stood between Westerners who found it hard to commit themselves and Easterners from lands where "commitment had gone to extremes."

Much of the discussion that ensued moved around the involvement of the writer in society and his role among his own people, not as nationalist but as a fellow of human beings to whom he was closest. Mr. Illyés, declaring his belief in the writer as teacher, went on to say that "we write for those who suffer as we suffer, and who ask for beauty as their remedy." Mr. Choi regretted that the younger Korean writers were abandoning "unconscious commitment"—the good kind—by tending to "depart from the attitude of closeness to their people." Pablo Neruda said that the poor in Latin America called upon writers, in effect, to "talk in the name of those who cannot write." He avowed himself a "fully committed poet"; call him a propagandist, he was one as Whitman and Hugo had been propagandists. "If the poet did not make himself the spokesman of the human condition, what else was there for him to do?" Mr. Tseng pointed out that Confucius had not willed to become a public figure; his writings, attracting 3,000 students, had made him one. Mr. Coutsoheras said that literature, the fruit of the social climate, "was itself a sort of public person." Mr. Csokor distinguished between three kinds of art: pure, committed, directed. Commitment was, as Gide had said, a factor—conscience—in the writer's being, which was aroused to response by given events. In religious art we saw directed art that was unobjectionable. In the sense that art provided men with a "central purpose" without which their lives would be empty "genuine art was always committed." The worst director of art, however, was the collectivity.

Not everybody agreed with the last dictum. Mme. Kamenova defined the writer as "a warrior on the social stage" who could not be absolutely independent because he was answerable to his people and had a duty to avoid pessimism, create "positive" characters, and point the way to a bright future. Mr. Csokor's compatriot, Miss Spiel, admired writers who took an independent political stand; not those who adopted other men's views. She asked that the writer resist a demand for commitment, but only on the grounds of principle, as Koestler and Sartre had done. Mr. Anoma Kanie believed that as a member of the human family the writer had an obligation to combat tyranny and to spread love and mutual understanding. Mr. Nghiem Xuan Viet saw the writer as artist and as fighter, judging him in the first role according to his contribution to beauty, in the second according to his sincerity; and adding that "a sincere writer might be mistaken in his faith." Valid commitment, said Mr. Herzfelde, was a matter of whom one was committed to fight against, fascists or non-fascists. P.E.N. had to be antifascist. (Mr. Tseng, in his political remarks, had held that in Mainland China there could be no intellectual honesty "so long as those fascist forces continue to exist.")

Arthur Miller was twice called upon by the chairman of the Round Table. At the morning session he began by saying that he would try to avoid abstractions and speak only out of his own experience. The fact that Brecht and Neruda were committed writers whose art could not be seriously questioned indicated that there was "something wrong with the question." * Mr. Miller had known American writers who had committed themselves publicly, signing manifestos, speaking at meetings, and yet no evidence of commitment could be found in their writings. He had known others who had never taken a public stand and whose works, nevertheless, indicated clear support of this or that concept of human society. As for himself, he had from time to time committed himself publicly and had written to express his commitment: "It has been in the blood and bone of my writing." He did not believe that his writing was either better or worse for that fact.

Mr. Miller believed that there existed an "implacable pressure on literature" to address itself to what is pertinent to the reader and to the public sitting in the theatre. When writers were "swept by their vision of something wrong in the world" there was no "either/or" about it; they were impelled from within to support or attack. He agreed that the writer could be "as stupid and foolish as anyone else in his political views." But it was the writer's role to express that "naked, naive, genu-

* Astonishingly, no Irish, British or American writer brought up the name of Yeats, Pound, Eliot or Wyndham Lewis, each in his own way a species of "reactionary."

ine response to reality" which men could hope to find only in literature. "The writer who is led into himself by his commitment is helped by that commitment. The writer who is led away from himself by his commitment is hurt by it."

When he spoke again Mr. Miller said *inter alia:* "The purpose of those present in speaking of the writer as a public figure is to save the writer from compulsion, from yielding to viewpoints that have not been given him by his spirit." Whether he should or should not commit himself was a matter of personal choice. "What I am pleading for," Mr. Miller went on, "is a certain toleration based on the fact and the knowledge that men in one country are in a different situation from men in another country. We, most of all, in P.E.N., should appreciate that fact, cling to it, believing in the good faith of one another and in a common wish to universalize our association; for it will do us no good if we do not grow in wisdom."

Mr. Bell, asked by the chairman to conclude the discussion, said that the writer knew truth only through his experience of life, and as his experience was incomplete, he could not know total truth. As for belief, it had to be tested in the light of the bewilderingly various realities of our complex civilization. Mr. Bell reiterated that doubt had "a prior claim."

This congress, he concluded, had sought to do what all intellectuals seek to do—to contribute to an open society. By open discussion its participants had sought to arrive at an understanding of one another. Commitment to the writer's vocation had here replaced commitment to ideology, to dogma.

The Latin-American session was unforeseen, and gave great satisfaction. Generous donors had enabled American P.E.N. to arrange for the presence of a distinguished representation from the great southern continent. Those writers, who rarely met (unless in Paris, which is still their cultural capital), had much to say to each other. At Arthur Miller's suggestion, they decided to say it in the presence of the entire congress. Like their meeting itself, their subject was *hors série;* they did not discuss the congress theme, they discussed their own problems, talking with a degree of feeling and sober realism which absorbed and deeply moved those who heard them.

At the closing session Mr. Silone, having expressed the thanks of all delegates for the style and warmth with which they had been welcomed, said that he was particularly glad to recall that what he himself had said had given rise to protest. If there was one thing he detested, it was a forced unanimity which was often meant to hide a real diversity of views. He and his Italian colleagues had, a day or two earlier, been interviewed on behalf of the Italian radio. They had been at special pains to stress the full freedom of utterance which had characterized this congress.

Lewis Galantière

New York
July 1967

P.E.N. Charter

The P.E.N. club affirms that:—

1. Literature, national though it be in origin, knows no frontiers, and should remain common currency between nations in spite of political or international upheavals.

2. In all circumstances, and particularly in time of war, works of art, the patrimony of humanity at large, should be left untouched by national or political passion.

3. Members of the P.E.N. should at all times use what influence they have in favor of good understanding and mutual respect between nations; they pledge themselves to do their utmost to dispel race, class and national hatreds and to champion the ideal of one humanity living in peace in one world.

4. The P.E.N. stands for the principle of unhampered transmission of thought within each nation and between all nations, and members pledge themselves to oppose any form of suppression of freedom of expression in the country and community to which they belong. The P.E.N. declares for a free press and opposes arbitrary censorship in time of peace. It believes that the necessary advance of the world towards a more highly organized political and economic order renders a free criticism of governments, administrations and institutions imperative. And since freedom implies voluntary restraint, members pledge themselves to oppose such evils of a free press as mendacious publication, deliberate falsehood and distortion of facts for political and personal ends.

Membership of the P.E.N. is open to all qualified writers, editors and translators who subscribe to these aims, without regard to nationality, race, color or religion.

The Writer as Independent Spirit

The overall theme of the New York Congress is *The Writer as Independent Spirit*. The purpose of this note is to make that theme explicit.

We should exaggerate if we said that all writers today felt that their independence as creative artists was threatened. Nevertheless, all writers, creative and other, participate in the malaise that reigns throughout the world. More than other men, they are in search of themselves, and they strive to discern a pattern in the life of our times. Their heads resound with such words as anxiety, alienation, the absurd, mimesis, cybernetics. They circle uneasily round their respective ideologies. They are aware that they live in a world administered by vast impersonal bureaucracies, public in some countries, a mixture of public and private in others, and they suspect that this phenomenon holds a special meaning for the writer, the intellectual inquirer and the artist. The Master of the King's Revels is now a minister of culture—unless, as in the United States, his function is shared among heads of rich foundations. There is gigantism in the university as in industry, in book publishing as in the electronic media, in magazine production as in human habitation.

To the American committee which met in New York in February and March of 1966 to draft the program of the New York Congress it seemed that a congress was something more than a colloquium; that when some five hundred writers from forty or more countries met, they would wish to speak and hear about subjects that concerned them universally. Our *ad hoc* committee chose *The Writer as Independent Spirit* as such a subject. It reflects their concern with forces which today may contain elements of menace, more insidious than censorship and dogmatism, to the writer's realization of his conception of his function and purpose. Our subject, or theme, having received the approval of the International President and the International Executive Committee, will be discussed at Round Tables, and open to comment from the floor, under the rubrics which follow.

I · THE WRITER IN THE ELECTRONIC AGE

Until the other day, "communication" meant to the writer mass culture, which was commonly discussed in terms of its effect, for good or for ill, upon what we have thought of traditionally as the culture of humanism. Today, linguists, social anthropologists, experts in "xerography" and prophets have entered the field. A "theory of communications" is being sought. The relations between verbal, visual and auditive communication are being studied. What is promised is not only the end of the printing press but a dissolution of the individual consciousness in a "cosmic consciousness." It is not inconceivable that the book will vanish; but what will be the role of the writer as independent spirit in that *saeculum felix et aureum?*

II · LITERATURE AND THE HUMAN SCIENCES ON THE NATURE OF CONTEMPORARY MAN

From time immemorial men have looked to the poet, the playwright, the essayist—in the past two centuries the novelist—to illumine for them the nature and spirit of man. Not measurement, analysis, investigation, but contemplation, self-knowledge, the creative imagination were sources of the works which cast that light. Today, it is suggested, men are turning away from literature to the social sciences and to psychology to learn what man—at least contemporary man—essentially is. We ask: is it true that literature is becoming a secondary source? that writers themselves are taking their ideas of man from the newer disciplines? that they tend to make society, indeed social problems, their subject, rather than man himself *sub specie aeternitatis?* If true, is there here a surrender of the writer's role as independent spirit?

III · THE WRITER AS COLLABORATOR IN OTHER MEN'S PURPOSES

The new literacy and the new media of communication have added new provinces to the universal republic of letters. The new reading public asks to be informed. The market for high-grade vulgarization has greatly expanded. What was once the occupation of the miserably paid hack, the *écrivain à gages,* has become the craft of skillful and respected writers. The document has almost done away with the essay and begins to supersede the novel. This, it is said, has the result that the magazine editor dictates the vocabulary, imposes a "house style," and decides what his contributors shall write—or, more likely, report on. The publisher, we are told, "originates" more and more books which call upon the skill but not upon the deeper resources of those who are commissioned to write them. The belle-lettrists form a progressively smaller minority in the community of writers.

We ask three questions: 1. Given the popularity of the "document," how does the domain of literature differ today from the wide field cultivated by Sainte-Beuve a century ago? 2. Have the book publisher and the magazine editor assumed prerogatives which do in fact trespass upon the writer's creative independence? 3. Does evidence exist that Gresham's Law (bad money drives out good) is operating; that bad writing is in fact now driving out good writing? Evidence that bad usage is driving out good usage in the written language?

IV · THE WRITER AS PUBLIC FIGURE

A very great English poet, Wordsworth (1770–1850), maturing in a time of turbulence, was terrified of social reform. Flaubert, unlike his friend George Sand, was anti-socialist in 1848. Neither committed himself publicly. On the other hand, in other times as in our own, examples of public commitment abound, both to simple humanitarianism and to rigorous ideology, out of sentiment and out of intellectual conviction. We see today in certain countries writers who demand freedom from political involvement and in others writers who take advantage of civic freedom to engage in political involvement. The question arises: does the committed writer's adoption of a public *persona* seduce him into the abandonment of his independence as a creative artist? Or is it through commitment that he makes himself "the amanuensis of the *Zeitgeist*"? Secondly, is it because of the light they shed on the spirit of man that we prize the works of a classic author, or is it because of the position he took for or against a significant thesis or movement of his age?

THE WRITER AS INDEPENDENT SPIRIT

Inaugural Session

Mr. Lewis Galantière (Chairman of the Congress): President Miller, Secretary General Carver, Chancellor Niles, Saul Bellow, distinguished guests from many lands, ladies and gentlemen of International P.E.N. —as president of P.E.N. American Center, the honor falls to me to bid you welcome on the occasion of the Thirty-fourth International P.E.N. Congress.

Before opening the proceedings of the congress I should like to read this telegram from the Mayor of the City of New York. Mayor Lindsay says:

Since I read occasionally, and fancy myself as a plain or garden variety of factual writer, I would enjoy some literary companionship. But the problems in this town seem to pile ever higher. In short, I cannot attend, but I do wish to extend my personal and official regards to your delegates, particularly those from abroad. And my best wishes for discordant, abrasive and thoroughly creative sessions.

I have also to read a letter from the Governor of the State of New York who writes to me:

As you are aware, prior commitments have made it impossible to be present in person at the opening session of the Thirty-fourth International P.E.N. Congress. I take this means therefore of saying to your distinguished colleagues that it is an honor to welcome them to the State of New York.

I am acquainted with the long record of International P.E.N. in defense of freedom of thought and expression. The central theme of the congress, *The Writer as Independent Spirit*, strikes me as most timely. The problem presented by one of your topics, *The Writer as Public Figure*, seems to me particularly acute in our day and I shall be interested to learn what emerges from your discussion of it.

It is above all because of my conviction of the importance of the writer's role as cross-fertilizer of cultures and civilization, and as promoter of world understanding that your congress interests me as Governor of this State.

Governor Rockefeller closes with his best wishes for a congenial and fruitful meeting.

We have had messages of good will from Kenneth Holland, president of the Institute of International Education, on behalf of himself and his staff, and from Henry Fischbach, president of the American Translators Association and a vice-president of the International Federation of Translators. I thank them both, as I do the Mayor and the Governor, in your name.

In February, I had the honor of inviting to the congress one of our international vice-presidents, the eminent philosopher, His Excellency the President of the Republic of India, Sir S. Radhakrishnan. He regretted that he would not be able to attend, and wrote: "I hope you will understand my commitments here and forgive me." Naturally, we do all understand. President Radhakrishnan has, however, sent us a special message by Madam Wadia, Founder of the All-India P.E.N. Center.

Madam Wadia, paraphrasing, said that President Radhakrishnan asked us to have the courage of our convictions and to voice them with all firmness and fearlessness, yet retaining the mellowing quality not just of tolerance but of acceptance and understanding of other points of view. In this troubled world we had many problems to face; he hoped that we would face them with the courage of the independent spirit that lived in each of us and must be heard in all we wrote.

Mr. Galantière, having thanked Madam Wadia, said that since P.E.N.'s two official languages were French and English, and since all speakers at this session would be using English, it was fitting that the representative of the host center use French.

It was in French, therefore, that he introduced the next speaker, Chancellor Niles, who addressed the congress on behalf of President Hester, of New York University. American P.E.N. owed much to the generosity with which the university had made available the extraordinarily well-equipped building in which they found themselves, the comfortable yet moderately priced student residences in which some five hundred delegates and those accompanying them were lodged, and the courteous and efficient staffs that were looking after their comfort.

Chancellor Niles spoke most interestingly about the growth of his university, which was founded in 1830, and its place in the cultural life of New York City; he closed by transmitting President Hester's wishes for a successful conference.

Continuing in French, *Mr. Galantière* introduced the Honorable Roger L. Stevens, chairman of the recently established National Council on the Arts and the Humanities. The Council was a public body, a creation of the United States Congress, established to supplement the support given by private institutions to literature and the arts, and to humanistic studies, in the United States. American P.E.N. was grateful for the assistance it had received and the liberty accorded it in the use of that assistance, in the organization of this congress.

Mr. Stevens said that the Council had been happy to play its part in making the congress possible. His own pleasure was the greater for finding himself in the midst of so many world-renowned writers. We lived in a time, happily, when the fame of a writer was not confined to his own country. St. John Perse had been translated into English, so had the great Urdu poet, Faiz Ahmed Faiz. John Steinbeck was only one of many American writers who were read in Russian. In the western hemisphere "Pablo Neruda, a giant of modern literature," had a great influence on the younger poets of the United States. Perhaps Shelley had been mistaken when he wrote that poets were the unacknowledged legislators of mankind, yet Mr. Stevens believed that "writers articulate the conscience of mankind and are in the front rank of those to whom we look for its ways of salvation."

Mr. Stevens then read the following message from the President of the United States:

It is a great pleasure for me, on behalf of the people of the United States, to extend to the members of P.E.N. International a warm welcome to our country. We are honored by your choice of the United States as the place of assembly for your Thirty-fourth Congress. Your worldwide association and its members have had a distinguished history during which time you have contributed unceasingly to the preservation of freedom of expression and the interchange of every writer's art.

The theme of your current congress, *The Writer as Independent Spirit,* is a most appropriate one, for I believe it defines the concern of writers everywhere. The world has always known times when the transmission of thought, as your charter puts it, has been threatened. It has known eras when the free exchange of ideas has been impossible. Yet the most powerful and noble movements of contemporary history are those on the side of removing the restrictions that weigh down the writer's creative spirit, and that impede his communication with his fellows in all lands.

Your meeting in the United States is a symbol of this great movement of the human spirit, and we Americans are proud to be your hosts. [Signed] Lyndon B. Johnson.

Thanking Mr. Stevens for his perceptive recognition of the role of the writer and for bringing to the congress the welcome of the President of the United States, *Mr. Galantière* introduced the international president of P.E.N., Arthur Miller. Mr. Miller's address, he said, would be followed by an address by Saul Bellow.

Address of the International President

Since this is the first P.E.N. congress at which, strictly speaking, I have the honor of presiding, I feel I am still in a position to ask your forbearance; my grasp of parliamentary procedure is about as steady as my French. But perhaps I can make up for these failings with the virtue of brevity, which, in a gathering of writers, is far more than the soul of wit; it is next to impossible.

First, I wish to express my personal regret that my predecessor, the Dutch poet Victor van Vriesland, has been prevented by his ill health from attending this congress. I know you will join me in sending him our affectionate good wishes.

We are a much-welcomed assembly. The head of the American Center, Lewis Galantière, has welcomed us, the Chancellor of New York University has opened to us these handsome and wonderfully equipped premises; Governor Rockefeller has put in a warm word for the State of New York, Mayor Lindsay for the City, and Roger Stevens for the United States Government. It is a pleasant duty to return thanks on your behalf.

The last P.E.N. gathering on American soil took place forty-two years ago, so I cannot vouch for what went on then. I imagine the delegates at that time regarded the organization as an attempt to create a sort of Republic of Letters. It seems fairly certain that in those days literary questions were still literary questions, just as an innovation in engineering or physics was still a purely scientific affair. In these forty-two years, however, revolution and counter-revolution and almost uninterrupted warfare, have impregnated every human activity with the question of the validity and prestige of competing social systems and nationalisms. Only from the viewpoint of another planet is it enough to know that a human being has managed to walk in space; on earth the important question is whether he is Russian or American. A feeling of sadness miraculously caught in a poem is not merely sadness now; disenchantment is not merely disenchantment. If it is a Russian poem these emotions are implicitly political, and in an American hardly less so. At least the world is inclined to think so.

In short, the integral beauty of a thing in itself, its degree of perfection as a created complex of inner tensions and resolution, is subordinate to its relevance to the survival and prestige of the social presumptions in which it was brought forth.

Which implies, of course, that at long last the work of the intellectual is important. And that is why so many people work so hard to regulate it. That is why in just about every country there is censorship in some form; books are burned or suppressed altogether. Writers are imprisoned, and P.E.N.'s Writers-in-Prison Committee rarely lacks customers.

So it is natural that P.E.N.'s reason for existence should seem completely bound up with its defense of the writer's right to express himself and to publish. When, in the 'fifties, American writers were being hounded by government committees and blacklisted, forced to write under pseudonyms or barred outright from movies and television and in some cases from publishing; when Portuguese writers are arrested, when Soviet writers are tried for the political implications of their works and sent to jail for long terms, the duty of P.E.N. is clear and unavoidable. When Yiddish literature in the Soviet Union is not permitted the same publishing accommodations as other literature; when the language of Catalonia is suppressed in Spain—these and unfortunately many other suppressive acts cry out for P.E.N.'s protests. But, important as this function is, it is not or ought not be P.E.N.'s sole reason for existence.

None of us comes here as a representative of his country. None of us is obliged to speak here as an apologist for his culture or his political system. In this congress, as in the preceding ones, the devout Communist, the militant anti-Communist, the apolitical, the anarchist, the Catholic, the Jew, the Protestant, Buddhist or Mohammedan, the realist and the surrealist, the drunk and the sober can come and leave behind the categories and turn their attention to the one problem which all of us share as human beings—the nurturing of culture. And I mean by culture, the faithful and profound rendering of the writer's awareness of his reality. Deprived of this kind of accounting, men lose their past, cannot deal with the present, and betray their future.

But P.E.N. is not yet doing this job. In the fifty-one weeks of the year between congresses, P.E.N. can work to become the cockpit of controversy, the free arena in over fifty countries, the leading edge of the wing that cuts the air. A P.E.N. center, if it is to become relevant to the promise of P.E.N., must become a place of confrontation, a place with a certain danger, so that the agony of this time is not spuriously covered over by an empty conviviality, but laid open to investigation.

P.E.N. is a curiosity among international organizations if only because it has endured so long. Not only endured but now it has grown and will continue to grow. I think this has happened in great part because it has refused, and rightly, to allow itself to become the agency of any political tendency. But it is a narrow mind which sees politics as the only or even the best means through which men can reveal themselves to each other. The fact is, politics is unmatched as a means by which to conceal ourselves. The view of P.E.N. is longer than this, and deeper than this. Because we are made up of so many different viewpoints, it is not necessary for us to celebrate the sadness in a Russian poem merely because it confirms our conception of Russian life; or the contempt and rebellion in an American poem because it does the same in regard to American life. Because P.E.N. is not engaged in political warfare, it ought to make more possible a view of literature as literature, as an expression of universal human conditions and feelings, universal human ideals. For if nothing else has come of these congresses, it is clear that even in bad French and broken English and stuttering Spanish, we do become comprehensible to one another. It is important that we meet not only in order to shake hands, but to revitalize our awareness of something that is as real, as palpable, and as decisive as the conflicts between our nations. It is the stubborn, underlying sameness of the human spirit whatever the variety of forms in which it is expressed. To universalize culture is our ultimate aim. It is our particular business as writers simply because no other group is in a position to care as much as we can care about it, and because it is in the nature of writing to reach out to the whole world. It is, perhaps above all, the ultimate way in which men will one day come to identify with one another and thus make the insanity of war less likely.

For many years now the question of the writer's commitment has been at issue, whether he ought or must or must not come down on the side of one social system or another, one nationalism, one revolutionary conception or another. P.E.N. is constructed—and its record in the past is convincing in this respect—as a means through which the writer may commit himself to mankind, to the defense of culture, and to its increasing prestige among the peoples. And this is the proper work of the P.E.N. center fifty-one weeks of the year.

It is for these reasons that I am disappointed that the expected delegation of observers from the Soviet Union has not arrived. In the absence of an official explanation it is inevitable to assume that it was feared the Sinyavsky-Daniel case would have brought down strong criticism from members of P.E.N. upon the delegation. And in all likelihood this would have been so.

Nevertheless, I would like to think that in such criticism there would have been something more than a political condemnation of the Soviet Union. International P.E.N. was the first to protest and condemn this trial and the sentences meted out. With every means at our command we attempted to mitigate the sentences and to help the accused. But at no time, least of all now, have we lost sight of the importance for the world, and the Soviet Union as well, of the future establishment of a Soviet P.E.N. center or centers. We are not looking for opportunities to castigate the Soviet Union, nor would it be in the spirit of P.E.N., implicitly or overtly, to set up especially difficult conditions for the entry of the Soviet writers into P.E.N. When the time comes that Soviet writers can subscribe to the principles of P.E.N.'s charter they will be welcome among us. The warmth of the reception this year in England and the United States for Andrei Voznesensky proves, I think, that no animus exists against a writer because he is a loyal citizen of the Soviet Union. Indeed, as I have tried to make clear, the very life of P.E.N., its very durability, rests upon its eagerness to welcome writers as writers rather than political ambassadors. Nevertheless, to forego insistence upon the right to write would be to violate the foundation of this organization.

It happens that we have an example at hand of the uses of P.E.N. that go well beyond its capacity to protest. By virtue of P.E.N.'s invitation Pablo Neruda is here. This great poet, whose influence in the United States has always been wide, and after forty years is widening still, has read his poems to New York, and soon will go to other cities here. The thousands of young Americans whose vision of poetry is deeply guided by Neruda's work, the teachers and critics, must surely take International P.E.N. into account now, not for a political reason, but because, quite simply, it has done its job of breaking down the separation of a great artist and a great civilization which, for over twenty years now, could only admire him from a distance. It is not necessary to propagandize Pablo Neruda, and politics could not be further from his mind as he moves among us. It turns out that art is important in this transaction; indeed, it is all that matters.

I hope that in the future, P.E.N. will do everything in its power and raise every cent it can to bring together the many writers, not all of them so famous, not all of them necessarily immortal, whose names we need to hear, and who need the stimulus of facing their audiences. The fact is that to many of us large parts of the creative world are unknown territory. The revolutionary experience of Asia and Africa, the rich literatures of Latin America must be made the patrimony of every cultured man. In a word, P.E.N. must offer to every man and woman who writes, a neutral ground, a kind of sanctuary where he will find support for that vision which is always in danger of being brought down by things, by technology, by suppression or sheer ignorance—the vision of man as the measure and center of all.

Address by Saul Bellow

It is absolutely essential in this age of immensely accelerated change to note transformations that affect us directly. It may not always be possible but we have no choice but to try.

The changes on which I would like to offer some remarks are those in the relations between public and writer in the English-speaking countries. I propose to begin with a short description of artist and public such as an avant-garde writer might have given thirty years ago. He would certainly have referred to himself as a highbrow. With a certain irony, but seriously nevertheless, he would have distinguished himself from the middlebrows, the apex of the culture, and from the lowbrow or no-brow, Philistine hater of all that was good and beautiful in the modern tradition. This is not to say that the highbrow writer loved his isolation or that he chose it out of pride or decadent class feeling. On the contrary, the division of cultures into high and low caused much bitterness and was considered by many to be dangerous to society and to civilization as a whole. Overlooking perhaps the humiliations of the poet under patronage, the modern vanguardist was nostalgic for the 18th century and the small, refined and aristocratic public of that age of masterpieces. The 19th-century public was already fully vulgarized, enthusiastic, perhaps, but coarse-grained: an audience of shopkeepers. The faults of this public were aggravated by commercial exploitation, by promoters who made vast fortunes in cheap novels and who brought mass culture into the world. The vanguard minority, by this account, grew steadily smaller. The specialist began to appear, a new sort of intellectual with little or no understanding of art and small sympathy for the life of the mind.

Finally, in the 20th century, to state the case as it was stated by a brilliant critic and observer, the late Wyndham Lewis—an authentic highbrow—civilization cut itself in two, driving into pens or reservations all that was most creative and intelligent. The vanguard writer, like the American Indian, was imprisoned in barren places, locked away in the Ivory Tower, deprived of human contacts and of influence. Probably all this would end in the total liquidation of all intellectual groups. Only a few twilight masterpieces by men like Joyce or Paul Klee would remain, and we would reach a stage of final degradation, the era of unrelieved stupidity.

This is in some way the description given by the Romantic of the bourgeois situation, not wholly unjustified but containing certain exaggerations. In this account the writer sees himself cut off from society, held in contempt by its rulers, separated from the people, longing to be reunited with them.

Wyndham Lewis was a thoughtful and original observer but it is apparent that he made any number of wrong guesses about the future. Intellectuals have not been liquidated. On the contrary, their power and influence increase continually and they are now spoken of with respect, even awe, as indispensable in government, as makers of educated opinion, as sources of symbolic legitimacy, replacing the clergy. Old Walt Whitman announcing "the priest departs, the divine literatus arrives" does not sound as unhinged as he did thirty years ago.

I do not refer to the *quality* of these literati—that is another matter —but to the growth of their influence.

On the eve of the Second World War the highbrow public was numerically insignificant. This is no longer the case. We now have a growing class of intellectuals or near-intellectuals, millions of college graduates. A university degree does not mean much, of course. It does however indicate exposure to high culture. At the same time we should bear in mind that a great deal of this literary high culture to which people have been exposed, the modern and most effective part of it, was created by highbrow geniuses—disaffected, subversive, radical— who rejected the average preferences of their contemporaries. The millions who go to the art museums today admire there the strangely beautiful, powerful painting of artists who worked in the thickening twilight of modernism.

Quick-witted promoters and managers have recognized that these masterpieces have great prestige, and that when a much-publicized picture has been hung, lines will form at the museums which are just as long as those at the Paramount Theatre.

The minority public is no longer that handful of connoisseurs that read *Transition* in the 'twenties, or argued about "significant form." We have at present a large itinerant community and something we can call, *faute de mieux*, a literary culture, in my opinion a very bad one.

For one thing, the universities have now embraced modern literature. Stony old pedants two generations ago refused to consider anyone newer than Browning. Their power was broken some time ago, and all universities permit the study of contemporary writers. Thousands of teachers turn out millions of graduates in literature. Some of these teachers are harmless enough, textual editors and antiquarians. Others are influential interpreters or misinterpreters.

It is in the universities that literary intellectuals are made, not on Grub Street, not in Bohemia. The mass media and the university-sponsored quarterlies have, between them, swallowed up literary journalism. The salaried professor will supply literary articles cheaply and has all but wiped out his professional competitors. Bohemia, too, has been relocated in new quarters, near to the university campuses.

The university therefore is producing quantities of literary intellectuals who teach, write or go into publishing houses. So far as I can see this new group, greatly influenced by the modern classics, by Joyce, Proust, Eliot, Lawrence, Gide, Valéry, etc., has done little more than convert these classics into other forms of discourse, translating imagination into opinion, or art into cognitions. What they do is to put it all differently. They redescribe everything, usually making it less accessible. For feeling or response they substitute acts of comprehension. Sometimes they seem to manufacture intellectual history, more congenial to them and to their students than art itself. Sometimes I think they are trying to form a model of civilized intelligence for the 20th century, an intelligence to which a more worthy art will one day be offered—the *Zeitgeist* permitting. I think the "dehumanization of art" of which Ortega speaks may reflect the demands made upon art by the literary intellectuals and may be in part a result of the pressure they put upon it for meanings.

Redescription can be intriguing and useful, and succeeding generations must, like Adam in the Garden of Eden, rename their beasts. Molière revealed the comic possibilities of this in *Le bourgeois gentilhomme* when M. Jourdain discovered with delight that he had all along been speaking prose. Americans take great pleasure in the comedy of terms. We pay psychologists to penetrate our characters and redescribe them to us scientifically, rationalizing consciousness on the verbal level at least. We are delighted to hear that we are introverted, fixated, repressed here or there, attached to our mothers thus and so. Such new accounts seem worth the money we pay for them. But what our critics seem to do is to redescribe downwards. They degrade the present age and deny creative scope to their contemporaries. They themselves are the only heirs of the modern classical writers. Our most respected men of letters identify themselves with Joyce, Proust, etc., and present themselves as the distinguished representatives, indeed the only representatives, of these masters. The agents, managers or impresarios of Henry James or the French Symbolists appear at times also to consider themselves their only legitimate successors and enjoy a certain genteel prestige. They are the "happy few" of culture. They are clear signs that intellectuals in what American universities call the Humanities are trying to appropriate literature for themselves, taking it away from writers. These intellectuals are like the young British princess who said to her husband during the honeymoon, "Do servants do this too? Much too good for them." Literature is too good for contemporary novelists, those poor untutored drudges. And what do these intellectuals do with literature? Why, they talk about it, they treasure it, they adorn themselves with it, they make careers of it, they become an *élite* of it, they make discourse of it. It is their capital, their material. They take from it what they need for their own work in cultural history, journalism, or criticism of manners, producing hybrid works, partly literary, sometimes interesting in themselves but postulating almost always the decadence or obsolescence of contemporary literature. They want to use the literature of the modern tradition to make something far better, a higher, more valuable, mental realm, a realm of dazzling intellectuality, of marvelous ideas, yielding new and original forms of personality.

Let me direct your attention to other consequences of the teaching of literature. In his latest book, *Beyond Culture,* Professor Lionel Trilling tells us that we now have a sizable group of people in the United States educated in the modern classics. He thinks they have not turned out very well. One sees his point. They seem to have it both ways. On the one hand they share the distaste of the modern classic writers for Western civilization, they are repelled by the effrontery of power and the degradation of the urban crowd. They have adopted the Waste Land outlook. On the other hand they are very well off. They have money, position, privileges, power, private schools for their children, elegant dental care, jet holidays in Europe, stocks, bonds, houses, even yachts, and with all this, owing to their education, they have a particular sympathy with the heroic artistic life, they have tastes and judgments formed by Rimbaud and D. H. Lawrence. What could be neater?

This may be the way things are in the modern world, a consequence perhaps of the decline in belief, a certain doubt about the worth of human actions. Thus in a short life one feels free to combine all things of value. People pursue luxury but try to keep, by some means, values conceived in austerity. They combine private security with rebellious attitudes, monogamy with sexual experiment, conventional family life with a Bohemian outlook, the *dolce vita* with the great books. Vice-presidents during the working day, they may be anarchists or utopians at cocktail time. In the higher income brackets, insulated from the dirt and danger of New York, they retain as a matter of course all the sentiments of alienation, honor bound to be sullen, ungrateful, dissatisfied, suspicious and theoretically defiant of authority. There is nothing very new in this. Dostoevsky observed that people who recited Schiller with tears in their eyes were also very good at managing their bureaucratic careers. No wonder Professor Trilling is upset. He sees that a literary education may be a mixed blessing, and that the critics and writers sent into the world by English faculties have not turned out very well.

What important function might they be performing? That question is answered by Irving Kristol in a recent number of *The Public Interest*. He points out that the literary intellectuals help shape the opinions of the educated classes and play a crucial role in defining the moral quality of our society. He says, "There is surely no more important task than to question or affirm the legitimacy of a society's basic institutions, to criticize or amend the original assumptions on which political life proceeds. How well equipped are our literary intellectuals for this job? Not, it must be confessed, as well equipped as they ought to be."

This, then, is the situation. Critics and professors have declared themselves the true heirs and successors of the modern classic writers. They have obscured the connection between the contemporary writer and his vanguard predecessors, and replaced the vanguard public with something else. They have projected the kinds of art and literature that suit them and have the power to recruit novelists who will meet their requirements. Novels are written which contain attitudes, positions or fantasies pleasing to the literary intelligentsia. These are, of course, given serious consideration. Literature is becoming important for what one can do with it. It is becoming a source of orientations, postures, life-styles, positions. The positions are made up of odds and ends of Marxism, Freudianism, Existentialism, mythology, surrealism, absurdism, *und so weiter,* the *débris* of modernism, with apocalyptic leftovers added.

It is believed that a correct position makes one illusionless, and that to be illusionless is more important than anything else. That it is enlightened to expose, to disenchant, to hate, to experience disgust. Wyndham Lewis had an excellent term for this last phenomenon—he spoke of the vulgarization of once aristocratic disgust by the modern romantics. One might add that the skepticism of the enlightenment has also been vulgarized and that it is thought blessed to see through the class origins of one's affection for one's grandfather or the hypocritical baseness at the center of friendships.

Nevertheless, there are friendships, affinities, natural feelings, rooted norms. People do on the whole agree, for instance, that it is wrong to commit murder, and even if they are unable to offer rational arguments for this they are not necessarily driven to commit gratuitous acts of violence. It seems to me that writers might really do well to start thinking about such questions again. Evidently they will have to do it without the aid of the critics. The critics are too romantic to deal with these problems.

A final word about the avant-garde. Genius is, without strain, avant-garde. To labor to create vanguard conditions is historicism. It means that people have been reading books of culture-history. As for the vanguard public, now assimilated by our literary culture and transformed into something else, we must for the time being do without it. The writer will have to believe that what he writes will evoke a public, that it will be summoned up by the force of his truth. The forms he invents will create a new public.

The Writer in the Electronic Age

Tuesday, June 14
FIRST AND SECOND SESSIONS

Marshall McLuhan, CHAIRMAN
Director, Center for Culture and Technology, University of Toronto

Iván Boldizsár
Editor, *The New Hungarian Quarterly*, Budapest

Haroldo de Campos
Co-editor, *Invencão*, San Paulo

R. Buckminster Fuller
University of Southern Illinois, Carbondale

Yves Gandon
President, P.E.N. Club Français
former president, Société des Gens de Lettres, Paris

Adolf Hoffmeister
President, Czechoslovak P.E.N. Club, Prague

Anoma Kanie
Ivory Coast P.E.N. (Second Session only)

Richmond Lattimore
Bryn Mawr College, Bryn Mawr

Kathleen C. Nott
London

Norman Podhoretz
Editor, *Commentary*, New York

Paul Tabori
Executive Director, International Film Writers Guild, London

The Writer in the Electronic Age

FIRST SESSION

Mr. McLuhan introduced the theme by saying that "Under conditions of electronic circuitry people become so profoundly involved in one another that the writer and his public assume altogether new relationships." The participants in this discussion, he said, would "probe, not package." They knew that a "happening" was definable as an "all-at-once situation without a story-line." Just so was electronic "information" an all-at-once occurrence. This was a situation understood by Edgar Allen Poe when he invented both the symbolist poem and the detective story.

Much earlier, the printing press had brought into being a previously non-existent phenomenon—the public, the writer's public. Montaigne was already aware of this: He owed a complete portrait of himself to *le public,* he wrote. Today, under conditions of xerography, the pre-printing age had returned: the reader, in effect, became his own publisher. The business world was already in this situation. Xerography "deals with entire *Gestalts.*" Associated with this was the computer which, though generally regarded as a storage system, was in fact an "instantaneous retrieval system" which simulated human memory. This instantaneous power of retrieving information permitted new discoveries "including the discovery of who we are"—for it was clear that human identity depended very much upon the instantaneous retrieval of memory. Still another characteristic of our age was brilliantly summed up in a sentence by Buckminster Fuller, when he wrote that the space capsule was the first totally designed human environment, one in which the planet accompanied the inhabitant of the capsule, who could not exist without the planet.

This, Mr. McLuhan went on, was very much the condition of the author in the electronic age. He now found himself working with "the entirety of human consciousness" as his datum. He could no longer merely express a private viewpoint. Electronic circuitry did not create a "mass audience"—the word was a misnomer; it brought about "the simultaneous involvement of a multitude of viewpoints"—which viewpoints were in fact a by-product of the technology of printing. Electronic circuitry had the effect that "everybody was affected by everybody at the same moment." It was significant that while Oriental society was being Westernized, Occidental society was being Orientalized, was going inward, becoming "profoundly entropic." The interest in Zen Buddhism and the drug called LSD represented only minor examples. Our fragmented, individualized Western consciousnesses were not being drawn inward by any ideology; it was electronics that created a "mood of inwardness." The "safe" automobile about to be developed was a form of padded cell. A newspaper report was a kind of surrealist poem. An editorial was a "fragmented mechanical form of separatism and individual-point-of-viewism." The new art forms, pop art, for example, tell us that "the total environment has to be dealt with as art."

Meanwhile, "the environment is a teaching machine, total and infallible," and the author is "a person who is going to be engaged in programming teaching machines."

Mr. Boldizsár, speaking in English, said that he felt "knocked out" by what he had just heard, as he had felt on first reading Spengler's *Decline of the West* several decades ago. He would add, for the moment, only that he had recovered from the knock-out delivered by Spengler.

Miss Nott said that she, too, had been about to refer to Spengler. Instead, she would ask a question. Were Mr. McLuhan's listeners being told that authors no longer had a future as "independent spirits" or that authors must learn to love and live with the computer? *The* (London) *Times Literary Supplement* had devoted articles to the computer in scholarship under a general title it had had the impertinence to call "Freeing the Mind." "Computer poetry" was not unheard of in England. Miss Nott had no objection to people playing with any toys they chose, but behind what they had just heard, she would say with respect, there was "a very dangerous and tendentious philosophy." Dangerous in the sense that like certain other philosophies—of Spengler, of Freud, of a good deal of Marx—it tended to produce what it prophesied.

Authors tempted to be discouraged by this sort of thing should remember history, and that the "history of good writing is really a kind of resistance movement." Miss Nott would suggest that media was a word not only of a mechanical connotation; it meant "means" as well; and in Western religious and psychological history means had never dominated, it was ends that were important. She did not wish to get away from Mr. McLuhan's subject. What he had said in his book *Understanding Media,* about print—that it imposed a linear or serial and visual aspect which readers transfer unconsciously to other things—was true. What he had omitted was that a good book was a kind of moral and aesthetic object; that the act of reading was solitary in a healthy sense, was in fact a semantically collectivist fact inducing personal mediation between author and reader. Here, on both sides, we had something which was omitted from Mr. McLuhan's exposition: the human personality in its subjective aspect. What Miss Nott had gathered was, chiefly, that environment was henceforward absolutely dominant—and irresistible.

That far fewer books might in the end be written, she was ready to think likely. She thought they might be better books. What she would not surrender was the spiritual, moral and social importance that lay in the kind of communion constituted by the act of reading.

Mr. McLuhan observed first that he had not intended to imply any fatality about the media he had dealt with: "One thing that media cannot bear is scrutiny." Means of "controlling and even dissolving them" were discoverable. Men decided to make these things; "we put them there to control us." As in "Miss Nott's famous book, *The Emperor's New Clothes,*" when one became aware of what was happening one could exercise control. To do that was to be autonomous, free; to ignore what was happening was to put oneself into the fatalistic hands of these phenomena. Under electronic conditions, "the tendency of artists is to move into the control tower, not ivory tower." The artist was the only person with enough courage to look at the present and perceive that it contained the future. He asked Mr. Fuller to comment.

Mr. Fuller began by saying that by reason of his deafness he had great trouble with electronics and much preferred reading. What he liked about a book was that "you can really sit there and think." He had been for many years a student of the patterns that took place in the "evolutionary expansion of man's capabilities." Man was unique in the extent and variety of his ability to "develop extensions of his functions." One of these was his means of communication. Other illustrations could be summed up by saying that in the United States, for example, each inhabitant was "using" 130 tons of copper, 10 tons of steel, 22 tons of concrete. Metaphorically, man was a far bigger animal than the dinosaur.

In its aspect of communication, this presented a certain interest for the writer. Socially and politically, the democracy of Jefferson differed from our own in the time then required for communication. It made a difference that Jefferson had had to say, "If we don't get a letter from our ambassador to Paris this year we shall have to—" etc. Another kind of difference was that representatives of the people, riding on horses to and from their parliamentary meetings were intimately in touch with the people. They lived in a decentralized world. Today there was much argument about the advantages and disadvantages of central government: this was not a political choice but a technological choice. Admirals could not escape it at sea, bureaucrats could not escape it on land. McLuhan's xerography was only an extension of broadcasting; both were one-way systems; the individual was unable to talk back; and this explained why institutes of public opinion were rampant. It explained why the seemingly swifter decision-making of dictatorships was sometimes favored. Mr. Fuller could see no escape from this domination of the "little man" except by a process of evolution.

Mr. Tabori, who followed, said that while he shared Miss Nott's cautious optimism about the writer's future, he was nevertheless impressed by the chairman's "warnings." He had been happy to hear from scientists at Cambridge University, England, that the combined national incomes of Britain, France and the United States would have to be spent to build a computer that could match the brain of a six-year-old child. That was hopeful. He was cheered also by the reflection that machines, too, could goof. The translation machine, for example, asked to put a common English phrase into Chinese, and then out of Chinese into French, performed this way: "Out of sight, out of mind" ended up as "Invisible, insane." As for what to do about it, he would recommend that writers do as was done in war by the most famous character in modern Czech literature, the Good Soldier Schweik. They should carry on passive resistance, exercise the wisdom of simulating stupidity.

Mr. de Campos, speaking in English, saying that he belonged to a group of poets in Brazil who had started a movement in the 1950s for a new kind of poetry, "concrete poetry," expressed his agreement with a good part of what Mr. McLuhan had said. Concrete poetry began with a notion of "space-time structure" instead of linear structure as the poet's syntactical field. The ideogram was its objective; analogical rather than logical analysis was its method of composition. The poet was, in Mr. de Campos' opinion, a "designer of language" in the sense of, say, industrial design. The Russian poet Mayakovsky might be cited as an example. The poet was the "engineer of day-to-day life." We lived in a time when the quantitative was instantly transformed into the qualitative; when there took place (as an Italian poet saw) a "dialectical exchange between the language of avant-gardist poets and the language of kids." The age of the literate was ended. The precursor of the present age in poetry—the poetry using all contemporary media—was Mallarmé, "the Dante of the electronic age," and Mayakovsky had built on Mallarmé as Marx had built on Hegel.

M. *Gandon* began by remarking that if certain participants were to speak at length, others would have to be brief. His own impression of what had been said was complex. He had been successively amazed, dazzled, bewildered, confused, and finally lost, feeling himself a Philistine in a company of learned men. The notes he had tried to take were useless. Yet he thought it might be possible to make certain statements reasonably, which was to say, simply.

What he admired in Professor McLuhan was the poet, the mystic of electronics. He admired mystics—up to the point where they frightened him; and a moment ago he had been frightened. He had thought he knew something about electronics; he had dealt at length with cybernetics in one of his novels and had even written in it of a *machina nuptialis*, a marriage machine. The machine, following the input of data about two people, decided whether or not they should marry, and its decision was without appeal. This, it now appeared, was the way things were to go. Well, why not, since it seemed that love matches always turned out badly.

But something else took place in the novel. Certain officials—the novel was set in a kind of totalitarian democracy—having decided that the marriage should not take place, had introduced into the machine an element that had falsified its decision. This much to demonstrate that M. Gandon knew whereof he spoke.

It had seemed to M. Gandon that Professor McLuhan must be an optimist, since he was a mystic who believed that electronics would benefit mankind. But he had gone on to say by what the writer would be replaced. M. Gandon had expected to learn by what the writer would *not* be replaced; and though Professor McLuhan might look down upon him for neglecting to take account of the admirable details in his exposition of the subject, M. Gandon still believed that the writer could not, in fact, be replaced.

One question raised in the Program Note prepared for the theme of this discussion asked if the book was fated to disappear. In France, at least, for all the spread of radio and television, the book-reading public had grown enormously. As in the United States, editions of "pocketbooks" were ten times greater than before.

Those who traveled in space capsules were likely to lose sight of the earth. M. Gandon envied them, but he remained an earth dweller.

Mr. Tram Combs of the Virgin Islands said that the chairman had explained that he was not forecasting the doom of the literate West; his books, however, displayed no anxiety on this score. All present were indebted to him for arousing their concern over the possible uses to which the new technology might be put. But in considering the damage that could result, comfort might be taken from the extraordinary capabilities of man's imagination and progress in the—was it 10,000 years?—since the great apes roamed the earth. The question to ask was how the new technology could be made to serve man's welfare. Past ages of great art had almost always been associated with great science and advancing technology. The latter had often served art by indicating new directions to art; this was very clearly the case of painting in the last and the present century. The new media of communication were already serving poets—the disc and tape recorders, for example—and today one could only say that writers had new worlds before them; they were not going the way of the dinosaur.

Dr. Hoffmeister, speaking in French, began by pointing out that there was a time when one put on one's glad rags to go to the theatre or the opera; today the man in the street could have them at home. Television screens were now replacing pictures on the wall; radios were replacing the family library, especially since so many lived in small apartments. The idea of delivering culture to one's domicile, like so much merchandise, could be carried to absurd lengths and would lead inescapably to the isolation of the individual, the breakdown of society. The more man lived amidst machinery, the greater was his need of human surroundings.

The socialist system—Dr. Hoffmeister spoke as a citizen of Czechoslovakia—did not contemplate the development of the individual outside of society; on the contrary, he was to develop in and through society. It was possible that the new art forms would have a collective effect, that they would become the very essence of the relations between highly individualized men. One obstacle to this goal deserved mention —time—an element from which, beyond all others, man suffered. It might be that machines would accelerate movement, contacts, communications to the limits of the possible, perhaps beyond the limits we now think of as unsurmountable; the fact remained, nevertheless, that man in our day had much less time at his disposal than his grandfather or his father had had. Did we really have time for poetry, art, leisure? Was there still time in this stimulating, irritating, disquieting present to savor the gentle irony with which authors and intellectuals confront those deep human frailties—love, money, selfishness? All one could say, despite the prognostications of an ominous future, was that a new era of humanism still lay before mankind in which man would continue to need the arts in order to manifest his superiority over electronics.

Mr. Lattimore began by saying that as a poet he did not like to classify, but he had put down the heading "communication" and the sub-heads, "editing," "creation," "distribution," and "recording." All this, he had scratched out, for it seemed to him that they were in fact independent, though some forms of art might tend towards their fusion.

First, editing. By this he meant selection, which involved rejection as well. Mr. McLuhan had spoken of a swarm of data that might be intolerable. It always was. There had always been "more world than we can take in."

Second, creation versus distribution or recording. Very much of what went on the air was the work of writers working in their "old solipsistic privacy." To Mr. Lattimore it seemed that the writer almost had to refuse to do anything but work as best he could, not in accordance with theory, but in obedience to a method which forced itself upon him. This was the writer's "real internal secret." An outsider might tell him what to write about, but it was intolerable that an outsider should tell him how to write. Either the writer would know what to do, or he was no writer.

Mr. Podhoretz had predicted that he would "have trouble with this machine." Skeptical of all apocalyptic expression, he was "glad to see that Mr. McLuhan couldn't get his machine to work either." The combination of apocalyptic temper and technological historicism was seductive and had indeed overwhelmed several participants at the Round Table. Mr. Podhoretz, for his part, would argue that although technology was very important in certain contexts, it was not important in the context of the future of "writing books as physical objects." Writers, including gifted philosophers and essayists, existed who were purveyors of information. This role had been pretty well exhausted— and by technology. And it might, as Paul Goodman had lately suggested, be a good thing, might have relieved literature of a burden.

As to television, Mr. Podhoretz believed that it had already "impaired the capacity for sustained attention to the printed word." Perhaps reading had always been difficult—an activity which presented spiritual and intellectual problems. The fact that book sales have increased in the face of the spread of television did not lessen Mr. Podhoretz's conviction that the latter had made reading "oddly more difficult."

Granting, now, these two things, that the electronic media were better purveyors of "sheer information" and that television lowered the reader's capacity for attending to the printed word, there was left in this context only a relatively slight and novel situation—one for which analogies had existed in the past and to which men had responded by refusing to be overwhelmed.

Mr. McLuhan, after recalling that Sir Samuel Hoare had once, in the House of Commons, dismissed a question about the Indian movement for Home Rule by saying that "India was passing through that phase which all countries pass through in such circumstances," called on the next speaker.

Mr. Boldizsár recalled that at the Thirty-third International P.E.N. Congress, in Bled, he had chaired a round table on *Literature and the Mass Media,* much as Mr. McLuhan was doing today. He had found himself defending the mass media against a certain snobbishness on the part of certain writers. Today he found himself defending all writers against Mr. McLuhan's "alluring and dangerous Utopia." Even more, against a vulgarized McLuhanism he had found sweeping the United States, particularly the college campuses, in the course of a three months' tour. This was in part the result of Mr. McLuhan's eloquent terminology, including such words as "circuitry." Mr. McLuhan was somewhat given to wit: Mr. Boldizsár thought it dangerous when the sense of his book, *Understanding Media,* was reduced to a pun.

As a man in love with television, he felt something needed saying against Mr. McLuhan's position. Watching American television, he had called it *horror televisionis;* this was before he learned that many Americans called their sets the "idiot box." He wished to point out that television had in fact—more than any other mass medium—created a new kingdom of dreams, a new reality; and that whereas the public lived in this new realm, the writers had not yet learned to enter it. But the writers would learn. Mr. Boldizsár had said in Bled that this was not the doomsday of literature, it was the beginning of a new literary rebirth. This he repeated today, not in opposition to Mr. McLuhan's dangerous ideas, but inspired by his ideas. Mr. McLuhan, by pushing his ideas to the absurd, had shown writers what not to do and where not to go. He had forgotten "the mystic of creativity."

The chairman, opening the session to questions from the floor, said he was amazed by the obsession with his ideas that seemed to exist among the panelists. He did not identify himself with the ideas he enunciated. Some he found ludicrous. They were not his opinions. His role was to invent "forms for probing the environment." Literary people tended to identify an expression with its author; "in the electronic age this was fatal." When he spoke this morning he was "simply trying to discover what was going on." He was changing his mind, finding out new things every day.

Mr. Pablo Neruda, called upon by the chairman, excused himself as a "rustic poet" who spoke poor English. His first emotional encounter with technology had occurred when, as a very young man, he read "two most beautiful poems by Walt Whitman on the locomotive." Another was when he read Hart Crane's poem on Brooklyn Bridge. Here were examples of "the union between what man makes and what the writer makes" which now, once again, was needed. As for the things man made, some of them were now causing the whole world to grow afraid. He remembered his own ecstatic sight, in his native Chile, when he was ten years old, of an airplane rising from the earth. He remembered also the sight, years later, of planes bombing his house in Madrid. Mr. Neruda begged to be excused for mentioning the subject of war; it was not before the Round Table, but when we talked of fearing technology we had to say that war was, after all, a thing all men feared today. And on the whole, it seemed to him that the old humanism was a better way of facing it, of eliminating distrust and fear, than the wonderful promises of science.

Mr. Wilhelm Girnus (P.E.N. Center, G.D.R.), speaking in French, thought that the computer could not replace the human personality. He believed that it was with man as a human personality that literature was concerned. Its function—to study man's involvement in reality and reach moral decisions about that involvement—was something science could not perform.

Mrs. Hilde Domin (P.E.N. Center, G.F.R.), speaking in English, said that Mr. McLuhan had spoken of the poet in a "control tower." We had had in the past the "ivory tower" and Virginia Woolf had substituted for it a "leaning tower" from which the poet, though he could not escape, looked down upon a broad social scene. Mrs. Domin believed that the poet must now descend from even this tower and participate in reality. But it was idle to pretend that the poet could "control" anything. She thought that control lay only in the "Pentagons" of our world. What was needed was a Nietzschean superman to overcome the trend of electronics and keep man human.

Mr. A. den Doolaard (Netherlands P.E.N.), speaking in English, said that this morning's discussion had suggested to him that as a center of communication in the electronic age, man seemed doomed to failure. When he thought of what he got from reading a volume of Mr. Neruda's poetry at home, and how little he had got from that great poet's remarks this morning, he had to consider the book an infinitely superior medium of communication to the spoken word electronically transmitted. He conceived of a time when man was abolished, when every infant at birth would be transistorized; in the intervals between news, weather reports and the rest, all men would from time to time absorb snatches of "permitted literature" automatically. He hoped, for his part, that that time would not come before he had retired into "the lost fortresses of poetry" where he could hear the bards of Yugoslavia, Crete, the American "hillbilly" country—and Washington Square.

Mr. Lawrence Lande (Canadian P.E.N.), speaking in English, asked three questions: First, how would it be possible to maintain and deepen the historic sense? Second, what would become of the love of old books as a tangible evidence of the past? Third, if we were to reflect that the book was a thing through which we communed with an author, in which we wrote marginal notes, over which we dreamt, how could we imagine that a strip of plastic tape could induce the feelings Keats had on first looking into Chapman's Homer? Finally, there was the aesthetic fact of a beautiful book: what, in the future, was to satisfy that sense?

SECOND SESSION

Mr. McLuhan introduced, as a new panel member, Mr. Anoma Kanie (Ivory Coast P.E.N.) and then invited remarks from the floor.

Mrs. Helen Rosenau (English P.E.N.) rose to say that she had observed two phenomena which appeared to indicate that we might already be in "a period of reaction to what has been described today." The first was that fewer scientists than humanists were seeking posts in the universities. The second was the publication of a book by Professor Hudson, of Cambridge University, in which the author argued that "creative people had a rather different type of intelligence from those in technology" and that the former were "the only scientists." This might indicate that "our problem is more transient than it appears."

Mr. John Simon (American P.E.N.) asked the chairman why he had given up the teaching of English literature to become Director of the Center for Culture and Technology at the University of Toronto.

Mr. McLuhan pointed out that print was the only medium for which formal educational study existed. It had created its own environment, called "the public." Other media had now created other environments in which print had to struggle. In order to save print from those media which were the "enemies of print" one had to go "outside the environment." He was himself a "print-orientated man" for whom the values of print were "supreme." He was surrounded by contemporaries for whom print was an "incidental and forgotten form." "Mono-medium people" were doing print "the worst possible service by ignoring its enemies." He had begun to study the new media with the help of Baudelaire, Rimbaud, "and above all Flaubert." Mallarmé had been "one of the greatest students of technologies," and Joyce had written, in *Finnegans Wake,* the "greatest handbook of media." T. S. Eliot, Wyndham Lewis and Ezra Pound had devoted "enormous attention to media and the grammars of media."

Mr. Emery George (Writers-in-Exile P.E.N.), speaking in English, began by saying that the "concern of literati with means of communication other than print" was nothing new. Professor Norbert Wiener, in his work on cybernetics, wrote that his study had been stimulated by the writings of St. Augustine. Leibniz had dreamt of constructing a communication theory. While there was some truth in the Balinese dictum, "We do not have art," and in the inference to be drawn therefrom that everything in the environment was "art," the environment was also "artifice." Only that could be called art which man created "with the intent of producing art" a German writer on cybernetics had written. It was true that the modern study of communication in all its aspects could be "very exciting." But it was also true that "information, theoretical criticism" provided a rational basis for agreement or disagreement. To this extent Mr. George would disagree with Saul Bellow's arguments against textual criticism in his address at the inaugural session. From which it followed that electronic circuiting should help men to become "not less human" but more human in the sense of becoming better acquainted with themselves.

Mrs. Elizabeth Janeway (American P.E.N.) asked leave to "move the discussion down from the level of morals and aesthetics" to a practical effect which electronics is having on the incomes (or should we say pittances?) of writers. This was the result of the growing practice of photocopying copyright material without the author's permission—a practice for which legislative sanction was being sought in the United States by non-profit organizations. The educational world was favoring it, the Authors League of America was opposing it. Mrs. Janeway directed all writers' attention to this menace. As with every technological advance, photocopying would perhaps do away with older methods. Mrs. Janeway would not deny that it contained potentialities for good; one of these was the possibility of bringing added income to writers who needed it most. Mrs. Janeway urged that in pursuing the objective of wider distribution, attention be given to the rights of every kind of free-lance writer, who lives by his work as well as by his wits.

The chairman said that publishers felt great anxiety about this problem.

Mr. Sutan Takdir Alisjahbana (Indonesian P.E.N.), speaking in English, remarked that men possessed by an idea tended to "accelerate" it, and felt that this might be the case of Mr. McLuhan. He had said that "the invention of phonetic literacy was a product of detribalization." He had then said that the development of the separate Anglo-Germanic languages had raised tribal walls and, further, that the nonphonetic writing of the Chinese had made the whole of China into one big tribal people. (Mr. McLuhan interrupted to say that one could not "detribalize with ideogrammic forms of writing." By "tribal" he implied a familial pattern of life; one without intense individualism. By "specializing the visual sense," the phonetic alphabet had the contrary effect.) Communication, Mr. Alisjahbana went on, was a function of society and culture. When men had only their hands and feet to grasp and move with, the extension of their culture was very limited. With the industrial civilization it became global. At the same time, it caused our writers to retire into themselves; caused some of them to call that civilization "absurd." The speaker urged the participants in the Round Table to persuade those present that the new worldwide civilization needed "a new avant-garde built on the achievements of science, economics and technology."

Mr. Wilfred Cartey (Trinidad), speaking in English, pointed out that there had thus far been no dialogue at this Round Table; each speaker had arrived with his firm conviction and had continued to maintain it. His sympathies were with the chairman, who had been attacked throughout. The chairman's role had been cast as that of a non-being, a machine, fighting a rear-guard action against the rest. He would say, for himself, that the writer's attitude to a new aspect of reality ought to be to infuse that reality with consciousness and emotion. Instead, writers here had declared that they were turning their backs on the electronic age. About television, for example, he would say that it was the writer's business to work with it, join forces with it, not to see it transformed into a "vegetable." For Mr. Cartey, the writer was the person to give quality to this thing he feared; the medium was of secondary significance. Its importance lay in the fact that it was a reality from which the writer should not run away.

The chairman, asking for comment on Mr. Cartey's remarks, went on to say that whereas in the movies or television the writer tended to be largely anonymous, in the printed medium his ego could be nourished. He called upon Mme. Victoria Ocampo, an international vice-president of P.E.N.

Mme. Ocampo (Argentine P.E.N.), speaking in English, led up to a question by an anecdote. A few years after the Second World War she had talked to Bertholt Brecht in Berlin. He had asked if, in her opinion, the Spanish-speaking peoples of Latin America "understood" the poet, García Lorca. Her answer was, as literature the mass of the people did not; emotionally, they did. Brecht had then said, "That is for me the great problem." And Mme. Ocampo asked this question: "Can this electronic age solve the problem put by Brecht?"

Mr. Boldizsár, speaking in English, offered Mme. Ocampo a positive answer. Television and radio had brought great poetry and other literature into the homes of "millions who had never heard about poetry." To this he would add from small experience of Latin America that books in general were not widely available to the masses and he assumed therefore that they were not widely acquainted with García Lorca. In this sense, he was "very much for the electronic age."

Mme. Ocampo explained her use of the word "masses" as including "people that believe they have culture"; people who, in her sense, catch up only after fifty years.

Man's voice, speaking in English, said that two separate issues seem to have been confused in this afternoon's discussion. One was the writer's relation to the new media. To the question, for example, should the writer write for television or should he boycott it, one could reply as one pleased. The other question had to do with the effect of the predominance of electronics on sensitivity, consciousness, habits of living and so on. In his view, Mr. McLuhan had exaggerated that effect. Of course it was huge, but the chairman talked as if one were witnessing "a kind of mutation not of culture but of the human species." This he did not believe, and he thought it bore no relation to the attitude writers should take to xerography or television. Indeed, he believed that xerography would make print more ubiquitous, not less. Except income, about which Mrs. Janeway had reminded them, there was nothing here for writers to worry about; there was a challenge to the printing press and to typesetters, but not to authors.

Miss Nott, commenting upon Mr. Tabori's suggestion that it would be "nice if at a P.E.N. congress we talked about the writer as writer," said that in that case the thing to do would be to advise the writer in the electronic age to ignore the electronic age. After all, these were only media that were being discussed. One didn't learn to walk by counting one's steps, or to breathe by counting one's breaths.

Mr. de Campos said he did not believe that "a writer surrendered his moral power of decision by committing himself to the new media." In his view, there was no difference between a computer and his pencil. The American poet William Carlos Williams had written that a poem was "a machine made of words," and he had not been sentimental about the machine in that statement.

M. Gandon, reminding the chairman that he had mentioned Mallarmé, quoted that poet to the effect that "everything had to end up as a book." It seemed to him that part of this discussion had been taking place in a vacuum. The impression had been given that writers had free access to television. That was, unhappily, not the case in France. There they had two sorts of writers: those who went on writing books while wishing, to some extent, to write for television, and those specialists who were the only writers to whom television was open. Was it in fact necessary to be a specialist to obtain access to television? Was this a new mode of expression which called for new skills? If so, M. Gandon regretted to say that all this talk was to no purpose.

Man's voice, speaking in English, referred to a "distressing statement" in the program which implied that the effect of universal use of the new media might lead to "a millennium in which the human being surrendered his individuality and was absorbed into a kind of cosmic consciousness." Did the chairman assume responsibility for that statement? Mr. McLuhan having answered, "Only in the sense of a probe, yes," the speaker protested that this "might not be a worthwhile goal" for a civilized man, that it was "not right to try to herd" writers into "any such ideology." He disliked the word "mass" and found it "tricky" to define. In his view, the writer had first of all to possess a sense of his own "human burden." He had to possess a personal mode of expression. The danger here was that a kind of fetish might be made of a technological device by such talk as "extending our conscious information" and so on.

Mr. Darko Suvin (Zagreb P.E.N., Yugoslavia) proposed to join those who had taken issue with the "bold, scintillating, seminal and somewhat self-contradictory ideas" of the chairman. It was not that he yearned for the "good old times" which had been neither all good nor all bad. The chairman had done all present a service by "identifying the situation where the technologists constitute our new environment, our windows on the new world"; they were, in the chairman's "pretty Joycean phrase, wearing mankind as a skin." He wished to point out that information and meaning were not the same thing. The commercial "jingle," because it conveyed only information, forced one to be conscious of the electronic device; listening to Mozart—or to Louis

Armstrong, as one's taste might dictate—one was primarily conscious of the music. The question, therefore, was whether writers for these media were to contribute a healthy skin or a diseased skin (to use Mr. McLuhan's metaphor). Whether "this casement" was to open on a world of the imagination or of finality. What we ask about the airplane—shall we see in it a triumph of human ingenuity or a bomb-carrier?—could also be asked about the media here discussed. Although himself a Marxist, Mr. Suvin saw the situation as "non-deterministic." Would the new media dictate "debased writing" or make possible creative writing, was the question.

Literature and the Human Sciences on the Nature of Contemporary Man

Wednesday, June 15

FIRST SESSION

Louis Martin-Chauffier, CHAIRMAN
member of the Académie des Sciences morales et politiques, Paris

Sutan Takdir Alisjahbana
Jakarta

Leon Edel
New York University, New York

Ralph Ellison
New York

Heinz Kamnitzer
Berlin (G.D.R.)

Cheik Hamidou Kané
Dakar

Rudolf Krämer-Badoni
Wiesbaden

Joost A.M. Meerloo, M.D.
New York

Leda Mileva
Sofia

Maurice Nadeau
Editor, *la Quinzaine Littéraire,* Paris

Ramon Parres, M.D.
Mexico, D.F.

Thursday, June 16

SECOND SESSION

Louis Martin-Chauffier, CHAIRMAN
Paris

Joseph W. Abruquah
Headmaster, Mfantsipim School, Cape Coast (Ghana)

Claude Arsac
Geneva

Ralph Ellison
New York

Jean Follain
Paris

Sei Ito
Tokyo

Cheik Hamidou Kané
Dakar

Maurice Nadeau
Paris

Ramon Parres, M.D.
Mexico, D.F.

Mihail Petroveanu
Bucharest

Literature and the Human Sciences on the Nature of Contemporary Man

FIRST SESSION

M. Louis Martin-Chauffier opened the discussion by reminding his colleagues that within the broad framework of the general theme of the congress, *The Writer as Independent Spirit,* they were asked to confine their statements to the particular subject before them: *Literature and the Human Sciences on the Nature of Contemporary Man.* In the chairman's view, there were a few scientists who could write and many more who could not; there were a few men of letters who were well grounded in one or another science and many who had no pretension to scientific knowledge. What was clear, meanwhile, was that scientists wrote in one way and men of letters in another way. Essentially, the subject before the table was the writer as such, and he could be described as a man with something to say who wrote in a personal style uninfluenced by passing fashions and able to survive them. His subject might be complex, but his language was eventually accessible to all: Proust came to mind as an example. One could say that the writer was in fact independent of the social or human sciences largely because the scientists had not the writer's gift of expression.

The writer was an artist; and an artist is one whose aim is to please himself and thereby to give pleasure to others. This had the result that what he wrote was inimitable; it could be parodied; it could not be copied with the intent which had prompted it.

Dr. Meerloo, speaking in English, said that he had been asked to put forward a few basic points for discussion. He would begin, therefore, by observing that all men, including the poet and the "revolutionary artist," were "born in a special language" and influenced as they grew up by concepts, modes of thought, and styles which were imposed by their environment. They were further influenced, as Charcot noted nearly a century ago, by the play of involuntary memory, in a way which caused them to reproduce, to "plagiarize" their unconsciously accumulated experience. This, too, inclined them to a special style. Among other influences in recent years were various branches of technology, including a kind of hypnosis exercised by television and the effects of mass production of the printed word. When, moreover, we were asked if man was an "independent thinker," our answer had to take account of the promptings of "the irrational" for "irrationality is a way of giving new meanings to things." Consideration of these four points, he believed, would reveal the extent to which the writer was able to create in a spirit of independence—particularly from the influence of the new electronic devices.

The chairman, before calling on the next speaker, redefined the subject as "the writer threatened in his inquiry into the nature of man"—man who remained unchanged while society changed, as we saw in our own times when cultural activities multiplied while the mass media tended more and more to diminish rather than elevate the human being.

Mr. Krämer-Badoni, speaking in French, began by citing examples of the tendency implied in their subject and summed up by saying that "Freud's purpose was not to offer models to writers; it was to cure the sick." The sick were among literature's most interesting characters. Shakespeare's contemporary, John Ford, in *'Tis Pity She's a Whore,* did not write "scientifically" about incest, his play was a tragedy about a desperate love-ravaged brother and sister; it was not a "case history" founded on "data" at all.

As a human being, Mr. Krämer-Badoni went on, one was both a personal and a social being; light was needed on the human condition, and needed precisely to aid man to live in the human community. But as an artist, one was still committed—even socially and politically committed. One suffered, took pleasure, was tracked by destiny, was an anarchist; one created symbols of these realities which science was incapable of creating; and as artist, as writer, one lived in a domain which science could not enter and which belonged wholly to art.

Mr. Ellison, who followed Mr. Krämer-Badoni, drew attention to the role played by contemporary sociology as "a substitute for art." In this role—not in his function of data-gathering and classification—the sociologist became a "manipulator" of the "mythology" which sociology has been engaged in creating. This had had the result of persuading some writers, some artists, to abandon their belief in "the autonomy of art." Such writers ceased to look into themselves, ceased to look to the accumulated insight that is contained in literature, for their knowledge of man and society; instead, they turned to the social scientists to learn from them what the human animal was, what human values were, in what direction literature should go, what the standards of artistic creation should be.

One of the "sacred functions" (so to say) of literature was precisely to take human experience apart, to re-live what was eternally human in the masterpieces of the past, both the rational and the irrational, and to give new form and meaning to the eternally human. This was a most important function; it—art, in fact—was man's chief means of preserving his humanity; and it was a function in which the social scientist could share only when—as now and again happens—he wrote as artist. Here in the United States, what was to be deplored was that many writers had lost courage when faced by "the heavyweight data of sociology." Man could not fulfill himself, sense his brotherhood, become aware of the wholeness of human experience if poets and editors —Mr. Podhoretz, for example, who believed that the novel was dead— agreed to turn over the function of describing life and defining human values, to "mindless machines."

Dr. Parres, speaking in English, said that many people appeared to feel themselves threatened by the machine in the electronic age. There might be some truth in the idea that the writer felt oppressed by the machine. But should we not bear in mind that to creative man—in the sciences as well as the arts—the important thing is the act of creation? The machine itself was an act of man's creation; and the purpose of its creation was surely to contribute to a better life for all men. Descartes had been quoted by Dr. Joost Meerloo. Dr. Parres disliked Descartes, who had divided man into body and soul. Instead of Descartes' "I think, therefore I am" he would suggest "I seek, therefore I am." Dr. Parres warned against using or quoting social data out of context. The function of the artist was, in his opinion, to look within himself; and the importance of the artist, the writer, lay in his giving deeper meanings and aesthetic expression to what he learned about man from looking into himself. Aggression was a psychological phenomenon, yet Dostoevsky had written more memorably about it in his novels than any scientist had done. And yet the writer, in common with the rest of us, including the psychiatrist's patients, could not live apart from the influences around him.

The chairman, before calling on M. Nadeau, observed that he had thus far listened to a succession of very interesting monologues. He would ask speakers to try to comment, when possible, on what they had already heard in order that out of exchanges of views a semblance of continuity and form might be given to the discussion.

M. Nadeau observed that Shakespeare, and in another age Balzac, had practiced psychology before the science of psychology existed. Writers had been preoccupied with the sentimental and the instinctual life of man long before the specialists—who of course had their place in society—had arrived with their instruments, methods and jargon. The savant sought to communicate information, the writer as artist had nothing to do with information; it was not his purpose to add to man's knowledge; and as to the writer's defining human values, as Mr. Ellison appeared to suggest, M. Nadeau was in two minds about that.

The writer's role was at one and the same time gratuitous and necessary, for the reason that he could not help writing what he felt and thought, and these were matters which the sciences could not express. Love, for example. Science was busy with love, analyzing, charting, measuring the duration of the orgasm; yet what could it tell us about a lover's feelings? Or death. Who but the writer could say what a particular person felt at any given moment about death? The only thing one might hope to derive from a confrontation of writers and scientists was perhaps a new definition of literature. Both sides had their place, ought to be acquainted, but neither should look up to nor down upon the other.

Mr. Edel referred to a remark by Mr. Krämer-Badoni to the effect that the artist was free to express his creative influence and his vision of the world. "But," Mr. Edel asked, "what of the invisible hammering at the artist by the mores of the times?" He had visited Thoreau's Walden Pond, hoping to commune quietly with nature: he had found there automobile trailers and heard the bawling of television voices. He had visited, in Italy, Hadrian's Villa, only to be surrounded by charming young Italians with transistor radios blaring. These, said Mr. Edel, were the powers arrayed against us.

To get away from a fictional war film on television he had turned to another station—only to see a film of real warfare. Was it too much to say that the public, that vast sponge, must end by ceasing to distinguish between reality and the unreal? That because of this, perhaps, people in New York City had only recently looked down from their windows and seen a woman murdered and had not called the police? Certainly, all this had relevance for the writer. He wrote for a public. The public was changing. It was desensitized, disassociated. "I think Mr. Ellison is right to say that sociology gives us an encapsulated and formalized picture of man." Mr. Edel put this down chiefly to the influence of advertising which he thought far more dangerous than Mr. Bellow's complaint that the academic intellectuals were talking literature to death.

What was the answer? Dr. Meerloo had hinted that writers were perhaps not independent. "I say we possess only the illusion of independence." The reading public would not help writers to make that illusion a reality; and what that implied, perhaps, was that the critic had today a greater duty and function than ever before. Perhaps also it meant that "part of the commitment of the writer is that he shall also be a critic, critical of all these conventions and horrors of our times." To which Mr. Edel added support for M. Martin-Chauffier's plea for a concern with style, purity of language, and a commitment to fight against the influence exercised by the semi-literate, formless and extravagant language of journalism and advertising. Real dangers existed, and the most dangerous was the desensitization of the individual, who was becoming a mere spectator of reality, not a participant in it.

Mr. Hamidou Kané, who spoke in French, said that as a Senegalese he represented an "oral rather than a written civilization" living in the midst of a world that was moving towards "totalization." For such a civilization, in such a world, the writer's function was particularly important. Whereas most of those who had studied the peoples of Black Africa had been ethnologists and anthropologists come from other continents, the African sensibility, African values, could be best expressed and interpreted by Africa's own poets and artists. It was in this that their importance for their own peoples resided.

Mme. Mileva spoke in English. Sharing what she called the optimistic—perhaps realistic—view that no effort of psychology and the social sciences could make of literature a mere by-product, she said that she sensed nevertheless a pessimistic undertone, particularly on the part of her American colleagues. They seemed baffled by electronics, cybernetics, the new psychology and the rest. The best Bulgarian writers had been ready to experience poverty and suffering, even death, to convey their message to their people. Why should writers fear scientific progress? Was it not better to accept the challenge and create an even higher and more significant literature?

Today we could turn deserts into palm-gardens. But we were able also to create vast and terrible deserts. We witnessed scientific achievements, but the word "war" remained in our dictionaries. Psychology explained the most subtle inner reflexes, but it was unable to cope with man's alienation, greed, indifference—a point well made by Mr. Edel. Obviously, this was not good enough.

Mme. Mileva then touched upon a point hitherto not discussed—whether the writer who took society rather than man himself as his subject, yielded up thereby some of his independence. It seemed to her that even the writer who chose to deal only with the human soul was, in spite of himself, dealing with society. This was true, for example, of Gogol, of Chekhov; true, in another time and setting, of Kafka. "Neither the writer as a person nor the characters he creates can escape society." As for a choice between shutting oneself up to write "only" about the soul, or going out-of-doors to survey the entire horizon of human relations, Mme. Mileva would say that there were many examples in modern literature of the first kind of writer producing a fleshless ghost. Without faith in man, without the will to make a better world, literature seemed to Mme. Mileva only an outcry of despair. To write outcries of despair was a form of disease, but one from which writers who crossed oceans and continents to take part in a P.E.N. congress could not be said to suffer.

Mr. Alisjahbana, speaking in English, said that the accelerated progress of science since the Renaissance had in recent years reached a phase of acute crisis in which the most important element was technology. All that was implied in this crisis of our civilization had to be understood before we sought to define the place of the writer. The resultant "expansion of man in time and in space" had been accompanied by a weakening of the religious sense, the sense of conscience, the integrating force of the human personality, to the point where we could say that contemporary man had been "hollowed out from within." Small wonder that mental illness was today the most prevalent illness, spreading wherever the industrial society took root, even in the "underdeveloped" countries. And with the rise of multiple new national states, new tensions had entered the field of politics. All this had been perceived by such social philosophers as Spengler in Germany and Ortega y Gasset in Spain.

Many writers had, in consequence, taken refuge in the life of the emotions and in poetic reveries. Others felt themselves the victims of the industrial society, and here it would seem that it was the writers of the United States who were least able to cope with their situation. We remembered how an earlier generation, the "lost" generation, escaped to Paris in the 1920s. We had seen Nelson Algren and Norman Mailer rejecting the industrial civilization. It was characteristic that some American writers now envied the social scientists.

But, in Mr. Alisjahbana's opinion, the social scientists themselves had failed to face the same challenge. The psychologists, the sociologists and the anthropologists could no longer talk together, so deep was the mire of terminology in which they were respectively caught. On the other hand, the "pure" scientists have had no language in which to communicate with the rest of us.

To *Dr. Kamnitzer,* speaking in English, it appeared that some of the previous speakers looked upon ignorance of the contemporary world, or unconcern about it, as "almost the hallmark of a poet." This prompted him to ask, how does a blind man find his way? Being himself a social scientist, he was apparently one of Mr. Ellison's terrible manipulators. But in his view it was not the social scientist, it was the poet, the playwright, the artist who posed the problem. If it was true (as the Program Note said) that "the writer no longer illuminates for man the nature and spirit of man" and that "literature may now be a secondary source," then it was the writer himself who was the source of his own dilemma. Today, it was not Hamlet but the human species that asked whether to be or not to be; it was not the poet, or the fittest, whose survival was in question, but our institutions. To adapt T. S. Eliot, "This is how the world ends, not with a whimper but with a bang."

If the writer was to influence his fellow man, he must be committed, and, "I am pleading that he commit himself." There was an "astonishing increase" of lack of purpose and of vision in some writing today. Some thought it "almost blasphemous" to deal with the miseries that exist. Brecht, who as a Marxist—which was his private concern—said that to write about trees was almost a crime when misdeeds were being performed; yet he himself wrote a beautiful little poem about a poplar planted in the midst of a devastated square in Berlin. He wrote, that is, of nature and humanity at the same time.

Dr. Kamnitzer noted that the program mentioned the existence of a hunger for documentation; there was also, however, a greater yearning for poetry than perhaps ever before, at least in his country. "Man is hungry for both bread and roses, and will turn away with scorn or sorrow if he is offered stones instead."

Mr. John Coutsoheras, President of the Greek P.E.N. Center, speaking in French from the floor, expressed his objection to the Program Note which asserted that not measurement, analysis and social research but only contemplation, self-knowledge and the creative imagination constituted the sources of past literature. In his view, the one did not exclude the other. The program referred also to a tendency on the part of contemporary readers to turn from literature to the writings of the sociologists and psychologists for light on the nature of contemporary man. Mr. Coutsoheras asked permission to summarize the views of Aristotle on this subject.

His audience would remember that Aristotle found the source of literature in mimesis, imitation of life; but not external life only; of the inner life as well: cruelty, pity (Ελησς), and the catharsis or purification of the passions. Aristotle did not stop here: he saw man as a social animal as well. From which it should be concluded that there was no need to fear that literature, in our time, would become a secondary form of writing merely because it was concerned with society. As the chairman said so well, the poet and the novelist create out of their imagination, and in a style, a language, that could not be written by sociologists.

SECOND SESSION

M. Louis Martin-Chauffier begged those at the Round Table to carry on a running dialogue and to refrain from pronouncing monologues. Because, he went on, time had been lacking at the first session to hear comments from the floor he would begin by allowing twenty minutes for this purpose.

Mr. den Doolaard said that for a writer to fear the loss of his independence of spirit to the sciences was unnecessary, provided the writer was able to "dominate the new things." He thought the social sciences were of use to the novelist. Zola, who took such voluminous notes, was an outstanding example. He agreed with Mme. Mileva that writers were members of society and with Mr. Coutsoheras' citation of Aristotle—that man was a political animal. For writers, the universe was their "grab bag"; they had only to take from it what they needed and disregard the rest.

M. Follain (French P.E.N.) quoted with approval Victor Hugo: "Form is substance risen to the surface." * Literature was a form that could not be displaced by any other art. True, traditional humanism appeared to be on the decline. Writers had found that Socratic reasoning was not enough; that they were more dependent upon the cosmic and the social than they imagined; but this constituted an enrichment, not a withering. The old self-confident psychology, too, had given way to a more fluid and mysterious psychology that was less sure of itself. The new sociology revealed a communion among men of which totali-

* "La forme c'est le fond qui remonte à la surface."

tarianism was a crude caricature. Meanwhile, the individual personality remained irreplaceable.

Many writers did tend to an easy abdication of their independence, did manifest what Jean Paulhan called a "terror" which prompted them to reject such words as "art" and "inspiration" and to adopt a fleshless jargon. But the rest, aware of their communion and their communication with the universe, were fortified by a more deeply grounded sense of independence.

Mr. Mansukhlal Jhaveri (All-India P.E.N.), spoke in English and summed up certain fundamental facts: A degree of give and take between the writer and society is inescapable; the writer nevertheless must have complete freedom of self-expression; he ought to have that spark we call genius, and to draw light from that spark he needed to have contact with life and to study life. He would not lose his independence of spirit if he chose to make use of the newer disciplines to obtain a surer assessment of man in the scheme of things—always provided that the object of his studies was man himself.

Mr. Tome Momirovski (Skopje P.E.N., Yugoslavia), speaking in English, observed that the creative writer's independence of spirit was in danger of vulgarization by the subjects offered him on this "limited and free contradictory planet." What was it that restricted his independence? The clamors and discords of the world? Was the solution to be found in a "synthetic or analytic theory of human totality?" In the long history of man's emancipation we seemed now to have reached a point of separation between the artist's personality and the social reality. A process of estrangement was going on which the writer could either try to conquer or from which he could seek escape into "self-deceptive neurosis."

Mr. Czeslaw Milosz (Writers-in-Exile P.E.N.) offered, in English, to "continue a dialogue" with M. Nadeau, Dr. Kamnitzer and Mr. Edel. There were people, he said, who explored Tolstoy's concern in *War and Peace* with such abstractions as freedom and necessity, the mass and the individual. There was his friend, a young (unnamed) Polish poet, who felt that poetry should not be "imprisoned" and whose ideal was the pre-Socratic age "when poetry and philosophy were one." Mr. Milosz opted for the zone between knowledge and literature; this zone, though it shifted from age to age, was a place of refuge from those social and political scientists whose forerunners were called publicists and who were today journalists using a complicated jargon and enjoying the prestige of university chairs. To find writers humbling themselves before these so-called scientists was surprising. Mr. Milosz saw no reason for the writer to be defeatist in the presence of a literature—the theatre of the absurd, say—that was turning to philosophical parable and investigation. The cause was not a weakness in literature, it lay in the existence of a crisis in philosophy itself, as a professor had written in a recent article entitled "American Philosophy is Dead."

Mr. Dragomir Nenoff (Writers-in-Exile P.E.N.), speaking English, said that we were in the presence of two schools, one which defended "the electronic reproduction of literature" while the other sought to "amplify the source of original ideas." He believed that they would ultimately be integrated; he would add that danger for the free spirit could come only from this table's excessive emphasis on the former and neglect of the latter.

Mr. Abruquah (Ghana) spoke in English. He described himself as headmaster of a school and as a social scientist. The scientists present, he said, had "tended to dazzle us by their excursions into technicalities." The writers had tried stoutly to defend their independence, though forgetting that they themselves, as writers, were the suppliers of the raw materials for the mass media. The fact was that one could not revert to a pre-scientific age. One could not say that science was "all wrong" because the Bible said that the universe was created in six days. What one meant to say, presumably, was that the role of literature was to breathe life into the clay of science.

Writers were in early times an aristocracy; they were the philosophers of their times. Writers today ought to take this leaf out of the book of their forerunners. "I am sure," Mr. Abruquah said, "that modern writers are better able to play the searchlight of truth on the nature of man" precisely because of what the social scientists (even though it was by "dissecting man into little classified entities") had added to the writer's knowledge. He felt, therefore, that there was no need for this controversy. The enduring works of literature would still be those which breathed life and soul into man.

Mme. Claude Arsac (Geneva P.E.N., Switzerland), a social scientist and the author of three novels, speaking in French, referred first to Mr. Edel's statement of the previous day that culture was widening but not elevating man, that men were being "desensitized." This was in her view particularly the case in the United States whose television, with its violence, murder and riots, was clearly inferior to that in Europe. It was plain that the writer could no longer shut himself up in an ivory tower. And though she saw in Marxism, "with its context of hatred and violence," a very meager source of inspiration, she would agree with Dr. Kamnitzer that the writer should be committed, *engagé*, at least to salvage true beauty in a soulless world. The mission of the writer was to create beauty, to lead men towards receptivity of the arts. She rejected the notion expressed at the first session—that the writer as a social being was wholly different from the writer as inescapably an anarchic individual. Not "anarchist" but "non-conformist" was the true description, and by non-conformist she meant "that man whose acts are the product of his essential nature." She took her stand with C. G. Jung and Bernanos against the Robot. And she would add Professor Gurevitch's warning, that when we exalt the inner life and contrast it with the externally social, we must be careful not to identify social life wholly with the anonymous mass, for the mass is unaware of the true community. The true social feeling, Mme. Arsac said, was intense and a form of inner communion with others. P.E.N. itself was an example —there was no reason for writers to fear competition from the sciences, precisely because literature was an art.

Mr. Ito (Japan P.E.N.), speaking in English, said that a Japanese psychologist had assured him that "nowadays we have no need of novelists in society. The psychologist will do everything they have done until now." He was shocked into reflection by this remark. The literary problem seemed complicated enough. But there was also painting, which seemed to have "lost its religious character" when art photography took to depicting "ideal things." Non-fiction had assumed the role of the novel in some respects. Some books of psychology unquestionably interested readers more than the ordinary novel did. In the Western world, certainly, the realistic novel had analysis and explanation of matter and human relations as its object, at least until Freud appeared and other changes took place. Psychoanalysis had brought out new relationships—between mother and son, father and daughter, for example; relationships inherent in nature. The aim of literature was to depict the whole man. And yet, could it be denied that in some sense scientific works did the job of the novelist?

In short, said Mr. Ito, one cannot deny either their value to the sciences or its value to literature.

Mr. Paolo Milano (Italian P.E.N.), speaking in English, took issue with the tendency to describe science as an approach to "single aspects of reality" and art as the "divine power to face man in his universality and reality in its totality." He doubted that writers—shifting their sights between cosmic reality and that individual, the "whole" man— knew what universality was. Secondly, the notion of "the influence of the sciences on art" seemed to him a defective formulation. For one thing, the writer was free, not obliged to draw upon the sciences for his understanding of reality. For another, the world of contemporary art and letters was, of itself, going about its work "in a scientific way." One thought of symbolic art, structural art, the anti-novel, the "non-fiction novel." What did this prove except that the artist was wondering if it was really possible to apprehend reality outside of the scientific approach, while the scientist, facing a single aspect of the reality he knew to be multiple, doubted the validity of his own limited search?

M. Petroveanu (Roumanian P.E.N.), speaking in French, asked if the problem before the Round Table was really as crucially urgent as it was made to appear? More than forty years ago the Roumanian poet and philosopher, Lucian Blaga, had related the vision of Picasso to non-Euclidean geometry and impressionistic painting to what he called *la psychologie abyssale*. In Renaissance times, the artist and the scientist were one. In the nineteenth century, thermodynamics and Comte's philosophy of positivism combined to found the theory of the will as motive force of the human comedy. Romanticism itself produced the "lucid hallucinations" of Poe and the "naive scientific optimism" of Victor Hugo. Today we saw psychoanalysis influencing the plays of the surrealists, Arthur Miller, Tennessee Williams, and Marxism the plays of Brecht and his school. At this point, M. Petroveanu took issue with Mme. Arsac's attribution of hatred and violence to Marxism, saying that Marxism was an instrument for man's liberation and even Catholic critics recognized that it had a humanistic aim, the aim of fusing essence and existence, which was indeed literature's own aim. That it could be misused was unquestionable; no one blamed Catholicism because the Jesuits had at one time made it an instrument of terror.

As to the subject before the Round Table, what counted was what the writer or artist did with whatever materials he used, and the essential question was what the means and ends were, of art and science respectively. The American poet Emily Dickinson had written

> A color stands abroad
> On solitary hills
> That science cannot overtake
> But human nature *feels*.

But the writer's subject was not only the ineffable, it was also human nature, and here literature encountered the sciences. The methods of science were not those of literature, they tended towards objectivity, or, as the Hungarian critic Lukács, put it, tended to "disanthropomorphize the world." Art, on the other hand, was a subjective form of access to reality, saturated with humanity and creating a wholly anthropomorphic world. The writer's language, meanwhile, was ambivalent: on the one hand a means of communication, on the other a means of creation, inventing new worlds and upholding aesthetic values. As communication it was only one among other means of informing mankind. Even when literature attempted to be purely impersonal and analytical—as in Flaubert, or the contemporary French "new novel"—and was fascinated by the objective process of science, it was still the product of an individual consciousness. This was why, though the writer might claim Marxism, psychoanalysis or another theory or science as his point of departure, his human implications outlived the scientific theories on which he founded his literary concepts.

In sum, literature transformed scientific ideas into the elements of myth; Balzac's own will endowed his characters with an energy that lent them the dimensions of mythical figures. It followed that the writer who subjected science to art was a conqueror; the writer who submitted art to science ensured his own defeat. Literature achieved its goal by devious paths which were not those of science. Fighting on its own terrain, with its own weapons, or even supplemented by weapons borrowed from science, it afforded us the fascinating spectacle of the human consciousness struggling with the problems of the life and death of man and society, and succeeding, in Huxley's words, "in revealing what is low in what is high, what is high in what is low, in the human condition."

Mme. Arsac intervened to explain that M. Petroveanu had misunderstood her. She had not meant to attribute the defects in United States television to Marxists. And though she had no wish to embark upon controversy, she would express the hope that one was free to believe there were more adequate and more fruitful ways than Marxism of trying to conciliate the essence of man with his existence.

The chairman announced a recess of fifteen minutes, after which seven speakers from the floor would be heard, each to speak no longer than five minutes.

Upon resumption, *Dr. David Abrahamsen* (American P.E.N.), took issue with Mr. Abruquah's metaphorical statement that "science is clay." He said to Mr. Ito that against his colleague who had no more use for novelists he would bring forward one hundred or one thousand psychologists who still saw a justification in novel-writing. As a psychoanalyst he would say that environmental influences (including those produced by electronic media) upon the human mind varied with the particular character of the individual concerned. He included here the character of writers. Lust for material gain was sometimes part of a writer's character. We ought not to forget, either, that for one writer who earned vast sums of money there were numberless writers who wrote without regard to money.

As to writers and the sciences, "if you are a good writer you have nothing to fear." There were great poets before Freud and after Freud; he had merely systematized our knowledge of "all the interests, ideas, and instincts which poets had written about." What counted was the personal integrity of the poet.

Man's voice, speaking in English, was critical of a phrase in the Program Note which read as follows: 'Today, it is suggested, men are turning away from literature to the social sciences and to psychology to learn what man—at least contemporary man—essentially is.' "I think," he said, "the implication—assumption, rather—that literature is an equally valid source of information as such is a wrong implication." After pointing out that literature and these sciences could properly "complement each other," the speaker went on to declare that "very few writers have been great thinkers as such; the writer has always taken ideas from the atmosphere around him" and that in fact "ideas again is the wrong word because the writer has always relied on experience." No writer, indeed, went to books of science to get ideas; "never was he that mechanical."

The chairman, expressing his agreement with Dr. Abrahamsen's statement on Freud's "systematizing" the thoughts and instincts of the poets, said that writers had much to learn from Freud's system but made a kind of use of it which Freud could not have made.

Dr. Henri-Jean Barraud (French P.E.N.) noted the omission in the Program Note of any mention of the philosophers as writers. He saw the writer not only as artist but also, in his own way, as philosopher. This was inescapable, though the writer expressed himself "in images" and the professional philosopher in concepts. The writer, meanwhile, did not explain himself, he merely suggested; he was "free to move between dream and reality"; where the two converged was in their sources, which for both science and literature were universal. Both had to reject pre-ordained attitudes and the objective of both was knowledge of man.

Dr. Barraud's second point was furnished by Mr. McLuhan's remark at Round Table I, that "history was the realm of nostalgia." This was an error; history was in fact the matrix of the future. European thought had been impregnated with Aristotle's ideas until the birth of the scientific spirit in the seventeenth century—the age which put an end to the communion that had till then united the philosopher, the artist and the writer. This point, said Dr. Barraud, was decisive, for here science had sought to impose mensuration and quantity upon those whose concern was with quality—the writer, the philosopher, the artist. Given the prodigious efficacity of experimental science, and the ideal of quality which animated the writer, we had "two absolutely separate worlds." Dr. Barraud believed that in maintaining the primacy of quality over quantity the writer could look forward to a splendid future.

The chairman, while appreciating Dr. Barraud's defence of philosophy, pointed out that contemporary philosophy was filled with jargon borrowed, in fact, from the vocabulary of science. He would distinguish between professional philosophers and those who were writers first—in France a Montaigne, an Alain. Did a man care or did he not care to write well, was the question. Dr. Barraud had spoken of history. M. Martin-Chauffier was a mediaevalist by education; he had great faith in historical documentation, much less faith in historical interpretation, which seemed to him valuable only insofar as the historian was a writer or a thinker, since the interpretations of historians were a product of their personal conceptions. Michelet's value, for example, lay in the truths he brought to the surface by his intuition, by the spirit that glowed within him. In speaking thus, he was speaking as one who was himself a historian.

M. Pham Viet Tuyen (Vietnam P.E.N.) spoke in French, first on literature and its publics. He took as examples a girl in a Vietnamese rice paddy singing a folksong, a Hong Kong housewife poring over an ancient story of chivalry, an American professor reading an essay on the independent spirit in the electronic age. None asked their authors to enlighten them on the nature of man; that was a question posed only by a small minority. They asked that literature, as wine does, or tea, give them pleasure, allow them to escape from the world of reality.

Secondly, as to science and literature. The light cast upon man's spirit by psychology or sociology was the product of an orderly presentation of disparate facts and was more or less faithful to reality, to life—that same life which the poet, the novelist, or the playwright sought to seize on the wing. For example, to understand the idealism of the present anti-war movement in the United States one would have to live here for a time. To communicate the aspiration for peace and liberty of the Vietnamese people one would need to have lived through the cruelties suffered by that people since 1959. Meanwhile, it was a fact that Homer still moved us and enlightened us; and whatever might be said of a literary work by a psychologist or a sociologist, that work could still produce a deeper effect than a work of science would produce. As for literary hacks and true writers, the hack might lose by studying the works of the new disciplines, but the talented writer would gain from this study. To take society as one's subject did not stand in the way of the creation of original and perhaps immortal characters.

Mme. Jean Durtal (French P.E.N.), after declaring that she brought the congress greetings from the Société des Gens de Lettres de France, pointed to eighteenth-century writers as the source of the ideas of liberty, and to nineteenth-century romantic and realistic writers as the inspirers of sociology. In our own age, she said, "a certain disequilibrium" had resulted from the separate paths followed by science and by literature. The result was a scientific development which filled man, at one and the same time, with fear and with hope. It was between these two emotions that Mme. Durtal saw the "true place of the writer." His role was to "decree that law of love without which the world could not evolve" and which was man's hope and the key to humanity. Warning the scientists against any effort to direct a world "whose directing belonged to the thinkers and writers we are," Mme. Durtal stressed that there existed only one problem—the "harmonious evolution of the world."

M. Nadeau, called upon by the chairman to comment, said, "Well, of course, I am for love, but after all. . . ." One of the Round Table's topics was the practice of borrowing from the sciences. An American, Oscar Lewis, had tape-recorded in Mexico the life of an urban family named Sanchez and then of a peasant family named Martinez. Here was a sociologist writers would do well to examine. Lewis was not a professional writer, he had used an electronic instrument, yet he had produced a work of art. A second example, created in the rarefied atmosphere of Paris, was the "new novel" which sought to return to reality by simply recording people's conversations and refraining from rewriting them. M. Nadeau would put the question—one he could not himself answer: How did these efforts achieve the quality of works of art?

Man's voice, speaking in English, said that the question was "very tough." Cutting—a form of editing—of the tape made the work of composition of Lewis' books analogous in kind to that of the movie director. There was intellectual, one might say, artistic intervention. There was also the intervention of translators, for if M. Nadeau read *The Children of Sanchez* in French, he read a translation of Oscar Lewis' English translation of the recorded Spanish. And not Spanish, merely, but Mexican dialect of Spanish.

The Writer as Collaborator in Other Men's Purposes

Wednesday, June 15
FIRST SESSION

Robert Goffin, CHAIRMAN
member of the Académie Royale de la Langue et de la Littérature
Françaises, Brussels

Jean Bloch-Michel
Paris

Philip A. Hope-Wallace
London

William Jovanovich
President, Harcourt, Brace & World, New York

Melvin Lasky
Editor, *Encounter,* London

Paolo Milano
Rome

Victoria Ocampo
Founder-Editor, *Sur,* Buenos Aires

Bogdan Pogačnik
Ljubljana

Elmer Rice
New York

Dolf Sternberger
Frankfurt-am-Main

Thursday, June 16

SECOND SESSION

Robert Goffin, CHAIRMAN
Brussels

Piero Chiara
Varese (Italy)

Marchette Chute
New York

Alberto S. Florentino
Publisher, 'Peso Books,' Quezon City (Philippines)

Philip A. Hope-Wallace
London

William Jovanovich
New York

Donald Keene
Columbia University, New York

Edward Lucie-Smith
London

Victoria Ocampo
Buenos Aires

Dolf Sternberger
Frankfurt-am-Main

The Writer as Collaborator in Other Men's Purposes

FIRST SESSION

M. Goffin opened the meeting by declaring that he had accepted the invitation to preside over this discussion willingly, but with some perturbation. The Program Note defining their theme was not altogether clear to him. He would like his colleagues' views about it and would begin by asking Mr. Elmer Rice to say how he defined it.

Mr. Rice's view was that the panel would discuss the effect upon writers of the new mechanized arts in which writers were employed in various capacities. He had himself, fourteen years ago, written an article entitled "The Industrialized Writer" which dealt with their subject and from which he hoped to be allowed to read.

Mr. Pogačnik, speaking in English, remarked that the writing they were asked to examine was not, he feared, the product of genius; it was in sum the writing produced by those who work in mass communication. The question was, nevertheless, how that considerable number of writers, whatever their talents, could maintain their "morality," could really remain honest and independent writers.

Mr. Sternberger, who followed, also spoke in English. His impression of their topic was somewhat broader than Mr. Rice's. He had supposed that the theme implied not so much media as masters; the writer in the service of a government, a doctrine, a commercial publisher, a theatre management.

Mr. Jovanovich looked upon the topic as defined in the program as implying that the writer was "constantly being violated." Why, for one thing, distinguish between writers and other men? For the moment, he would suggest that the writer stop being "sentimental about himself."

Mme. Ocampo, speaking in French, was of the opinion that the new media had in fact faced writers with a problem of conscience, a moral problem. It was clear that these "terrible means of communication" could be used either for good or for ill. On this point, she was wholly in agreement with Mr. Sternberger.

M. Bloch-Michel began by agreeing with Mr. Jovanovich: who were these "other men" against whom the writer was arrayed? Meanwhile, the theme as put to them could be defined in two ways. First, was it true that the conditions in which the writer wrote and published were now so different that they threatened the writer's spiritual independence? For example, publishers had always commissioned books. Second, was it true that the fact of having to serve the exigencies of the new technological means—the cinema, radio, television—had been followed by loss of the writer's independence?

Mr. Hope-Wallace saw, first of all, a fairly simple distinction between writing as journalism and writing as art. As journalist, one hired oneself out and accepted the conditions implied in that fact, including the "emendations of editors." Writing for a *good* newspaper, one was not seriously interfered with. Cutting of copy was, in his experience, the only serious form of editing. On the other hand, while writing as an artist was a kind of "self-indulgence," he did think it ought to be "inviolable as far as possible." The conditions of journalism had to be accepted, even when editorial cutting of a review of a play (for example) hurt the writer, the play, and the actor of whom mention was perhaps deleted. But those were different kinds of editing. The Program Note mentioned "house style." Mr. Hope-Wallace knew of a magazine whose editors regularly boiled down "personal pieces" by many journalists and produced an article which falsified the original contributions. This practice was growing and he thought it a danger to the writer's independence.

Mr. Lasky agreed that the distinction drawn by Mr. Hope-Wallace was important, though he would add that there was a "high journalism" which was better than "low art." He asked if the habits and tendencies of "tampering, cutting, censoring, twisting, rewriting" in mass journalism could be sealed off from the editing of the manuscripts of poets and other creative writers? He felt that there was no accident here; that this was "connected with a lack of respect for the word and the independence of the writer."

Mr. Milano, speaking in English, suggested that the core of the problem was whether there was anything inherent in the mass media which hampered the writer's freedom of expression. He asked if the participants round the table should not explore such questions as "What *is* a television show?" "What *is* a broadcast in the present state of civilization?" "What *is* mass publishing?" There were people who said that no idealism, no degree of intelligence, could make a televised production of Sophocles' *Antigone* anything but a betrayal, because of the very nature of the medium.

Mr. Hope-Wallace quoted the Italian dictum, *traduttore tradittore.* Why, he asked, was a television performance of *Antigone* necessarily worse than an English translation of the Greek? Dante, for example, was probably untranslatable into Bantu. Whatever the medium of communication, one had to make allowances. The radio producer could properly say to the writer, "You are writing for people who are not reading, they are viewing and listening; therefore you must 'put the noun here and the verb there.' " That curtailment of the writer's liberty was necessary in defense of the art of television production. Television was not the only medium with limitations which stood in the way of transcription or translation of a complexity known as "a masterpiece."

Mr. Sternberger stressed, first, that the products of the media were most often the work of a team and not of an individual, and secondly that the writer, whatever his line—confessor, entertainer, storyteller— was one whose business was "all men's business" and not narrowly the business of a mass medium.

The chairman reminded the panel that brevity was essential if they were to make progress, and that their subject was "the confrontation of the writer with the difficulties he encountered." In his opinion, the most important thing to ask was whether the writer was to follow the public or was to write in a form with which the public would later catch up. He would take the American poet Emily Dickinson, by way of illustration—a woman who was able to persuade editors to publish only six short poems in her lifetime, whereas fifty years after her death fifty books had been written about her. Mallarmé had written: "We are the melancholy opacity of our future ghosts"; and in dedicating a poem to Théophile Gautier he had written: "The poet is the hero of the posthumous expectation." So much for the writer and the public.

Mr. Rice believed that ideas he had published in 1942 were still valid and would read some of them into his remarks. When he had first joined the Authors League of America, in 1914, its members were novelists, playwrights and poets. Later had come the Screen Writers Guild and the Television Guild. The League's earliest preoccupation had been with copyright, royalties, and subsidiary rights. With the rise of the cinema and, later, radio and television, came problems of trade unions, conditions of employment, and blacklists (exclusion of writers on pretext of ideological loyalties, true or alleged). The cinema and radio-tv writers' material concerns had prompted them to withdraw from the Authors League and to found their own professional associations. The meaning of this was unmistakable: it reflected the accelerated shift of the writer from independent creator to wage-earner. Today, the Authors League membership did not include the tens of thousands who earned their living as salaried writers on newspapers, trade publications, and in advertising and public relations. It was only in the fields of book publishing and the theatre, and to some extent in magazine publishing, that the American writer remained a really independent writer. Under the pressure of mechanization and standardization, writing had ceased very largely to be "a self-instituted and highly personal" pursuit. Even the degree of independence still enjoyed was precarious by reason of well-known changes in the publishing trade. As for the New York theatre, it had shrunk from 280 plays produced in 70 theatres in 1926 to 60 plays in 30 theatres in the season 1965–66.

To leave time for other panelists, Mr. Rice said he would stop here and ask his audience to reflect on these facts.

M. Bloch-Michel asked leave to say that he did not believe that the chairman's quotations from Mallarmé constituted a valid definition for literature taken as a whole. One could not say that the writer wrote for himself alone and without regard to the reception his work would obtain. M. Bloch-Michel cited Dickens as one who wrote for his public. Writers might be said to be of two kinds, those who wrote for themselves (whether or not with the future in mind) and those who made an immediate impact upon the public.

As to that impact, Dickens—not to speak of the undeservedly neglected Eugène Sue, who had influenced Dostoevsky among others—was able to influence the broad reading public through the *feuilleton,* through publication by installments. This was no longer possible in the present age. For the *feuilleton* had been replaced by television and the radio, in which a Dickens and a Sue would, if now alive, be active. Would this limit them as independent spirits? M. Bloch-Michel thought not; and this was to him the core of the problem. The broad fact was that no writer was forced to work for these media. The Mallarmés of our time wrote in their studies while the others, avid for contact with and influence over the public, subjected themselves to the exigencies of television.

Mr. Jovanovich began by identifying himself as not only a writer but also a publisher. In his opening statement he had spoken of sentimentality and they had had a good deal of it at the Round Table on the electronic age. Mr. Podhoretz had referred to Mr. McLuhan's difficulty in making his electronic devices work. That was not a failure of technology but of human beings, indeed of humanism. Mr. Jovanovich had recently heard the subject discussed at a meeting of the well-known German writers—Gruppe 47—under the title, "Is the Writer Suffering from Technology and Affluence?" At that meeting, as at this one, the suggestion had been made that the writer had a role as model and guide to play. In his view, the writer had never had this role and did not have it today. It was a sentimental notion to which all writers seemed to be inclined. Mr. Milano's worry about television seemed to Mr. Jovanovich excessive. Anyone who had read the medieval morality and miracle plays—they were retained in university curricula not as literature but as part of cultural history—would recognize two things about them: they were written and played for the masses, and most were "worse than today's television scripts."

It was well known that people were reading more books today than ever before; less well recognized that those who spent all of their spare time watching television had never read books before television came in. Mr. Jovanovich believed that nothing ought to survive unless it was viable and feasible.The disappearance of literary forms—the literary epic, for example—was not new. If the novel disappeared it would not be because the "purposes of other men" had brought that about. If the essay died (Mr. Jovanovich was an essayist) it would be because it could no longer find a public. He believed, contrary to Mr. Rice, that there were probably more, and not fewer, good writers today than fifty years ago; the evidence was there in the fact that the reading of books had increased. Nor did he agree that rewriting in editorial offices imperiled all literature; there were "an awful lot" of bad writers in the world. In his opinion, "one necessity for the writer was to be tough-minded about his own art." Writers who wanted to be "model and guide" to other men ought to take care not to be confused.

Mme. Ocampo said that they had in Argentina a great and untranslatable writer named Jose Hernández. His book, *Martin Fierro,* was read by every Argentine able to read; his poems were known by heart, even by those who could not read. But there was also Jorge Luis Borges who was thirty years winning recognition—not among the masses—as a great writer. Here were two examples of the variety of ways in which writers spoke to their fellow men. As for mechanical media, Mme. Ocampo would refer only to Dylan Thomas' *Under Milk Wood,* which he had described as "a piece written for voices." With a collaborator, she had translated it into Spanish, had read it to a troupe of actors and had worked a fortnight with them over it. In the beginning, they had been bewildered; in the end they were enthusiastic. Of course it was hard for the masses to grasp—and by "masses" Mme. Ocampo did not mean illiterates, she meant people who could read and were assumed to be able to understand what they read. *Under Milk Wood,* a magnificent play, had been written expressly for the radio.

The chairman called for comments from the floor.

Mr. James Ngugi (Kenya), speaking in English and referring to a remark made in passing by Mr. Hope-Wallace, said that there was no Bantu language as such, there were the Bantu languages. Swahili, for example, was one of them. As to limitations of vocabulary, English and French books had been translated into some of these languages. Mr. Ngugi went on to say that "We in Africa do not think that art is sacred . . . and our aim is to use any medium we can to reach our people." For his own part, he was prepared to rewrite any poem to reach his audience.

Mme. Claire Sainte-Soline (French P.E.N.) said that, having been obliged recently to read many novels, she had remarked that in the contemporary novel action seemed to have diminished in importance, the span of time had grown progressively shorter, the scene was shrinking (sometimes to the limits of a bed) and the number of characters was declining. It would appear, therefore, that as a source of information the novel was not what it had been. It was now television that opened up the world to us. Zola, in *le Ventre de Paris,* had described the great Paris market halls: today, television did that. What, this being so, was nowadays the aim of the novel? To study the individual— and she did not mean *an* individual in all his complexities. And to do this, the novelist was using a very meticulous, very precise style. Mme. Sainte-Soline could therefore not agree with the statement in the Program Note for Round Table III, that *"l'oeuvre bien écrite cède la place au travail bâclé."* * In her opinion, it was the long old-fashioned novel that was hurriedly and badly written, where incident counted far more than purity of language. She would add, finally, that "prerogatives" did hamper the writer's independence. Book clubs, general editors of series of books, did propose that authors write to order. Authors held back, complained to their friends that they were going to write a book they did not wish to write; and a week later they were able to persuade themselves that they themselves had chosen the subject. This was not true of novels, of course, which no publisher could order according to his prescription.

Miss Rosamond Lehmann (English P.E.N.) agreed with all that Mr. Hope-Wallace had said and much of what Mr. Jovanovich had said, except that for the latter's "sentimentality" she would substitute "self-

---

* The Program Note asks a question: "Does evidence exist . . . that bad usage is driving out good usage in the written language?"—EDITOR'S NOTE.

consciousness." If she understood what had been said, the idea was that writers did or had to write with one eye on the public. That did not seem to her true of creative writers, who wrote under "some imaginative compulsion which was to give themselves pleasure" and that their aim was to give pleasure to their readers. While they were writing, what the reader might think was not of much consequence; they had to do what they were doing. Dickens, and Shakespeare, too, wrote under this "colossal imaginative compulsion" and both were universal because they gave pleasure.

Mr. Sternberger thought it would be useful to decide at this point "what we were talking about." There had been talk of the writer and mass media, relations between the writer and the publisher, categories of writers, journalists versus artists. He would propose to go back to the theme set them, mysterious as it was: *The Writer as Collaborator in Other Men's Purposes*. "Other men's purposes" was the subject. In this connection, Mr. Sternberger would call attention to the range of literature, which was greater than the sum of art plus journalism. There was the literature of scholarship, there was pamphleteering, there was the essay on non-literary subjects, social, political and the rest. Looking at these subjects one saw that some were more "exposed" than others to the phenomenon of collaboration. One great example was the seventeenth-century philosopher and political theorist, John Locke. He was an ideologist who deliberately served the cause of England's "Glorious Revolution" of 1688. It *inspired* him. Or Dante. He venerated the holy Roman Emperor, Henry VII, and sought to help him unify the Empire against the Pope. What mattered was whether the writer was or was not in sympathy with the purpose in which he collaborated.

Mr. Lasky began with a publisher's anecdote about Sinclair Lewis addressing a college class in "creative writing." Lewis had asked all those present who aspired to be writers to raise their hands. All raised their hands; upon which Lewis asked, "Why are you not at home writing?"

Those round the table were here collaborating in the purpose of the author of the theme and the three "dramatic" questions which sought to make the theme explicit. He proposed to answer those questions. Thinking about them last night he had answered yea to all three. Today, more troubled, he was answering nay. His position was summed up in a word he had learnt from a Heidelberg professor, *Janein*, "Yesno."

The first question referred to the wide public interest in information, in "the document." It asked if the domain of literature was now wider than when Sainte-Beuve wrote a century ago. Taking the American critic and essayist, Edmund Wilson, as a writer of analogous breadth, Mr. Lasky would answer that there had been no essential change: there had been change in the substance of the works examined and the styles of the two ages. One could venture to add that just as Truman Capote had been inspired by a newspaper cutting to write *In Cold Blood* so perhaps had Dostoevsky been inspired by a press cutting to write *Crime and Punishment*. But when one remembered Saul Bellow's reference at the inaugural session to "an imaginative response to a problem of life," and saw that Capote had reduced this to a documentary and journalistic—high journalistic—response, one could answer yes, everything has changed.

On the second question, whether or not publishers and editors had assumed extraordinary prerogatives, Mr. Lasky was tempted to say no; clashes between authors and publishers or editors had always taken place. Mr. Lasky referred to incidents involving, successively, Thomas More, Spinoza, Diderot, Voltaire. Only that morning he had had a cable from the British novelist Colin MacInnes, whose manuscript he had edited slightly before coming away from London. The cablegram read: "Eliminate your flabby semicolons restore my splendid dashes."

The third question was more important: it asked whether or not bad writing was nowadays driving out good? Good writing had always been uncommon, bad writing common. But editors of mass media did perplex their contributors. A friend had told him this story. Back in New York after several years as foreign correspondent, the friend had outlined to his editors ideas for an article he had in mind. "Great!" said the editors. "We'll make it a long 'cover' story." Their first move was to order a cover from the painter, Artzybashev. Four weeks later, after reading the "cover" story, the editors decided that the subject was worth only a "shortie" made up of a few of the writer's anecdotes. Then, again changing their minds, they decided it should be of medium length with two photos. Having already written two versions, the writer had nightmares while working on the third. "It's very simple," said the senior editor to whom he complained; "the story should go 'da *dat,* a *ta,* da *dat;* da *dat,* a *ta,* da *dat.'* " Whether that rhythm represented good style or bad style, Mr. Lasky would not presume to say; it did, however, describe a style that had its function. The following was an example of one journalistic style among others:

. . . And so, as the war grinds on and monsoon clouds mount overhead like leaden mushrooms, the political crunch shapes up."

This was not just a literary lapse. It stood for "a meaningless language, a kind of systematic sloppiness which befogs any type of thinking about serious questions." It was a product of mediocrity wedded to arrogance and ignorance. It called for more concern than the wrinkling of a supercilious nose by a Mandarin whose field was seventeenth- or eighteenth-century English.

Only this morning Mr. Lasky had read a magazine article on the U. S. Government's "Peace Corps"—those young Americans who go into the newly developing countries to work side by side with what Europeans call "the peasants," the humble people. "What was boiling at Peace Corps headquarters in Washington?" the article asked. The "hot line" was that the good old U.S.A. should "start exporting revolution." There was a "worldwide demand for revolution"; why should not the Peace Corps be "in the revolution racket"? Another thing: "I want love in the Peace Corps package; I equate love with commitment," a Washington figure said. This, Mr. Lasky pointed out, was not merely depressing. Such language made thinking and deciding about serious problems literally impossible. Would anybody deny that the great political questions could be decided only in the kind of language used by Aristotle, Machiavelli, John Locke? Today we worried about the drug habit: marijuana, LSD: we should be worrying about a language now become stupefying and degenerate.

Mr. Pogačnik commended Mr. Ngugi on his clarification concerning the Bantu languages, and, mentioning that he came of a country—the Republic of Slovenia—of only 1,500,000 people, stressed the importance of language, literature, and the arts in maintaining a people's national being.

Mr. Jovanovich asked what this had to do with other men's purposes, and *Mr. Lasky* answered that the writer did not create the style all by himself. If Truman Capote wrote a non-fictional reportage and not a novel, it was because "he was listening to his publisher"—and not in a commercial or vulgar sense; he had listened also to the *Zeitgeist*.

Mr. Jovanovich retorted that Capote "wasn't under any pressure" and *Mr. Lasky* replied that Capote, as every writer did, was "collaborating with other institutional purposes." *Mr. Jovanovich* said again, "I don't think he could write that book as a novel," to which *Mr. Lasky* answered, "Well, conceivably," though he believed that "the stress of forces often push a man" to adopt a form, or a subject, or to write in a style not "normally" of his choice. As for its relation to other men's purposes, communication between human beings was itself a communication of purposes. When the President of the United States had to communicate with the body of democratic public opinion, he was obliged to take account of the language that was being fed them, the language required for communication with them. If he succumbed wholly to that "LSD language," however, he would cut himself off from communication with other peoples who were not subjected to that language.

Mr. Jovanovich saw no evidence of a brutalization and vulgarization of language and the press beyond what the United States had known in the past; indeed he believed that the language of the American people was "better" than at any time before and that the American press was more serious, less vulgar now than in 1910. If Burke in eighteenth-century England, or the Founding Fathers in 1776, spoke and wrote as they did, the reason was that they "wrote prose for 2,000 or 5,000 people." And if today the public language was "horrifyingly degenerate" this was not a phenomenon peculiar to the United States. Their colleague Sternberger had written a little book on the "vocabulary of inhumanity" which showed what had been done in these times with the German language.

At this point the chairman called for comments from the floor.

Mrs. Barbara Tuchman (American P.E.N.) spoke warmly against the notion that any writer was obliged to use the language described by Mr. Lasky as degenerate, or to choose a subject under pressure—certainly not when writing a book. A writer who compromised, who surrendered his independence of spirit, would do better to become a bank clerk. Nor was it necessary for an American in high political office to use such language; Adlai Stevenson had not used it, nor had Woodrow Wilson.

Man's voice, speaking in English, offered another example of collaboration in other men's purposes. Luther had said in one of his tracts that the language of the tract was one he had learnt by listening with care to the talk of peasant women in the market place. This was the language Luther had sublimated in his version of the Bible. The speaker felt that when writers spoke for those who were illiterate, they were serving as the instrumentalities through whom bad language became good language. The banalities manipulated by Robert Frost were one example. William Carlos Williams offered another. Dante's shift from Latin to the vernacular was a third. The purpose lay in the key word—to communicate. Dante (*Inferno,* canto XXII), and Goethe here and there were characterized by "hip and LSD periods" in their careers.

SECOND SESSION

M. Goffin, having asked Mr. Hope-Wallace to sum up the position at which the first session had closed, *Mr. Hope-Wallace* repeated the substance of Mr. Lasky's answer to three questions put before them in the congress program: (1) despite the widespread demand for information, the field of literature was not noticeably broader now than a century ago; (2) editorial "prerogatives" nowadays taken could properly be resented by writers of imaginative works, but writers who "hired themselves out" did not have the same freedom; (3) on the whole, bad writing was driving out good writing. Agreeing with Mr. Lasky on all three points, Mr. Hope-Wallace said as regards the third that various social pressures but also the "bad thinking and untruthfulness" of "a certain kind of journalism" were responsible for the poorer writing.

Mr. Wieland Herzfelde (P.E.N. Center, G.D.R.), speaking in English, said that writing was a craft as well as an art. Problems which did not arise for the craftsman did, however, confront the artist. The test came when the writer had the choice of either glibly writing down something that did not express his belief or, alternatively, struggling to write what he sensed inwardly but could not immediately express.

As to co-operating with others, if there was a common conviction between those who co-operated, there was no difficulty. An advertising writer might agree that the common purpose was not to judge the quality of a toothpaste but to persuade people to buy it. A different kind of relationship existed when one man wrote and another—critic or editor—sat in judgment. Here it was difficult to generalize: the editor was often helpful in his guise of critic. One could perhaps say only that the honest writer rejected editorial emendations he could not agree with.

Mr. Lucie-Smith remarked about advertising, first that it was a word for "mechanized selling" and secondly that the text was here a subordinate factor, the copywriter and the designer, working together, were "inventors of images." If anybody was prepared to live in a society in which advertising existed, it was "very difficult to moralize honestly about it." Professor Herzfelde had talked, in effect, about pen and paper. Little as Professor McLuhan's discourse had pleased Mr. Lucie-Smith, McLuhan had been right to talk of the new means of communication. Many successful authors now used the tape recorder. Was their product not to be called "literature"? If these questions were going to be subjected to moral analysis, Mr. Lucie-Smith thought it would be well to decide "what sort of morals we're going to talk about."

Mr. Keene began by objecting that till now the talk had not been of the writer as collaborator but rather of the writer as victim. There were many writers—of course by no means all—who were willing collaborators. Mr. Auden must have been happy to collaborate with Stravinsky on *The Rake's Progress*. Queneau's *Exercices de Style,* published by Gallimard, was a triumph of virtuosity in collaboration between author and book designer; recently published works by Michel Butor showed how the writer could profit from collaboration with the graphic arts. There was also the writer as teacher, and collaboration with one's students was not to be contemned. Saul Bellow had spoken ironically of the writer at the university: intentionally or not, he had himself profited more than most writers from the situation he satirized.

The situation in many American universities of the "poet in residence" had often been thought of as limiting the poet's freedom to write. This was nonsense. In every society, the poet's career involved his reading of poetry by others: why not by students? In Japan, poets had for centuries earned their living by reading aloud other men's poetry and helping them to write better poetry.

Then there was the writer as translator. As a member of the American P.E.N.'s committee on translation, Mr. Keene had recently served on its jury to award the annual American P.E.N. Translator's Prize. They had read fifty works by American and British translators, from many languages. The quality of translation had been deplorably low. A poor translation was not necessarily better than no translation at all. The jury had had difficulty in finding a translation worthy of the $1,000 award. A Paris publisher had spoken to him of a translation from the Japanese so bad that it could not be published: *"Ce n'était même pas du français."* This had brought to mind the thought that co-operative translation should be possible. "Ideally, we should all learn foreign languages and do some translating, for as writers we are more capable than others of writing our own language." There were today fewer people able to translate from Japanese into English than when he had complained of the shortage of such translators at the Tokyo Congress of P.E.N. in 1957. From Chinese, there were perhaps only three or four who could translate into proper English. Writers already eminent could not be expected to devote five years to learning a difficult Oriental language; but there were "enormous possibilities of collaboration, particularly in poetry." The pleasure and inspiration which writers (not to say the reading public) would derive from such translation was not to be disdained. P.E.N. would do well to encourage collaboration to this end.

Finally, there had been an inclination yesterday to speak of the writer and the publisher as if they were enemies. Actually, we were in the presence—as a number of literary quarterlies testified—of the writer as publisher all over the place. These publisher-editor-writers had a particular responsibility; it was to encourage (or, it may be, discourage) Asian and African writers who were creating new literatures and should be helped in their task. Special issues on Japanese, Filipino, or Thai literature were a mistake: stories and poems from such sources should not be lumped together in a national issue as a kind of patronizing "good deed." Who would go to a concert of nothing but American music? Those translations should be published as literature in normal issues and be required to survive comparison with writings from other languages.

The writer was said to be a reader as well. Who among us read the excellent magazine published in Uganda and called *Transition?* Or the first-rate miscellany brought out in Calcutta? They were more worth reading than the third-rate books we reviewed in our press. Mr. Keene would mention two great living writers who read Oriental literatures: Borges, in Argentina, and Mr. Keene's friend, Octavio Paz, the great Mexican poet (ambassador to India at this moment), who experimented with Japanese and Chinese poetic forms. "Such writers are the best kind of readers, those who make writing worthwhile."

Miss Chute said that she could not qualify as a victim. Being what was called a scholar, she had no way of collaborating in other men's purposes. She could collaborate only as reader. The scholar was debarred from listening to any other voice than that of his documents; and perhaps a principal reason for the existence of universities was that they provided a sheltered place where the scholar could be secure in the fulfillment of his purpose.

Now and then a scholar found that he had chosen a subject the public wanted to read about. Miss Chute's life of Shakespeare was an instance. The public's interest in her book had enabled her to visit England for the first time; there she found that she had written about England better out of the documents than she could have done from seeing it. She wrote mainly about poets, and mostly because she was interested in "a great talent being bent out of shape by the need of money." Shakespeare, because he had a trade—acting—which brought him a livelihood, was free to write as he chose; the proof was that he had not found it necessary to follow a great success like *Hamlet* with another play like *Hamlet.* His friend Ben Jonson had failed as an actor and knew no other trade than writing. Jonson's four great plays had been written for Shakespeare's company; thereafter, he had spent his life looking for patrons and his great talent had run thinly away like water in sand.

It was not wrong for a writer to have a trade. Two of the great American poets of this century had worked for insurance companies. T. S. Eliot, after years of reading the European press for a London bank, became an editor. Another of Miss Chute's subjects, the English poet who came first after Shakespeare, Geoffrey Chaucer, was a civil servant. Having a trade, she believed, could not change the fact that— for her, anyway—writing was the greatest joy in the world. One might be lucky if one did not need to do anything else; but there was evidence enough that paying one's way by working at something else did not limit the privilege nor diminish the delight of writing.

Mr. Florentino, speaking in English, said that he represented a young nation, the Philippine Republic, which had been a democratic republic for 20 years after 46 years of American occupation and 350 years of Spanish domination; a country of 7,000 islands and 27,000,000 people. He could perhaps be said to "represent" any young African or Asian nation of small area, for it was to him a shock to be "thrown into a conference where the subject matter, the viewpoint, and most of the participants" were European and American. The electronic age was not the Filipinos' worry; their lack was an electric lamp to read by. Their problems were not the threat posed by the mass media, nor serving other men's purposes, nor the degradation of their language. To the contrary, their problems were the lack of a market, the search for a literary language—there were many former colonial nations which had not yet decided what their literary language should be. As for subjection to publishers, the problem was to establish one's own publishing trade in the face of the books and magazines (and television) flooding them from abroad. Not the end of the Gutenberg era but "our entry into it" was their problem.

These points, Mr. Florentino hoped, would encourage the organization of a future conference or seminar on the arts-and-letters problems of Asia, Africa, and perhaps also some of the Latin American countries.

Mr. Lasky, asked to comment on what had preceded, said that the forms of collaboration cited were less simple than appeared. To believe that sincerity of itself created good writing was sentimentality. Mr. Herzfelde, if memory served, had said in sum that bad writing was somehow the consequence of a bad cause, and that the gods of literature would ensure that a good cause would issue in good writing. This was a fallacy. Yesterday, Mr. Sternberger mentioned two great "committed" writers—Milton and John Locke—who had spoken for diametrically opposed causes. The same could be said for those two "brilliant stylists," Marat and Robespierre. One might contrast Trotsky, a genius as phrasemaker and historian, with the "leaden and almost illiterate" Stalin. In their struggle it was the genius who lost.

New York had long been assumed to be governed from three hateful streets: "Wall Street which exploits us, Broadway which manipulates us, Madison Avenue which brainwashes us." Mr. Lasky had wondered as a child if advertising was really necessary, if this vulgarity was not supererogatory. The political scientists told us no, that it was an essential social mechanism. Mr. Lasky would not want to be an ad writer, but if he was one his aim would be to do "a professional job which had certain social consequences." Over the years, he had seen advertising copy—in the weekly *New Yorker,* for example—whose ideas and images were in some respects wittier, livelier, more amusing than some of the writing printed around the advertisements. Certainly ad writing had grown more professional, more sophisticated. The copy written for the self-avowedly "second largest" American car-hire company, for example. If its writer was one of those who lived by a trade and wrote also "for himself"—a condition of which Miss Chute had approved—then he was in Mr. Lasky's view potentially capable of producing great comic novels. Perhaps that writer was wasting his time; but he was demonstrating that ad writing could contribute to the gaiety of the nations.

M. Bloch-Michel went back to the question whether bad writing was driving out good. He said it was evident that those who wrote for the cinema or for television were forced to adjust themselves to the techniques involved. Those techniques, however, were themselves the creators of forms, aesthetic forms, which were absolutely new. There existed an art of the radio, of television, of the cinema, which bore no relation to, simply, speech, drama, photography. And inevitably these forms influenced literature, not at all by imposing a bad style of writing but by causing literature to create its own forms in response to the forms created in the process of employing the resources of those media. We saw in France a whole school of novelists who, deliberately or not, had transferred to the printed page processes which were born of those media. Robbe-Grillet's novels, for instance, were inspired by what we may call the "narrative in pictures," a form altogether different from traditional literary narration. A writer like Michel Butor, though by no means altogether successfully, had been producing books in which he was experimenting with the literary possibilities suggested by the multiplicity of sound channels used in radiophonic and stereophonic communication.

These means of communication, therefore, exercised other influences than the one suggested by Mr. Lasky. It was quite true that their influence on journalism was disastrous. But more writers than one might believe were engaged in purely formal experimentation. A kind of reversal was taking place. Forms which to some extent contained a contradiction of literature were leading writers to engage in purely literary experiments. To this extent, then, M. Bloch-Michel would say: no, bad writing was not driving out good. One might or might not care for the very sophisticated, highly skilled writing that resulted; one could not deny that it was excellent literature.

M. Goffin, asking permission to comment on M. Bloch-Michel's remarks, said that he took the contrary view. First, because the public was driven by the new literature to "more facile forms." It was true—a kind of "law of literature"—that poets had to live through a period of purgatory before they were read. And yet it was also true that in every successive age it was the poets who shaped and represented their people —the poets, not the politicians. Verlaine had been condemned to two years in prison by a Belgian minister of state: Who remembered the minister? Who did not know Verlaine? Victor Hugo wrote against Napoleon III and went into exile in Belgium. There, in two lines, he immortalized a man otherwise forgotten—the legislator who had put this question in Parliament: "When will the individual known as Victor Hugo be expelled?" And Hugo had written:

> Pour comble de malheur, les animaux parlèrent:
> Un certain Ribaucourt m'appelle "individu."

Mr. Lucie-Smith said that he would try to put together several things that had been said by the last three speakers. First, as language was the "barometer of a society" one couldn't say a language was sick without saying that the society was sick. Moralizing literary critics often used language as a stick with which to beat society. Collaboration could be either a stumbling block or a stepping stone: the first forced a writer out of his natural track, the second served as a means of getting him to a place where he couldn't have got on his own. As for advertising, Mr. Lucie-Smith would repeat that the ad writer was "less concerned with words" than people supposed, and that advertising was an aspect of contemporary culture, was the "meshing together of the seen and the heard, of the word (printed or spoken) and the image." In a world in which everything was being synthesized, one couldn't be sure that literature was not "as much a sequence of images as it was of words on a page." This was the television writer's problem.

Mr. Lucie-Smith suggested that literature did not always fill the same function in every society. The role of the poet, which the chairman had exalted, was no longer the same. In Russia, Voznesensky and Yevtushenko, in America, Allen Ginsberg, wrote poems which were meant to be read aloud in public. Mr. Lucie-Smith would ask, therefore, if at this table the writer was not assumed to be still playing a role he had grown out of?

Mr. Chiara, speaking in French, observed that his French colleagues, who represented perhaps the "most living part of European culture," had sufficiently made known the "Mediterranean points of view." Italian writers looked towards French literature and on the whole shared its ideas on the relations between writers and contemporary society. His own view was that social problems constituted only "a moment in the development of the human community, whereas man was something real, unique, the object of philosophy, of literature, and of art." For him, therefore, social problems were not necessarily of the same character as the personal experience of the individual writer.

Mr. Sternberger said he would say a word about a "fortunate field" of collaboration, that between writer and the politician in the German Federal Republic. During the general elections of 1965 a group of prominent professional writers had decided to campaign for the Social Democratic Party, despite the fear of certain party functionaries that they might take an excessively highbrow approach to the electors. In the G.F.R., where "the politicians and the writers were divided classes, so to speak, and where politics could show no such writers as Churchill and de Gaulle," this intervention was fortunate. The United States, in the persons of the late President Kennedy, Arthur Schlesinger, and others, had its examples. As to advertising, Mr. Sternberger pointed to American political slogans: New Deal, Fair Deal, New Frontier, Great Society, and the rest. He would approve of writers collaborating in suitable verbal inventions of this kind.

Mr. Keene said that the impression appeared to have been given that literature of high quality must necessarily enjoy lower sales—and esteem—with the general public than works of low quality. This was not the case in Japan where perhaps "a thousand times as many writers as in the United States" were able to live—some of them surprisingly well —from their writings. In the late 1940s the writer with the highest income, the novelist Tanizaki, was proposed for, though not ultimately awarded, the Nobel Prize. Poets were highly respected and 200 poetry reviews were published in Japan. Contrary to Western experience, in Tokyo it is the best newspaper, not the worst, that has the largest circulation. What was happening in Japan was worth looking into by P.E.N.

The chairman felt that in the United States there was perhaps a certain neglect of the minor European literatures. Belgium had both a French P.E.N. and a Flemish P.E.N. Center. The Hungarians were about to publish an anthology of Belgian poetry, as the Russians had already done. Czechoslovak and Yugoslav groups had proposed exchanges of anthologies to the Belgian P.E.N. M. Goffin urged that the English-speaking P.E.N. centers encourage the translation of poetry from the less-favored languages.

Mr. Hope-Wallace said that they had a "very strange problem in England." Shakespeare's language was growing archaic to the point of unintelligibility for the mass of the people. This was not the case of Shakespeare in Germany, thanks to the Tieck-Schlegel translation of a century and a half ago; the Russian mass audience, too, was "far more aware of Shakespeare" than were the poet's own compatriots. Should one "modernize" Shakespeare as the King James Bible had been modernized? Was this dangerous, or was it useful?

Mr. Sulaksana Sivaraksa (Thailand P.E.N.), speaking in English, saw the source of many difficulties in the control of mass media by "vested interests and pressure groups" in the democratic countries and by Party authorities in the Communist countries. "Biased and prejudiced groups" controlled and manipulated more and more of the highly concentrated Western press, which, at the same time, was "infiltrated by pro-Communist elements under the cover of liberalism." The cultural purge that was taking place in Mainland China was the fifth since 1951. Mr. Sivaraksa expressed the wish that the congress protest against the "suppression of the creative impulse in a country which has contributed so much in the past" to all creative arts. The Chinese P.E.N. Center in Tibet [sic] had published a report on the current purge; a copy had been sent to the International Secretariat of P.E.N.*

Mme. Ocampo expressed her agreement with Mr. Lasky, who had said that sincerity of itself was not enough. Sincerity, she said, had "only one translator into the language of literature, and that was talent." But talent itself, if not accompanied by conscience, produced lamentable things—propaganda, lies.

Mr. Matej Bor, former president of Slovenian P.E.N., Yugoslavia, and president of the 33rd International P.E.N. Congress (Bled, July 1965), speaking in English, was convinced that useful statements had

* There is no Tibetan P.E.N. center (and none in Mainland China).

been made at this session. He confessed however that he found the formulation of their theme somewhat unclear. On the question of "distortion" of language, he thought that writers were ceasing to produce "finer products" because they so often provided only "raw material for the other arts," e.g., television and cinema. He would agree with M. Bloch-Michel that these new arts were influencing contemporary writing, though he could not agree that the influence was always good. To adopt the techniques of the screen play lowered the quality of the novel by causing the novelist to lend less attention to "meditation" and inducing him to concentrate on the writing of images.

To this Mr. Bor would only add an expression of regret that the remarks by his colleague, Mr. Pogačnik, on "commitment" had not stimulated more comment, and that Mr. Coutsoheras' motion at the meeting of the Executive Committee for a resolution on the danger of atomic catastrophe had been ruled out as a political and not a literary subject.

Woman's voice, speaking in English, made two points, of which the first concerned writers who earned their living by another trade. She was herself in the teaching profession and would agree that there was no "dichotomy" between what teachers "research in and what they write on." Even so, the writer who "debased his wares" in an advertising agency could find that this way of earning a living was not a help but a hindrance to him as a writer. In her view, if a writer had to live by another trade the best kind of trade was one that had nothing to do with writing, something that enriched one's experience and helped to "objectivize" one's writing.

Her second point concerned refugees from the smaller countries who had learnt a second language. Could they not turn to translation, and was this not an idea with which P.E.N. should concern itself?

Miss Chute agreed with the thought that a writer's livelihood was best earned by work "you love to do, that will pay you, and that is not writing."

Mr. Alexandru Balaci (Roumanian P.E.N.) thanked the chairman for his reference to the Roumanian translations of Belgian poets, both French and Flemish. Turning to the question of the novel *versus* the currently popular document, he said that the latter would not replace the former any more than the machine would replace the writer. There was a story to the effect that a translation machine, having produced two different versions of an extract from Shakespeare, had said, "I do not know which to choose" and had blown up.

On the question, do publishers and editors trespass upon the writer's freedom to create? the answer was that no true poet would ever write jingles, no true novelist would become a reporter, and no true playwright would give up the theatre for the music hall. Gresham's Law, that bad money drove out good, had no application to literature.

M. Anoma Kanie (Ivory Coast P.E.N.) summed up his impression of what had been said thus far, in these terms: "If the writer felt himself threatened in our times, the reason was that man as man felt himself threatened by what science and technology were offering him." We had given birth to a monster whom we could not understand and did not know how to live with. The fault lay not with technology but with man himself who had been lulled to sleep by his own past achievements. Man's mission was to remember that he was, as Christians say, created in the image of God and meant to seek the truth and dominate his condition. The writer's task was, at bottom, man's task: to strive for reforms and never to content himself with temporary solutions. The same task faced all who were present at the congress.

The chairman said that before calling on Mr. Lasky again he had a story to tell. Here in New York, in 1940, he had been at work on a play with the great poet, Maeterlinck. The poet had just sold an article to *Liberty* magazine for which he had been paid $2,500. M. Goffin had been present when a representative of the magazine arrived to ask Mr. Maeterlinck to agree to certain changes in the article. Maeterlinck's answer was that there could be no talk of changes. He always knew what he wanted to say and he had written exactly that. To which the magazine man had retorted: "You know what you want to say, Mr. Maeterlinck, but the magazine knows what its readers want to read."

Mr. Lasky began by going back to Mr. Sternberger's problem of the services which a writer can lend to political groups, whether groups of his own conviction (in which case we spoke of "commitment" and "sincerity") or groups which paid him well or which it amused him to serve momentarily (when we spoke of "irresponsibility"). The relationship between a writer's ingenuity and his irresponsibility could be expressed in something playful, harmless, when he dealt with a literary composition; it had another result when he was producing political formulations.

Thirty years ago, as a student, Mr. Lasky had heard the then leader of the American Communist Party, Earl Browder, give voice to a slogan with which he profoundly disagreed but which he wished—as Oscar Wilde had once done on hearing a *bon mot* dropped by the American painter, Whistler—that he himself had thought of. It was this: "Communism is twentieth-century Americanism." In those days, Paul Robeson was singing folk songs out of the American past. Browder and Robeson were manifesting their cultural devotion in a way they thought consistent with both communism and Americanism. Mr. Lasky's admiration went out to Browder's imaginative fusion of ingenuity and irresponsibility. And yet there was here a tragic element also, for many Americans had believed that what Browder said was true. Another example was Franklin Roosevelt's "We have nothing to fear but fear itself," this at a time when there was war to fear, fascism, social decay. . . . The slogan served a purpose, but one had always to look carefully at the function and consequences of slogans. A very good poet had coined the word *"Négritude."* This was expressive of an aspect of the African personality; but its political and social consequences were not in every case constructive. In short, where "ingenuity becomes a prison and irresponsibility a deception" one would prefer a duller, less sloganized way of political expression.

Mr. Lucie-Smith said that he was struck by the salutary reminder given by earlier speakers of the "extent to which writers in smaller literatures have remained the guardians of the national identity and of the national soul." He had often noticed, in translations of works from those literatures, "a kind of richness of social identity" which was no longer found in English novels. He took it that those writers were alert not to betray their nations because they knew that a "trust" was placed in their hands. A writer who wrote in a quasi-universal language— English—was conscious of "being pushed to the margins of society." He mattered less to his own society, therefore he felt freer to indulge in writing which might involve compromise (the mass media, etc.). Meanwhile, Mr. Lucie-Smith would "hold on to" Mme. Ocampo's distinction between good writing and good conscience. This, too, was perhaps easier in a smaller literature and there was a real sense in which he envied Mr. Florentino.

Mr. Combs thought that the ability to formulate slogans was "one of the greatest social powers of the writer" and deserved thinking about. In today's world there were two men who thought of themselves as poets and had the most tremendous impact on their societies, which they stirred by their words. One was Mao Tse-tung, the other was Luis Muñoz Marín, of Puerto Rico, whose leadership was in part the result of his gift for creating slogans. In this connection, Mr. Combs would recommend to poets the practice of writing in brief forms—the Japanese *haiku* was an example—because, the poems being easily remembered, they could enrich men's lives.

Mr. Leslie Konnyu (Writers-in-Exile P.E.N.) noted that the question of refugees writing translations in English had been raised. Such a program existed in Europe and here in America; an example was the *American–Hungarian Review* which published Hungarian literature in English and also English and American literature in Hungarian. It had brought out a book on modern Hungarian literature and a history of American–Hungarian literature.

Mrs. Vera Blackwell (English P.E.N.) was a translator from the Czech, specializing in dramatic literature and more recently doing the plays of Vaclav Havel who, with two other writers, had been denied passports to attend this congress by the Czechoslovak Government. She had been faced with the following difficulty—that English theatre managers demanded not translation but adaptation to the ready comprehension of the British public. There were always political and other local overtones in the text which were difficult to transplant. In the case of two plays by Havel, this problem had not yet been solved. What, asked Mrs. Blackwell, was the answer? Havel had been performed in eighteen German theatres, in Sweden, in Finland, and twice in Vienna. Why could he not be done in either England or America?

The chairman regretted that time was lacking for discussion of this interesting question and found himself obliged to close the session, with thanks to all participants.

The Writer as Public Figure

Friday, June 17
FIRST SESSION

Douglas Young, CHAIRMAN
University of St. Andrews, St. Andrews (Scotland)

Daniel Bell
Columbia University, New York

Chang Ho Choi
Seoul

A. den Doolaard
Hoenderloo (Netherlands)

Gyula Illyés
Budapest

Rosamond Lehmann
London

Arthur Miller
New York

Pablo Neruda
Valparaiso

Ignazio Silone
Rome

Hsu-pai Tseng
Taipei

SECOND SESSION

Douglas Young, CHAIRMAN
St. Andrews

Daniel Bell
New York

A. den Doolaard
Hoenderloo

Jean Follain
Paris

Rosamond Lehmann
London

Horia Lovinescu
Bucharest

Arthur Miller
New York

Pablo Neruda
Valparaiso

Ignazio Silone
Rome

The Writer as Public Figure

FIRST SESSION

Professor Young outlined the procedure he would follow and quoted extracts from the Program Note on the theme to be discussed, first by those seated at the table and thereafter by members of the audience who had put down their names for this purpose. All writers, the chairman said, were public figures in the sense that readers formed more or less vague notions about their personalities. Actually, a writer was an individual who wrote for himself; the reader, too, read as an individual, and not consciously as a member of "the reading public." In the theatre, the situation was somewhat different: the playwright wrote with an audience in mind, and the playgoer's reaction was influenced by the simultaneous reactions of the rest of the audience. For these reasons Mr. Young inclined to disagree with the suggestion in the program that the writer consciously adopted a *persona*.

Mr. Illyés, speaking in French, said that a strange notion of the writer's role in society was revealed by the almost pathological demands which readers made in the letters they wrote to authors, as illustrated in his own experience. In the inter-war period he had published his diary of a visit to Russia. A Russian nursery gardener had written to ask that he send, as a gift and by devious means—Hungary having at that time no diplomatic relations with Moscow—500 slips of frost-resistant Siberian peach trees. Then there was the young lady—every writer had heard from her at one time or another—who demanded that he justify at length the behavior of a character she found destestable. And the older woman who, having read what you wrote, discovered that you were soul mates and proposed a regular weekly correspondence. One of his distinguished colleagues had described to him

The Reader as Aristocrat, the nobleman for whom a book he read sitting by the fire was a private communication; honor required that it be held confidential, wherefore this reader tore out each leaf as he finished it and threw it on the fire.

Dante had not written to earn a living, but to inform, to teach. How could a writer teach if he was not independent, if he was answerable to those he taught? And if Mr. Illyés were asked, Has the writer in our times the right to teach? he would answer yes, decidedly; for without this right there would be no writers—and no readers.

What was the situation today? Was the writer free to speak to his pupil? There were those—the booksellers, the money-changers—who said that writers and readers formed two opposing camps. Mr. Illyés was not impressed. Every literature was the product of its age; we seemed to be living in a commercial age, a time of trouble and of hopes in which clarity of vision and good writing were growing rare. We had exigent publishers; but the Muses too were exigent. We did not write today for readers in padded chairs who yawned as they read; we wrote for those who suffered as we suffer and who asked, as their remedy, for truth and beauty, at whatever cost.

Mr. Silone, speaking in French, began by citing the title of a book, published a few years ago by a young Italian essayist, *The Eclipse of the Intellectuals.* In astronomy, he said, an eclipse was an event of short duration; the eclipse described in the book was intended to be as good as permanent. This paradox was associated with an outdated sociology which argued that in the industrial society, the social question —the reactions between capital, labor and the state—was one in which intellectuals as such could play only a secondary role; they were merely the servants of three forces now confronting one another, namely, the state, the private monopolies, and the "revolutionary organization."

Historically, the intellectuals had already been pulled down from their throne in 1848; it was then that they first became "a simple ornament of society, instruments employed to attain other men's purposes." Bismarck had said that only a little money sufficed to buy poets or prostitutes. Probably that was an exaggeration, but there were times when the psychology of the intellectuals seemed to confirm the Iron Chancellor's words, for their psychology was a product of the life most of us lived, which led to narcissism and to servitude—at least as seen from the outside.

In our own times, we had been living with the phenomenon of totalitarianism. Now, if we were to forget polemics and were to take that term in its strict historical and scientific connotation, as a concept of a society in which politics was dominant, in which all else was subordinated to the totalitarian state, it would follow of itself that the theory of the intellectual as the servant of a higher power was perfectly and definitively embodied in the totalitarian state. We would agree that in that state the intellectuals—including the writers—were in fact materially well treated in exchange for their services as instruments of propaganda. They were organized into shock troops to urge on the bringing in of the harvest on the collective farms, the clearing of virgin lands, the inauguration of a new five-year plan. And they did duty abroad as well—work not so tiring, but propaganda work just the same: showing themselves publicly with the revolutionary avant-garde, signing manifestos, whether aware or unaware of their significance, and acting generally like so many freeloaders on the modern ship of state. Meanwhile, the idea of art and of literature expressed in these functions and manifestos could not but be rather narrow—a reflection of official slogans and orders.

But even in this age we had seen other things. We had seen occasions when certain kinds of social problems—the liberty of the individual, national independence, etc.—were dealt with by free intellectuals acting in the name of the people. And when had we seen this? Whenever the vast class organizations had remained silent on those subjects. There had been episodes in recent decades when the political scene had been dominated by the initiative of intellectual groups, or even individual intellectuals. This was particularly visible in colonial lands where tribal organization was rudimentary and the few intellectuals, although educated abroad, had remained faithful to their peoples and had led them against the colonial powers. *"Négritude,"* for example, was an invention of intellectuals. The defense of the national interest, the struggle against the totalitarian state with its social bureaucratization and its abolition of spontaneous creativity, had been their work. In every such country the weaker links in the chain of totalitarianism had caused the chain to break: the peasantry, the religious communities, the cultural groups and individual leaders. Thus we had had the *White Rose* in Nazi Germany; the *Non mollare* group in Florence, Croce himself in Italy's fascist period. We would never forget the Petoefi clubs in Hungary and the small *Poprostu* circle in Poland, in 1956. Today, in Spain, we were pinning our hopes on the student mass and the faculties of the universities. There had been books that had won battles in this struggle—*Dr. Zhivago* was one.

Only he who had lived through such struggles could know the cost, in doubt and in anguish, in resistance against temptation, in the breaking of ties with a regime to which one had been bound by the very fibers of one's being—the cost of struggling against a regime built on the foundation of a socialist economy. The worst was not police persecution, nor hunger, nor calumny; it was the infamous charge of treason leveled and believed by simple honest souls, one's own friends among them.

But on our own side, too, in the traditionally democratic countries, conditions had also developed which called for intervention by the intellectuals, including those who normally remained aloof from political involvement. In these states, too, the national conscience had been confronted by urgent problems which existing political institutions did not suffice to analyze and to solve. The traditional groups and parties, the established machinery of government, seemed of a sudden paralyzed. They stood inert, passive, as if waiting for the fever to subside and the routine processes to resume their operation. This was what had led to the collapse of the French Fourth Republic. Who among us would forget that when the Algerian War came, and the parties and organs of government revealed their flabbiness, it was the intellectuals who redeemed the honor of France?

Here in the United States, against a different social and economic background, we saw that the students and intellectuals were in the grip of a like malaise in connection with the conflict in Vietnam. It could of course be argued that the realities were more complex than they realized; that the reiteration of moral and intellectual declarations was not enough to manage the business and resolve the contradictions of the world in which we live. But the freedom permitted those who protest was itself one of the rules of the debate—and was in its own way a refutation of affirmations that might turn out untrue.

Since, said Mr. Silone, he found himself talking about war and peace, he would close by quoting Clemenceau's well-known dictum, that war was too serious a subject to be left to generals.

Mr. den Doolaard said that he intended to be controversial and concrete. He too objected, as the chairman had done in his opening remarks, to the question about the writer's adoption of a *persona;* his objection was against the notion that the committed writer was play-acting: "Frequently, the commitment and the literary work are two facets of the same personality." It was not because Zola was a "committed" writer, nor even because he was a man of courage who had dared defend Dreyfus in the face of a mob, that Mr. den Doolaard admired Zola's best novels. On the other hand, he would deny that Zola had adopted a *persona,* acted a part. His commitment was a fact of his nature, "he couldn't do otherwise." Another example was a writer of our own day, Romain Gary, who had written *les Racines du ciel (The*

Roots of Heaven), defending mankind symbolically in a novel in which he purported to defend African elephants.

Mr. den Doolaard was not happy, moreover, with the implication in the Program Note that for a writer to be committed was somehow not desirable. Did not the P.E.N. Charter—which he had translated into Dutch—commit all P.E.N. members to do their utmost to banish hatred between races, classes, and peoples? Whether one accepted a commitment or not was a personal decision; one was or was not "a fighter"; and the decision was not (as the Program Note implied) a matter only of sentiment or intellectual conviction, it was more than anything a matter of that mysterious element called "conscience." It might also be a matter of upbringing and tradition—as, probably, in the great Faulkner's cautious position on desegregation of blacks and whites. Mr. den Doolaard himself had been a "committed" anti-fascist and as such had been evicted from four countries before the war. Since the war, since Hiroshima, he had been fighting against nuclear armament. And he would stress this fact: "You don't find it literally in my work, but it's all behind my work." We were threatened with annihilation; and that was why he was a committed writer.

Miss Lehmann said that she had been haunted all week by some lines of W. H. Auden: "Private faces in public places are wiser and nicer than public faces in private places." That really was the problem. Brought up as she had been in a home with strong literary and musical traditions, taking as the models of her youthful ambitions such English novelists as Jane Austen, Mrs. Gaskell, and George Eliot, Miss Lehmann's ideal had been to write books and remain at the same time "extremely private; in fact, as they did, anonymous." To sign one's books with a *nom de plume* seemed to her something "liberating." She still believed this. But when, being still very young, and having published her first novel under her own name, and that novel, *Dusty Answer,* having become a best-seller, she had been terrified. Since then she had not been able to reconcile her concern to look inside herself to find herself with what had become her public image—the person publishers wanted to send on lecture tours, urged to speak on the radio, and the rest. A writer's *raison d'être,* she thought, was to write, to go on writing as truthfully as possible. Henry James had said that it was in the waste of time, of passion, of curiosity, of contact that the true initiation began. Idling about, absorbing without having to give out—what Keats had called the poet's "negative capability"—that was the way the writer's time should be spent.

True, James had also said, "In the destructive element immerse," and this might mean, do speak on platforms. Here the danger was that one might begin to believe one's opinions were 'important. In Miss Lehmann's view, great writers had often held very foolish opinions. Besides, the temptation grew to look at one's public image—in fact, to construct one's public image. Miss Lehmann would suggest that a good theme—sub-theme, at least—for a future P.E.N. congress would be "the writer as a silent spirit." The American poet Marianne Moore had said that one should above all learn to be silent, to listen, to make possible "promptings from on high." "From on high" meant for Miss Lehmann "from within." And so, for a future congress, she envisaged "a lot of small rooms with round tables, and around each table perhaps a dozen writers sitting in absolute silence for about twenty minutes or half an hour. And at the end of that time each of these writers would be allowed to speak one sentence. I think we'd find some tremendously good ideas, or perhaps one good idea, would come out of that."

Mr. Choi, speaking in English, began by saying that the Korean writer did not write for the entertainment of the ruling classes nor as propagandist for the governing parties; he wrote as spokesman for his people, a people who had in the past lived in poverty and oppression. Before the era of Japanese rule (1910–1945), the royal Court had imposed Chinese scholarship, and Chinese literature was their only literature. Under the Japanese colonial regime, only the Japanese language and literature had been taught, and in the war years freedom of expression had been ruthlessly repressed. Thus, although there had been certain great vernacular poets in an earlier age, it was only since 1945 that the Korean writer had been able to think, feel and speak for the people.

If there was "commitment" here, Mr. Choi said, it was unconscious and instinctive, not deliberate. Mr. Choi believed that "conscious commitment" was dangerous; that it led to loss of independence by the creative artist. On the other hand, he felt that the younger Korean writers tended to depart from the attitude of closeness to the people. In his view, it was only by living with the people that the writer could safely commit himself without loss of his spiritual independence.

The chairman announced that the broadcasting networks had asked to interview a number of those present, including Mr. Nasciamento (Brazil), Mr. Ngugi (Kenya), Mr. Kané (Senegal), Mr. Abruquah (Ghana), and Mme. Ocampo (Argentina). He then called upon Mr. Pablo Neruda.

Mr. Neruda, speaking in French, said that after listening to the earlier statements—so interesting and touching—made by certain colleagues, he had had a little surprise. He had thought that we had left the cold war behind—that war which had been "so terribly hard for writers on both sides." Apparently he had been dreaming, since there were famous writers present for whom that war was still on. He would say only this about cold war between writers. He had visited all the socialist countries, those countries which capitalist writers called totalitarian. He had visited all the capitalist countries. Everywhere, he had talked to writers. He had found under both social systems writers who were happy and other writers who were unhappy. But he would have to say, in all sincerity, that he had found many more unhappy writers in the capitalist countries. His own wish was that all writers, whatever their beliefs, their function as writers, their prominence or anonymity, be able to live and to create in a condition of happiness.

Mr. Neruda's own country, Chile, had been "invented" by a sixteenth-century poet named Ercilla who had found himself among the restless conquistadores sent from imperial Spain. Ercilla was the author of a long and most beautiful epic called *La Araucana;* a Renaissance man whose mission was to celebrate that imperialistic conquest. This soldier-poet had seen the tragic fate suffered by those Araucanian Indians, he had witnessed their heroic defense of their land, their religion, their ways and their lives. Chile, in a word, was born of a poem written by a poet whose mission was to exalt the heroes of his side and who ended by exalting the proud spirit and the prowess of a people destroyed by their conquerors. From that moment, the spirit of Chilean writers had never ceased to be a spirit of independence.

To return now to the subject before the Round Table. If one took, for example, Whitman and Rimbaud, and ignored their views about politics and society, one might imagine that they had not been concerned with politics, with society. And yet Rimbaud's whole being was marked by a tragic rejection of the society of his time. Whitman's whole personality was penetrated with the tragic epoch and the fervor he felt for Lincoln's cause. He was essentially a man stirred to the depths by that great commotion, just as Rimbaud was essentially the creature of an inner conflict between himself and the capitalist society of his own tragic times.

Mr. Neruda had wandered through all the villages and mines of his country, which extended from below the Equator almost to the South Pole. Everywhere, the Chilean people had come forward to talk to him —often only with their eloquent glance. People in other Latin American countries had done the same. And what they had said, in effect, was, "Talk in the name of those who cannot write." Mr. Neruda had undertaken this mission with humility and with pride. His poetry had been written with anguish, but in the hope that his own opposition to war and to injustice would contribute to change in Latin America. And he would ask only this: If the poet did not make himself the spokesman of the human condition, what else was there for him to do?

In sum, he was "the fully committed poet," convinced that man's future was a future of liberty, creation, dignity, and justice. Call him a propagandist, he was one as Whitman and Hugo had been propagandists. There was a poet he had loved as he had loved no other poet— Federico García Lorca; a man of deep pride, who had refused to commit himself. They had been intimate friends. In the Spanish Civil War, Lorca had been sacrificed by what had been called "socialist totalitarianism." Mr. Neruda still carried this wound "in my literature, in my poetry, in my conscience." It was then that he had said to himself, "Lorca did not commit himself, but I will—in order that this may not happen again."

Mr. Bell said he would speak of the writer of works of the imagination and the sensibility, though at the risk perhaps of wounding the vanity of such writers. He spoke also primarily as a sociologist and would point out that "what one calls a writer today is a new kind of person on the social scene." In earlier times, those who sought to symbolize feelings had been mainly the priest, employing ritual, and the bard, using myth and legend and the recurrent themes of tragedy. The modern writer was born of two phenomena. One was the emphasis now placed on experience and immediacy in contrast to past concern with revelation, authority, tradition, and even reason. The other was the new emphasis on the self in contrast to the group, on the "I," *le moi*, as it touched on truth. The writer, meanwhile, was not an isolated being; he lived in a social milieu, was part of a circle, foregathered with others. Nothing about him—his imagination, his art, his style of life— served men as a model.

Because tension was always present between self and society, writers played a social role—not as play-acting but as an obligation to themselves and to others. In playing this role the writer was subject to lures (the self being a powerful magnet); he was often seduced by the idea of power; he became an ideologist, an apologist, often a self-righteous moralizer. Much of this—even what was best in it—he rationalized by the idea of commitment; and when he did so, commitment became a mystique. "Committed . . . commitment": the word was always used abstractly, rarely with a simple intention, a well-defined relationship. It could, at worst, indicate a posture; could become what the American philosopher William James had called "the ascension of the faith ladder" in which possibilities were indistinguishable from probabilties and the ladder was converted into certainties. One definition of the ideological writer was "the man who runs down the street shouting, 'I've got an answer, who's got a question?'"

The situation was somewhat better in the advanced industrial societies; here, at least, one could say that the writer faced an important problem—his relation to the politicians, to power, to the technological intelligentsia. As regards the political relationship, there was the temptation to allow the "I" to be subverted. And here, Mr. Bell would interject that the question was not whether the writer was happy or unhappy; he might be happy or unhappy for many reasons. The ultimate political question was whether the writer was free or not free, purged or not purged, in prison or not in prison.

As to the writer and the technological intelligentsia, the complication arose out of the fact that the writer's essential questions about the quality of life were now bound up with matters of detail which he was ill-equipped to deal with. For example, the whole complex of problems involved in life in the large city was something beyond the writer's ken, yet he wrote about it without being aware of the limitations of his knowledge. All men were more or less in this predicament, and Mr. Bell would suggest that if there was here a role for the writer it was essentially to emphasize the note of doubt rather than commitment. "Alienation," he remarked, had become a "camp" word; Mr. Bell thought it could often be a positive virtue. Alienation was "a distancing of oneself from an event." To distance oneself was to create a degree of self-consciousness. And in so doing, one could perceive that the claims of doubt became prior to the claims of faith. Miss Lehmann had cited Keats' notion of "negative capability." Keats, also, had spoken of Shakespeare's ability to remain in uncertainty without any irritable reaching for faith or reason. Goethe, too, had said, "Doubt pleases me no less than knowing." Mr. Bell would offer the idea, then, that the role of the writer as public figure was perhaps to remain in a state of doubt.

The chairman, at this point, called for comments from the floor.

Mr. Aleksis Rannit (President, Writers-in-Exile P.E.N., member, American P.E.N. and Estonian P.E.N.) began by remarking that at Round Table III, on the previous day, the writer as collaborator with non-writers had been accused of creating original but irresponsible slogans. He would add that, as public figures, there were also writers who could be described as "spokesmen expressing political opinions." While many writers of this age had courageously resisted sinister political forces, others had begun by resisting Hitler only to accept Stalin; hating one gangster and venerating the other. Such writers, he suggested, should be "simply overlooked as public figures." Few had shown Silone's ethical and civil courage in rejecting all dictatorships. In general, Mr. Rannit would say that the writer as a public figure had betrayed the people.

Mr. Coutsoheras, speaking both as poet and as member of the Greek Parliament, believed that the writer was caught within the framework of national and worldwide statism. History taught that mythology and folklore were born in societies dominated by the idea of a god or gods. Greek literature had been written for men, but men as citizens, and man (Protagoras had said) was the "measure of all things." Roman literature bore the stamp of the *res publica romana.* The chairman's clepsydra forbade him to follow history in detail, but in the modern age we believed in a natural law, in a quasi-social contract, in the bourgeois and his social milieu as the dominant influence on creative literature. Mr. Coutsoheras mentioned all this as evidence that literature, so far from losing, profited by the social climate, was the fruit of the social climate, was itself a sort of public person. Would Aeschylus have been able to write *The Persians* if he had not fought at Marathon? Would Sophocles and Euripides have given us their ideas of man and humanism if they had held themselves aloof from the life of their times? Was it not because Dante was a political man that he had written *The Divine Comedy?* The writer could not escape participation in the life of his society, for it was the social milieu that guided his sensibility, his humanism, and his lyricism. This was the credo of a poet who was also a deputy for Athens.

Mrs. Hilda Domin, after quoting three poets who had celebrated the beauty and consolation of trees, quoted Confucius to the effect that when language is incorrect the arts cannot prosper, when that happens the laws cannot be applied, and what then follows is that the people are thrown into confusion; therefore writers should be free to write. She would add that a writer could be "committed" as a person and still write pure poetry; and that every writer "should try to appoint himself controller of the public language of his country," should be the "custodian of the true meaning of reality." Beyond this, she would press for the defense of writers against states that imprisoned them.

Mr. Tseng offered the view that the writer was an individual integrated into a community, and whatever he wrote influenced his community. In this sense he was inevitably a public figure. Whether his public *persona* could seduce him from independence as a creative artist depended upon the strength of his conviction and his character. In China's 12,000 years of history, one supreme example of a great philosopher, a great writer who was also a great public figure, stood out.

Confucius was a teacher who had attracted 3,000 students. He had not willed to become a public figure, his writings had made him one; and nobody would presume to say that this had seduced him into the abandonment of his independence.

Mr. Tseng would take the liberty of mentioning that his own family had had, under the Chin dynasty, a philosopher and writer—he was a commanding general, as well—who had been an incorruptible public figure. Today we found the creative impulse contested or suppressed by scientism, which sought to "computerize" men's minds, and by ideology, which was ambitious to "re-make human minds." In the Soviet Union, Sinyavsky and Daniel were in prison; across the border, in Mainland China, literary writing was being made an instrument of political control. Intellectual honesty "could not be assured so long as these fascist forces continued to exist." And writers had to come down from the ivory tower and fight against them. Mr. Tseng had written a report on these acts in China which was available to his colleagues.

President Miller, having been called on by the chairman, said that he would confine himself to his own experience of these matters rather than try to formulate dicta, although he thought it was not possible to say that a writer who was committed was necessarily doing injury to his art, any more than an uncommitted writer (whatever that might mean) was either helping or hurting his art.

On the one hand we had examples of committed writers—a Neruda, a Brecht—whose art could not be seriously questioned. On the other hand there were writers of high art who felt that "commitment was a jail." Something, therefore, was wrong with the question. Here in the United States, writers had lived through great changes in the attitude to commitment. In the depression years of the 1930s it was common for American writers—at least, a "very vocal minority" among them—to declare themselves committed to one form or another of the socialist ideology. In considering this it had to be borne in mind that, traditionally, the American public had ignored its writers. The writer as a public figure in the United States was a rare phenomenon until quite recently. By "public figure" Mr. Miller meant not a writer whose name was well known, but one "whose opinions on public matters might be of political importance." The poet Robert Lowell had spoken out on the Vietnamese conflict; depending on the citizen's views, the whole country had either shuddered at his statement or cheered it; that was something remarkable in this country, where writers who took a public position on a political question had previously been either ridiculed or ignored.

Mr. Miller had, in the past, known American writers who spoke publicly, or signed manifestos, and whose writing, nevertheless, showed no spiritual commitment to anything. He had also known writers who had never declared themselves, never signed a petition, and whose work contained evidence of clear commitment to one or another concept of human society. Therefore it appeared to him fruitless to try to equate the achievement of a writer with his degree of commitment—assuming that one would respect both points of view and concede that both kinds of writer wrote in good faith. As for himself, he had committed himself publicly from time to time and had written to express his commitment: "It has been in the blood and bone of my writing." He did not think that his writing was either better or worse for this fact, or that any writer made a deliberate choice of commitment or non-commitment.

Some writers were "swept by their vision of something wrong in the world"; they were impelled to support or attack, in their work. The subject did not fall in the either/or category; there was no imperative about it. Mr. Miller would add his belief, however contradictory this seemed, that the reader, or the playgoer, was likely to be moved by whatever "most powerfully impinged on his own social and personal problems." Insofar as this was true, it would mean that when a writer addressed himself to a reality of his times, his "commitment" would have an effect on the public reception of his work. People were more stimulated by, and critics accorded more importance to, a play which dealt vividly with the perplexities of today's living, than by a play, however beautifully written, which had no connection with what men were worrying about, in the street, the factory, or the bedroom. Mr. Miller believed in the existence of this "implacable pressure on literature to address itself to what is pertinent"; and he believed in the writer's commitment "to be the eye that sees the reality of the moment."

He agreed that the writer could be "as stupid and as foolish as anyone else in his political viewpoints"; he believed also that it was "in the nature of the writing we want to read, that it be individual—the writing that sucks us in and makes us want to go on." We were all victims of politeness, of standardized concepts. The role of the writer was "to speak from the center of his soul," to express that "naked, naive, genuine response to reality" which men could hope to find only in literature. "The writer who is led into himself by his commitment is helped by that commitment. The writer who is led away from himself by his commitment is hurt by it."

Mr. Silone asked permission to clarify points made in his earlier statement. He had spoken with admiration of the intellectuals who had successively opposed fascism, nazism, colonialism, the Algerian War, and the present war in Vietnam. And of the Poles and Hungarians who had retained their love of freedom. And of Pasternak, and Sinyavsky and Daniel. None of this had been prompted by a "cold-war mentality" or intent to keep the cold war alive. Anybody who thought that to pronounce the name of Pasternak was to revive the cold war was himself the prisoner of that mentality.

Secondly, on the word "totalitarianism." Mr. Silone had said unmistakably that he was not using it in the vulgar pejorative sense, but rather in the objective, juridical and historical sense—the sense of a regime under which the public authority had full power over man and society, decided what was beautiful and what ugly, what was true and what false. We were, happily, witnessing a modification of this extreme form, in several of the peoples' democracies of eastern Europe and even in the U.S.S.R., and we hoped that the result would be the transformation of totalitarian socialism into democratic socialism.

Finally, a word on the broadening of representation in the ranks of International P.E.N. Mr. Silone favored the entry of Soviet and Chinese writers into this free association where the life of literature and of the arts was freely and frankly discussed, without mental reservations and with, naturally, mutual respect. His own respect was entire, towards all the world; and he would add, if Mr. Neruda permitted, towards Mr. Neruda himself.

Mr. Bell, commenting on Mr. Miller's remarks, said that he shared most of his views but would draw one distinction. Certainly it was important that the writer should say "I feel the truth, I see it, I must speak it." But when a writer made his "naive response to reality" he did two things: he expressed, and he affirmed. His expression might be naive; his affirmation was a form of judgment. The difference was like that between knowledge and opinion. Opinions were not always founded on knowledge; writers often affirmed when they thought they were merely expressing. The question arose, did they always have the degree of knowledge, the degree of judgment, or the "aspect of mind" that was necessary to the judgment made in their affirmations? Where they did not possess these attributes, there was always the risk that their commitment was a mystique by which they justified a belief that whatever they affirmed was the truth.

Mr. Franz Theodor Csokor (President, Austrian P.E.N.), speaking in English, expressed his pleasure at finding himself for the first time in the country of the Declaration of Independence, the country of the late "young and wonderful" President Kennedy. On the theme of the congress he would say that literature had "three terms: pure, committed, and directed art." We looked most readily for free or independent writing to poetry; and yet in our time the "strongest impressions we have received of pure poetry have come from committed poetry such as Celan's "Fugue of Death" and Bertolt Brecht's "Hauspostille" which have lasted longer than even Rilke's "Duinese Elegies." And was not this poetry charged by one of its profoundest lines—"*Alles Vollkomene faellt zum Uralten*"—which was to say, "All that is perfect becomes part of the age-old"? Here the poet was his own patron. "The piper pays himself and calls his own tune." As to committed writing, it was enough to remember André Gide's statement, that there was a factor in the writer's being—his conscience—which was aroused, was stimulated to response, by certain kinds of events. We could say, therefore, that it was only in the case of directed art that the writer wrote in obedience to a purpose "outside his own private sphere." Mr. Csokor would recall that the visual arts have always been influenced—even directed—by religious and social institutions, and without necessarily lowering their quality.

The decisive factor was always the personality of the patron, and where the patron was a collective body the chances of quality resulting were lessened. Yet even here progress had been made. A kind of adult education had taken place. More people, nowadays, knew something of the evolution of art and had some habit of looking at art. Art had a social function, was in a way a social science. It was "generated by the forces prevalent in its time." It gave meaning to things otherwise unexplained. It sought and provided men with a "center of purpose" without which their lives were empty. In this sense alone, "genuine art always was and will be committed."

Mr. den Doolaard, speaking as a deeply committed writer, asked permission to extend Mr. Miller's reference to categories of committed and uncommitted writers—in the interest of the spirit of tolerance. During the German occupation of Holland, a young Dutch poet had left Amsterdam, where famine reigned, to live in a farmhouse, and there, well-fed and unconcerned, he had written the "most wonderful poem that we possess in modern Dutch literature." Such writers might not be the salt of the earth, but they were the angels invisible to us; and if their race died out the world would be lost.

SECOND SESSION

Mr. Lovinescu, speaking in French, began by complimenting the Program Committee of American P.E.N. upon its "intelligent choice of a subject which aroused universal interest." He had been particularly struck by the care taken to explain their concern with "forces which today may contain elements of menace, more insidious than censorship and dogmatism, to the writer's realization of his function and purpose." However, about the Committee's statement that writers, more than other men, "strove to discern a pattern in the life of their times," Mr. Lovinescu found himself in two minds. There had been great writers who remained apart from that search for a coherent pattern which was "the supreme fruit" of art and the highest expression of its dignity. Every civilization was the product of man's struggle to introduce his own human order into the "mystery of an impersonal world," his will to reshape the world in his own image. It was this tragic, because precarious, enterprise that marked man as the supreme artificer—literally the creater of the artificial.

Today, it would seem, some of the greatest writers, fascinated by the non-human, the irrational, or, to use a fashionable term, the absurd,* either from lack of faith in the creative function of man, or because they were lured by the void, had abandoned their predecessors' *raison d'être* and given themselves up to the terrible and dangerous enterprise of summoning the unsummonable, the world from which man was absent.

It would be stupid to sit in moral or aesthetic judgment on a phenomenon so characteristic of our ailing times. What we could do, however, was to look seriously at the problem of the writer or artist as a public figure; the artist as a man committed. Every writer who refused to believe in the possibility of a human order, was in Mr. Lovinescu's view, non-committed. And he would describe as committed every writer who embraced a religion, a political ideology, an "instinctive humanitarianism"; who, in other words, had not lost his faith in man and who sought, consciously or unconsciously, to "lend a human visage to the great impersonal All." The confrontation was not a quarrel of generations, or of schools, but a confrontation of mental and spiritual structures. From this viewpoint, a Marxist and a Catholic writer (both

---

* What is absurd, said Mr. Lovinescu parenthetically, is to call a world from which man is absent "absurd," for without man the world is neither good nor bad, neither absurd nor reasonable; it merely is.

committed) had more in common than a Catholic writer had with an uncommitted, though equally anti-Marxist writer.

Books such as Léon Daudet's *Le stupide dix-neuvième siècle,* and more recently a degraded type of political writing, had demonetized certain expressions: faith in man, man's dignity, the artist's responsibility. One pronounced them nowadays with a certain feeling of embarrassment; but precisely for this reason, Mr. Lovinescu felt it necessary to stress that commitment did not, for him, imply a beatific and grandiloquent optimism. To the contrary, it presupposed a severe, manly, even bitter, sometimes despairing and yet noble discipline—to use more of those embarrassing words.

Where was truth to be found? In the work of the committed, the uncommitted, the independent writer? In the writer who was the slave of fashion? The question itself was a quibble. Mr. Lovinescu, himself "structurally a committed writer," was nevertheless forced to recognize that in our times the most heart-rending cries, the most authentic pictures of human frailty confronted by a faceless and nameless universe, had been heard and made known thanks to artists who had lost their faith in God, in man, and even in art. Was this, Mr. Lovinescu asked, the art of the future? Was it perhaps the last manifestation of a cycle about to close? He would not presume to answer but would instead leave with his listeners the image of a small statue ("no bigger than that"), unearthed in a strange and remote corner of his country where the remains of every European culture since paleolithic times were to be found, layer upon layer—a statuette which archeologists and artists agreed to call "The Thinker." This primitive idol sat with its elbows on its knees; and though its head was held up by bestial hands, in the receding forehead, the great arch of the eyebrows, the empty eyesockets, one saw a creature gazing with terror at an immense, unknown, and hostile world. Stronger than its terror, however, there was in that glance a curiosity, a desire to know and to understand, that made of this figure a fraternal being, a vivid symbol of mankind.

Mr. Won Ko (Korean P.E.N.), speaking in English, confessed that he was unable to define the words "public figure" and that the topic discussed seemed to him "not to make very good sense." In China and in Korea the man of letters, above all the poet, had always passed examinations to serve his country. He had, in consequence, been a leader, admired by his people for his scholarship, his wisdom, creative ability, and purity of mind. Today they had two Korean literatures, one in the North, the other in the South, written in the same language. The works he had been able to consult in the Library of Congress in Washington revealed that contemporary North Korean literature was unmistakably composed of propaganda. Stories and poems were filled with praise of the government leader, the ruling party, the Soviet ally, and with expressions of hostility against what they called the "enemy of peaceful peoples." North Korean writers were controlled by their Communist party, were expected to deceive the people, and many since 1945 had been killed for refusing to do that. Were such official writers to be called public figures? In South Korea "everything was the opposite, except for the language."

A writer, Mr. Won Ko believed, was a kind of messenger carrying a new message to each man. He lived in a universal republic of understanding and friendship. He was not politically influential, and even when he wrote an anti-war poem he wrote as a poet. Poetry was, as Paul Valéry had written, "the spirit of our holidays."

Miss Henrietta Drake-Brockman (Melbourne P.E.N., Australia) had been particularly interested in the remarks made by delegates from the developing countries. Australia was the "last voice in the Western civilization." Its own distinctive literature went back only twenty years. Australian writers were imbued with the independent spirit, if only because they had had to fend off the British tradition—though their wholehearted allegiance was to Britain and to Western culture. As writers, however, they had had to compete with books from abroad and to suffer the fact that Australian literature was not taught in their universities. The speaker herself had delivered a lecture on Australian grammar as long as twenty-five years ago. Meanwhile, although she and her colleagues would prefer, as Miss Lehmann had suggested, to be private persons, they had had to do the contrary in Australia—take to television, the lecture platform, and the press, for the good of Australian literature. Their commitment—to speak of that—was to their country; and indeed upon this their capitalists and their Communists were pretty well united; though a majority of the Australian writers followed what could be called "the Labour point of view" and many, incidentally, were defenders of the aborigines. Only lately had they begun to be public figures in the sense defined by Arthur Miller.

Mme. Anna Kamenova (Bulgarian P.E.N.), speaking in English, was happy to think that light was shed on the problem before them in this place where statements from so great a variety of delegates could be heard and compared. The prevailing feeling seemed to be that "the writer should not estrange himself from his public." Her own impression was that the public, if not private, influence of the writer was growing—the influence of his books, she meant; for as a person he might sometimes be found disappointing.

Today, as the emblem of American P.E.N. symbolized, the pen had broken the sword. The writer was playing a role as the spiritual interpreter of his people. No longer the remote contemplator, the unbiased observer, he was a warrior on the social stage. To this extent the writer could be called a public figure. But he could not be said to be "absolutely independent" for he was answerable to his readers and to his nation. Mme. Kamenova would emphasize, however, that this role of warrior or prophet could not be performed by writers who produced only characters incapable of coping with the very evident difficulties of contemporary life, or by pessimists who saw only the seamy side of life. The writer had to know how to bring out latent forces, shape positive characters, show the road that led to a bright future.

M. Follain believed that unconditional commitment was as "reprehensible" as indifference or the ivory tower. In France a great writer, Maurice Barrès, had dishonored himself by writing newspaper articles, during the First World War, on the bayonet, which he dubbed "Rosalie" and about which he wrote: "Gay Rosalie should cut open the enemy's belly, and that belly should be cut open joyously." Then there had been Valette, publisher and editor of the *Mercure de France,* and not altogether a fool. When Paul Léautaud had protested against his stupid pseudo-patriotism, Valette had answered: "I can't be intelligent while the war is on. I'll be intelligent when it's over." Nor would M. Follain agree that a writer should dirty his hands on pretext of obedience to party discipline. On the other hand, indifference was equally unacceptable. Among the nineteenth-century writers whom M. Follain loved was his fellow-Norman, the great Flaubert—who had never seen what was going on: not in 1848, and even less the meaning of the Commune of 1870. He was not alone in this in 1870; not even Victor Hugo had been really aware of the significance of the Commune. "Down with unconditional commitment! But also with indifference!"

Mr. Valery Tarsis (Writers-in-Exile P.E.N., London), speaking in English, began by saying that he carried a great moral responsiblity, for he was pleading the cause of Sinyavsky and Daniel, among other writers in Russia. From this statement he would exclude the six "so-called" observers who were to have appeared on behalf of the Soviet Union of Writers. He had learnt "with great indignation" that the Writers Union, in expressing its approval of the sentencing of Sinyavsky and Daniel, had had "the gall" to say that they spoke for all members of the Writers Union. Even Communist writers in the West—Aragon and others—had been shocked.

Mr. Tarsis wondered if there could be room in P.E.N. for the representatives of an organization, the "sole purpose of which is to serve a totalitarian government as the chief instrument to police the writers."

He was himself a writer, a poet; the world of politics was strange and foreign to him. But politics were forced upon all writers behind the "Iron Curtain." Communist politics explained the award of the Nobel Prize in 1965 to Sholokhov, the novelist who had openly demanded that Sinyavsky and Daniel be shot. Mr. Tarsis was "ashamed of" the Nobel Prize; "I am ashamed also," he declared, "of the speech of Mr. Pablo Neruda"; he was proud of "the speech of Mr. Silone."

"I want to say to Mr. Pablo Neruda," Mr. Tarsis went on, "that we [should] really proclaim not only a Cold War but a Hot War to the Communist countries. We owe to the Russian people . . . a Hot War." Reading an "inspiring document written by the gallant young Yugoslav scholar, Mihajlov" Mr. Tarsis had thought of his young friends in Russia. Those who lived in the free world and belonged to this "illustrious organization" could wield the "tremendous power of public opinion" and the Communist rulers could "no longer ignore it."

Mr. Sandor Weöres (Hungarian P.E.N., statement paraphrased in English by Mrs. Amy Weöres). Concerning the fame and image of the writer, Mr. Weöres made the point that certain poets of high quality could not, by reason of their writing in languages known only to their own peoples, become public figures without the intervention of able translators. There were numerous poets in Yugoslavia, in Russia, in China and in Japan, living and dead, who would have been "public figures in the best sense of that term" if translators had come to their aid; moreover, translation of their works would have contributed "an added dimension" to world literature and to "our spiritual concepts." As things were, they remained known to few outside their homelands.

Miss Hilde Spiel (Austrian P.E.N.), speaking in English, observed that several delegates had seemed to urge their listeners to participate in politics, not only as citizens but in virtue of their talents and even in obedience to certain traditions. This, it seemed to Miss Spiel, required that the writer be ready to adopt other people's views and that he assume other people's responsibilities. The first was detrimental to the writer's craft, the second frequently out of character.

Miss Spiel would plead for the writer who resisted a demand for commitment at whatever risk; not an unqualified plea, for the resistance should be founded upon a moral code. She would not advocate certain kinds of eccentricities, even on the part of the poet whom Conor Cruise O'Brien, in a current article, had called the greatest poet of our day. For example, she thought Günter Grass was entitled to beat his tin drum for the Socialist Party in the current German elections. She admired every writer who took a political stand. But Grass was wrong to attack the writers of the Weimar Republic for not sinking their differences on political and social questions. And she would ask if the writer's task was not to think independently and dangerously (as Koestler and Sartre had done). She would close by quoting Emerson who had said that every reform was once a private opinion, and it was only by private opinions that problems were solved.

Mr. Edgar Johnson (a former President of American P.E.N.) said that he had listened for three days, not with indifference but with, at times, impatience and rebellion. He had heard prophets robed in pseudo-scientific dress, "croaking an abracadabra of jargon according to which this audience should be terrified by technology, silenced by sociology, crushed by computerized knowledge, immolated on a pyre of mass media." There had been some voices of protest and defiance, most had been voices of respectful worry and fear. More than fifty years ago the American historian and man of letters, Henry Adams, had invented a "law of history" with which he had frightened himself. Twenty years ago, H. G. Wells declared that the mind of man had reached the end of its tether; and Mr. Johnson doubted that he had been consoled by Bernard Shaw's telegram: "Don't worry. If man destroys himself God will replace him with something better." Today Samuel Beckett saw the human race as living in garbage cans or buried up to the neck in sand. For himself, Mr. Johnson was not waiting for a Godot who never came, nor did he believe many writers were waiting.

Professor McLuhan had symbolized the past, its history and literature, as a rear-vision automobile mirror, ignoring the fact that knowledge of the past was indispensable to an understanding of the present and as a guide to the future. McLuhan saw the past as static; Mr. Johnson saw it as constantly changing, some elements receding and others moving forward; and if he saw it thus, it was because he was in the driver's seat, looking ahead and knowing where he was bound.

Of course the materials of knowledge had grown more complex. Of course computers were extraordinary instruments. But the problems they solved were problems put to them by human minds. Mr. Johnson's objection was not to them but to the assumption that man could not make them serve him for his enlightenment and must, instead, be dominated by them.

We were told derisively that art did not progress, only science progressed; whereas the truth was that the insight and vision of the great writers had taught things which the psychologists were only now beginning to stumble upon. If Proust and Thomas Mann and Eliot and Joyce told us things that Wordsworth and Cervantes had not said, the reason was that each was supreme in his own realm and that literature did not need constant correction, as science did. Man, Mr. Johnson concluded, would continue to grow in understanding.

The chairman made the following announcement: "Mr. Valery Tarsis, of the Center for Writers-in-Exile, wants me to say that when he spoke of 'hot war' he meant hot ideological war. We are grateful for this clarification."

M. Anoma Kanie said that the question being debated had been succinctly put at the first session by Mr. den Doolaard: could the fact of a writer's commitment have a harmful bearing on his creative work? Mr. Miller had said that the problem was falsely posed. The fact was that the writer, as an independent spirit, was free to express himself as he pleased, provided he was faithful to his ideal, which was to serve truth and beauty. Truth, which was the writer's ultimate aim, was obviously not a formal but a variable thing; and to the extent that the writer discovered truth, he was committed to affirm and support it. It had also been said at the morning session that the writer should follow the dictates of his conscience. M. Kanie believed that when a writer committed himself, and continued to consult his conscience, he was reaffirming his independence of spirit. A writer was a member of the human family; he expressed the deepest feelings of man; his task was to combat tyranny and hatred and to ensure the triumph of love, truth, and mutual understanding.

Mrs. Ingeborg Drewitz (German P.E.N. Center, G.F.R.) said that the practice of publicity was driving the writer to make of himself a public figure, often against his will. We all knew the historical process that destroyed feudalism and brought about a "harsh individualism" with the result that in our day the individual had lost his pride and his sense of security. This condition, in turn, had yielded to the socialistic aim of a particular kind of Utopia. On the one hand we had the complex dreams, feelings, intellectual values of that iceberg of which only a small part was visible—the human person. On the other hand we had the security of the collectivity. Both existed; both had their systems. Mrs. Drewitz believed that the writer was becoming more and more "the teacher of society" and that, for her part, a society of moral individuals was to be preferred to a society led by "those brutal and infernal characters who have seven skins more than anybody else."

Mr. Miller said that he would try to draw together certain ideas that had been emphasized or repeatedly voiced at this session.

Earlier in the week, Marshall McLuhan, an inhabitant of a highly technological society, had said in effect that the age of linear culture, the age of print, was being superseded by an age of circuitry, of electronics. The next day, on the same platform, a group of Latin-American writers,* some of whom had never met before, spontaneously declared that in all their different countries—without exception, as Mr. Miller recalled—the principal problem was to teach the people to read. On both occasions, men had spoken honestly; they had reflected a reality. McLuhan's problem was to go beyond reading; the Latin-American problem was to reach the stage of reading. Each pronounced his own truth. And so it was with commitment: there was no single truth.

Mr. Miller could conceive of himself living in an illiterate society and being moved to want to teach—because the people wanted to know. He could conceive of being obsessed with the idea of being alone —almost alone—as a man who possessed knowledge and lived in a sea of ignorance. In such a situation, how could he refrain from commitment?

He could also conceive of a writer who lived in Paris, London, New York, surrounded by literacy and fed by commercialized messages of every kind, by artificial concepts that had no relation to any sort of reality—a writer who felt that it was his duty to draw his readers' attention to underlying facts about human nature and about the society they were living in.

The purpose of those present, in speaking of the writer as public figure, was to save the writer from compulsion, from yielding to viewpoints that had not been given him by his spirit. Whether he should or should not commit himself was, Mr. Miller thought, a matter of personal choice.

Soon after the American Revolution, theatres were opened in Philadelphia and New York. As an academic exercise, Mr. Miller had read plays which had been performed in those theatres. The characters were either British or American. The British were portrayed as effete, opinionated, condescending—all in all, quite unattractive. The Americans were simple fellows: peasants, perhaps, with a native wit; honest, physically strong, easily tricked; but their native honesty always won through. Nobody had imposed these concepts, though possibly the audience would not have tolerated a kind, understanding, valiant Englishman. There was a kind of commitment here, long before the word (as we use it) was known. It might have been imposed by public opinion, or by the Americans' own idea of reality, their own moral values.

"What I am pleading for," said Mr. Miller, "is a certain toleration based on the fact and the knowledge that men in one country are in a different situation from men in another country. We most of all, in P.E.N., should appreciate that fact, and cling to it in this discussion, believing in the good faith of one another and in a common wish to

* See *The Situation of the Latin American Writer*, p. 109.

universalize our association; for it will do us no good if we do not grow
in wisdom."

Mr. Jyotirmoy Datta (Calcutta, India) pointed out that two views
had been expressed about commitment and that delegates from Kenya,
Korea, and the National Republic of China had supported the writer
as a committed artist. Mr. Bell had proposed a state of perpetual
doubt. Miss Lehmann had suggested that the writer be silent and re-
ceptive. Mr. Datta's view was that one should write the best poem possible and hope for an audience. He would say to Mr. Bell that the right
to doubt ought to include the right to change one's mind; for a man
who had no beliefs was not a man at all. In the West, the situation
seemed to be that artists found it hard to commit themselves; in the
older countries commitment had gone to extremes.

Mr. Boldizsár asked permission to refer to previous discussion of the
remarks of "the noblest figure among us," Ignazio Silone. Because he
respected Silone, and respected the truth as Silone did, he wished to
comment—after making a personal remark—on what was a delicate situation. He was a Hungarian. Hungary had been mentioned. There
might be some present who were thinking: "Boldizsár is a Hungarian.
Is he silent because he fears that if he speaks he will be persecuted
when he gets home?" That would be nonsense.

The fact was that Mr. Boldizsár was not now and had never been a
Communist. He was speaking now because Silone had referred to the
events in Hungary of ten years ago. Mr. Boldizsár had been one of the
intellectuals who had signed "the resolutions of the revolutionary committee." Silone was one of the idols of his youth; his *Bread and Wine*
had been passed from hand to hand in the fascist days of Hungary
where that book had been a proof of human dignity and a source of
faith in the future. Today, he would argue with Silone on only one
point: his omission to include in his survey of events the changes that
had been taking place in East Europe. Certainly, as regards Hungary
specifically, he was wrong to put every kind of totalitarianism, past and
present, "into the same bag." Today there were four Hungarian delegates at this congress. None was ever asked to sing a hymn of praise.
None was a party member. Ten or twenty years ago, none of them
could have come to New York.

This was important for them. It was important for their readers in
Hungary. Gyula Illyés not being present in the auditorium, Mr. Boldizsár would say that he was the "greatest living personality in Hungarian
literature"; his authority went beyond Hungary's frontiers. For him
and for literate Hungary—which was to say 99 per cent of the nation—
the presence here of a Hungarian delegation was an event of high im-

portance; a symbol of change not to be ignored by any intellectual. *The chairman* felt that Mr. Boldizsár's statement was very pertinent to P.E.N.'s general purposes. He could testify to its validity from personal experience in Budapest. He would add, as one who had been a guest in earlier years of the Soviet Writers Union, that many Russians did not have "seven skins," as had earlier been implied. They were warmhearted; they were no more responsible for their government than was Mr. Young, a Scot, "for the English government in London."

Mme. Mileva felt compelled to address a personal question to Mr. Miller concerning the resolution on peace offered at the meeting of the International Executive by Mr. Coutsoheras of Greece. Mr. Miller— "with some right," said Mme. Mileva—had moved the resolution out of order on the grounds that it dealt with politics. Her question was, did Mr. Miller find Mr. Tarsis' remarks unpolitical and not out of place at a P.E.N. meeting? To the question, she would add a protest— against his slander of the Soviet Union and the Soviet Writers Union. She would not protest that he was not free to express a personal opinion —either about a Soviet body or when he said, "I am ashamed also for the speech of Mr. Pablo Neruda." As for what Mr. Tarsis said against Bulgaria—where, incidentally, there was not one writer in prison today —Bulgarian writers did not need to be defended by anyone, least of all Mr. Tarsis. "But," Mme. Mileva went on, "I protest against the chairmanship of this Round Table which allowed a purely political statement absolutely contrary to the Charter of P.E.N."

The chairman reminded Mme. Mileva of a dramatic event in P.E.N.'s forty-five years of life, the Dubrovnik Congress of 1934, where analogous protests were made by the Nazis who had turned up as delegates of the German P.E.N. They had demanded that German anti-Nazis in exile be expelled from the congress. When H. G. Wells, who presided, refused, they had marched out of the hall. Mr. Young reminded the audience that "they love not liberty who fear license." It was, in his opinion, far better that members say exactly what they think and what their experience leads them to say, than to follow procedures which lead to false understandings: "We want a true understanding."

Mr. Miller said, on Mr. Coutsoheras' intervention, that it was made at a meeting of the Executive and in the form of a resolution to be adopted as the official expression of that body. As such, it was out of order. Mr. Miller would add his own view that it was moreover a pointless proposal. People were "against war" the way they were "against sin." Of course we were against war. But what could P.E.N. do about it? P.E.N. could do only specific concrete things, and one thing it could not do was to make peace. As President of International P.E.N., he thought that members did not want the Executive Committee to spend its time passing vain resolutions.

M. Nghiem Xuan Viet (Vietnam P.E.N.), speaking in French, declared that he would offer a few personal ideas. First, that the writer owed it to himself to follow his deepest instincts, guided by a disinterested search for truth and beauty. If he was a born artist, he would remain within these limits; if a born fighter, he would enter the arena. He had only to follow his innate bent, and the fact of committing himself would have no ill effect upon his creative independence. In fact, it was in the climate of struggle—convinced, sincere struggle—that he would find the total development of his personality.

The second question, on what basis we should esteem an author, ought to be answered as follows. As artist, we judged him according to his contribution to beauty and creativity; as fighter, according to his sincerity. A sincere writer might be mistaken in good faith. Although present-day means of information permitted us to be better informed, the writer sincerely concerned to inform his own people would take pains to learn the facts. In the case of Vietnam, he would visit that country, study its language, make certain that he refrained from praising what he would condemn if he knew the truth—about Mao Tse-tung, for example, or Castro.

The speaker asked leave to say a word on the war in his country. Well-known writers were condemning it who had not asked themselves how it began nor by what means it could be brought to an end. The Vietnamese asked them to learn the facts about the "so-called liberation movement" in Vietnam itself. This, he believed, would persuade them that half-measures were no more adequate to avoid catastrophe in Vietnam than when Hitler was annexing territory in Europe before the outbreak of the war. Subversion was a great danger; the atomic bomb destroyed life, but subversion destroyed the soul, the social order, the freedom of man. Liberty should be the first concern of the writer, for the writer was more or less responsible for the public conscience.

Mr. Nicanor Parra (Chilean P.E.N.), speaking in English, said that he was not a member of any political party, nor a "committed" writer. He would say, however, for people who believed that only propaganda literature could be published in the socialist states, that this no longer seemed to be the case. His own poems, which some Western critics regarded as "nothing but nihilistic nonsense," had been translated into Russian and published by the Soviet Writers Union.

Miss Shirland Quin (English P.E.N.) made the point that while George Bernard Shaw was certainly a public figure, she believed that he would "not have submitted to being called 'committed.' " He had gained much from his public status, for he was a man who needed conflict to keep his wit sharpened. Miss Quin remembered that Shaw, having disputed an ethical view expressed by the founder of P.E.N., Mrs. Dawson Scott, had later admitted laughingly that she had been right and that he had intervened only to spur her on to arguing her own case more persuasively. Of course there had been writers—D. H. Lawrence or T. E. Lawrence, for example—"to whom public life meant devastation of their creative powers." And she thought Miss Lehmann's suggestion of silence, in the sense of "stillness of the spirit," was all-important. Finally, there was "no such thing as 'the writer' "; there were writers as there are plants in the garden, each needing its own variety of nurture.

Mr. Frank Doczy (Melbourne P.E.N., Australia), asked if a writer could be at one and the same time committed and an independent spirit, and how one was to look upon writers who changed their commitments?

Mr. Bell confessed himself confused by a question which asked if the revolving door was set up to judge political positions. Questions put abstractly were hard to answer cogently. He would point out—perhaps pedantically—that modern philosophy had for some years been trying to teach us to avoid abstract nouns. "Consciousness" or "commitment" was not "a state of being" by itself. Only relational terms were meaningful: consciousness *of* something, commitment *to* something. This new introduction of an "activity principle" in understanding knowledge was all that he wished to emphasize at the moment.

Mr. den Doolaard's admonition came to this: let the writer commit himself to writing. Thereafter, he could support causes, provided he did not fritter away his life on them.

Dr. Kamnitzer, remarking that members appeared to be free to discuss politics outside the International Executive Committee, said that the writer as public figure was "obviously not disassociated from politics." Mr. Miller's position on Vietnam was widely shared in Europe "and we are grateful for the stand he has taken." Secondly, he said, the audience had been asked to support a "regime whose Marshall Ky is a follower of Adolf Hitler": he could not understand the applause which had greeted that speech. Thirdly, he could not, "for the life of me" understand how this "illustrious gathering could by-pass the bombardment in Vietnam by phosphorus bombs."

M. Georges Charaire (French P.E.N.) said that all writers were in some sense "engaged" or committed. Valéry had written that the creative act committed a writer's entire being. To commit oneself implied freedom to commit oneself; commitment under duress was not true commitment. The story was told that General de Gaulle had one day telephoned M. Debré to ask him what time it was. "Whatever you say, General," Debré had answered. Writers were people who told us the time, and each had his own chronometer. This was the writer's essential freedom. If constraint existed, it came from the public, or the publisher, or from commercial or political pressures. When that happened, writers ceased to exist.

M. Charaire had no fear of pressure from the sciences. They were, in fact, less strong today than in the ages of primitive science, of sorcerers. He confessed to uneasiness about electronic media, however; for by tempting the writer to reach a very wide public, they tempted him to lower his standards; to reply, in effect, "Whatever you say, General."

M. Nghiem Xuan Viet said that he would remind the delegate from East Germany that machines existed for the fabrication of false news.

Mr. Wieland Herzfelde said he believed that change of commitment could be either honest or dishonest. He was committed in a way he believed consonant with the International P.E.N. Charter. It all depended upon whom one was fighting against—fascists or non-fascists: "P.E.N. cannot be otherwise than anti-fascist."

M. Jacques Fiechter (Geneva P.E.N., Switzerland) began by assuring his audience of a warm reception in the near future by the Geneva P.E.N. Center. He believed that the New York Congress had been a success from three points of view. First, the International Executive Committee's activity; second, despite the danger of "verbal inflation," work had fairly and honestly been done, and above all, men and women from the four quarters of the world had met in a friendly atmosphere and learnt to understand and respect one another. Best of all was the demonstration that P.E..N represented a great source of hope in our time. Six hundred years ago, a charter had been written in three Swiss valleys in which one would find enunciated the principles which P.E.N. was striving to implant and revive. To find at this congress that despite struggle, error, war between peoples and religions, those principles were still upheld, convinced Mr. Fiechter that—adapting a line from Victor Hugo—"P.E.N. will have the last word."

Mr. Bell, asked by the chairman to close the discussion, said that he would try to do what Mr. Miller had done halfway through—to see if common themes had emerged.

First, the writer and commitment. It might be helpful to ask, how would this debate have looked thirty years ago? Thirty years ago one committed oneself to a line, a specific political position. Today we were talking of commitment to the vocation of the writer. This would seem to imply that passion about politics was still not "a religious situation." Mr. Bell thought it an "advance" in the sense that total commitment to a political line was no longer demanded. Commitment to the writer's vocation had, in this congress, replaced commitment to ideology, to dogma.

Second, concerning the writer's notion of truth. It might help to look at the scientist's notion. One did not talk of Russian science, American science, Bulgarian science, as the Nazis had talked of German science; one talked of physics, or chemistry, or biology. Scientists sought to attain objective goals. The writer's objective was necessarily somewhat different: he was a Bulgarian writer, an American writer, a Russian writer. He worked in a language and in a culture particular to his people. The writer knew truth by experience; the scientist, by trying to transcend experience and to find "common norms." This lent special importance to a point made by Mr. Miller. A writer had to guard against the notion that he spoke total truths, because his experience was not total, it was incomplete and tentative. This did not mean—and by recommending an attitude of doubt, Mr. Bell had not meant—that belief did not exist. It meant only that faith had to be tested, and therefore doubt had "a prior claim."

It was in this perspective that he had offered his remarks. This P.E.N. congress had tried to do what all intellectuals try to do—to create an open community. By an open community and open discourse, we had sought to arrive at an understanding of one another.

The Situation of
the Latin-American Writer

Wednesday, June 15
SPECIAL SESSION

Emir Rodriguez Monegal, CHAIRMAN
Uruguay

Homero Aridjis
Mexico

Manuel Balbontin
Chile

Haroldo de Campos
Brazil

Carlos Fuentes
Mexico

Alberto Girri
Argentina

Juan Liscano
Venezuela

M. A. Montes de Oca
Mexico

Carlos Martínez Moreno
Uruguay

Pablo Neruda
Chile

Victoria Ocampo
Argentina

Juan Carlos Onetti
Uruguay

Nicanor Parra
Chile

J. Guimaraes Rosa
Brazil

Mario Vargas Llosa
Peru

The Situation of
the Latin-American Writer

Mr. Rodriguez Monegal, speaking in English, took the chair at what he explained was a session *hors série,* which he and his fellow Latin Americans had spontaneously proposed and their North American hosts had been happy to arrange. He introduced to the congress audience those on the platform: M. A. Montes de Oca (Mexico), Nicanor Parra (Chile), Victoria Ocampo (Argentina), C. Martínez Moreno (Uruguay), Carlos Fuentes (Mexico), M. Vargas Llosa (Peru), Haroldo de Campos (Brazil), Manuel Balbontin (Chile), Homero Aridjis (Mexico). Other Latin-American writers were present in the audience and they would speak. The chairman explained that in view of the presence of a majority of the delegates to the congress from other countries, speakers would use, not their native Spanish or Portuguese, but the P.E.N.'s two official languages, English and French.

Mr. Martínez Moreno, speaking in French, began by saying that it was necessary to use the now universal term "underdevelopment" in discussing the situation of the Latin-American writer. It was significant, he said, that Spanish was not one of P.E.N.'s official languages. In Latin America, underdevelopment had created for the writer a problem of "incommunication." The Latin-American writer was cramped, hemmed in, in his effort to bear witness to his times. His life was spent far from the great active centers of culture. He existed through intermediaries of various kinds. His quasi-anonymity rendered it difficult for him to gain recognition at home as a professional man of letters. The number of Latin-American writers who could live by their writing was very small. Of course this situation was different in the different republics accordingly as the literary markets, the publishing houses, the number of inhabitants differed in each country. Each writer could testify only as to the material conditions in his own country. That Latin-American unity which all of them so ardently desired and projected in all they wrote was still a distant prospect. They all knew what stood in its way; but it was harder to know how, and to be able, to overcome the obstacles. The writers themselves had at times exaggerated their differences, exasperated them, and even kept them alive—with the result that in each republic writers had been thrown back upon themselves, disunited, reciprocally ignorant and ignored.

In this sense, the importance of the present P.E.N. congress was easy to measure. Mr. Martínez Moreno was convinced that each of their P.E.N. centers should be strengthened, beginning with recognition of the fact that each Latin-American center had its own particular weakness. He thought no one would be offended if he said that the Uruguayan Center was very weak.

There was also the anachronism of an official culture out of touch with the living cultures of the Latin-American countries. Class feeling, what Gide had called "delayed communion" was perhaps partly responsible. Writers suffered from delayed recognition by official circles. It was not that authors demanded official places in the Establishment . . . places as cultural attachés, for example. What they demanded was recognition as the living representatives of a living culture. And it was a sad truth that in all their republics official culture was a kind of pantheon—official reviews, official consecration, official obsequies. A writer had to be dead, or at least reduced to silence, to be awarded a place in this pantheon. There was no simultaneity of living and operative culture, on the one hand, and officially paraded and exploited cultural values on the other hand. For this reason Latin-American writers had to become better acquainted, gain a hearing for themselves, write in order to put an end to "incommunication."

Mr. Parra, speaking in English, said that he would not deal with generalities; he would give a concrete example of cultural relations. In 1965 he had published a book in Argentina of which the publisher sent to him, in Chile, 100 copies. To this day the Chilean postal authorities had not been legally able to deliver those books to him: "In other words, books are not let into the country, not even if the author is a Chilean."

Mr. Liscano, speaking in French, referred first to the fact that the market for books was very limited in the Latin-American countries, whence it followed that the possibilities of being published were also limited. There existed two poles, so to say, of publishing. In the southern area, there were publishing houses in Buenos Aires, Montevideo, and Chile. In the north there was Mexico City. Between the two, from Panama to Bolivia, there were practically no book publishers and Mr. Liscano, as a Venezuelan, could testify that it was extremely difficult for a writer to become known because to arrange for publication in Mexico or in the southern centers was not easy. Only one Venezuelan writer had a wide reputation outside his country—Rómulo Gallegos, whose novel *Doña Barbara* had been translated into some twenty languages; and this thanks in large part to a prize awarded that novel in Spain in 1928.

One solution might be the establishment of a single "Bolivarian" publishing house to serve the markets of Panama, Venezuela, Colombia, Ecuador and Peru. What was certain was that without a publishing trade, writers could not go on writing. At the age of twenty, everybody started writing; to go on without being published was a heroic task, and the lack of publishers in the "Bolivarian" countries was the prime reason why so many writers emigrated to Europe or to New York.

Mr. Vargas Llosa, speaking in French, said that he was a little embarrassed in describing the writer's situation in Peru. The congress had heard, the day before, an interesting discussion on the writer in the electronic age. Peruvian writers' concerns were very far removed from that problem. Their problems were, in a sense, problems of the Stone Age. How things looked to young Peruvians who felt the urge to write, to make a career of literature, he would try to describe briefly.

The career of writer in Peru was one of frustration. The reason was that in a country with Peru's historical, sociological and economic conditions, the social importance of literature was almost nil. Half the population could neither read nor write. Another half lived in "asphyxiating" conditions on the edge of cultural life—workers in shantyvilles, peasants, people with no margin to spend on books or whose degree of schooling was too low for literary reading. The educated minority with enough income to buy books and finance a cultural life— the Peruvian governing class—had never interested itself in things cultural, had been traditionally suspicious of culture, in contrast to what went on even in most other Latin-American countries. In a word, the country had no reading public, therefore no publishers; the Peruvian writer was a kind of freak, a figure picturesque but abnormal. Young people who wanted to write were confronted by a kind of moral and psychological "dissuasion machine."

Most Peruvian poets, playwrights and novelists were deserters, people who published a book or two and then gave up; deserted the literary life. And why? Because if they had persevered each would have become a kind of outcast, a derelict. Of course some did persevere. How? By going into exile; they had no other defense against the "dissuasion machine." There were different kinds of exile of which the traditional form was to take refuge in a foreign land, even in other Latin-American lands. It was almost symbolic that Peru's two greatest writers, El Inca Garcilaso de la Vega and the poet Vallejo, died in exile. This was physical exile, but there was also spiritual exile. One dug oneself in against indifference or hostility. This was inescapable where a writer was not buoyed up by a national traditional culture. Writers who needed cultural nourishment had to read foreign works, integrate themselves in foreign cultures—English, French, "even American." To reject such integration was a kind of patriotism, perhaps, but it was also to ensure oneself a narrow and an impoverished culture.

An example of spiritual exile at the beginning of this century was the Peruvian poet, José Mariá Egurén, who never left Lima and wrote of Nordic gnomes and fairies, of flora and fauna foreign to Peru. Another kind of exile was that of the great poet, Cesar Moro, who lived in France and in Mexico and had chosen to write in French, a foreign language—and this very great poet had not once mentioned Peru in his poetry.

The Peruvian writer who chose to confront reality at home had to live in an unbearable state of tension and run the greatest risks. First the risk of deserting literature. Second, the risk of living a double life, a life handicapped by the need to seek a livelihood outside of literature —literature being in Peru a non-social function. Third, politics. The speaker had often been asked in Europe, "Why are so many Latin American—especially Peruvian—writers politically committed; militants?" The answer was that to feel oneself part of such a society was very difficult. A writer tended to rebel, tended naturally to be moved by a sense of political responsibility and to point to other men's responsibilities. His own miserable condition as writer made him automatically a defender of others who were in misery. It led him to see that those who turned their backs on their responsibility for these miseries were precisely the governing class—who could buy books but didn't; who had the means to make Peru a worthy country, but didn't.

And this risk comported still another—the subordination of their literary vocation to their will to change the social situation. Many writers felt that this was the just and honorable thing to do. And this too was a way of deserting literature and frustrating the writer in oneself.

True though all this was, many Peruvian writers would probably protest that the panorama the speaker had sketched was far too pessimistic; they were not at all discouraged by the reality of Peruvian conditions. Because of them, he would end on an optimistic note. The difficulty, the vacuum, the negligence and deficiencies in that reality were for those writers a challenge and an encouragement to act. This was a heartening thing and led writers to achieve ambitious ends. And he would conclude by saying that the Peruvian situation was, despite everything, favorable; because many examples in literary history demonstrated that it was in decomposing societies that rich, ambitious and total literatures had been born.

Mr. Fuentes, speaking in English, began by remarking that the congress seemed to have been discussing whether or not the writer was in fact a sort of dinosaur whose place, function and influence were doomed to vanish. As regards Latin America, it was true that there was no technology and that the mass media were a hindrance rather than an aid to communication. It was a fact that in countries—this was true of most of Latin America—where there was no legislature, no political party, no workers' union worthy of the name; where the mass media were in the hands of the "most catastrophic merchants one could imagine," it became the writer's business to say those things which history and the mass media did not say.

Here Mr. Fuentes saw a challenge to the writer—and to language, the instrument he works with, the importance of which could not be exaggerated. In his country, Mexico, language had been kidnapped, so to say, by the *status quo* incarnated in the paradoxically named Party of Revolutionary Institutions. It was very common, in Mexico, to find a landowner speaking of "agrarian reform," a banker speaking of the "proletarian revolution," everybody taking shelter under the banner of "the revolution," "the left," etc. What the writer could do about this was problematical; one knew how Hitler had kidnapped a language and destroyed all means of personal and social communication, obliging the postwar writers to create a new German language. In the United States, what McCarthy had represented was essentially a kidnapping of language, an attack upon institutions with the weapon of adjectives and epithets.

Mexican writers had tried for a time to withdraw quietly and cultivate their gardens. They had overlooked the domination of the whole social structure by the pyramid of power built on the fearful conjunction of Aztec autocracy and Spanish Jesuitism. The inactive intelligentsia had been Mexico's only liberal sector until, quite recently, those in power demanded that they render public homage to authority. First came the campaign against the book, *Los Hijos de Sánchez (The Children of Sanchez),* edited from tape-recordings of life among the lowly by the North American, Oscar Lewis. The book was condemned as pornographic; the famous liberal and creative publishing house, Fonda de Cultura Mexicana, was crippled by the removal of its director, Arnaldo Orfila Raynal, on the chauvinistic pretext that he was an Argentine, a foreigner, and the charge that the book was anti-social because it was critical of the government—a "crime" punishable by twenty-five years in prison. Finally, in the spring of 1966 the government accused the traditionally liberal (but limited in academic freedom) University of Mexico of "anti-national" cultural activities: examples were the performance of plays by Beckett and Ionesco, music by Alban Berg and Schoenberg, and public readings of works by "decadent" foreign poets. In sum, we had here a radical corruption of language which had the effect of almost total submission of the Mexican intelligentsia to the *status quo.*

Mr. Fuentes concluded from these events that "in Latin America, fidelity to language is the sole permanent defense." There had been talk at the congress of the "pure" versus the "committed" writer, Mallarmé versus Dickens. He believed that both were the defenders of the writer as independent spirit, whether proclaimed in their works or from a public platform. In Latin America, this distinction was meaningless. The speaker believed that a Neruda or a Borges, a Carpentier or an Asturias, an Octavio Paz or a Cortázar, committed or uncommitted, all contributed to the same defense.

Meanwhile, there was another influential condition in Latin America—a heritage of historic schizophrenia. The speaker meant by this Utopian promises in the area's origins, corrupted and negated by what soon followed. (Vasco de Quiroga's foundations in Michoacán, for example, were inspired by Sir Thomas More.) The epic nature of the continent's history (lost paradise, noble savage, etc.) had collided with eschatological expectations, and between the two "our personal, concrete, every-day life practically disappeared." Thus, there remained to the writer today the task of "creating a sense of the present."

Finally, Mr. Fuentes would point out that in Latin America, literature was "paralyzed by the fact that reality is more literary than fiction in most of our countries." Could one imagine more incredibly fictive, literary figures than the dictators: Santa Anna, Rosas, Francia, Trujillo, Batista? What was terrible in this historical vigor was that it imposed an "absolutely fatalistic, deterministic chronology." Perhaps the Latin-American writer could, by his imagination, perform the modest but important task of obliterating that fatality, creating a "simultaneous virtuality of space."

Mr. de Campos, speaking in English, said that he would deal with the Latin-American avant-garde, to which he himself belonged, in the movement for concrete poetry, since the early 'fifties. He believed that the avant-garde, and particularly its connections in the various Latin American centers, was not well known. In Portuguese-speaking Brazil, for example, few people knew so important a writer as Borges, fewer still knew Cortázar, a mere handful had heard of Vicente Huidobro. He himself would like to become acquainted with the friends of his colleagues here present.

In Brazil, the writers of concrete poetry had undertaken experimentation "in a committed way," on the model of Mayakovsky and Brecht. They believed, as the former had put it, that "without revolutionary form there was no revolutionary art." Moral commitment and technical innovation went hand-in-hand. At the same time, earlier Brazilians had incorporated concrete techniques in their work as for example, Bandeira, Drummond de Andrade, Ricardo, Braga, Murilo Mendes and, to a certain extent, Cabral de Melo Nato. Mr. de Campos and his friends had republished a poem dating from 1870, Sousa Andrade's *O Guesa Errante* which brought to mind "our Neruda's" *Canto General,* especially in a section entitled "O Inferno de Wall Street." This rediscovery was in the speaker's opinion as important as "T. S. Eliot's rediscovery of the English metaphysical poets." It was an attack on North America's mixture of capitalism, puritanism and progress, written in an elliptical, polyglot kind of verse, and employing a montage technique of political events, newspaper reports and literary references, to produce an ironic insight into the beginnings of modern North America.

Latin-American poets, Mr. de Campos said, would have to take account of technology, enlarge their vocabularies, and use new resources of communication—the placard or poster poem, for example. The old book forms were unfit for wide communication.

Mr. Montes de Oca, asking forgiveness for his imperfect English, was convinced that the Spanish American writer's criticism of his own society was more effective than any praise of his society. Neruda, Vallejo, Octavio Paz and other vigorous talents had made important contributions to the universal poetry of our times. He believed in the future of a Latin-American literature.

Mr. Martínez Moreno said that in Uruguay the independent writer had for some years been a man who troubled those in power because they knew that it was easier to make use of a party clerk than of an artist. This explained what Vargas Llosa had called their "traditional suspicion of culture." But another problem that had been raised here, the narrow dimensions of the literary market, was one which, as a Uruguayan writer, he felt he must talk about.

Mr. Martínez Moreno had often spoken of "the strain of a creative writer's second occupation." The mass media created an appearance of fictive equality between a writer—Graham Greene, for example—who was wholly free to write, and another who, like Juan Carlos Onetti, was a civil servant. Readers bought books without knowing anything of the economic and cultural circumstances in which they were written. The theatregoer applied an identical scale of values to a play by Arthur Miller and a play by a perhaps solitary dramatist of his own country. Of course this was inescapable, and in fact Latin-American writers did not protest; they did not want to be pitied, they wanted to be read. But it was hard to think how this initial inequality could be righted.

Mme. Ocampo, speaking in French, proposed to say a word about the situation in Argentina and was happy to think that what she said would be on the optimistic side. A writer she greatly admired, Vargas Llosa, had spoken of the distressing situation of the Peruvian writers. Mrs. Ocampo, having devoted a lifetime to the writer's world, was able to share his sentiments.

In her country, books by Argentine writers were more in demand than ever before. Young writers, writers without the great following of a Borges or a Cortázar, were doing very well. She would mention—because it was only just to do so—that they had in Argentina a "Fonda Nacional de las Artes" which helped talented young writers to find publishers—in fact it helped painters as well. The Fonda distributed books throughout the provinces, not in the mere hope of finding readers for them but because the readers were there; Mrs. Ocampo had been impressed by the books they asked to read, both Latin American and European. She was happy to take part in the work of the Fonda and to say a word about it here.

Mr. Balbontin, speaking in English, began by saying that "the independence of the author was a fact no one would dare dispute." It was acknowledged as his inalienable right and as socially indispensable. But it had not been clearly defined. Latin-American authors, specifically, suffered from a "form of coercion" which seriously limited their independence. It lay in the ignorance of Europeans and North Americans about their works. This was true, incidentally, as regards the writers of all developing countries.

Latin America was a vast continent. Chronologically, it was the third area in which democratic and republican forms of government had been established. It had a Nobel Prize poet in the late Gabriela Mistral of Chile, and at least four potential Nobel Prize men: Neruda, Carpentier, Borges and Asturias. Its social and educational levels were high in many places—though it was the "indirect victim of the black legend built around Spain in the sixteenth century." Yet Spain was more fortunate than Latin America, for the latter was rarely mentioned in the world's textbooks or its press.

Mr. Balbontin felt that this international meeting of P.E.N. should reflect upon the fact that the writer's independence was closely related to the degree of men's knowledge of his world. We had still what he would call "confidential circulation" of Latin-American literature: small editions of books and, "for reasons unknown," the non-inclusion of Spanish among P.E.N.'s official languages. The Chilean P.E.N. Center asked International P.E.N. to "bring to a happy conclusion" four basic Latin-American aspirations, as follows:

1. The inclusion of Spanish literature in the curricula of all universities in the countries where P.E.N. centers are present.
2. The inclusion of Latin-American texts in the curricula of secondary schools.
3. The fostering of joint ventures between Latin-American publishers and other publishers with a view to bringing out translations of classic and modern Latin-American literature.
4. The nomination by International P.E.N. of a commission, made up of Latin Americans and others, to draw up "a basic collection of 100 best books of Latin-American literature, for translation by selected P.E.N. members," the same to be offered to American, French, British and German publishers.

The chairman asked leave, before calling on Mr. Neruda, to make three points in connection with Mr. Balbontin's proposals. As to language: It was because English and French were P.E.N.'s only official languages that the speakers at this session had been obliged to use "broken English or synthetic French." Secondly, Mr. Rodriguez Monegal had been asked by Miss Carolyn Kizer, of the United States National Endowment on the Arts, to say that a plan had already been approved by its chairman, Mr. Roger L. Stevens, to contribute towards the translation of perhaps 100 selected Latin-American works into English. The chairman's third point was that Mr. Balbontin's proposal was in fact a motion which, if those present agreed, would be presented to P.E.N. [It was so agreed.]

Mr. Neruda, who followed, spoke in French. After warmly endorsing Mr. Balbontin's proposals he went on to express the hope that out of the congress itself—and not only the Latin-American session—there would come a determination to intensify the life of all P.E.N. centers. We had seen, at this congress, the vitality that resulted from the unity of our diverse spirits and expressions; we had witnessed a great manifestation of creative life. Why should not this spirit be stimulated in each of the member countries? Surely we believed that writers should organize themselves. Surely none of us was in favor of isolation and division among writers. Reminding his audience of Mr. Vargas Llosa's forceful and interesting remarks, and of the powerful picture of Peruvian life drawn in his latest novel, Mr. Neruda said he would suggest that Vargas Llosa take the lead in founding a P.E.N. center in Peru—a wish, indeed, which had been expressed to Neruda by other Peruvian writers. To this he would add, as regards all P.E.N. centers, that they be made up of true writers. He did not mean by this that he was against the social functions a P.E.N. center might carry on; only that the literary life was the important life.

Meanwhile, the crucial thing in Latin America was to obtain respect for the writer. His own intimate friend, the great poet Vallejo, whom he had seen daily in their Paris days, had—it was horrible to relate— died of hunger, without ever an offer of help from his own country. And once dead, he had been given a fantastic state funeral. There were many ways of obtaining respect for the writer. Their illustrious friend, Mme. Ocampo, had long ago set an example with her review which was one of the great manifestations of culture in Argentina. In Mr. Neruda's own country their greatest poet, Gabriela Mistral, a woman born of poverty-stricken parents who throughout her life had remained faithful to her social class without ever departing from the greatest personal dignity, had set a higher value upon her poems about the martyred Chilean poor—and the poor were still there, everywhere in Latin America—than upon the poems her readers loved best.

Latin-American writers were magnetized by two poles: universal culture and the condition of their own peoples. The question before them had been, for whom am I writing? For the few, those who knew the names of Mallarmé and Rimbaud, or for the peoples of their continent? "You are a committed writer," people were constantly saying to Mr. Neruda, either with approval or with fury. He was indeed committed; for he carried on his back the shadow of sixty or eighty million Latin-American illiterates. His ambition was, as Gabriela Mistral had put it, "to give shoes to little children in the Antarctic winter of Chile."

This was a great tradition and it went back to the first strike by Chilean workers in 1848. If he spoke of it, the reason was that almost all Chilean writers had inherited this tradition. As Fuentes and Vargas Llosa had indicated, literature could not refrain from taking up a position which sought to endow the world with justice, freedom, the creative spirit. By giving their own peoples such works, Latin-American writers would be giving them to all men.

Mr. Rafael Tasis (Catalan P.E.N.), speaking in French from the floor, asked permission to remind the audience that his native city, Barcelona, was the capital of Spanish-language publishing and that Latin-American works were welcomed by its publishers with great enthusiasm. He paid homage to Mme. Ocampo as the great publisher of modern literature in South America and reminded her that, following the Spanish Civil War of thirty years before, Spanish publishers had emigrated to Latin America and established important firms, particularly in Mexico and Argentina. This consequence of the Spanish catastrophe was, for publishers in Spain, a matter of pride.

The defense of their language and their culture required that publishing houses be planted wherever Spanish was spoken. And since at present it was not easy for Chileans, Bolivians, Peruvians to be published at home, they should be published in neighboring countries and in Spain, wherever publishers were to be found.

Mr. Tasis would add a word about Catalan literature. Many of its writers, too, lived in exile in Central and South America. He himself had been published in Mexico. Like those to whom he spoke, the Catalans were struggling to defend their literature, their language and their culture, and on their behalf he expressed his support for Mr. Balbontin's proposals.

Mrs. Aridjis (Mexico: speaking in English for Homero Aridjis) said that the maximum printing of a volume of poetry in Mexico City, even though the volume was destined for all Latin America, was only 2,000 copies. It would be larger, except for the defective distribution system (to which Mr. Parra had referred). In Mexico, critics tended to judge poetry largely on their personal antipathies and friendships in literary circles. Further, unless the poet wrote about national heroes, especially of the pre-conquest past, he was likely to be stigmatized as a foreigner, unpatriotic. Meanwhile, almost all writers had to engage in other work —many became civil servants—to ensure their livelihood. And in that case, they had to be careful not to offend the government by what they wrote. To be a writer in Mexico was a kind of martyrdom and demanded great courage.

President Miller, invited to comment, said he would mention four things that he had learnt at this session. First, all that had been said here had put such problems as "the writer in the electronic age" into a different perspective by recalling the existence of worldwide poverty and illiteracy. Second, P.E.N. itself had before it the job of raising the prestige of the writer and the intellectual in countries where it was so low. Latin-American writers themselves, and Latin-American foreign correspondents, could begin by making known the respect and admiration shown for living Latin-American literature at this congress and in the European and North American literary press. Existing P.E.N. centers could make this known, and as Pablo Neruda had suggested, new P.E.N. centers could be formed in Latin America to ensure that this became known. Other P.E.N. centers could find ways to stimulate such awareness—and not only about Latin-American writing.

Mr. Portella (reporting for the Cuban News Agency) rose to answer Mr. Neruda's question of why Alejo Carpentier, President of the Cuban P.E.N., was not here. Mr. Portella had inquired and been informed that the American invitation had arrived too late; to which the speaker added that it was "not easy" for Cubans to travel to "the Western civilization." *

The chairman, in his closing remarks, saw as the most important result of this meeting the revelation that Latin-American writers had to fight not only against an adverse professional situation but also in the midst of dynamic changes to which they could contribute by their creative work and their critical outlook on a "cruel, hard reality." The fact that they had been able to come together in so large and distinguished a group was itself evidence of the utility of International P.E.N. He wished to express their thanks, together with his own, to American P.E.N. for affording them this occasion to describe their situation before writers from all other continents.

---

* Mr. Carpentier was personally invited on February 25, 1966, and a general invitation was addressed to the secretary of the Cuban P.E.N. Center on the same date. A second letter was sent to the distinguished Cuban writer on April 28. All invitations remained without acknowledgment. As to entry into the United States, the way had long been prepared by American P.E.N., to whose president the State Department's Coordinator of Cuban Affairs wrote on June 22, 1965: ". . . the Department would not object to the participation of a Cuban delegation in the 1966 conference." Applications for visas from Cuban delegates, he added, would be treated "in the same manner as those of applicants from other countries."—[Editor.]

Closing Session

Saturday, June 18

Mr. Galantière, Chairman of the Congress, said that he would not attempt to sum up a week so crowded with variety, novelty, and incident. The themes put before the delegates had been discussed with a warmth and an earnestness which confirmed their relevance to the writer in our times—with one limitation, however. The electronic age was not everywhere a problem for the writer—at least, not yet. The Philippine delegate, Mr. Florentino, had reminded his listeners of parts of the world where the writer was cut off from his people by a degree of illiteracy which, since it discouraged publishing as a trade, severely restricted his chances of appearing in print. President Miller had made the same point in the course of the brilliant Latin-American meeting—a meeting the host center had not planned and for which it was immensely grateful to the writers from the great southern continent who had spontaneously organized it. The problem raised by Mr. Florentino and perceived by President Miller was perhaps one which ought to be taken up by a future International P.E.N. congress or seminar.

At this congress, political views had intruded themselves more noticeably than at previous congresses. The government of a great nation had, most regrettably, been attacked by a speaker unfamiliar with the traditions of P.E.N. during the session on the writer as public figure. With this exception and another which the chairman had found excessive in its acrimony—discussion of the theme had been limited to its literary and moral aspect and been marked by entire frankness and respect for diversity of opinion and sentiments. This, Mr. Galantière believed, the record would confirm.

Among those who had accepted an invitation to address the closing session was the eminent essayist and director of the Literature Section of UNESCO, M. Roger Caillois.

M. Caillois transmitted to International P.E.N. and to the American Center the compliments of M. Maheu, director general of UNESCO, on the "magnificent success of the congress." He thanked General Secretary Carver and his translation committee for their recommendation of works written in certain languages of limited diffusion, to be translated and published under the auspices of UNESCO. Also as of particular interest to UNESCO, M. Caillois took this occasion to express the satisfaction with which he had observed the development of a spirit of co-operation between P.E.N. and COMES (the European Community of Writers).

Two years ago, at the Oslo Congress, M. Caillois had taken the liberty of saying that P.E.N. would not be complete until the inheritors of Cervantes and Quevedo and the inheritors of Tolstoy and Dostoevsky had taken their seats in this association. He had followed P.E.N. efforts to fill the Soviet seats and knew that if his hopes had not yet been realized, the fault was not P.E.N.'s. He was happy, meanwhile, to render homage to the good will and firmness with which Arthur Miller had guided the negotiations looking to this end.

The presence of numerous writers from continents hitherto inadequately represented in P.E.N. deliberations—Latin America, Asia, Africa—gave him much satisfaction. He was aware that this was the result of the unremitting efforts of Lewis Galantière and the help he had obtained for this purpose from enlightened American foundations. This "growing ecumenism" of P.E.N. was most gratifying to UNESCO; the reception at the United Nations, tendered the delegates jointly by the U. S. Mission and American P.E.N., was a fitting consecration and symbol of that ecumenism.

The congress had been asked to deal with the broad theme of "the writer as independent spirit" and to discuss factors in the life of letters which seemed today to threaten the writer's independence. One of these was the assertion, more and more widely heard, that writing—if not, indeed, the press itself—might prove to be a parenthetical phase in the history of mankind which was about to close; that it was menaced by sound (the radio) and by the image (photography); the latter in the illustrated weeklies, the films, and television.

M. Caillois saw in this argument a certain disregard of a need older than printing, older indeed than writing itself. This was the need to select, in the transient flow of human expression, those utterances which deserved to be remembered, used again, kept indefinitely in circulation. This ambition, one might say, which was characteristic of poetry, of proverbial dicta, even before men wrote at all: was it too much to believe that just as it had preceded the written word, so it might outlive writing? M. Caillois saw here the essence of the writer's purpose, the essence of the art of letters; and the dual character of the word *letters* was demonstrated in that it conveyed the sense of "character" both in forming letters and in writing as an art.

At the congress, also, a kind of fear had been expressed of the machine, a creation now thought of as possessing the powers of the human mind and the sensibilities of the human person. Although many present at the congress had assumed it to be greater in America than in Europe, M. Caillois had found this fear even more pronounced at a colloquium of Les Rencontres Internationales held last autumn in Geneva. There it had been presented as almost mythological; speakers endowed machines with all sorts of qualities, beginning with memory and intelligence. How could a machine possess memory? Did a phonograph disc possess memory? The machine resembled man in this, that it received an impression and retained it; it was "programmed." The difference was that it was man who programmed it. Man, outside the machine, made a decision. He chose and grouped two words; not arbitrarily—the machine could do that. He grouped them in such ways that they possessed a *new semantic value,* a value that prolonged and heightened the old meanings of each separate word.

The congress had discussed a third subject, disturbing in various ways, it seemed, to many who discussed it: the cry for help of suffering mankind and its relation to the writer's commitment. The question was asked, "What do you mean by 'the masses'?" Any dictionary defined mass as a body, a weight, inert matter. If we talked about society, therefore, we would have to define mass as that which, in any society, acted, was effective, by virtue of its weight and only its weight. And which, consequently, acted as a brake, retarding every impulse, every invention, every ferment.

Nor did this mean that mass was found only in the greater number. It was present in a crowd, could be present in a school, an avant-garde, a clique, round a café table—wherever there were prejudices, wherever those prejudices seemed to be bold, daring, though they might in fact be the contrary—as paralyzing as the rules of an academy.

Here were reasons why independence was necessary to the writer; and to be independent he had to be free. But freedom was never freedom in a void. The writer's freedom had to march hand-in-hand with free choice of a responsibility. History was filled with examples of total commitment. One example was Demosthenes; Dante furnished us another; the Calvinist poet of the Wars of Religion in France, Agrippa d'Aubigné, was a third. And what was the result? When we read *les Tragiques* of Agrippa d'Aubigné the fact that he was anti-Catholic was meaningless to us. Who now cared whether Dante had been Guelph or Ghibelline? What remained was the beauty of their writings; and as Valéry had put it, once the things they stood for had been forgotten, swept away by history, the monument remained, the work was still there.

As to the responsibilities which had to be accepted before the writer could be, in any serious sense, free, M. Caillois would place first among them the responsibility to his language. There were many schools of contemporary writing which sought to evade these . . . servitudes; sought to escape from prosody, logic, syntax, and even articulated language. They would do well to bear in mind Kant's dove which, finding it hard to battle the resistance of the air, longed to fly in a vacuum—in which it would have dropped to earth. Then there was the writer's responsibility to his fellow men, which demanded that he work against what was permanent in them and for what was the best one could expect of most of them. To widen the gamut of their emotions, deepen their consciousness, their self-knowledge, their appreciation of the beauty of life's mysteries. In a word, whatever the commitment the writer entered into, he would always need to keep his distance from day-to-day events, and in particular political events.

By way of conclusion, M. Caillois recited a parable of Taoist inspiration which told of an emperor who had determined to build a temple such as the world had never before seen. An architect having built him such a temple, the emperor asked how he had done it. "First," said the architect, "I went alone into the forest, and having meditated three days I emptied my mind of all thought of styles, fashions and the approval of the critics. After another three days I dismissed from my thoughts the precepts of the masters and the historical examples to be found in our textbooks. Three more days and I became indifferent to Your Majesty's opinion, your praise or your blame. Then came three days at the end of which the verdict of posterity ceased to concern me. And in the last three days I no longer knew what a temple was: I had a vision of the temple perfectly designed, and I was free to build it."

At least in theory, said M. Caillois, we had here a supreme rule which might offer practical guidance to the writer.

Mr. Silone, who followed and spoke in French, said that he had the agreeable task of expressing, though in a tongue not native to him, and possessing a vocabulary of polite usage that was in any case somewhat limited—expressing his thanks to their American hosts, to David Carver, and to Arthur Miller for the style and warmth with which all had been welcomed to this congress. Looking back on it, he had every reason to be content. He was particularly glad to recall that what he himself had said had given rise to protest, for if there was one thing he detested above all others it was a false, a forced unanimity which was often meant to hide a diversity of views. When, a day or so before, he and his friends of the Italian delegation had been interviewed by the Italian radio, they had been at pains to stress the full freedom of speech which had characterized the congress. Mr. Silone had said: "This congress differed in one detail from others. Not one political figure, no minister of education, no mayor, no public authority spoke from this platform." This, said Mr. Silone, is the most striking impression that I take home.

Dr. Glanz-Leyeless, speaking in English on behalf of the Yiddish P.E.N. Center, reminded his listeners of the world-renowned writers produced by "a literature that is surrounded by many perils, that walks among many pitfalls"—a Sholem Aleichem, a Peretz, and in our time Isaac Bashevis Singer. He thanked his hosts for their hospitality, and, rendering special thanks to President Miller for the reference in his opening address to the condition of Yiddish literature in the Soviet Union, Dr. Glanz-Leyeless expressed the hope that his remarks would contribute to the restoration of the full cultural and religious rights of the Jewish minority in the Soviet Union.

M. Léon Damas, of French Guiana, after expressing the satisfaction he had derived from his presence at the congress, evoked the names of his two great colleagues in the founding of the school of poetry known as *"Négritude,"* Aimé Césaire, of Martinique, and President Senghor, of the Republic of Senegal. The subject of this congress, the independence of the writer, had been their joint concern. He wished to say to Rosamond Lehmann, to Pearl Buck, to Arthur Miller and to Roger Caillois that their messages had been heard by him and his friends and had helped them in realizing their goal. It was thanks to Mr. Galantière's invitation that he had been enabled, for the first time, to attend a P.E.N. congress. In Africa as well as in Paris, he would urge that Africa march hand-in-hand with P.E.N.; indeed, his listeners would learn next year at the Abidjan Congress how eager President Houphouët-Boigny, of Ivory Coast, was to do so.

Mr. Michal Rusinek, of the Polish P.E.N., speaking in French, said that we lived at a dramatic moment in the history of mankind, a moment so filled with great inventions, exercising a pressure so powerful, that the bewilderment of contemporary man was not at all astonishing. Admiration and anxiety were the characteristics of our attitude to the world around us. On the one hand we were uncertain of ourselves, on the other hand, too sure of ourselves. What could the role of literature be on this agitated planet? The fact was that literature had outstripped technology. It had discovered the "mysteries of human emotions" even while it continued to celebrate the luminaries of our past, from Homer to Mickiewicz and beyond. Could it be true that literature was about to become a secondary source of our knowledge of mankind? Mr. Rusinek's own observations convinced him of the contrary. In closing, he would express his thanks to their American hosts and would remind all present that while P.E.N. signified "Poets, Essayists, Novelists" it also had the meaning, in French, of *"Paix entre nous,"* peace among us.

Dr. Hoffmeister said that he had a brief message to deliver on behalf of his center. It had been their custom for six years, when preparing to participate in a P.E.N. congress, to compile a bibliography of works written in the country of the congress, translated into Czech and into Slovak and published in Czechoslovakia. This year, it was the turn of American literature to receive this homage. Dr. Hoffmeister took particular pleasure in delivering this message and assuring all P.E.N. members present that copies of the bibliography were being sent to all P.E.N. centers.

Mr. Galantière begged Dr. Hoffmeister to transmit American P.E.N.'s thanks to the Czechoslovak P.E.N. Center for this generous and touching mark of the warm friendship between the two literary communities. It came as a surprise, and when one thought of the planning, the scholarly scruple, the co-operation of so many hands that had gone into it, the least one could say was that the surprise was overwhelming.

President Miller rose to make the concluding remarks, which we give in *oratio recta.*

President Miller. I am going to speak in a more or less impressionistic manner about this congress, and I already know that by the time I sit down I will regret not having said some things that I will not have remembered. Perhaps you will forgive me for speaking badly but from the heart.

I don't want to forget to thank our valiant and accurate interpreters. (*Applause*) And my personal gratitude to Mr. Silone whose spirit has given me a certain determination not to lose track of the main point. (*Applause*)

Only that which is dead is no longer in danger. This organization is showing signs of new life. Therefore the dangers to it increase. Listening to the debates here, the thought of Mr. U Thant has come into my mind; you will allow me to express my great admiration for him. I want to say also what a vast distance mankind seems to have yet to go before it will be capable of taking a really human view of itself. We all know that the United Nations, as an example, is for the most part paralyzed because the interests of the great powers, many of them irreconcilable from month to month and year to year, are such that all the good will and wisdom in the world seem to avail nothing and we stand helpless before a succession of one disaster after another.

In P.E.N. it need not be so. We do not come here representing armies. Or revolutions. Or counter-revolutions. We come here because it is important to us that there be one place at least where a man can speak in a human voice. I am as passionate in my beliefs as most men are. I do not agree, probably, with three-quarters of what has been said here. I have been impelled a dozen times a day to rise and destroy arguments that I have heard. I have done that from time to time, but always out of a deep concern that nothing—nothing—should be done here that can hurt P.E.N. For example, I do not think that this is the platform from which to call for a heating up of the cold war. (*Applause*)

This in no way implies that I would be a party to any dilution of the P.E.N. Charter which pledges us to defend freedom of expression. But it does imply that I am opposed to linking our Charter to the overthrow of any government. We are not a political organization. But we live in a time which has a terrible curse upon it.

For more than twenty years we have been indoctrinated with one method of discourse and one method only. It is the destruction by each of the other. "We or they" is the slogan, even as over our heads hangs a universal destruction that will spare none of us. If P.E.N. does nothing else, it must learn—and this will be hard to learn—how to see through the political clichés of the moment to the essential human truth that those clichés hide and in some cases are designed to hide.

As a private citizen, I have often protested injustice, war, and other acts which I judged to be inimical to the welfare of people. I intend to go on doing that. In this organization I, along with you, must seek at all times to emphasize that which is common to us all, to isolate that which separates us; to face that which separates us and try with all our forces to resolve our differences. There are differences that cannot be resolved: let us put them at the back of our minds and let us proceed with those we can resolve. (*Applause*)

Now I want to say something about a tendency I have noticed during this past week, a relationship between the membership and the leadership. It is quite obvious that there are no magicians in the upper echelons of P.E.N. I'm an amateur president. I spend most of my time alone, writing. I have no interest whatever in becoming a leader, a chairman, or anything of the kind. When I see members behaving as though, from on high, there will come some gratuitous solution of their problems, it tells me that we need a new perspective on International P.E.N.

Here is an example. On Tuesday I was having dinner with Latin American writers, six or seven of them, and I learned that some had never met before. We talked on, the conversation was getting interesting, and before we knew it, it was announced that the restaurant was closing—the hour was late. Someone suggested that we continue next day in somebody's hotel room. I suggested that the Latin Americans use this hall and that their talk be recorded on tape. This was done and I learned a great deal about them; they learned a great deal about each other. Nothing was more natural than that, having gathered from all parts of their immense continent for the first time, they should have taken advantage of the P.E.N. congress to talk seriously about their problems.

Chance had provided the occasion, after long years of relative isolation. And the thought came to mind that I might ask everybody here, when you return home, each to his own country, will you sit down and ask yourselves, if you were president of your P.E.N. center what would you do for your center, with your center, in your center?

It turns out that in Latin America there are some problems that can be solved without money, or with little money. Those writers want to see each other again. It can't require much money for a Peruvian to spend a week in Venezuela, a Venezuelan to meet a Peruvian in Argentina. Or, I was told that some centers need books, magazines. Well, that can't be insuperable. We in P.E.N. have learned the value of personal encounters—that they alone are enough to give P.E.N. a reason for being.

I think that perhaps the most important thing P.E.N. can do is to open itself to youth. This seems to me point number one on the agenda of every center. If your membership does not represent the younger writers, if P.E.N. can't make itself relevant to youth, it is on the way to death, not to life. (*Applause*) And I can't tell you how to do that. I don't know Belgium, or Bulgaria, or Chile. That is your job. P.E.N. is not a club for retired people. (*Applause*) You have witnessed for yourselves, and I can confirm, that for the Americans this congress has been a good thing, it has drawn the attention to P.E.N. of many American writers who were either ignorant of P.E.N., or cynical about it, or indifferent to it. But this new interest will not last unless American P.E.N. can make itself relevant. American P.E.N., at its next meeting, will have to learn to make itself relevant to our younger American writers. And this will have meaning for the whole of P.E.N. because it is no good pretending that what happens in American literature does not have influence outside this country.

Now for myself I only want to tell you that I have been very happy to know how warm you feel toward me and I regret if at times I have been abrupt with anyone. If that has happened, I ask you to forgive me. It was simply an attempt to keep things moving. I want to thank Mr. Galantière and Judge Isaacs and the whole group in American P.E.N. who made what I think is a glorious thing of this congress. And my thanks to everybody who participated. (*Applause*)

Mr. Galantière said that it gave him much pleasure to close the session, as it had opened, on a fraternal note. He would read an English translation of a message just received from Giancarlo Vigorelli, of Rome, General Secretary of the Community of European Writers, who cabled:

To the writers from all over the world present at the P.E.N. Congress in New York COMES sends warmest wishes for good work and ever better results and hopes for an ever stronger defense of the rights and duties of dignity and free expression for all writing and all writers.

COMES rejoices in and is honored by our collaboration. It takes particular satisfaction from our common action in the Sinyavsky affair. We maintain that the honorable mission to Moscow of our respective secretaries general, in spite of expected negative results, was neither useless nor sterile. Deeply regretting my inability to take part in your congress, on my own behalf and in the name of the president of COMES, Giuseppe Ungaretti, I beg President Miller, the international vice presidents of P.E.N. and General Secretary Carver, as well as all delegations, to receive my most cordial personal greetings.

There being no further business, Mr. Galantière declared the Thirty-fourth International P.E.N. Congress closed.

L'ÉCRIVAIN EN TANT
QU'ESPRIT INDEPENDANT

L'ECRIVAIN
EN TANT QU'ESPRIT
INDEPENDANT

Compte-rendu du XXXIVe Congrès
du P.E.N. International
12–18 juin 1966

New York

Avant-propos

1. LE P.E.N. INTERNATIONAL

Le public lettré n'est pas sans avoir entendu parler du P.E.N. International, cette association d'ecrivains qui fut fondée à Londres en 1921 et qui réunit aujourd'hui environ 8000 membres groupes en 79 centres ou "clubs" dans 58 pays. Il est probable, cependant, qu'il n'a qu'une idée assez vague quant à la nature et aux buts du P.E.N. C'est pourquoi, avant d'aborder le sujet du congrès de New York, nous croyons utile de répondre brièvement à la question, "qu'est-ce au juste que le P.E.N.?"

Le nom du P.E.N. tire sa signification des mots anglais: *Poets, playwrights—Essayists, editors—Novelists.* L'on sait que *playwright* veut dire auteur dramatique et *novelist* romancier. *Editor* n'a pas le sens d'éditeur mais de rédacteur ou rédacteur-en-chef. Quant à *essayist*, ce mot devait englober tout écrivain chez qui la pensée et l'imagination créatrices se rencontrent pour produire des oeuvres admises comme faisant partie de la littérature, quelque soit le classement que leur réservent les bibliothécaires. Il va sans dire que le philosophe Croce, qui fut président international du P.E.N., n'était pas moins homme de lettres que son prédécesseur, le romancier Galsworthy. Aujourd'hui, bon nombre d'essayistes consacrent leur talent à satisfaire à la soif d'information et d'explication des gloires et des miseres de l'époque actuelle que ressentent tant de nos contemporains.

La réponse à la question, "qui fait partie du P.E.N." se trouve dans la Charte qu'on lira plus bas: "tout écrivain, rédacteur ou traducteur qualifié" qui souscrit aux buts définis dans la Charte, "sans distinction de nationalité, de race, de couleur ou de religion."

Si nos membres sont groupés dans plus de centres (ou communautés littéraires) que de pays, c'est que notre terre connaît plus de cultures, plus de langues qui produisent des littératures vivantes, qu'elle ne compte d'Etats—même de nos jours. Aussi avons-nous trois centres en Suisse, quatre en Yougoslavie, trois en Afrique du Sud; en Belgique un centre d'expression flamande et un autre d'expression française, au Canada un centre français et un anglais. Il existe un centre yiddish, un autre compose d'ecrivains en exil; sur le vaste continent australien deux centres, deux aussi aux Etats Unis. Le P.E.N. est représenté en sept Etats de l'Europe de l'Est, en Afrique, en Amérique latine et en Asie. Pour ne parler que des îles, il y a des centres en Nouvelle Zélande, à Ceylan, en Indonésie, Islande, Irlande (Dublin et Belfast), à Cuba, en Jamaïque et à Porto Rico. Des congrès P.E.N. ont eu lieu en maintes villes d'Europe occidentale, en Yougoslavie, à Tokyo, à Rio de Janeiro, à New York. Le congrès de 1967 se tiendra ce mois-ci (juillet) à Abidjan, en Côte d'Ivoire.

L'idée du P.E.N. a jailli dans l'esprit généreux d'une romancière anglaise, Mme Catherine Dawson Scott, en 1921. On a un peu oublié que la guerre de 14–18 avait, elle aussi, connu des horreurs, enfanté des haines, qui avait pour résultat—pour un certain temps du moins— d'atténuer les passions des hommes. L'idée de Mme Dawson Scott était que les écrivains du monde entier devaient se réunir pour encourager les effort que l'on faisait alors pour édifier un ordre international basé sur la justice et avec l'espoir d'établir une paix durable. Elle soumit son idee à John Galsworthy qui en reconnut les mérites et fonda le P.E.N. anglais avec le concours, entre autres, de H. G. Wells et de George Bernard Shaw. Galsworthy persuada Anatole France d'accepter la présidence du centre français. Maurice Maeterlinck fut un vice-président international. Thomas Mann présida le centre allemand à sa fondation. Le siège international fut établi à Londres et c'est là que se tint le premier congrès international en 1923. Au deuxième congrès, tenu à New York l'annee suivante, vingt pays étaient representés. Quarante-deux ans plus tard le congrès qui fait l'objet de ce volume réunissait plus de six cents écrivains venus de cinquante-neuf pays.

Les buts de Mme Dawson Scott—comme ceux de bien des hommes et des femmes de coeur en cette période d'après-guerre—étaient lointains et abstraits; mais au cours des années qui suivirent, le P.E.N. vit ses objectifs devenir de plus en plus concrets. D'une part, le P.E.N. était tout designé pour servir de porte-parole de la communauté littéraire universelle quant commença la suppression de la liberté d'expression, l'incendie des livres, la détention arbitraire et la "liquidation" d'écrivains par des régimes totalitaires dont la sauvagerie allait alors croissant. D'autre part, il y avait la tendance naturelle des membres du P.E.N. à "parler boutique" dès qu'ils se réunissaient.

Au Congres de Dubrovnik (Raguse) en 1933, le centre allemand, déjà nazifié, demandait péremptoirement l'expulsion des membres allemands anti-nazis. Les délégues ayant repoussé cette proposition, le centre nazi réagit en se retirant du P.E.N. International. C'est à ce moment que le P.E.N. organisa pour la première fois l'aide aux écrivains réfugiés, oeuvre qu'il poursuit encore aujourd'hui et dont le dernier grand effort eut lieu entre l'instauration des régimes communistes en

Europe occidentale (1945–48) et les sequelles du soulèvement du peuple hongrois en octobre-novembre 1956.

En même temps, le P.E.N. n'a pas cessé d'intervenir en faveur d'écrivains qui, sur la base d'accusations fabriquées de toutes pièces, ont été jeté en prison pour "offense contre l'Etat", ce crime qu'on appelait autrefois lèse-majesté ou *Majestätsbeleidigung*. La Corée du Sud, la DDR (Allemagne de l'Est), l'Espagne, la Hongrie, l'Indonésie, le Portugal, la Tchécoslovaquie, l'URSS, la Yougoslavie figurent parmi les pays auprès des autorités desquels le P.E.N. est intervenu, soit en protestant énergiquement, soit en intercédant, selon les cas. Là ou il existe un centre P.E.N., c'est toujours par son intermédiaire que l'intervention se fait. Cette fonction permanent est exercée par le Comité des Ecrivains en Prison du Secrétariat international, dont Mlle Rosamond Lehmann est présidente.

Quant aux questions professionnelles sur lesquelles le P.E.N. se penche, il est logique que dans les réunions des centres locaux on se préoccupe surtout de problèmes qui touchent plus particulièrement la communauté littéraire locale, tandis que le P.E.N. international s'occupe de questions dont l'intérêt littéraire est universel. Voici quelques uns des "thèmes" proposés aux réunions internationales:

l'art de la prose	le théâtre de notre temps
la critique	l'auteur et le public
la traduction	la littérature à l'âge de la science
l'écrivain et la sémantique	l'écrivain et le cinéma
tradition et innovation	les intellectuels dans le monde contemporain
jeunesse et littérature	l'écrivain et la société

Entre autres activités, le Secrétariat international publie *Arena*, un périodique consacré à des traductions en anglais de textes actuels écrits dans des langues dont la diffusion est limitée, et une anthologie annuelle de poètes membres du P.E.N. Chaque année il recommande à l'UNESCO des oeuvres écrites dans des langues peu favorisées afin qu'elles soient traduites en français et en anglais. Son Fonds international des écrivains décerne des prix annuels pour des oeuvres écrites dans ces langues, et en assure la traduction en anglais.

Enfin, il est bon de rappeler que le P.E.N. est la seule association mondiale d'écrivains. Les gouvernements, l'UNESCO et la presse le reconnaissent comme porte-parole de la communauté littéraire universelle.

2. LE CONGRÈS DE NEW YORK

Lors de la séance de clôture l'éminent essayiste, Roger Caillois, directeur de la section littéraire d'UNESCO, a été heureux de relever le caractère oecuménique d'un congrès où figuraient soixante écrivains venus de quinze pays asiatiques, vingt-trois auteurs latino-américains et neuf representants des communautés littéraires de l'Afrique Noire. Parmi ces participants se trouvaient des observateurs invités de onze pays où il n'existait pas encore de centres du P.E.N. Les sept centres de l'Europe de l'Est avaient envoyé vingt-sept délégues dont quatre du P.E.N. Zentrum Ost und West (DDR). Nous notons avec regret que trois délégués tchécoslovaques se sont vu refuser leurs passeports, et que la participation de six observateurs de l'Union des écrivains soviétiques a été brusquement annullée à la veille du congrès. Nous avons également été déçus que le centre P.E.N. cubain n'ait pas accusé réception des deux invitations qui lui avaient été adressées par le centre américain. Le Zentrum Ost und West ayant proposé une résolution tendant à interdire que des congrès du P.E.N. aient lieu dans tout pays qui refuserait l'accés aux membres quelconques du P.E.N., le centre américain obtint son accord pour la motion de remplacement suivante, qui fut acceptée à l'unanimité par le Comité exécutif international:

Le P.E.N. international déplore les mesures prises par tout gouvernement qui ont pour effet d'empêcher des membres du P.E.N. à quitter leur pays ou à entrer dans un pays étranger pour assister à un congrès du P.E.N., à une réunion du Comité exécutif international, ou toute autre rèunion tenue sous les auspices du P.E.N. auquel ils ont été conviés.

Le terme "déplore" établit que le P.E.N. reconnaît qu'il ne lui est pas possible d'imposer sa volonté à des gouvernements souverains Mais cette résolution manifeste que le P.E.N. n'entend pas se réunir dans des pays qui ne rempliraient pas ces conditions. Nous sommes heureux de reconnaître que l'Administration Johnson avait donné pleine satisfaction dans ce domaine.
Arthur Miller a donné la note à ce congrès en disant au cours de son allocution présidentielle:

Aucun de nous n'est venu ici comme représentant de son pays. Aucun de nous est obligé, en se présentant ici, de faire l'apologie de sa culture ou de son système politique. Dans ce congrès comme dans les précédents, le communiste convaincu, l'anti-communiste militant, le non-politique, l'anarchiste, le catholique, le juif, le protestant, le bouddhiste ou le mahométan, le réaliste et le surréaliste, le saoûl et le sobre peuvent venir et laisser derrière eux leurs catégories et tourner leur attention vers le seul problème qui nous préoccupé tous en tant qu'êtres humains—l'enrichissement de la culture. Et par culture j'entends la manière sincère et profonde avec laquelle l'écrivain exprime ce que représente pour lui réalité. Privé de ceux qui rendent compte de cette façon, l'homme perd son passé, ne peut faire face au présent et trahit son avenir.

Le P.E.N. est résolument apolitique, mais il ne faut pas en conclure que les points de vue politiques soient de se fait absents de ses débats. Par exemple, au congrès de Bled de 1965, la délégation japonaise avait présenté une motion plaidant pour la cessation des hostilités au Viet-Nam. Quoiqu'une écrasante majorité des délégués ait été individuellement favorable au contenu de cette motion, elle avait été repoussée pour la raison qu'une motion d'ordre politique n'était pas à sa place dans les délibérations d'un organisme littéraire. A New York une motion contre l'armement nucléaire, proposée par le distingué président du centre grec, avait également été refusée; les délégations yougoslaves et bulgares avaient protesté contre cette décision.

Au congrès de New York, dans les échanges de discussions au cours des séances de travail, des délégués s'étaient vu entraîner à faire des remarques d'ordre politique.

Nos collègues de Viet-Nam, du centre Tai-peh, de Corée du Sud, de la Thaïlande parlerent sur un ton mesuré de problèmes qui les touchent de très près, ce qui est bien compréhensible. Le bien-aimé Ignazio Silone, qui a passé sa vie à lutter contre l'injustice et l'inhumanité, a fait une déclaration dont l'argumentation impeccable ne cachait pas sa position politique. Pablo Neruda, également défenseur de la justice et de l'humanité, lui a donné la réplique avec courtoisie et fermeté. La talentueux Valery Tarsis, membre de fraîche date du P.E.N., et peu au courant de ses traditions, dépassa les bornes de la bienséance en faisant des remarques personnelles, et en sonnant l'appel à une reprise de la guerre chaude contre l'Union soviétique ("contre l'idéologie" expliqua-t-il plus tard). Ceci ne plut pas aux délégués et provoqua la déclaration suivante du Centre des écrivains en exil (anti-communistes):

Le Centre des écrivains en exil est composé de membres dont les conceptions politiques et philosophiques sont variées. Les opinions que Valery Tarsis, qui est membre de la branche londonienne du centre, a exprimées après la séance de la Table Ronde du vendredi 17 juin, ne coïncident pas nécessairement à celles des autres membres. Après la déclaration publique de M. Tarsis, qui ne correspond pas aux intérêts de notre organisation, qui est en contradiction avec ses buts fondamentaux, et qui nuit à la cause pour laquelle elle combat, son appartenance a été sérieusement mise en cause par d'autres membres de notre organisation.

Il est intéressant de relever à l'intention de ceux qui auraient pu craindre que ce seraient les délégations communistes qui feraient intrusion dans des domaines politiques, qu'au contraire ce fut le côté anti-communiste qui s'en rendit responsable. Pablo Neruda et le Dr. Kamnitzer répondirent à ces interventions.

Le titre de ce livre est tiré du thème général du Congrès—l'*Ecrivain en tant qu'esprit indépendant*. Le Comtié exécutif international doit donner son assentiment à tout thème choisi pour un congrès du P.E.N. C'est tout à l'honneur du P.E.N. international qu'au sein de ses organes dirigeants, qui réunissent côte à côte des écrivains d'une soixantaine de pays aux systèmes sociaux les plus variés, aucune voix ne se soit élevée pour exprimer des doutes quant à la bonne foi du centre organisateur quand il leur proposa un thème qui de prime abord pouvait paraître une provocation. Les remarques du programme au sujet du thème choisi, que se trouve à la page 153 expriment avec suffisamment de clarté que l'on attendait du congrès qu'il se penche sur certains phénomènes scientifiques, économiques et sociaux nouveaux et qu'il étudie jusqu'à quel point ces forces étaient susceptibles de menacer l'indépendance de l'écrivain.

Si personne n'a réclamé contre ce thème au cours du congrès, c'est parce qu'il correspond à la tendance innée de chaque écrivain authentique, à être libre d'exprimer sa propre expérience de la vie et comment il réagit à cette expérience. En attendant, les membres du P.E.N. sont d'avis que la diversité des opinions philosophiques et des aspirations sociales va avec la liberté individuelle de l'écrivain d'écrire et de publier.

En compulsant le programme annexé, les lecteurs remarqueront que les organisateurs n'ont prévue que deux discours, l'un étant l'allocution présidentielle d'Arthur Miller, l'autre l'assaut brillant et sans réserve de Saul Bellow contre ce qu'il considère être la tendance des facultés des lettres des universités américaines et anglaises de s'approprier et d'accaparer ce qu'elles avaient naguère rejeté et frappé d'anathème—la littérature vivante. Ces deux discours exceptés, le congrès prit la forme de Tables Rondes autour de chacune desquelles dix participants discutaient un sujet donné, la discussion étant suivie d'interpellations venant de la salle. Notre index des orateurs (identifiés) montre que 116 délégués et invités ont eu l'occasion d'exprimer leur opinion.

Cette manière de faire a été adoptée afin d'éviter l'ennui que provoquent des discours qui se succèdent plusieurs jours, alors que la capacité d'attention des auditeurs diminue de jour en jour. A ce point de vue, il est indéniable que ce système a été un succès. On l'avait également adopté dans l'espoir raisonnable que les séances seraient animées par des débats continus entre participants. Dans ce domaine, les résultats furent différents selon les tables.

La Table Ronde I, sous la présidence du professeur Marshall Mc-Luhan, avait à traiter de *l'Ecrivain à l'âge électronique*. Grâce à sa virtuosité, McLuhan est parvenu à stimuler, même à exciter ses compagnons de table, et s'il a pris la parole plus souvent qu'il n'est l'usage pour un président, ce ne fut pas sa faute. A deux exceptions près, ses collègues virent en lui—ce qu'il affirma ne pas être le cas—un ennemi du livre, et peut-être même un penseur dont le système menaçait la liberté d'esprit, ce qui fit que dans les discussions à la première Table Ronde on trouva presque toujours McLuhan d'un côté, ses interlocuteurs de l'autre.

Bien des délégués furent comme piqués de la tarentule par ce sujet, qui fut souvent évoqué et repris au cours des séances suivantes. Des écrivains de pays en voie de développement, où le nombre des illettrés est grand et l'édition dans son enfance, trouvèrent que ce sujet était typiquement "occidental" et ne les concernait pas. Des Européens trouvèrent que les Américains étaient terrorisés par cet ogre, quoiqu'il semblât que personne d'autre que Miss Nott n'avait étudié ce sujet sérieusement, et que seul M. Gandon en avait fait le sujet d'une satire. (Buckminster Fuller, qui connaît d'instinct le sujet en tant qu'ingénieur et visionnaire, se tint à l'écart d'une discussion qui pouvait lui paraître à côté de la question). Au cours de la séance de clôture, M. Caillois apporta une petite correction: lors d'un colloque des Rencontres internationales de Genève il avait entendu des Européens exprimer la même crainte superstitieuse à l'égard de la diablerie électronique. En général il semble ressortir que les Européens ont pris M. McLuhan moins au sérieux que ne l'ont fait des participants américains et anglais.

M. Louis Martin-Chauffier présida la seconde Table Ronde, qui discuta la question: Les "sciences humaines" menacent-elles d'évincer la littérature de son rôle immémorial, qui a été de trouver l'ultime définition de la nature spirituelle de l'homme? La littérature est-elle en train de devenir une "source secondaire" pour la connaissance de l'âme humaine? Plus d'une fois le distingué président dut intervenir pour encourager ses collègues à dialoguer plutôt qu'à faire des monologues. L'occasion leur en fut fournie par le défi lancé par M. Ellison, qui prétendit carrément que la nouvelle sociologie et la nouvelle psychologie se croyaient appelées à remplacer la littérature, que le sociologue était devenu le "manipulateur" d'une "mythologie" de sa propre création, et qu'au lieu de chercher en eux-mêmes et dans les trésors accumulés de la littérature, pour trouver ce qu'est l'homme, les écrivains eux-mêmes commençaient à se "détourner de l'art" et à demander la réponse aux savants.

Le Dr. Parrès, psychiâtre, admit que Dostoïevsky avait "écrit de l'agression" d'une manière plus mémorable qu'aucun psychologue ne l'avait fait. M. Nadeau, l'historien du surréalisme, affirma que Shakespeare et Balzac avaient "pratiqué le psychologie, avant que la psychologie n'existât." Tout le monde parût d'accord, au sujet de la suprématie de l'art.

Cependant, Mme. Mileva paraissait mettre la société avant l'être humain comme sujet de la littérature, le Dr. Kamnitzer voulait que le Hamlet de nos jours fut "l'espece humaine" toute entière, la majorité etait nettement contre la retraite de l'écrivain dans la "tour d'ivoire," nettement d'opinion que l'écrivain avait des choses à apprendre des scientifiques, et cependant l'on était d'avis que dans les cas où il se servait de concepts scientifiques, c'était quand même, comme le disait M. Petroveanu, "les implications humaines" dans son oeuvre qui survivaient aux théories sur lesquelles il prétendait fonder son oeuvre. Personne ne parla des savants de notre époque dont les théories exercent en ce moment une influence profonde dans certains milieux littéraires—les philologues Jakobson et Saussure, l'anthopologiste Lévi-Strauss, le sociologue marxiste Althusser, ne furent pas mentionnée.

La Table Ronde de M. Robert Goffin avait à se pencher sur un thème dont la signification ne ressortait pas de prime abord—*L'Ecrivain collaborateur dans les desseins d'autrui.* Afin de l'éclairer, trois questions furent posées: Est-il vrai que l'éditeur, le rédacteur-en-chef, le "produceur" (cinéma, télévision, théâtre) menace l'indépendance de l'écrivain en l'obligeant à se directives? Est-ce que, par conséquent, le travail bâclé remplace l'oeuvre bien écrite? Est-ce que le besoin d'information sur les gloires et les misères de notre temps est devenu si impératif que les talents créateurs sont entraînés à écrire des oeuvres qui font appel plutôt à leur maïtrise professionelle qu'à la profondeur de pensée et à l'imagination?

Le président-poète commença par demander prudemment à ses collègues ce qu'ils pensaient de tout cela, et obtint des réponses des plus variées.

Même si le thème était mal formulé, les discussions furent chaudes, et les interlocuteurs savaient de quoi ils parlaient. L'idée que l'augmentation énorme des besoins en écrits "informationnels" était en train d'attirer les écrivains, qui de ce fait ne produisaient plus d'oeuvres d'imagination, ne trouva pas d'écho auprès des participants.*

M. Jovanovich fit observer que "la disparition de formes littéraires n'avait rien de nouveau", et que si le romain venait â disparaître, on ne pourrait en accuser personne d'autre que les écrivains eux-mêmes. Mlle Lehmann fut d'avis que ce n'était pas la demande du public qui obligeait les écrivains à produire. Pour elle, l'écrivain créateur subit une sorte de "contrainte imaginative", qui le pousse à faire ce qu'il doit faire, sans se préoccuper du lecteur.

M. Lasky répondit par une expression entendu à Heidelberg *janein,* "ouinon". Il est possible qu'une coupure de journal ait inspiré à Dostoïevsky *Crime et Châtiment* comme cela avait été le cas pour *In Cold Blood* (De sang froid) de Truman Capote; mais malgré cela ce que Capote écrivait était du "haut-journalisme" (que M. Lasky préfère à la "basse littérature"), ce n'était pas ce que M. Saul Bellow avait réclamé dans son allocution—"une réponse imaginative à un problème de la vie".

Les éditeurs at les rédacteurs-en-chef se sont-ils attribué des prérogatives exagérées? M. Lasky a envie de répondre non, quand il se rappelle qu'il a toujours existé des tiraillements entre écrivain et éditeur, mais il ne répondra à la question que quand elle sera rapprochée de la troisième, est-il vrai que le travail bâclé remplace l'oeuvre bien écrite? Considérant que la bonne qualité a toujours été exceptionnelle, on serait tenté de répondre, non. Mais c'est un fait que les rédacteurs "tripotent" la copie, et ceci implique "un manque de respect pour les mots et pour l'indépendance de l'écrivain". En Amérique, l'anglais des périodiques est devenue "stupéfiant et dégénéré" au point qu'il est devenu littéralement impossible de réfléchir et de prendre des décisions sur des problèmes sérieux (il cite des exemples). M. Goffin raconte qu'il avait été présent quand, il y a 25 ans à New York, un rédacteur avait demandé à Maeterlinck de revoir son texte parce que "bien que vous sachiez ce que vous désirez dire, nous savons ce que le lecteur désire lire". M. Hope-Wallace confirme qu'à Londres on pratique couramment le tripotage de manuscripts, coupures etc. afin d'obtenir un "style maison". Ce qui en résulte est "mal écrit" car c'est le produit de ce qui est "mal

* A la Table Ronde "électronique," M. Podhoretz avait cité avec approbation l'essayiste Paul Goodman, qui avait exprimé l'opinion que si la télévision se chargeait de tout ce qui touche l'information, cela délivrerait la littérature d'une corvée.

pensé et mensonger". M. Lucie-Smith alla plus loin en avançant—comme Confucius avant lui—qu'une langue malade venait d'une société malade. Tout à l'opposé, M. Jovanovich affirma qu'on n'avait encore jamais aussi bien écrit en Amérique, Mme de Sainte-Soline avança que le roman français contemporain était écrit dans un style méticuleux qu'on ne pouvait pas trouver dans les romans démodés du siècle dernier, qui étaient bâclés à la hâte et remplis d'incidents. Les éditeurs commandent des livres, dit-elle, et les écrivains ne demandent pas mieux que d'accepter leurs propositions.

M. Jovanovich est d'avis que l'expression "dans les desseins d'autrui" prouvait que l'écrivain "s'apitoyait sur son propre compte", Mr. Bloch-Michel et Mme de Sainte-Soline sont d'accord avec lui. Pour M. Bloch-Michel, le cinéma et la télévision sont des formes artistiques qui influencent forcément les écrivains qui choisissent de travailler pour elles (personne n'est obligé de le faire), et nous avons également pu constater que, paradoxalement, elles influencent la littérature elle-même. Mme de Sainte-Soline fit remarquer que la télévision avait mieux rendu l'atmosphère des Halles de Paris que ne l'avait fait Zola dans *Le ventre de Paris*. Dès le moment où les romans ne donnent plus une image de la société, que leur décor se réduit à une pièce ou même à un lit, et ne mettent en scène qu'un personnage ou deux, il incombait à la télévision de remplir la brèche. M. Sternberger releva qu'il y avait d'autres sortes de maîtres que ceux qui employaient des écrivains, par exemple des gouvernements, des doctrines, des engagements. En Allemagne de l'ouest, les membres socialistes du célèbre Groupe 47 avaient soutenu de leurs écrits la dernière campagne électorale. John Locke et Milton avaient choisi de servir une cause; Dante avait essayé d'aider l'Empereur Henry VII à réunir le Saint Empire Romain contre la papauté.

En attendant, dans le domaine des organes de masse il s'agissait le plus souvent d'un travail d'équipe qui se base sur la collaboration. M. Hope-Wallace fit remarquer que c'était inévitable qu'en télévision le rôle de l'écrivain fût moins important puisqu'il "écrivait pour des gens qui ne lisent pas". Cette déclaration ainsi que celle de M. Bloch-Michel paraissent répondre négativement à la question si bien posée par M. Milano—y a-t-il quelquechose *d'inhérent* aux organes de masse qui limite la libertè de l'écrivain?

M. Herzfelde est persuadé que la collaboration est honorable quand il existe une "conviction commune" entre collaborateurs. M. Keene releva l'esprit de collaboration qui régnait entre Auden et Stravinsky, entre Queneau et Butor et les artisans qui réalisaient leurs livres, entre les traducteurs de poésie et ceux qui "possèdent" les langues (il ne fit pas spécifiquement allusion à ce qui se passe couramment en Amérique où les meilleurs poètes traduisent la poésie russe assistés par des intermédiaires qui leur enseignent métaphores russes, symboles, intonations, conventions métriques, etc.).

Avant de se séparer, les participants eurent encore l'occasion d'entendre M. Florentino, des Philippines, leur parler d'un monde où les problèmes de l'écrivain sont bien différents de ceux qu'on venait de discuter, d'un monde où les problèmes sont ceux d'un peuple qui ne sait pas lire, d'un pays ou il n'y a pas de lampe sous laquelle lire, et où il n'y a pas de marché pour les livres. Le président de la Table Ronde fit alors un appel pour que l'on fasse davantage de traductions "de langues moins favorisées"—"un rappel salutaire", souligna M. Lucie-Smith.

C'est à la Table Ronde présidée par le professeur Douglas Young au sujet de *L'écrivain en tant que personnalité publique* que les controverses politiques dont il a été question plus haut se firent jour. Ces points de vue peuvent être lus plus loin dans le texte et n'ont pas besoin d'être repris ici-même, mais on peut noter que M. Silone avait expliqué dans sa replique, qu'il avait voulu s'opposer à "la théorie de l'intellectuel au service d'une puissance supérieure". Loin de lui l'idée de réveiller la guerre froide, il était pour l'entrée des écrivains chinois et soviétiques dans cette association libre, où l'on discutait de la vie de la littérature sans réserve mentale, et dans un esprit de respect réciproque.

Mlle Lehmann fut la seule qui chercha à traiter le sujet du point de vue de l'écrivain, de sa fonction et de son métier. Citant le vers de W. H. Auden: "des figures privées dans les endroits publics sont plus sympathetiques que des figures publiques dans les endroits privés", il lui semble que l'écrivain qui est interviewé au sujet de son opinion sur des événements publics, qui fait des conférences et apparaît sur le petit écran, risque de finir par croire que son point de vue est important, "or de grands écrivains ont parfois des opinions stupides". La raison d'être de l'écrivain est d'écrire, il serait préférable qu'il passe son temps à "absorber sans avoir à produire", qu'il fasse preuve de ce que Keats appelle sa "capacité négative". Un bon sujet pour une prochaine Table Ronde serait "l'écrivain, personnage silencieux", 20 minutes de silence, chaque participant ayant droit à une seule phrase. Elle est persuadée qu'il pourrait en résulter de très bonnes choses.

Mlle Lehmann n'a pas été choquée par la question: l'écrivain qui milite en faveur d'une idéologie ne va-t-il pas se voir attribuer une *per-*

sona publique, qui pourrait le tenter de vouloir adopter le rôle qu'on lui attribue? D'autres qui prirent la parole à ce sujet eurent vite fait de le rejeter, quoiqu'ils condamnèrent certains cas particuliers, comme par exemple M. Follain qui critiqua sévèrement l'exaltation sadique d'un Maurice Barrès qui, pendant la guerre de 14–18, avait célébré la baïonnette et souhaité qu'on "pourfende joyeusement le ventre" de l'ennemi allemand.

Quant à savoir si l'idéologie d'un écrivain classique était un facteur dont on tenait compte aujourd'hui pour juger de sa valeur—Dante opposé à la papauté, Hugo humanitaire, Stefan George prônant l'élite—M. Caillois fut le seul à juger cette question digne d'intérêt au cours de la séance de clôture. Le sujet qui revint constamment à la surface fut "l'engagement". Que signifiait-il? Etait-il un danger absolu, ou tout au moins un danger pour l'écrivain (par quoi l'on entendait en général le poète, le dramaturge ou le romancier)?

M. Lovinescu proposa une définition assez large: est engagé tout écrivain qui n'a pas perdu sa foi en l'homme; est non-engagé celui qui refuse de croire à la possibilité d'un ordre humain. Il souligne qu'engagement ne signifie pas "un optimisme béat et grandiloquent" mais plutôt une discipline sévère, parfois sans espoir. Cela ne veut pas dire qu'on ne trouve jamais la vérité dans les oeuvres d'écrivains non-engagés. Quoiqu'il fût lui-même un écrivain engagé, il reconnait que les cris humains les plus déchirants, les plus authentiques images de la faiblesse humaine, sont, de notre temps, l'oeuvre de ceux qui ont perdu toute foi, même en l'art.

De ce qui fut dit ensuite, on peut conclure que le définition de M. Lovinescu fut jugée acceptable. A une exception près, tous les participants étaient des "croyants"—et même M. Bell croyait au doute philosophique. M. Bell fut seul à condamner l'engagement public tel que ce terme est employé dans les grands débats sur les problèmes du jour. Personne ne cita Luther ("Dieu me vienne en aide, je ne puis faire autrement"), même M. Bell ne rappela pas la phrase de Cromwell, ce dictateur si fortement engagé ("je vous en supplie, par les entrailles du Christ, pensez que vous pouvez vous tromper"). M. Bell commença par rappeler que depuis que l'homme ne trouvait plus l'explication de son être propre et de son univers dans la Révélation et les traditions, mais allait la chercher dans sa propre expérience, il avait existé une tension entre lui et la société. De nos jours son *ego,* son "moi" est exposé à certaines séductions—puissance, idéologie, moralisme étroit— qu'il a rationalisées et appelées "engagement". Il est bien qu'un écrivain puisse dire: "je sens la vérité, je la vois, je dois l'exprimer". Mais en disant ceci il ne fait pas qu'exprimer, il affirme. Il est comme un homme qui court dans la rue en criant: "j'ai une réponse, quelqu'un a-t-il une question?" Si sa réponse n'est pas le produit d'un certain degré de connaissance, de jugement et de disposition d'esprit, son engagement risque de n'être rien de plus qu'une croyance. Il ne faut pas mépriser les croyances, mais correspondent-elles toujours à la vérité? Pour M. Bell, le rôle de l'écrivain en tant que personnalité publique est avant tout de remettre en question la foi et l'engagement, donc de rester dans un état de doute.

Les vues de M. Bell furent écoutées avec respect, mais ils semblent ne pas avoir fait de convertis. M. den Doolaard qui avait commencé en disant que "l'engagement et l'oeuvre littéraire sont souvent les deux faces de la même personnalité" et qu'il n'aimait pas l'affirmation du programme qui semblait impliquer qu'il n'était pas souhaitable que l'écrivain fût engagé, ne se contredit pas en ajoutant plus tard: "Que l'écrivain s'engage d'abord à son oeuvre, ce n'est qu'après qu'il pourra soutenir des causes". M. Datta (qui avait rétorqué à M. Bell qu'un homme qui ne croyait à rien n'était pas un homme du tout) exprima sa conviction "qu'on devait écrire le plus beau poème possible et espérer qu'il trouverait des lecteurs". Il se trouve entre les écrivains de l'Ouest qui ont de la peine à s'engager et ceux de l'Est venant de pays où "l'engagement est devenu extrême".

La plus grande partie de la discussion qui suivit tourna autour des rapports entre l'écrivain et la société, et du rôle de l'écrivain au sein de son propre peuple, non pas en tant que nationaliste mais en tant que compagnon des hommes qui lui sont les plus proches. M. Illyés est convaincu que le rôle de l'écrivain est d'enseigner, et continue: "nous écrivons pour ceux qui souffrent comme nous avons souffert, et qui se tournent vers la beauté comme vers le remède suprême." M. Choi regretta que les jeunes écrivains coréens soient en train d'abandonner leur "engagement inconscient" (la bonne espèce d'engagement) et aient tendance à se distancer du peuple. Pablo Neruda déclara qu'en Amérique latine les pauvres faisaient appel aux écrivains pour qu'ils "parlent au nom de ceux qui ne savent pas écrire". Il avoue être un poète "complètement engagé", et il veut bien qu'on l'appelle même un propagandiste, il en est un comme Whitman et Hugo avant lui. "Si le poète ne se faisait pas le porte-parole de la condition humaine, que lui resterait-il à faire?"

M. Tseng fit remarquer que Confucius ne désirait pas devenir une personnalité publique, mais ses écrits, qui avaient attiré trois mille étudiants, l'avaient rendu tel. M. Coutsoheras dit que la littérature, fruit d'un climat social, "était en elle-même une sorte de personnalité publique". M. Csokor fait la distinction entre art pur, art engagé et art dirigé. L'engagement serait, selon Gide, un facteur—la conscience—qui est réveillé par les événements. L'art religieux est un art dirigé que nous pouvons admettre. Dans le sens que l'art procure à l'homme un "centre d'intérêt" sans lequel sa vie serait vide, un art authentique sera toujours engagé. Le pire patron pour l'art est cependant la collectivité.

Tout le monde ne fut pas d'accord avec cette affirmation. Mme Kamenova qualifia l'écrivain de "guerrier sur le champ de bataille social" qui ne pouvait être absolument indépendant parce qu'il était responsable envers son peuple. Son devoir était d'éviter le pessimisme, de créer des personnages "positifs" et de montrer le chemin vers un avenir meilleur. Mlle Spiel, compatriote de M. Csokor, admire les écrivains qui font preuve d'indépendance dans leurs opinions politiques et méprise ceux qui adoptent aveuglément les opinions des autres. Elle aimerait que l'écrivain sache résister à un engagement "forcé" en s'appuyant sur des principes comme l'avaient fait Koestler et Sartre. M. Anoma Kanie croit que le devoir de l'écrivain, membre de la famille humaine, est de combattre la tyrannie et de répandre l'amour et la compréhension mutuelle.

M. Nghien Xuam Viet voit l'écrivain dans le double rôle d'artiste et de guerrier; dans le second on le jugera selon sa sincérité, et il ajoute "qu'un écrivain sincére peut se tromper". Selon M. Herzfelde, la valeur de l'engagement dépend de qui l'on s'est engagé à combattre, fasciste ou non-fasciste. Il faut que le P.E.N. soit anti-fasciste. (M. Tseng avait prétendu, au cours des controverses politiques, qu'il ne pouvait exister aucune honnêteté intellectuelle en République populaire de Chine "tant que ces forces fascistes existent").

Le président de la Table Ronde a deux fois fait appel à Arthur Miller. Dans la séance du matin, ce dernier avait commencé par dire qu'il éviterait d'être abstrait et ne parlerait que de son expérience propre. Le fait que Brecht et Neruda soient des écrivains engagés dont la qualité artistique ne pouvait être mise en question prouvait que la question était mal posée.*

M. Miller a connu des écrivains américains qui s'étaient engagés publiquement, qui signaient des manifestes et parlaient en public, et dont les oeuvres ne contenaient pourtant aucune trace de leur engagement. Il en a connu d'autres qui n'avaient jamais pris publiquement position et dont les oeuvres exprimaient néanmoins telle ou telle conception de la société humaine. Quant à lui-même, il s'était de temps à autre engagé publiquement, et l'avait exprimé dans ses écrits. Cela

---

* Il est étonnant de constater qu'aucun écrivain irlandais, anglais ou américain ait cité les noms des "réactionnaires" Yeats, Pound, Eliot ou Wyndham Lewis.

avait été "la chair et le sang de mes oeuvres", mais il ne croyait pas que cela les avait rendues ou meilleures ou moins bonnes.

M. Miller estime que la littérature subit une "pression implacable" qui la pousse à se préoccuper de ce qui touche le plus le lecteur et le spectateur. Quand un écrivain est "entraîné par la vision qu'il a de ce qui ne va pas dans le monde" il n'a pas le choix, il est forcé intérieurement d'attaquer ou de défendre. Il est bien d'avis qu'en ce qui concerne ses opinions politiques, l'écrivain peut-être "aussi stupide et naïf que n'importe qui d'autre". Mais le rôle de l'écrivain est d'exprimer cette réponse à la réalité nue, naïve et authentique "que les hommes ne peuvent espérer trouver que dans la littérature". "L'engagement est un puissant auxiliaire pour l'écrivain à qui il a permis de se trouver lui-même, il est néfaste pour celui qu'il a entraîné loin de son "moi".

Quand M. Miller reprit la parole au courant de l'après-midi, il dit entre autres: "L'intention de ceux qui ont parlé ici de l'écrivain en tant que personnalité publique, a été de le sauvegarder de toute contrainte, de l'aider à ne pas se laisser séduire par des opinions qui ne lui ont pas été dictées par sa propre conscience; qu'il s'engage ou non est l'affaire d'un choix personnel. Je plaide en faveur d'une certaine tolérance, fondée sur le fait que nous savons que la situation des hommes d'un certain pays est différente de celle des hommes d'un autre pays. Nous, membres du P.E.N. plus que quiconque devons tenir compte de ce fait, nous y cramponner, croire à la bonne foi de tout un chacun, et au désir commun de rendre notre association universelle, car cela ne nous fera pas de bien si nous ne croissons pas en sagesse."

Le président donna alors la parole à M. Bell afin qu'il close la discussion. M. Bell dit que pour connaître la vérité, l'écrivain ne disposait que d'une seule source, son expérience de la vie; cette expérience étant incomplète, il ne pouvait connaître la vérité totale. Quant à la croyance, elle devait être constamment remise en question, à la lumière des réalités de notre civilisation complexe dont la variété déroute. M. Bell réitère que "le doute doit garder la priorité".

Ce congrès—conclut-il—a essayé de faire ce que tous les intellectuels essaient de faire, contribuer à une communauté ouverte. Par des discussions ouvertes, les participants ont cherché à se comprendre les uns les autres. Dans ce congrès, l'engagement à une idéologie, à un dogme, a été remplace par l'engagement à la vocation d'écrivain.

La séance latino-américaine n'était pas prévue au programme, et donna pleine satisfaction. De généreux donateurs avaient permis au P.E.N. américain de faire en sorte que le grand continent sud-américain soit représenté par une délégation distinguée. Ces écrivains qui ne se rencontrent que rarement (excepté à Paris qui est toujours leur capitale culturelle) avaient beaucoup à se dire. Comme leur suggéra M. Miller, ils décidèrent de le dire en présence de tout le congrès. Leur sujet— comme leur séance—fut hors série, ils ne discutèrent pas les thèmes du congrès, mais leurs propres problèmes, parlant avec un niveau de sentiment et un réalisme sobre qui charmèrent et émouvèrent tous ceux qui les entendirent.

Dans la séance de clôture, M. Silone exprima la reconnaissance des délégués pour la chaleur et le style avec lesquels ils avaient été accueillis. Il était spécialement content que ce fût ce qu'il avait dit lui-même qui ait provoqué des protestations. Il déteste l'unanimité forcée qui sert souvent à cacher une diversité d'opinions. Ses collégues italiens et lui avaient été interviewés quelques jours avant par la radio italienne. Ils avaient tout particulièrement insisté sur la parfaite liberté de parole qui avait caractérisé ce congrès.

Lewis Galantière

New York
juillet 1967

Le Charte du P.E.N.

Le P.E.N. affirme que:

1. La littérature, si elle connaît des nations, ne connaît pas de frontières, et les échanges littéraires doivent rester en tout temps indépendants des accidents de la vie politique des peuples.

2. En toutes circonstances, et particulièrement en temps de guerre,
le respect des oeuvres d'art, patrimoine commun de l'humanité,
doit être maintenu au-dessus des passions nationales et politiques.

3. Les membres de la Fédération useront en tout temps de l'influence
qui pourrait dériver de leur personne et de leurs écrits en faveur
de la bonne entente et du respect mutuel des peuples. Ils s'engagent
à faire tout leur possible pour écarter les haines de races, de classes
et de nations et pour répandre l'idéal d'une humanité vivant en
paix dans un monde uni.

4. Le P.E.N. défend le principe de la libre circulation des idées à
l'intérieur de chaque nation et entre toutes les nations; chacun de
ses membres a le devoir de s'opposer à toute restriction de la
liberté d'expression dans son propre pays ou dans sa communauté.
Il se déclare pour une press libre et contre une censure arbitraire
en temps de paix. Le P.E.N. affirme sa conviction que le progrès
nécessaire du monde vers une meilleure organisation politique et
économique rend indispensable une libre critique des gouvernements et des institutions. Et comme la liberté implique des limitations volontaires, chaque membre s'engage à combattre les abus
d'une presse libre, tels que les publications délibérément menson-
gères, la fasification et la déformation des faits à des fins politiques
et personnelles.

Est susceptible d'être admis comme membre du P.E.N.:—Tout écrivain,
rédacteur, éditeur et traducteur souscrivant à ses fins, quelque soit sa
nationalité, race, couleur ou réligion.

151

L'Ecrivain en tant qu'Esprit Indépendant

Le thème général du Congrès de New York est le suivant: *L'écrivain en tant qu'esprit indépendant.* Ces notes ont pour but de rendre ce thème plus explicite.

Il serait exagéré de vouloir prétendre que tout écrivain aujourd'hui se sent menacé dans son indépendance en tant que créateur. Il n'en est pas moins vrai que tout écrivain, créateur ou non, participe au malaise qui règne dans toutes les sociétés. Plus que les autres hommes, l'écrivain est à la recherche de soi-même; il tente de reconnaître un ordre cohérent dans le monde actuel. Dans sa tête, des mots tels que *anxiété, aliénation, l'absurde, mimésis, cybernétique,* résonnent. Les écrivains de notre temps tournent avec inquiétude autour de leurs idéologies respectives. Ils se rendent compte qu'ils vivent dans un monde régi par de vastes bureaucraties, publiques dans certains pays, à la fois publiques et privées dans d'autres, et ils se doutent que ce phénomène a une signification particulière pour l'écrivain, pour le savant et pour l'artiste. L'Intendant des Menus Plaisirs du roi s'appelle maintenant ministre de la culture—à moins que, comme c'est le cas aux Etats-Unis, les directeurs de dotations ne se partagent ses fonctions. On retrouve le gigantisme partout, à l'université aussi bien que dans l'industrie, dans le monde de l'édition aussi bien que dans celui de l'électronique, dans la production de magazines et dans les habitations des êtres humains.

Le comité du P.E.N. américain qui s'est réuni à New York pour esquisser le programme du Congrès de New York estimait qu'un congrès était quelquechose de plus qu'un simple colloque; que quand six cent écrivains de quelque soixante pays se réunissaient, ils voudraient traiter et entendre traiter des sujets qui les concernent universellement. Notre comité a choisi *L'écrivain en tant qu'esprit indépendant* comme étant précisément un de ces sujets. En effet it reflète son inquiétude devant les forces qui aujourd'hui semblent menacer, plus insidieusement que ne le font la censure ou le dogmatisme, la réalisation des conceptions de l'écrivain quant à sa fonction et sa raison d'être. Notre thème ayant été approuvé par le président international et par le Comité international executif, il fera l'objet de discussions autour de tables rondes, ouvertes aux questions posées par les délégués qui voudront y assiter, et portant sur les sujets suivants.

I · L'ÉCRIVAIN À L'ÂGE ÉLECTRONIQUE

Il y a peu de temps encore, le mot "communication" correspondait pour l'écrivain averti à la notion de "la culture de masses" et à l'action—positive ou négative—que celle-ci pouvait avoir sur l'avenir de la haute culture traditionnelle de l'humanisme. Dernièrement, les linguistes, les anthropologues, les experts en "xérographie" et les prophètes s'en sont mêlés. On cherche à établir une "théorie de la communication". Les rapports entre les communications verbales, visuelles et auditives sont à l'étude. Ce que certains nous promettent, c'est non seulement la fin de l'imprimerie mais également la dissolution de la conscience individuelle dans une "conscience cosmique". Il est concevable que le livre soit appelé à disparaître. Reste la question: quel va être le rôle de l'écrivain en tant qu'esprit indépendant dans ce *saeculum felix et aureum?*

II · LA LITTÉRATURE ET LES SCIENCES HUMAINES DEVANT L'HOMME CONTEMPORAIN

De tout temps les hommes se sont tournés vers le poète, le dramaturge, l'essayiste—et depuis deux siècles vers le romancier—pour qu'il les éclaire sur la nature et l'esprit de l'homme. A la source des oeuvres qui projetaient cette lumière il n'y avait ni mensuration, ni analyse, ni enquête sociale, mais bien contemplation, connaissance de soi et imagination créatrice. Aujourd'hui, nous dit-on, l'homme se détourne de la littérature pour s'adresser au sociologue et au psychologue afin de savoir où se trouve l'essence de l'homme—ou du moins celle de l'homme contemporain. La question que nous posons est la suivante: est-il vrai que la littérature est en train de devenir un texte d'ordre secondaire? que les écrivains eux-mêmes s'adressent aux disciplines nouvelles pour en tirer leurs idées sur l'être humain? qu'ils tendent à prendre pour sujet la société ou même des problèmes sociaux au lieu de l'homme lui-même *sub specie aeternitatis?* Et si tout cela est vrai, doit-on voir ici une sorte d'abdication de l'écrivain en tant qu'esprit indépendant?

III · L'ÉCRIVAIN EN TANT QUE COLLABORATEUR DANS LES DESSEINS D'AUTRUI

Le degré d'instruction plus élevé dans tous les pays ainsi que les nouveax moyens de communication ont ouvert des provinces nouvelles à la république des lettres. Ce public neuf veut être informé. La haute vulgari-

sation trouve aujord'hui un marché universel. Ce qui autrefois était
le travail mal payé d'un écrivassier est devenu aujord'hui le métier
d'écrivains excellents et respectés. Le document remplace l'essai et il
menace (a-t-on dit) de détrôner le roman. Cet état de choses semble
avoir pour résultat que c'est l'éditeur de magazine qui dicte le vocabulaire, impose un "style maison" et décide quels seront les sujets sur
lesquels ses collaborateurs écriront. On nous dit que de plus en plus
c'est l'éditeur qui "conçoit" des ouvrages (en en proposant le sujet et
allant parfois même jusqu'à en fournir la trame), qui font appel à
l'habileté des écrivains qui s'y engagent plutôt qu'à leurs ressources
intérieures. Dans la communauté des écrivains, les belles-lettriens représentent une minorité qui va en diminuant.

Nous posons les questions suivantes: 1. Etant donné la popularité du
"document", en quoi le domaine de la littérature diffère-t-il aujourd'hui
du vaste champ cultivé par Sainte-Beuve il y a un siècle? 2. L'éditeur
de livres et le directeur de magazine se sont-ils attribué des prérogatives
qui, en fait, empiètent sur l'indépendance créatrice de l'écrivain? 3.
Avons-nous des preuves que la loi de Gresham (la mauvaise monnaie
chasse la bonne) est valable en ce qui nous concerne, et que l'oeuvre
bien écrite cède la place au travail bâclé?

IV · L'ÉCRIVAIN EN TANT QUE PERSONNALITÉ PUBLIQUE

Wordsworth, un très grand poète anglais qui vécut à une époque tu-
multueuse (1770–1850), était terrifié par la perspective de la réforme
sociale. Flaubert, contrairement à son amie George Sand, fut anti-sociali-
ste en 1848. Ni Wordsworth ni Flaubert cependant ne s'engagèrent
publiquement. Par contre, les exemples d'engagement public abondent,
qu'il s'agisse d'humanitarisme simple ou d'idéologie rigoureuse, que ce
soit par sentiment ou par conviction intellectuelle. Aujourd'hui nous
voyons dans certains pays des écrivains qui revendiquent le droit de
rester en dehors de la vie politique, tandis que dans d'autres pays se
trouvent des écrivains qui profitent de la liberté civique pour entrer
activement dans des débats publics. La question qui se pose est la
suivante: l'écrivain qui adopte ainsi une "persona" publique se trouve-
t-il gêné dans son indépendance créatrice? ou doit-on dire, au contraire,
que c'est précisément par son engagement qu'il se constitue "le secrétaire de son époque"? Deuxième question: estimons-nous l'oeuvre d'un
auteur classique pour la lumière qu'il a jetée sur l'esprit humain ou en
raison de la position que cet auteur a prise pour ou contre une idée
de son temps?

L'ÉCRIVAIN EN TANT
QU'ESPRIT INDEPENDANT

Séance d'Ouverture

13 juin

M. Lewis Galantière (Président du Congrès)—Monsieur le Président Miller, Monsieur le Secrétaire général Carver, Monsieur le Chancelier Niles, Monsieur Saul Bellow, invités distingués de nombreux pays, Messieurs et Mesdames du P.E.N. international, c'est à moi, en tant que président du centre du P.E.N. américain, que revient l'honneur de vous souhaiter la bienvenue au trente-quatrième congrès international du P.E.N.

Avant de déclarer ce congrès ouvert, je tiens à vous lire ce télégramme du Maire de la cité de New York. Monsieur Lindsay nous dit:

Comme il m'arrive parfois de lire, et comme je me considère sans façon comme une sorte d'écrivain de tous les jours, j'aurais eu beaucoup de joie à me trouver en compagnie de mes co-auteurs. Mais les problèmes de cette cité ont tendance à s'accumuler. En bref, je ne puis être des vôtres, mais je tiens à exprimer mes salutations officielles à vos délégués, spécialement à ceux venant de l'étranger. Tous mes voeux pour des séances pleines de discorde et de frottements, et profondément créatrices.

J'ai aussi à vous lire la lettre dans laquelle le Gouverneur de l'Etat de New York vous souhaite la bienvenue dans ces termes:

Comme vous le savez, des engagements antérieurs m'ont empêché d'être présent à la séance d'ouverture du 34ème congrès international du P.E.N. Je prends donc la plume pour exprimer à vos distingués collègues que c'est un honneur de leur souhaiter la bienvenue dans l'Etat de New York.
Je connais les longues annales du P.E.N. international dans la défense de la liberté de pensée et d'expression. Le thème principal du congrès, *l'écrivain en tant qu'esprit indépendant,* me paraît très opportun. Quant au problème de *l'écrivain en tant que personnage public* que vous traiterez parmi d'autres,

il me semble qu'il est spécialement aigu de nos jours, et cela m'intéressera beaucoup d'apprendre quel sera le résultat de vos discussions à ce sujet.

C'est avant tout parce que je suis convaincu de l'importance du rôle de l'écrivain en tant qu'élément fertile de la culture et de la civilisation, et en tant que promoteur de la compréhension entre les peuples, que votre congrès intéresse le gouverneur de cet Etat.

Le gouverneur Rockefeller termine sur des voeux pour une réunion sympathique et féconde.

Nous avons reçu des messages bienveillants de Kenneth Holland, président de l'Institut international de l'éducation, en son nom et en celui de ces collaborateurs, et de Henry Fischbach, président de l'Association américaine des traducteurs. Je les remercie ainsi que le Maire et le Gouverneur en votre nom à tous.

En Février, j'ai eu l'honneur d'inviter à ce congrès l'un de nos vice-présidents internationaux, Son Excellence le président de la République indienne, Monsieur S. Radhakrishnan, l'éminent philosophe. Il a beaucoup regretté ne pouvoir être de nôtres et a écrit: "j'espère que vous comprendrez que je suis pris par mes obligations ici, et que vous m'excuserez". Naturellement nous le comprenons. M. Radhakrishnan nous a cependant envoyé un message spécial par l'entremise de Madame Wadia, fondatrice de l'All-India Center du P.E.N.

Madame Wadia, ayant pris la parole, paraphrase le message du Président Radhakrishnan, qui nous exhorte à avoir le courage de nos convictions, et à les exprimer avec fermeté et sans crainte, mais sans acerbité, non seulement en faisant preuve de tolérance, mais surtout en acceptant et comprenant les autres points de vue. Dans ce monde troublé où nous sommes confrontés à de nombreux problèmes, il espère que nous les envisagerons avec le courage que nous donne l'esprit indépendant qui repose en chacun de nous, et qui doit s'exprimer dans tout ce que nous écrivons.

M. Galantière remercie Madame Wadia, et dit que, comme les deux langues officielles du P.E.N. sont le français et l'anglais, et que tous les orateurs de cette séance parleront anglais, il estime convenable que le représentant du centre qui accueille parle français.

C'est par conséquent en français qu'il présente le prochain orateur, le Chancelier Niles, qui s'adresse au congrès au nom du président Hester de l'Université de New York. Le P.E.N. américain doit beaucoup à la générosité avec laquelle l'Université a mis à sa disposition ce bâtiment extraordinairement bien équipé où le congrès se trouve réuni, ainsi que les résidences d'étudiants confortables et à prix modérés où sont logés près de 500 délégués et ceux qui les accompagnent, et le personnel courtois et efficace qui se préoccupe de leur confort.

Le Chancelier Niles décrit d'une manière fort intéressante la croissance de son Université, qui fut fondée en 1830, et la position qu'elle occupe dans la vie culturelle de la cité de New York. Il termine en transmettant tous les voeux du Président Hester pour une conférence pleine de succès.

M. Galantière présente, toujours en français, l'Honorable Roger L. Stevens, président du Conseil national des arts et des humanités qui a été créé depuis peu par le Congrès des Etats-Unis dans le dessein de compléter l'aide que les institutions privées accordent à la littérature, les arts et les études humanistes aux Etats-Unis. Le P.E.N. américain est très reconnaissant pour l'aide qu'il a reçu, et pour la liberté totale dans laquelle il a pu utiliser cette aide en préparant le congrès.

M. Stevens dit que le Conseil a été heureux que sa participation ait pu contribuer à rendre ce congrès possible. Il est lui-même d'autant plus content que cela lui permet de se trouver au milieu de tant d'écrivains connus. Nous vivons heureusement à une époque où la renommée d'un écrivain n'est pas limitée à son propre pays. St. John Perse a été traduit en anglais de même que le grand poète urdu Faiz Ahmed Faiz. John Steinbeck n'est qu'un des nombreux écrivains américains qui est lu en Russie. Dans l'hémisphère occidental, Pablo Neruda, "ce géant de la littérature moderne" jouit d'une grande influence sur les jeunes poètes des Etats-Unis. Shelley s'est peut-être trompé quand il a affirmé que les poètes étaient les législateurs non reconnus de l'humanité, mais M. Stevens croit pourtant que "les écrivains articulent la conscience de l'humanité, et sont au premier rang de ceux sur qui nous comptons pour la mener sur les chemins du salut".

M. Stevens passe alors à la lecture du message suivant du Président des Etats-Unis:

C'est pour moi un grand plaisir de souhaiter une chaleureuse bienvenue aux membres du P.E.N. international, au nom du peuple des Etats-Unis. Nous sommes très honorés que vous ayez choisi notre pays comme lieu de rencontre pour votre 34ème congrès. Votre association s'étend sur le monde entier et ses membres ont une histoire glorieuse, au cours de laquelle vous avez contribué sans relâche à préserver la liberté d'expression, et l'échange entre toutes les branches de l'activité des écrivains.

Le thème du congrès actuel, *l'écrivain en tant qu'esprit indépendant,* est très approprié, car il me semble définir les préoccupations des écrivains de partout. Le monde a toujours connu des époques pendant lesquelles, selon les termes de votre charte, la transmission des idées a été menacée. Il a même connu des périodes où le libre échange des idées était impossible. Et pourtant les mouvements les plus nobles de l'histoire contemporaine sont ceux qui avait comme but d'écarter les restrictions qui entravent l'esprit créateur de l'écrivain, et qui l'empêchent de communiquer avec ses collègues des autres pays.

Votre réunion aux Etats-Unis est un symbole de ce grand mouvement de l'esprit humain, et nous, Américains, sommes fiers de vous recevoir.

Après avoir remercié M. Stevens pour avoir reconnu avec tant de pertinence quel était le rôle de l'écrivain, et pour avoir apporté au Congrès le message de bienvenue du Président des Etats-Unis, *M. Galantière* présente M. Arthur Miller, Président international du P.E.N. dont l'allocution sera suivie par celle de M. Saul Bellow.

Allocution du Président international

Etant donné que c'est le premier congrès du P.E.N. auquel il m'est, strictement parlé, accordé l'honneur de présider, je me sens obligé de vous demander toute votre indulgence; mes notions de procédure parlementaire sont à peu près aussi sommaires que mon français. Mais je vais peut-être compenser mes faibles de ces côtés-là par la vertu de la brièveté, ce qui semble presque une gageure dans une assemblée qui réunit des écrivains.

Tout d'abord je tiens à exprimer mes regrets personnels que l'état de santé de mon prédécesseur, le poète hollandais Victor van Vriesland, l'ait empêché de participer à ce congrès. Je sais que vous vous joignez à moi pour lui envoyer nos bons voeux affectueux.

Vous avez remarqué avec quelle cordialité cette assemblée est reçue. Le président du Centre américain. Lewis Galantière, nous a souhaité la bienvenue, le Chancelier de l'Université de New York nous a ouvert tout grand les portes de ces locaux admirablement équipés, le gouverneur Rockefeller a exprimé l'accueil chaleureux de la part de l'Etat de New York, le maire Lindsay a fait de même pour la Cité de New York, et Roger Stevens pour le Gouvernment des Etats-Unis. C'est un devoir agréable de les remercier en votre nom.

La dernière réunion du P.E.N. sur sol américain a eu lieu il y a 42 ans, ce qui fait que je ne puis me porter garant pour ce qui s'y est passé alors. Je m'imagine qu'à cette époque les délégués prenaient notre organisation pour une tentative de créer une espèce de République des lettres. En tout cas les questions littéraires de ce temps étaient encore des questions littéraires, de même que des innovations techniques ou physiques étaient encore du ressort de la science. Pendant ces 42 années, cependant, les révolutions, les contre-révolutions et les guerres presque ininterrompues, ont imprégné toute activité humaine de questions concernant la validité et le prestige de systèmes sociaux et de nationalismes qui se font concurrence. Vu d'une autre planète, le fait même qu'un homme soit arrivé à marcher dans l'espace est un événement important; sur terre, la question importante est de savoir s'il est russe ou américain. Un sentiment de tristesse, miraculeusement capté dans un poème est maintenant autre chose que de la tristesse, le désenchantement n'est de nos jours plus un désenchantement. S'il s'agit d'un poème russe, on implique que ses sentiments sont politiques, et s'il s'agit d'un poème américain, on le fait presque autant. Du moins, le monde penche à penser ainsi.

En un mot, la beauté intégrale d'une chose en elle-même, son degré de perfection en tant que produit complexe de tensions et de résolutions intérieures, est subordonnée aux rapports qui existent entre elle et le prestige ou la survivance des présomptions sociales qui forment le cadre dans lesquelles elle a été produite.

Ce qui implique qu'avec le temps le travail de l'intellectuel acquiert un certaine importance. Et c'est pourquoi tant de gens s'acharnent à le réglementer. C'est pourquoi dans presque tous les pays il existe une forme ou une autre de censure; des livres sont brûlés ou tout à fait supprimés, des écrivains sont emprisonnés, et le Comité du P.E.N. des écrivains en prison manque rarement de clients.

Voilà pourquoi il peut sembler naturel que la raison d'être du P.E.N. soit étroitement liée à ses efforts pour défendre le droit de l'écrivain de s'exprimer et d'être publié.

Quand, dans les années cinquante, des écrivains américains ont été harcelés par des législateurs, qu'ils ont été mis sur des "listes noires" et forcés d'écrire sous des pseudonymes et que l'accès au cinéma, à la télévision et dans certains cas aux éditeurs, leur a été barré; quand des auteurs portugais sont arrêtés, quand des écrivains soviétiques passent en jugement à cause de ce que leurs oeuvres pourraient impliquer dans le domaine politique et qu'ils sont condamnés à des peines de prison à long terme, le devoir du P.E.N. est évident, et il ne peut y échapper. Quand la littérature yiddiseh ne se voit pas accorder en Union soviétique les mêmes facilités de publication que les autres littératures, quand la langue catalane est supprimée en Espagne ces faits—et malheureusement de nombreux autres de ce genre—appellent les protestations du P.E.N. Mais, tout importante que soit cette fonction, elle n'est pas et ne doit pas être la seule raison d'être du P.E.N.

Aucun de nous n'est venu ici comme représentant de son pays. Aucun de nous n'est obligé, en se présentant ici, de faire l'apologie de sa culture ou de son système politique. Dans ce congrès comme dans les précédents, le communiste convaincu, l'anti-communiste militant, le non-politique, l'anarchiste, le catholique, le juif, le protestant, le bouddhiste ou le mahométan, le réaliste et le surréaliste, le saoûl et le sobre peuvent venir et laisser derrière eux leurs catégories et tourner leur attention vers le seul problème qui nous préoccupe tous en tant qu'êtres humains, l'enrichissement de la culture. Et par culture j'entends la manière sincère et profonde avec laquelle l'écrivain exprime ce que représente pour lui la réalité. Privé de ceux qui rendent compte de cette façon, l'homme perd son passé, ne peut faire face au présent et trahit son avenir.

Mais le P.E.N. ne remplit pas encore cette mission. Pendant cinquante et une semaines par an entre deux congrès, le P.E.N. pourrait se faire le champ de bataille de la controverse, l'arène ouverte en plus de cinquante pays, le tranchant de l'aile qui coupe l'air. Pour être fidèle aux promesses du P.E.N., chaque centre pourrait devenir un lieu de confrontation, un endroit non exempt de danger, de manière que l'angoisse de notre époque ne soit pas cachée par l'écran factice d'une vaine cordialité, mais soit ouverte aux investigations.

Parmi les organisations internationales, P.E.N. représente une curiosité, ne serait-ce que parce qu'il a duré si longtemps, il n'a pas seulement duré mais il a crû et continuera à croître. Je pense que c'est dû en grande partie au fait qu'il a refusé, avec raison, de devenir l'agent d'une quelconque tendance politique. Ce n'est qu'un esprit étroit qui considère que la politique est le seul moyen, ou le meilleur, de permettre aux hommes de se révéler les uns aux autres. Le fait est que la politique n'a pas son pareil comme moyen de se cacher. Le point de vue du P.E.N. est plus étendu et plus profond que cela. Parce que nous réunissons tant de points de vue différents, nous n'avons pas besoin de célébrer la tristesse d'un poème russe rien que parce que cela confirme notre conception de la vie en Russie, ou d'admirer le mépris et la rébellion d'un poème américain, pour une raison analogue. Puisque P.E.N. n'est pas engagé dans la lutte politique, cela lui devrait être plus facile de voir la littérature en tant que littérature, c'est-à-dire une expression de la condition et des sentiments humains universels, de l'idéal humain universel.

Même si ces congrès n'avaient servi à rien d'autre, il est évident que malgré notre mauvais français, notre anglais écorché et nos balbutiements espagnols, nous nous sommes fait comprendre les uns des autres. Il est important que nous ne nous réunissions pas seulement pour échanger des poignées de mains, mais que nous donnions une nouvelle vitalité à la conscience que nous avons de quelque chose qui est aussi réel, aussi palpable et aussi décisif que les conflits entre nos nations. Il s'agit de la ressemblance fondamentale et indéracinable qui existe entre les esprits humains, quelle que soit la forme dans laquelle ils se manifestent. Notre but suprême est de rendre la culture universelle.

C'est la tâche qui nous est particulièrement réservée, à nous écrivains, simplement parce qu'il n'existe aucun autre groupe qui s'en soucie autant que nous pouvons nous en soucier. Cela réside dans la nature même de l'oeuvre littéraire de tendre à atteindre le monde entier. Et c'est, peut-être avant toute chose, le moyen suprême qui permettra un jour aux hommes de s'identifier les uns aux autres, et de ce fait rendre moins probable l'insanité des guerres.

Depuis bien des années la question de l'engagement de l'écrivain a été à l'ordre du jour; doit-il ou ne doit-il pas prendre parti pour un système social ou un autre, pour un nationalisme, une conception ré-volutionnaire ou un autre? P.E.N. a été conçu, et l'histoire de son passé ne laisse aucun doute à ce sujet, comme un moyen par lequel l'écrivain peut s'engager pour l'humanité, pour la défense de la culture universelle et pour faire comprendre chez tous les peuples que cela importe. Voilà qui me semble être la véritable tâche de chaque centre du P.E.N., cinquante et une semaines par an.

C'est pour ces raisons que je suis navré que la délégation d'obser-vateurs d'Union soviétique qui était annoncée ne soit pas arrivée. Dans l'absence de toute explication officielle, il faut supposer que l'on craignait que le cas Sinyavsky-Daniel n'attire sur une délégation sovié-tique de fortes critiques de la part de membres du P.E.N. Et il est probable que cela aurait été le cas.

Néanmoins, j'aimerais croire que dans de telles critiques il y aurait eu quelque chose de plus qu'une condamnation qui engage les écri-vains de tous les pays et surtout les écrivains de l'URSS. Le P.E.N. in-ternational a été le premier à protester, et à condamner ce procès, et les sentences prononcées. Par tous les moyens à notre disposition nous avons essayé de faire adoucir les sentences et d'aider les accusés. Mais à aucun moment, aujourd'hui moins que jamais, nous n'avons perdu de vue l'importance pour le monde et pour l'Union Soviétique, de créer à l'avenir un ou des centres du P.E.N. soviétiques. Nous ne cherchons pas des prétextes pour administrer une correction à l'Union Soviétique, ce n'est pas non plus dans l'esprit du P.E.N. de poser des conditions spécialement difficiles pour l'admission d'écrivains soviétiques, que ce soit d'une façon ouverte ou larvée. Quand le moment sera venu où les écrivains soviétiques pourront souscrire aux principes de la Charte du P.E.N., ils seront les bienvenus parmi nous. La réception chaleureuse qui a été accordée cette année à Andrei Voznesensky en Angleterre et aux Etats-Unis est la preuve, me semble-t-il, qu'il n'existe aucune animosité contre un écrivain rien que parce qu'il est un loyal citoyen de l'Union Soviétique. J'ai plus d'une fois exprimé mon sentiment que l'existence même du P.E.N. et sa solidité reposent sur son empressement à accueillir des écrivains en tant qu'écrivains et non en tant qu'ambassadeurs politiques. Néanmoins, renoncer à insister sur le droit d'écrire équivaudrait à violer les principes fondamentaux de notre organisation.

Par hasard nous avons sous la main un exemple de l'action positive dont le P.E.N. est capable qui va bien au-delà de sa capacité de protester. Grâce à l'invitation du P.E.N. américain, Pablo Neruda est parmi nous. Ce grand poète, qui a toujours eu une influence aux Etats-Unis qui ne fait que grandir depuis quarante ans, a fait lecture de ses poèmes à New York, et ira bientôt dans d'autres villes de notre pays. Les milliers de jeunes américains qui se laissent guider par Neruda dans leur manière de voir la poésie, les professeurs et les critiques, doivent certainement tenir compte maintenant de ce qui fait le P.E.N. international, non pas pour des raisons politiques, mais parce que tout simplement il a rempli sa mission de briser la barrière qui séparait ce grand artiste d'une grande civilisation qui depuis vingt ans ne pouvait l'admirer que de loin. Il n'est pas nécessaire de faire de la propagande pour M. Neruda, et pendant qu'il est parmi nous la politique est bien loin de ses préoccupations. Il ressort que dans cette transaction, la chose qui importe, c'est l'art, et c'est là vraiment la seule chose qui compte.

J'espère qu'à l'avenir le P.E.N. fera tout ce qui est en son pouvoir, et récoltera le plus de fonds possible, pour réunir les nombreux écrivains —pas tous aussi fameux, pas tous immortels—dont nous devons apprendre à connaître les noms, et qui ont besoin d'être stimulés par la rencontre avec leurs lecteurs étrangers. Il est indéniable que pour beaucoup d'entre nous de grandes parties du monde créateur restent des territoires inconnus. Les expériences révolutionnaires de l'Asie et de l'Afrique, la riche littérature de l'Amérique latine, doivent devenir le patrimoine de tout homme cultivé. En un mot, le P.E.N. doit offrir à chaque homme et à chaque femme qui écrit, un terrain neutre, une sorte de sanctuaire où il trouvera un soutien pour cette vision qui est toujours en danger d'être détruite par les choses, par la technique, par la répression ou par pure ignorance—la vision de l'homme en tant que mesure et que centre de l'univers.

Allocution de M. Saul Bellow

Dans cet âge de transformations immenses et accélérées, il est essentiel de noter celles qui nous touchent directement. Cela n'est pas toujours facile, mais nous devons tout au moins essayer de le faire.

Les changements sur lesquels je désire faire quelques commentaires sont ceux qui se sont produits dans les rapports entre le public et les écrivains dans les pays qui parlent anglais. Je commence par une courte description de l'artiste et du public dans la perspective d'un écrivain d'avant-garde américain d'il y a trente ans. Lui-même se serait certainement qualifié de *highbrow**. Avec une certaine ironie, quoique sérieusement, il aurait tracé une ligne de démarcation entre lui et les *middlebrows,* lesquels, à vrai dire, se croient les sommets de la culture, et les *lowbrow,* ces philistins qui sont censés détester tout ce qui est beau et bon dans la tradition moderne. Cela ne veut pas dire que l'écrivain *highbrow* aimait l'isolement dans lequel il vivait, ni qu'il l'avait choisi par orgueil ou par un sentiment décadent des classes. Au contraire, la subdivision de la culture entre les "hauts" et les "bas" causait beaucoup d'amertume, et nombreux étaient ceux qui pensaient qu'elle représentait un danger pour la culture et pour la civilisation dans son ensemble.

Ce poète d'avant-garde éprouvait une certaine nostalgie pour le 18e siècle et pour le public aristocratique, raffiné et restreint de cette époque productive de chefs-d'oeuvre, mais il ne pensait pas aux humiliations que comportait ce genre d'existence. Le public du 19e siècle était plus enthousiaste peut-être mais plus grossier, c'était un public de boutiquiers. L'exploitation commerciale a vite fait d'augmenter encore cette vulgarisation. Certains lanceurs d'affaires firent fortune avec le roman à bon marché et avec le temps le monde a connu la culture de masse. Voilà pourquoi la minorité d'avant-garde ne cessa de diminuer. C'est également cette période qui vit naître le spécialiste, une nouvelle sorte d'intellectuel, qui n'avait que peu de compréhension des choses de l'art, et peu de sympathie pour la vie de l'esprit.

Pour finir, au 20e siècle, il se produisit le phénomène qu'a si bien décrit le brillant observateur et critique, feu Wyndham Lewis, que je qualifierais de *highbrow* authentique: "la civilisation se scinda en deux parties, et tout ce qui était intelligent et créateur fut refoulé dans des enclos et des réserves." Comme les Indiens d'Amérique, l'écrivain d'avant-garde fut parqué dans des lieux stériles, enfermé dans des tours d'ivoire, privé de contacts humains et d'influence. Le résultat final sera probablement la liquidation totale de tous les groupes intellectuels; quelques chefs-d'oeuvres d'hommes comme Joyce et Paul Klee emergeraient de ce crépuscule, et nous atteindrons un état de dégradation finale: l'ère de la stupidité irrémissible.

Cette description a des points communs avec celle que donnaient les

* *highbrow,* "front haut", homme de grande culture; *middlebrow,* de culture moyenne; *lowbrow,* primaire, "front bas".

romantiques et ce qu'ils appelaient le monde bourgeois: pas totalement injustifiée, mais certainement exagérée. D'après Lewis, l'écrivain serait un proscrit de la société, méprisé par ceux qui gouvernent, séparé du peuple et brûlant de retrouver le contact avec ce dernier.

Wyndham Lewis était un observateur attentif et original, mais il est évident qu'il s'est bien trompé dans ses prophéties. Les intellectuels n'ont pas été liquidés, bien au contraire, ils voient augmenter leur puissance et leur influence, et on les considère maintenant—avec un respect mitigé de crainte—comme indispensables aux gouvernements, comme fabricateurs de l'opinion des gens instruits, une source de légitimité symbolique, jouant le rôle tenu auparavant par le prêtre. La prophétie de Walt Whitman: "le prêtre sort; entre le divin homme de lettres" qui semblait il y a 30 ans être le fruit d'un esprit dérangé, paraît de nos jours justifié.

Je ne parle pas ici de la *qualité* de ces hommes instruits—car ceci est une autre histoire—mais de l'accroissement de leur influence.

Avant la guerre de 39–45, le public de l'écrivain était insignifiant quant au nombre. Ce n'est plus le cas aujourd'hui, car nous nous trouvons en face d'une classe qui ne cesse de croître: celle des intellectuels ou des quasi-intellectuels; des millions d'étudiants sortent de nos universités et de nos collèges. Il est vrai qu'un grade universitaire ne veut pas dire grand'chose, mais il indique, tout de même, que l'on a été exposé à la lumière d'un foyer de haute culture. Nous ne devons pourtant pas oublier qu'une grande partie de cette haute culture littéraire à laquelle nous sommes exposés—la partie la plus moderne et la plus active—est due à ceux qui avaient rejeté l'approbation de leurs contemporains. Les millions de visiteurs de nos musées d'art admirent aujourd'hui la peinture étrangement belle et puissante d'artistes qui ont travaillé dans l'aube obscure du modernisme.

Des hommes d'affaires avertis et malins ont bien vite découvert le prestige dont jouissaient ces oeuvres d'art, et que quand on exposait un tableau sur lequel il avait été fait une bonne publicité, les queues se formaient aux portes des musées aussi longues qu'à celles des plus grands cinémas.

Cette minorité cultivée est plus étendue aujourd'hui que la poignée de connaisseurs qui, dans les années vingt, lisaient les revues d'avant-garde et discutaient sans fin sur la "signification de la forme".

Car il existe de nos jours une communauté littéraire nombreuse, et quelque chose que nous appellerons, faute de mieux, une culture littéraire—d'ailleurs fort médiocre, à mon avis. D'abord, les universités ont inscrit la littérature moderne à leur programme. Il y a deux générations encore, des pédants sclérosés refusaient d'admettre un auteur quelconque qui fût postérieur à Browning ou à Leconte de Lisle. Ils ont perdu la partie; aujourd'hui, toutes nos universités acceptent que l'on étudie les auteurs contemporains. Des milliers de professeurs fabriquent des millions "d'ès lettres".

Certains de ces professeurs sont parfaitement inoffensifs, ceux qui étudient des textes, les annotent et en donnent des éditions. D'autres ont plus d'influence, ce sont ceux qui les interprètent—ou les trahissent.

Ce sont les universités qui produisent les intellectuels littéraires, non pas les plumitifs ni la bohême. Le journalisme littéraire a été entièrement accaparé par les organes de masse et les revues publiées par les presses universitaires. Le professeur est prêt à fournir des articles littéraires à bon marché et dans ce domaine il a presque totalement supplanté ses concurrents de la corporation des écrivains. La bohême a aussi pris de nouveaux quartiers; elle s'est établie dans le quartier des *campus* universitaires.

Nous voyons donc que l'université produit des quantités d'intellectuels littéraires qui deviennent professeurs, écrivains ou directeurs de revue. Pour autant que je puisse m'en rendre compte, ce *nouveau* groupe, fortement influencé par ces classiques modernes que sont Joyce, Proust, Eliot, Lawrence, Gide, Valéry et autres, n'ont past fait grand-chose d'autre que prendre ces classiques et essayer d'en faire la matière de leurs leçons. Ils traduisent l'imagination en opinions, ils débitent l'art en forme de "cognitions": il faut que tout soit dit autrement; ils redécrivent tout; en général tout cela devient moins accessible. Aux sentiments et aux élans ils substituent des actes réfléchis. Parfois ils semblent fabriquer l'histoire intellectuelle, qui leur convient mieux que l'art même. C'est comme si leur but était de créer le modèle de l'intelligence du 20e siècle. Une intelligence qui verrait naître un jour un art plus digne d'elle—pour autant que le *Zeitgeist* le permette. Je pense que la "déhumanisation de l'art" dont parlait Ortega, est née des exigences que les intellectuels littéraires posent au domaine artistique, et résulte en partie de la pression qu'ils exercent sur ce dernier pour obtenir une "signification".

Cela peut être un exercice fort intéressant, intelligent et utile, que de redécrire les choses; chaque génération doit—comme Adam dans son jardin du Paradis—donner de nouveaux noms à ses animaux. Dans *Le bourgeois gentilhomme*, Molière nous révèle les possibilités comiques, nées de la découverte par M. Jourdain qu'il fait de la prose sans le savoir. Les Américains apprécient beaucoup la "comédie de la terminologie". Nous attendons des psychologues qu'ils pénètrent en nous et nous redécrivent d'une manière scientifique tout ce qu'ils y trouvent. Nous sommes enchantés d'apprendre que nous sommes introvertis, que nous avons des fixations, des complexes de ceci ou de cela, que nous sommes attachés à nos mères de telle ou telle manière. D'apprendre cela noir sur blanc vaut bien l'argent que cela nous coûte. Mais ce que nos critiques font, c'est redécrire en allant vers le bas, dénigrer les temps présents et refuser de reconnaître que leurs contemporains soient capables de créer quelquechose de nouveau. Ils se présentent comme étant eux-mêmes les seuls héritiers des écrivains classiques modernes. Je parle d'un genre d'hommes de lettres des mieux cotés qui s'identifient avec Joyce, avec Proust, et se présentent comme les représentants distingués—les seuls représentants—de ces maîtres.

Ces agents, managers et impresarios d'Henry James ou des Symbolistes français paraissent parfois se considérer comme leurs seuls successeurs légitimes, et jouissent d'un certain prestige de bon ton. Ils sont les *happy few* de la culture. La tendance des intellectuels—dans le domaine de ce que les université américaines appellent les humanités—d'essayer d'accaparer la littérature, de l'enlever aux écrivains, se manifeste avec netteté. Ces intellectuels ressemblent à la jeune princesse britannique qui avait dit à son mari au cours de leur voyage de noces: "Est-ce que les domestiques font la même chose? C'est bien trop bon pour eux". La littérature est trop bonne pour les romanciers contemporains, ces pauvres êtres qui peinent tout seuls à leur vile besogne. Et qu'en font les intellectuels, de la littérature? Ils en parlent, ils s'en parent, ils s'en servent pour faire carrière, ils deviennent une élite, et ils en font des discours et des conférences. Elle est leur capital, leur matière première. Ils en sortent juste ce qu'il leur faut pour leurs travaux critiques, journalistiques ou historiques, et produisent des oeuvres hybrides, quasi-littéraires, intéressantes en elles-mêmes parfois, mais toujours affirmant la décadence et la désuétude de la littérature contemporaine.

Ils veulent utiliser la littérature de tradition moderne pour en faire quelque chose de bien mieux, un domaine mental plus élevé et plus précieux, un domaine d'intellectualité éblouissante d'idées merveilleuses, d'où sortirait une forme nouvelle et originale de la personnalité.

Je voudrais attirer votre attention sur d'autres conséquences, encore, de ce genre d'enseignement de la littérature. Dans son dernier livre *Beyond Culture* ("au-delà de la culture"), le professeur Lionel Trilling nous révèle que nous disposons actuellement aux Etats-Unis d'un groupe important de personnes qui ont été formées aux disciplines de la littérature moderne classique. Il trouve que ces personnes n'ont pas très bien tourné, et on comprend son point de vue: elles paraissent avoir gardé le beurre et l'argent du beurre. D'une part, comme aux écrivains modernes classiques, la civilisation occidentale leur répugne; l'effronterie des gens au pouvoir et la dégradation des populations urbaines les dégoûtent, ils observent tout cela comme s'ils se trouvaient dans une région dévastée. Et d'autre part, eux-mêmes sont dans une fort belle situation. Ils ont de l'argent, une position, des privilèges, de la puissance, des écoles privées pour leurs enfants, des soins dentaires perfectionnés, des vacances en Europe, des actions, des obligations, des maisons, et avec tout cela, et grâce à leur instruction, ils sont d'une sympathie toute particulière pour l'héroïque vie de l'artiste, leurs goûts et leurs jugements ont été formés à l'école de Rimbaud et de D. H. Lawrence. Peut-on se représenter quelquechose de plus raffiné?

Voilà peut-être ce qui se passe dans le monde entier, et cela vient peut-être de ce qu'on ne croit plus assez en rien, qu'on doute de la valeur des actions humaines. Ainsi, dans notre courte vie, nous nous sentons libres de combiner et de garder toutes les valeurs. On recherche le luxe tout en conservant, d'une manière ou d'une autre, des valeurs qui ont été conçues dans l'austérité. On cherche à combiner la sécurité de sa personne avec des attitudes révolutionnaires, la monogamie avec les expériences sexuelles, la vie de famille conventionnelle avec un point de vue bohême, la *dolce vita* avec les grandes lectures. Président-directeur-général pendant la journée, on est anarchiste à l'heure de l'apéritif. Habitant les quartiers les plus calmes de New York, isolés de la boue et des dangers de la rue, ils gardent tout naturellement tous les sentiments d'aliénation, ou se font un point d'honneur d'être maussades, ingrats, insatisfaits, soupçonneux et théoriquement défiant toute autorité! Ceci n'est rien de neuf, et Dostoïevsky avait déjà fait remarquer que les gens qui récitaient du Schiller avec les yeux pleins de larmes étaient doués aussi pour pousser leur carrière bureaucratique. Il n'y a rien d'étonnant à ce que le professeur Trilling regarde tout cela d'un oeil pensif. Il constate qu'une éducation littéraire n'est qu'un bienfait tout relatif, et que les critiques et les écrivains des facultés des lettres ne sont pas les mieux réussis.

Quelle est cette fonction importante qu'ils remplissent? M. Irving Kristol répond à cette question dans un numéro récent du *Public Interest*. Il relève que les intellectuels littéraires contribuent à former l'opinion des classes cultivées, en définissant les caractéristiques morales de notre société. Je cite: "il n'y a pas de fonction plus importante que de mettre en question ou d'affirmer la légitimité des institutions fondamentales de la société, de critiquer ou de réformer les prétentions qui sont à l'origine des événements de la vie politique. Nos intellectuels littéraires sont-ils bien préparés à cette fonction? Il faut avouer qu'ils ne le sont pas autant qu'il serait souhaitable".

Voilà donc la situation. Les critiques et les professeurs déclarent qu'ils sont les véritables héritiers et les successeurs des écrivains modernes classiques. Ils ont volontairement fait l'obscurité sur les rapports qui existent entre les auteurs contemporains et leurs prédécesseurs d'avant-garde, et ils ont remplacé le public d'avant-garde par quelque chose d'autre. Ils ont fait ressortir des arts et des lettres seulement ce qui leur convenait, et cela a été en leur pouvoir de recruter des auteurs qui se plient à leurs exigences. Il paraît des romans qui reflètent les attitudes, les notions ou les fantaisies qui plaisent à l'intelligentsia lettrée, auxquels on voue une attention toute particulière. La littérature prend de l'importance selon ce qu'on en peut faire ou ne pas faire. Elle devient une source d'orientation, de poses, de styles de vie, d'opinions, qui sont le produit d'un bric à brac de marxisme, de freudisme, d'existentialisme, de mythologie, de surréalisme *und so weiter,* les reliquats du modernisme avec quelques rogatons apocalyptiques.

On part de l'idée que quand on a pris position d'une manière correcte on perd toutes ses illusions, et que c'est là la chose qui importe le plus. Que c'est faire preuve d'un esprit averti que de démasquer, de désenchanter, de haïr, d'éprouver du dégoût. Ce phénomène a été fort bien décrit par Wyndham Lewis qui dit que les romantiques modernes ont vulgarisé le dégoût qui était autrefois l'apanage de l'aristocratie. On peut ajouter que le "scepticisme de celui qui sait" a également été vulgarisé, et que l'on considère comme un bienfait par exemple d'être conscient que l'affection que l'on porte à son grand-père provient de la classe sociale où l'on est né, ou que l'amitié est un sentiment bassement hypocrite. Néanmoins il existe des amitiés, des affinités, des sentiments naturels, des normes stables. Les gens s'entendent, par exemple, pour admettre que le meurtre est illicite, et même s'ils ne son pas capables de le prouver par des arguments rationnels, ils ne sont pas pour cela entraînés à des actes de violence gratuits. Il me semble qu'il serait bon que les écrivains se remettent à penser à ces questions. Ils devront évidemment le faire sans l'assistance des critiques, car ceux-ci sont trop romanesques pour envisager des problèmes de ce genre.

Pour terminer, un mot sur la notion d'avant-garde. Le génie est d'instinct d'avant-garde. Vouloir créer de toutes pièces des conditions d'avant-garde, c'est faire de l'"historicité", c'est piocher les livres d'"histoire culturelle".

Quant au public d'avant-garde, qui a été assimilé par notre culture littéraire et transformé en quelquechose d'autre, nous devons pour le moment nous en passer. Il faut que l'écrivain soit persuadé que ce qu'il écrit évoquera un public, et que celui-ci sera appelé par la force de la vérité. La forme qu'il inventera créera un public nouveau.

L'écrivain à l'âge électronique

mardi 14 juin
PREMIÈRE ET DEUXIÈME SESSIONS

Marshall McLuhan, PRÉSIDENT
directeur du Center for Culture and Technology, University of Toronto

Iván Boldizsár
directeur du *New Hungarian Quarterly*, Budapest

Haroldo de Campos
directeur de *Invencão*, São Paolo

R. Buckminster Fuller
University of Southern Illinois, Carbondale

Yves Gandon
président du P.E.N. club français,
ancien président de la Société des gens de lettres, Paris

Adolf Hoffmeister
président du P.E.N. tchécoslovaque, Prague

Anoma Kanie
P.E.N. de la Côte d'Ivoire (deuxième session seulement)

Richmond Lattimore
Bryn Mawr College, Bryn Mawr

Kathleen C. Nott
Londres

Norman Podhoretz
directeur de *Commentary*, New York

Paul Tabori
directeur de la *International Film Writers Guild*, Londres

L'écrivain à l'âge électronique

PREMIÈRE SÉANCE

Dans son introduction du thème, *M. McLuhan* déclare qu'à l'âge électronique, les hommes sont si intimément mêlés les uns aux autres, que les rapports entre l'écrivain et ses lecteurs sont devenus entièrement nouveaux. Les participants à cette discussion, "veulent approfondir plutôt qu'apposer des étiquettes". En effet, chacun sait qu'un *happening* peut être défini comme une "situation établie d'un seul coup sans canevas préalable". Il en est de même pour l'information électronique, qui est un événement "tout d'un seul coup". Edgar Allen Poe avait compris cette situation lorsqu'il inventa à la fois le poème symboliste et l'histoire policière.

Bien avant ce dernier, l'imprimerie avait créé un phénomène qui n'existait pas auparavant—le public, le public sollicité par l'écrivain. Montaigne déjà s'en était rendu compte: il écrivit que c'était au public qu'il devait un portrait complet de lui-même. Aujourd'hui, grâce à la xérographie, l'époque pré-gutenbergienne est de retour: en effet, le lecteur est devenu son propre éditeur. Le monde des affaires se trouve déjà dans cette situation depuis un certain temps. La xérographie reproduit des structures entières des "Gestalt." Il en est de même pour l'ordinateur, généralement considéré comme un système à emmagasiner, mais qui en fait représente un "système de rappel immédiat" imitant la mémoire humaine. Ce don de faire surgir instantanément des informations a permis de nouvelles découvertes, y compris celle de savoir qui nous sommes—car il est bien évident que l'identité humaine dépend profondément de la mémoire immédiate. Une autre caractéristique de notre époque a été brillamment résumée en une seule phrase par Buckminster Fuller: "la capsule spatiale est le premier environnement humain créé de toutes pièces, un environnement dont l'habitant est accompagné par la planète sans laquelle il ne saurait exister."

Et ceci, continue M. McLuhan, illustre remarquablement la condition de l'écrivain à l'âge électronique. Les données de l'écrivain sont en fait "l'ensemble de la conscience humaine". Il ne lui est plus possible d'exprimer un simple point de vue personnel. La "circuiterie" électronique n'a pas créé "l'audience de masse"—ce mot ne veut rien dire— mais "la confrontation simultanée d'une quantité de points de vue", et ces points de vue sont un sous-produit de l'imprimerie. L'électronique a pour effet que "tout le monde est affecté par tout le monde au même moment". Il est à noter que parallèlement à l'occidentalisation de l'Orient, l'Occident est en train de s'orientaliser, d'aller à l'intérieur de lui-même, de devenir "profondément entropique". L'intérêt provoqué par le bouddisme Zen et la drogue appellée LSD n'en sont que des exemples mineurs. Ce n'est pas par telle ou telle idéologie que nos consciences occidentales fragmentées et individualisées sont encouragées à l'introspection; c'est l'électronique qui a créé "une tendance à l'intériorité". L'automobile "de tout repos" que l'on est en train de développer est une sorte de cellule matelassée. Un reportage journalistique est devenu une sorte de poème surréaliste, l'éditorial est "une forme mécanique et fragmentée de séparatisme, de point-de-vuisme individualisé". Les nouvelles écoles artistiques comme par exemple l'art "pop", nous apprennent que "l'environnement total doit être traité comme un art".

Cependant, "l'environnement est une machine à enseigner totale et infaillible", et l'auteur "une personne dont la mission sera de programmer des machines à enseigner".

M. Boldizsár, le premier à commenter, parlant anglais, déclare qu'il a été mis *knock-out* par ce qu'il vient d'entendre, sensation identique à celle qu'il a subie en lisant *Le déclin de l'occident* de Spengler il y a plusieurs dizaines d'années. La seule chose qu'il peut ajouter pour l'instant, est qu'il était remis du coup d'assommoir de Spengler.

Mlle Nott déclare qu'elle aussi allait faire allusion à Spengler. Au lieu de cela, elle poserait une question. Le pubic de M. McLuhan doit-il comprendre que les auteurs n'ont plus d'avenir en tant qu'esprits indépendants et que les écrivains doivent apprendre à aimer l'ordinateur et à vivre avec lui? *Le Supplément littéraire* du London Times a en effet consacré un certain nombre d'articles à l'ordinateur dans le domaine de l'érudition, sous un titre collectif qu'on avait eu l'impertinence de nommer "la libération de l'esprit". "La poésie de l'ordinateur" n'est pas inconnue en Angleterre. Mlle Nott n'a aucune objection envers ceux qui veulent s'amuser avec les jouets de leur goût, mais après avoir entendu ce que M. McLuhan vient de déclarer, elle voudrait faire remarquer respectueusement qu'il y avait là une "philosophie très dangereuse et tendencieuse". Dangereuse en ce sens que—comme celle de Spengler, Freud ou Marx, par exemple—elle a tendance à faire de ce qu'elle prophétise une réalité.

Les auteurs qui se sentent découragés par ce genre de choses devraient se souvenir de l'histoire, et se rappeler que "l'histoire de la bonne littérature est en fait une sorte de mouvement de résistance". Mlle Nott suggère que *media* n'est pas seulement un terme à connotation mécanique: il veut aussi dire "moyens"; et au cours de l'histoire de la religion et de la psychologie occidentale, les moyens n'avaient jamais pris la première place, c'était le but qui importait. Mlle Nott ne veut pas s'éloigner du sujet de M. McLuhan. Ce qu'il dit dans son ouvrage *Understanding Media* au sujet de la chose imprimée—qu'elle imposait un aspect linéaire, sériel ou visuel que le lecteur transférait inconsciemment à d'autres choses—est vrai. Ce qu'il a omis de dire, c'est qu'un bon livre est une sorte d'objet moral et esthétique; que l'acte de lire est un acte solitaire—dans le sens positif du terme—une action sémantique collective qui conduit à un rapport personnel entre l'auteur et le lecteur. Pour l'un et pour l'autre M. McLuhan a négligé l'aspect de la personnalité humaine subjective. Ce que Mlle Nott a surtout retiré de cet exposé est que l'environnement était dorénavant absolument dominant —et irrésistible.

Il est fort probable qu'avec le temps on écrira bien moins de livres. Mlle Nott pense cependant que ceux qui seront écrits risquent d'être de meilleurs livres. Ce dont elle se refuse à faire l'abandon, c'est l'importance spirituelle, morale et sociale qui existe dans la sorte de communion que constitue l'action de lire.

M. McLuhan fait remarquer tout d'abord qu'il n'avait en aucune façon eu l'intention de soulever une impression de fatalité quant au *media* dont il avait parlé. "Une chose que les media ne peuvent pas supporter, c'est d'être analysés minutieusement". On peut découvrir des moyens de les "contrôler, ou même de les annihiler". Ce sont les hommes qui ont décidé de créer ces choses; "nous les avons créées afin qu'elles nous contrôlent". Comme dans l'ouvrage célèbre de Mlle Nott, *Les habits neufs de l'Empereur*, dès qu'on se rend compte de ce qui se passe, on peut exercer un certain contrôle. Faire cela veut dire qu'on est autonome, libre; ignorer ce qui se passe équivaut à se livrer fatalement aux mains de ces phénomènes. Avec l'avènement de l'électronique, "l'artiste a tendance à prendre domicile dans la tour de contrôle, et non plus dans la tour d'ivoire". L'artiste est la seule personne qui possède suffisamment de courage pour ouvrir les yeux au présent et percevoir l'avenir qu'il contient. M. McLuhan demande à M. Fuller ce qu'il en pense.

M. Fuller commence par déclarer qu'en raison de sa surdité, l'electronique lui cause des problèmes et il préfère de beaucoup lire. Ce que la lecture lui apporte, c'est "qu'on peut là vraiment rester tranquille et réfléchir". Pendant de longues années il a étudié les motifs qui revenaient régulièrement dans "l'évolution et l'expansion des capacités humaines". L'homme est unique par ses capacités multiples et variées à "développer et étendre ses fonctions". Les moyens de communication sont une de ces fonctions; une autre peut par exemple être caractérisée par le fait que chaque habitant des Etats-Unis "emploie" 130 tonnes de cuivre, 10 tonnes d'acier, 22 tonnes de béton. Métaphoriquement parlant, l'homme est un animal autrement plus énorme que le dinosaure.

Socialement et politiquement parlant, la démocratie de Jefferson se distinguait de la nôtre par les délais plus grands des communications, cette différence est illustrée par le fait que Jefferson était obligé de dire: "Si nous ne recevons pas de lettre de notre ambassadeur à Paris cette année, il nous faudra . . .". Une autre différence était que les représentants du peuple faisaient à cheval le voyage pour prendre part aux sessions parlementaires, ce qui les mettait en contact étroit avec leurs électeurs; ils vivaient dans un monde décentralisé. Aujourd'hui, on parle beaucoup des avantages et des désavantages d'un gouvernement central: ceci n'est pas un choix politique, mais un choix technique. Les amiraux ne peuvent y échapper en mer, et les bureaucrates ne peuvent y échapper sur terre ferme. La xérographie de McLuhan n'est qu'une extension de l'émission radiodiffusée; les deux représentent un système à sens unique; l'individu ne peut répondre; et ceci explique pourquoi les instituts de sondage de l'opinion publique se multiplient. Cela explique également pourquoi la possibilité apparente de prendre des décisions plus rapides paraît favoriser parfois la dictature. M. Fuller reconnaît que seul un processus d'évolution parviendra à libérer "le petit homme" de cette domination.

M. Tabori, succédant à M. Fuller, déclare que tout en partageant l'optimisme prudent de Mlle Nott quant à l'avenir de l'écrivain, il se trouve néanmoins impressionné par les "signaux d'alarme" du président. Il a été rassuré d'apprendre par des savants travaillant à l'Université de Cambridge, en Angleterre, qu'il faudrait combiner les revenus nationaux de la Grande-Bretagne, de la France et des Etats-Unis pour construire un ordinateur qui corresponde au cerveau d'un enfant de six ans. Il y a de l'espoir là-dedans. Une autre chose qui le réjouit est l'idée que les machines, elles aussi, peuvent se "gourer". Par exemple, la machine à traduire à qui on demande de traduire une phrase simple d'anglais en chinois, puis de chinois en français, donne le résultant suivant: *out of sight–out of mind* (l'équivalent anglais de "loin des yeux–loin du coeur" qui se dit: "hors des yeux–hors de l'esprit") a donné: *invisible–insane* (invisible–fou). Et si on lui demande ce qu'on peut y faire, M. Tabori recommande que les écrivains agissent de la même façon que le *Bon Soldat Schweik,* personnage célèbre de la littérature moderne tchécoslovaque, pendant la guerre: faire de la résistance passive et être assez malin pour faire l'idiot.

M. de Campos, parlant anglais, qui appartient au groupe de poètes brésiliens qui font partie du mouvement nouveau, celui de la "poésie concrète", proclame qu'il est en grande partie d'accord avec M. McLuhan. La poésie concrète est partie de la notion d'une "structure espace-temps" remplaçant la structure linéaire dans le domaine de la syntaxe poétique. Son but est l'idéogramme; sa méthode de composition est l'analyse analogique plutôt que logique. A son avis, le poète est un "dessinateur de langage" dans le même sens que "dessinateur industriel". Le Russe Maïakovsky en est un excellent exemple. En effet, ce poète fut un "ingénieur de la vie vécue au jour le jour". Nous vivons à une époque où la quantité se transforme instantanément en qualité et où, ainsi que l'exprime un poète italien, un échange dialectique s'établit entre le langage des poètes d'avant-garde et celui des enfants. "L'ère de l'homme de lettres est révolue. Le précurseur de la poésie contemporaine—la poésie qui utilise tous les moyens qui nous sont offerts aujourd'hui—est Mallarmé, "le Dante de l'âge électronique"; et "Maïakovsky a bâti sur Mallarmé comme Marx avait bâti sur Hegel".

M. Gandon, commence par remarquer qu'afin que certains orateurs puissent parler longuement, d'autres se doivent d'être brefs. Son impression de ce qui a précédé est complexe. Tour à tour émerveillé, ébloui, ahuri et confondu, il ne sait finalement plus très bien où il en est, et il a l'impression d'être le philistin rétrograde qui se trouve au milieu de personnages extrêmement savants. M. Gandon a essayé de prendre des notes, tout à l'heure, mais celles-ci ne lui sont d'aucun secours, étant illisibles. Toutefois il pense pouvoir dire certaines choses raisonnablement, c'est-à-dire simplement.

Si M. Gandon admire tant le professeur McLuhan, c'est qu'il voit en lui le poète, le mystique de l'électronique. Il admire les mystiques jusqu'au moment où elles lui font peur; et tout à l'heure, il a eu un peu peur. Il croyait qu'il savait ce que c'était que l'électronique. Il s'était même beaucoup occupé de cybernétique dans un de ses romans, parlant entre autres d'une *machina nuptialis,* la machine à marier. Il s'agissait dans ce roman d'introduire dans la machine un certain nom-

bre d'informations sur les deux fiancés, et la machine décidait sou-
verainement si ce mariage était possible ou s'il ne l'était pas. Il paraît
que dans l'avenir, c'est comme ça que ça se passera. M. Gandon n'y voit
pas d'inconvénient, après tout, puisqu'il paraît que les mariages
d'amour se terminent toujours mal.

Seulement il se passait autre chose, dans ce roman. Certaines personnes officielles—car il s'agissait d'une sorte de démocratie totalitaire
—ayant intérêt à ce que ce mariage n'eût pas lieu, introduisaient un
élément dans la machine qui faussait le résultat complètement. Tout
cela, ajoute M. Gandon, pour prouver qu'il sait de quoi il parle.

M. Gandon avait d'abord pensé que le professeur McLuhan était un
optimiste, puisqu'il était un mystique qui croyait que l'électronique
apporterait à l'humanité tous les biens possibles et imaginables. Mais
il avait poursuivi en expliquant par quoi l'écrivain serait remplacé. M.
Gandon pense qu'il aurait mieux valu dire par quoi l'écrivain ne serait
pas remplacé; et bien que M. McLuhan risque de le mépriser parce
qu'il ne fait pas du tout état des admirables précisions que ce dernier a
données dans son exposition du sujet, M. Gandon continue à croire
fermement que l'écrivain ne saurait en fait être remplacé.

Une des questions soulevées dans le programme décrivant le thème
de cette session est celle de la disparition possible du livre. En tout état
de cause, malgré l'influence grandissante de la radio et de la télévision
en France, le public qui lit a énormément augmenté. Quant aux Etats-
Unis, le nombre des éditions de livres de poche a pour le moins décuplé.
A force de se promener dans les capsules spatiales on peut perdre le
sens de la terre que nous foulons tous les jours, et M. Gandon, tout en
enviant le sort des aéronautes, reste pour l'instant sur la terre.

M. Tram Combs (Virgin Islands), déclare que le président a expliqué qu'il ne prédisait pas la fin de l'homme de lettres occidental;
et pourtant, il n'existe dans ses ouvrages aucune inquiétude à ce sujet.
Tous ceux qui sont présents ont une dette de reconnaissance envers lui
pour les avoir amenés à se préoccuper de l'usage que l'on allait faire des
nouvelles techniques. Cependant, tout en pensant aux dégâts qui pourraient en résulter, on peut se sentir réconforté par les possibilités extraordinaires de l'imagination humaine et par le progrès de l'homme—combien d'années ont-elles passé depuis que les grands singes parcouraient
la terre: est-ce 10.000? La question est celle-ci: comment la technique
nouvelle peut-elle ajouter au bien-être de l'homme? Les grandes époques
artistiques du passé allaient presque toujours de pair avec les grandes
époques scientifiques et le progrès technique. La technique a souvent
servi l'art en lui indiquant de nouvelles directions à suivre; tel fut très
nettement le cas de l'art plastique aussi bien au siècle passé qu'au nôtre.

Les nouveaux moyens de communication sont déjà au service des poètes —le disque et le magnétophone par exemple—aussi ne peut-on dire qu'une seule chose, aujourd'hui: l'écrivain a des mondes nouveaux qui s'ouvrent à lui, et il n'est pas en train de suivre le même chemin que celui des dinosaures.

Le Dr. Hoffmeister, parlant français, commence par rappeler qu'il fut un temps où les gens se mettaient sur leur trente-et-un pour aller au théâtre ou à l'opéra; aujourd'hui, l'homme de la rue peut les recevoir à domicile. Les écrans de télévision prennent sur le mur la place des tableaux à cadres dorés, et les haut parleurs ont remplacé les bibliothèques, car les bibliothèques sont devenues la malédiction des petites pièces. L'idée de livrer la culture à domicile telle une marchandise, peut mener jusqu'à l'absurde, et conduirait inévitablement à isoler l'individu, à le faire rompre avec la société. Plus il sera entouré de machines travaillant pour lui, plus l'homme aura besoin de réconfort humain.

Parlant en tant que citoyen tchécoslovaque, le Dr. Hoffmeister relève que le système socialiste ne concevait pas que l'individu puisse s'épanouir en dehors de la société, mais bien au contraire par la société, et dans son sein. Les nouvelles formes de l'art auront, peut-être, un effet collectif et deviendront en tous cas l'essence même des rapports entre des hommes très individualisés. Cependant, le Dr. Hoffmeister s'en voudrait de ne pas mentionner un obstacle à ce but—le temps—un élément dont l'homme, plus que tout autre être, souffre. Les machines auront beau accélérer le mouvement, les contacts et les communications jusqu'à la limite du possible, peut-être même au-delà des limites que les hommes considèrent encore comme infranchissables, il n'en demeure pas moins que l'homme de notre époque a beaucoup moins de temps que n'en avaient son père et son grand-père. M. Hoffmeister se demande s'il nous reste encore du temps pour la poésie et l'art et pour l'oisiveté qui est tellement agréable et douce. Vivant dans l'ambiance excitante, irritante et affolante de l'actualité immédiate, aura-t-on encore le temps de savourer l'ironie légère et néanmoins présente dont font preuve les intellectuels et les auteurs face aux faiblesses profondément humaines: l'amour, l'argent et l'égoïsme? Finalement, tout ce que le Dr. Hoffmeister peut dire, en dépit de ces sombres perspectives, c'est qu'il ne doute pas qu'une fois encore s'ouvre une ère de grand humanisme où les hommes auront autant besoin de l'art que de l'air qu'ils respirent afin de prouver leur supériorité sur la machine électronique.

M. Lattimore déclare que le poète en lui se refuse à faire des classifications, mais il avait néanmoins inscrit dans son carnet un titre: "communications", et par-dessous les sous-titres "édition", "création", "distribution" et "enregistrement". Mais il a finalement effacé tout cela, car il lui semble qu'il s'agit là d'éléments entièrement indépendants les uns des autres, bien que certaines formes artistiques tendent à en provoquer la fusion.

D'abord, "édition". Par cela, M. Lattimore entend l'action de choisir qui comprend celle de rejeter. M. McLuhan a parlé d'un pullulement de documentation qui risque de devenir intolérable. Mais cela a toujours été le cas. Il y a toujours eu, "sur cette terre, plus d'éléments qu'il n'est possible d'assimiler".

Deuxièment, la "création" par opposition à la distribution ou à l'enregistrement. Une grande partie du matériel diffusé par les ondes est le résultat du travail effectué par les écrivains "dans leur propre soipsisme". M. Lattimore est d'avis que tout écrivain doit refuser de faire quoi que ce soit qui l'empêche de travailler au mieux de ses possibilités, et ce non pas en se conformant à des théories, mais bien selon la méthode qui s'impose à lui. Tel est le "véritable secret personnel" de l'écrivain. Quelqu'un de l'extérieur peut lui demander d'écrire sur un sujet quelconque; mais il est impensable qu'il lui dise *comment* l'écrire. L'écrivain sait comment il va s'y prendre, sans cela il n'est pas un écrivain.

M. Podhoretz avait prévu qu'il aurait des "problèmes avec cette machine". Sceptique envers tout ce qui touche à l'expression apocalyptique, il est heureux de voir que M. McLuhan ne parvient pas non plus à faire marcher sa machine. La combinaison du tempérament apocalyptique et de l'historisme technologique est séduisante, elle a en fait ahuri plusieurs participants à la Table Ronde. Cependant, bien que la technologie soit très importante dans certains domaines, M. Podhoretz estime qu'elle ne l'est pas en ce qui concerne l'avenir "où l'on écrirait un livre comme on fabrique un objet matériel". Il a existé des écrivains, des philosophes et des essayistes doués qui ont été des pourvoyeurs d'information. Ce rôle tend de plus en plus à disparaître, de nos jours, remplacé qu'il est par la technologie. Et, comme l'a dit Paul Goodman dernièrement, il se pourrait que ce soit une bonne chose en fin de compte, que la littérature soit de ce fait débarrassée d'une corvée.

Quant à la télévision, M. Podhoretz pense qu'elle est déjà parvenue à "réduire la capacité de se concentrer d'une manière continue sur une page imprimée". Il se peut que la lecture ait toujours été quelquechose de difficile—une activité présentant des problèmes spirituels et intellectuels. Et le fait que la vente de livres ait augmenté parallèlement avec le développement de la télévision ne parvient pas à convaincre M. Podhoretz que cette dernière n'ait pas rendu la lecture encore "drôlement plus difficile".

Si l'on admet ces deux faits—les moyens électroniques sont de meilleurs pourvoyeurs d'information pure, et la télévision a diminué la capacité de concentration sur le caractère imprimé—M. Podhoretz estime que la situation d'aujourd'hui n'est que légèrement différente de celle de naguère, que des difficultés analogues avaient déjà surgi par le passé et que la réaction de l'homme avait été celle de refuser de se laisser dominer.

Après avoir rappelé qu'à la Chambre des Communes, Sir Samuel Hoare avait une fois rejeté une question au sujet du mouvement pour l'autonomie de l'Inde par ces mots "L'Inde est en train de vivre une phase par laquelle passent tous les pays qui se trouvent dans les mêmes circonstances", M. *McLuhan* fait appel au prochain orateur.

M. *Boldizsár* rappelle à l'assistance qu'au 33ème Congrès international du P.E.N. à Bled, il avait présidé à une Table Ronde traitant de *"la littérature et les media de masse"* comme M. McLuhan aujourd'hui. A cette occasion, il avait défendu les media de masse contre un certain snobisme de la part de certains auteurs. Aujourd'hui, il se trouve en train de défendre tous les auteurs contre "l'utopisme alléchant et dangereux" de M. McLuhan. Plus encore, il les défend contre un vaste mouvement de McLuhanisme vulgarisé qui fait rage aux Etats-Unis, surtout dans les universités, ainsi qu'il a pu s'en rendre compte au cours d'une tournée de trois mois dans ce pays. Ceci est dû partiellement à la terminologie percutante de M. McLuhan qui comprend des termes tels que "circuiterie". M. McLuhan a tendance à vouloir faire de l'esprit, et M. Boldizsár trouve dangereux de réduire le sens de son ouvrage *Understanding media* à un simple calembour.

Amoureux de la télévision comme il l'est, M. Boldizsár estime que certaines objections doivent être faites à la position de M. McLuhan. Au début, M. Boldizsár appelait la télévision *horror televisionis,* et ceci jusqu'au jour où il découvrit que les Américains eux-mêmes l'appelaient "la boîte à crétin". En fait, plus que n'importe quel autre *medium,* la télévision a créé un nouveau royaume du rêve, une nouvelle réalité, et bien que le public d'aujourd'hui vive déjà dans cette ère nouvelle, les écrivains n'ont pas encore appris à en faire partie. Mais ils apprendront. Au Congrès de Bled, M. Boldizsár avait dit que ce n'est pas la fin du monde pour la littérature, mais bien le début d'une renaissance littéraire. Et il le répète aujourd'hui, non pas en opposition aux idées dangereuses de M. McLuhan, mais plutôt inspiré par elles. En poussant ses théories jusqu'à l'absurde, M. McLuhan a démontré aux auteurs quels chemins suivre et où ne pas aller. Il a oublié avec tout cela "le mystère de l'acte créateur".

Le président, enjoignant le public à poser des questions, se déclare sidéré par le fait que les participants à la Table Ronde semblent être obsédés par ses idées. Il ne s'identifie pas aux idées qu'il énonce. En fait, certaines lui semblent parfaitement grotesques. Elles ne représentent pas son propre avis. Son rôle est d'inventer des "moyens de sonder l'environnement". Les hommes de lettres ont tendance à identifier une expression à celui qui en est l'auteur, ce qui est fatal en cet âge électronique: Tout ce qu'il a fait en parlant ce matin, était "d'essayer de découvrir ce qui se passe". En effet, lui-même change d'avis tous les jours, en raison de ses découvertes constantes.

Appelé par le président à prendre la parole, *M. Pablo Neruda* s'excuse de ne parler l'anglais que très mal et se qualifie de "poète rustique". Le premier choc émotif que la technique lui ait procuré était dû à "deux poèmes de très grande beauté de Walt Whitman sur la locomotive", lorsqu'il était encore un tout jeune homme. Un autre poème qui produisit un effet analogue fut celui de Hart Crane dont le sujet était le pont de Brooklyn. Il s'agit là d'exemples de "la rencontre entre l'oeuvre de l'homme et l'oeuvre de l'écrivain" qui, une fois de plus, est nécessaire. En ce qui concerne les oeuvres de l'homme, certaines d'entre elles sont en train d'effrayer le monde entier. M. Neruda se souvient de l'extase qui s'empara de lui à l'âge de dix ans, dans son pays le Chili, lorsqu'il vit un avion se soulever et prendre de l'altitude. Il se souvient également des avions qui, des années plus tard, bombardèrent sa maison à Madrid. Le poète s'excuse de faire mention de la guerre, qui n'est pas à l'ordre du jour de la Table Ronde, mais si l'on parle de la peur que l'on a de la technologie, il faut dire que la guerre est, après tout, une des choses dont les hommes ont le plus peur. Il lui semble que plus que la science et toutes ses merveilleuses promesses, l'humanisme de toujours est une des meilleures façons d'y faire face, et d'éliminer la méfiance et la peur.

M. Wilhelm Girnus, du P.E.N. de la République Démocratique Allemande, parlant français, est d'avis que l'ordinateur ne peut pas remplacer les personnalités humaines. Pour lui, la littérature doit se préoccuper de l'être humain en tant que personnalité. L'ordinateur ne peut jamais nous dispenser de chercher et de trouver des décisions morales, c'est-à-dire des engagements de l'homme envers la réalité.

Mme Hilde Domin, du P.E.N. de la République Fédérale Allemande, parlant anglais, dit que M. McLuhan avait parlé du poète dans la "tour de contrôle". Dans le passé, on avait la "tour d'ivoire" que Virginia Woolf avait transformée en une "tour penchée" de laquelle le poète, bien qu'incapable de s'en échapper, avait une vue d'ensemble sur une vaste scène sociale. Mme Domin estime qu'aujourd'hui le poète doit sortir de cette tour et participer à la réalité. Mais il serait vain de prétendre que le poète peut "contrôler" quoi que ce soit. Le contrôle appartient seulement aux "Pentagones" de notre monde. Pour venir à bout des tendances de l'électronique et faire que l'homme reste un être humain, on aurait besoin d'un surhomme nietzschéen.

M. A. den Doolaard, du P.E.N. hollandais, dit, en anglais, que la discussion de ce matin lui avait suggéré que l'homme en tant que centre de communication de l'âge électronique était voué à l'échec. En comparant le profond effet causé par la lecture d'un volume de poésie de M. Neruda, chez lui, et le peu d'effet que lui avaient fait les remarques du grand poète ce matin, il en déduit que le livre est un moyen de communication infiniment supérieur à la parole retransmise électroniquement. M. den Doolaard imagine le jour où l'homme sera aboli, où l'enfant sera transistorisé, dès sa naissance; entre les nouvelles, les prévisions météorologiques et le reste, l'homme devra de temps en temps absorber automatiquement des petits bouts de "littérature autorisée". Pour sa part, M. den Doolaard espère que ce temps ne viendra pas avant qu'il se soit retiré dans "les forteresses perdues de la poésie" où il pourra entendre les bardes de Yougoslavie ou de Crète, des contrées "hill-billy" des Etats-Unis—et de Washington Square.

M. Laurence Lande, du P.E.N. canadien, parlant anglais, pose trois questions: d'abord, comment est-il possible de maintenir et d'approfondir le sens de l'histoire? Deuxième, qu'adviendra-t-il de l'amour des vieux bouquins comme preuve tangible du passé? Troisièmement, si nous songeons que le livre est un élément au travers duquel nous communions avec son auteur, que nous remplissons de notes marginales et qui nous fait rêver, comment imaginer qu'une bande de plastique puisse nous procurer les sentiments que Keats ressentit à la première lecture de l'"Homère" de Chapman? Finalement, il y a le fait esthétique que représente un beau livre: qu'est-ce qui va, à l'avenir, satisifaire ces sens?

DEUXIÈME SÉANCE

M. McLuhan présente un nouveau participant à la Table Ronde, M. Anoma Kanie (P.E.N. de Côte d'Ivoire), puis invite le public à participer à la discussion.

Mme Hélène Rosenau (du P.E.N. anglais) déclare avoir observé deux phénomènes qui semblent indiquer que nous nous trouvons aujourd'hui déjà "dans une période de réaction à ce qui a été décrit ce matin", le premier est qu'il y a plus de professeurs de lettres que de professeurs de science qui postulent des situations dans les universités; le deuxième est la publication d'un livre du professeur Hudson, de l'Université de Cambridge, dans lequel l'auteur déclare que "les hommes créateurs ont un type d'intelligence passablement différent de celui des hommes qui se consacrent à la technologie", et que ce sont en fait les premiers qui sont véritablement des hommes de science. Ceci semble vouloir dire que "notre problème est plus passager qu'il ne le paraît".

M. John Simon (du P.E.N. américain) demande au président pourquoi il a abandonné l'enseignement de la littérature anglaise pour devenir le directeur du Centre de culture et technologie de l'Université de Toronto.

M. McLuhan fait remarquer que le texte imprimé est le seul moyen qui fait l'objet d'un enseignement formel. Il a créé son propre environnement, appelé "public". Aujourd'hui, d'autres moyens ont créé d'autres environnements dans lesquels le texte imprimé doit lutter pour survivre. Afin de sauver le texte imprimé de ces moyens, qui sont les "ennemis de l'imprimé", il faut "sortir de l'environnement". M. McLuhan lui-même est un homme orienté du côté du texte imprimé et pour qui les valeurs en sont "suprêmes". Il se voit entouré de contemporains pour lesquels l'imprimé est une "forme fortuite et périmée". "Les hommes à mono-medium" rendent "le pire des services à l'imprimé en voulant en ignorer les ennemis". M. McLuhan a commencé l'étude des nouveaux media à l'aide de Baudelaire, Rimbaud, et surtout Flaubert. "Mallarmé fut l'un des plus extraordinaires disciples de la technologie", et *Finnegans Wake* de James Joyce est le "manuel des media" le plus remarquable qui soit. T. S. Eliot, Wyndham Lewis et Ezra Pound ont consacré "la plus haute attention aux media et aux grammaires des media".

M. Emery George, du P.E.N. des écrivains en exil, parlant anglais, commence par dire que le souci des hommes de lettres au sujet des moyens de communication autres que le texte imprimé ne représente rien de nouveau. Dans son ouvrage sur la cybernétique, le professeur Norbert Wiener écrivait par exemple que son étude avait été stimulée par les écrits de St. Augustin. Leibniz déjà rêvait d'établir une théorie de la communication. Bien qu'il y ait une part de vérité dans le dicton de Bali—"nous n'avons pas d'art", et dans la déduction que tout, dans l'environnement, était "art"—l'environnement est "artifice" également.

Un écrivain allemand traitant de cybernétique a écrit que "ce que l'homme crée dans l'intention de produire de l'art peut être appelé art". Il est vrai que l'étude moderne de la théorie des communications sous tous leurs aspects peut être extrèmement passionnante, mais il est vrai également que l'information et la "critique théorique" procurent une base rationnelle pour un accord ou un désaccord. Sur ce point, M. George n'est pas d'accord avec les théories de Saul Bellow contre la critique des textes dans son discours à la séance inaugurale. D'où il ressort que la circuiterie électronique doit aider l'homme à devenir non pas moins humain, mais plus humain dans le sens qu'il doit apprendre à mieux se connaître lui-même.

Mme Elizabeth Janeway, du P.E.N. américain, demande que la discussion cesse un moment de planer dans des sphères de morale et d'esthétique pour se préoccuper un peu de l'effet pratique que l'électronique semble avoir sur le revenu (ou plutôt la maigre pitance) des écrivains. Trop souvent des écrits qui jouissent du *copyright* sont photocopiés sans la permission de l'auteur—aux Etats-Unis, des organismes bénévoles essaient de sévir contre ces pratiques en obtenant des sanctions légales. Mme Janeway attire l'attention de tous les écrivains sur ce danger. Comme tous les progrès techniques, la photocopie parviendra à faire disparaître les méthodes plus anciennes, ce qui pourrait même comporter certains avantages, ne serait-ce que d'augmenter le revenu des écrivains qui en ont le plus besoin. Mme Janeway prie instamment que tout en faisant des efforts pour augmenter la distribution, on n'oublie pas les droits des auteurs qui travaillent à leur propre compte, et qui vivent du produit de leur travail autant que de leurs activités intellectuelles.

Le président fait remarquer que ce problème préoccupe énormément les éditeurs.

M. Sutan Takdir Alisjahbana, du P.E.N. indonésien, parlant anglais, remarque que les hommes qui sont possédés par une idée ont souvent tendance à "l'accélérer", et il a l'impression que tel est le cas de M. McLuhan. Après avoir déclaré que "l'invention de la phonétique était un résultat de la détribalisation", il avait ajouté que le développement des différentes langues anglo-germaniques avait élevé des murs entre tribus et que l'écriture non-phonétique des Chinois avait fait de la Chine entière un grand peuple tribal. (M. McLuhan l'interrompt pour expliquer que la "détribalisation"—et par tribal il entend ici un mode de vie familial sans individualisme intense—ne peut pas être le fait d'un mode d'écriture idéogrammique mais bien celui de l'alphabet phonétique, qui "spécialise le sens visuel", donc individualisé.)

M. Alisjahbana poursuit son exposé en déclarant que la communication est une fonction de la société et de la culture. Quand les hommes n'avaient pour tout instrument que leurs mains et leurs pieds, leur culture était très limitée. Avec l'avènement de l'industrialisation elle est devenue globale. Par réaction, les écrivains actuels ont tendance à se retirer en eux-mêmes, et à qualifier cette civilisation d'absurde. M. Alisjahbana prie instamment les participants à la Table Ronde de persuader le public ici présent que la nouvelle civilisation mondiale a besoin d'une "nouvelle avant-garde fondée sur les accomplissements de la science, de l'économie et de la technologie".

M. Wilfred Cartey de Trinidad, parlant anglais, fait remarquer que jusqu'à présent il n'y avait pas eu de véritable dialogue à cette Table Ronde; chaque orateur s'y était assis fermement convaincu de ses propres idées, et les avait maintenues inchangées. Sa sympathie va au président qui a été attaqué sans répit, et auquel on a attribué le rôle d'un anti-être, d'une machine qui se bat à l'arrière-garde contre le reste. Pour sa part, M. Cartey estime que l'attitude de l'écrivain face à une réalité nouvelle devrait être d'essayer de lui donner une conscience et une émotion, mais les écrivains ont bien au contraire déclaré ici même qu'ils tournaient le dos à l'âge électronique. Par exemple, en ce qui concerne la télévision, il pense que c'est à l'écrivain de travailler avec elle, de joindre ses forces, afin de l'empêcher de végéter. De l'avis de M. Cartey, c'est à l'écrivain qu'il appartient d'améliorer la qualité de cette chose qui lui fait peur. Ce n'est pas le medium en lui-même qui a de l'importance, mais le fait qu'il existe, qu'il soit réel, et l'écrivain doit oser le regarder en face.

Le président invite le public à commenter les remarques de M. Cartey et ajoute que si, dans le domaine du cinéma ou de la télévision, l'écrivain reste la plupart du temps dans le plus sombre anonymat, son moi est hautement entretenu par le texte imprimé. Il demande à Mme Victoria Ocampo, vice-présidente internationale du P.E.N. de prendre la parole.

Mme Ocampo (du P.E.N. argentin), en anglais, raconte une anecdote qui mène à une question. Quelques années après la deuxième guerre mondiale, elle eut une entrevue avec Bertholt Brecht à Berlin. Il lui demanda si, à son avis, les peuples de langue espagnole d'Amérique latine "comprenaient" le poète García Lorca. Sa réponse fut la suivante: littérairement parlant, non, mais émotionnellement, oui. Brecht dit alors que pour lui, ceci était le grand problème. Et Mme Ocampo pose la question suivante: "L'ère électronique peut-elle trouver une solution au problème posé par Brecht?"

M. Boldizsár donne une réponse affirmative à Mme Ocampo. La télévision et la radio ont apporté la poésie et la littérature au domicile de millions de gens qui n'avaient jamais entendu parler de poésie. Il ajoute que selon sa propre expérience—aussi brève soit-elle—de l'Amérique latine, le livre n'est en général pas largement accessible aux masses et dès lors il présume que García Lorca n'est pas très répandu. Dans ce sens, il est très en faveur de l'âge électronique!

Mme Ocampo explique qu'en employant le terme "masse" elle comprend "ceux qui croient qu'ils sont cultivés"; c'est-à-dire des hommes qui ne sont à la page que cinquante ans après les autres.

Voix d'homme, parlant anglais: que deux problèmes distincts ont été embrouillés, dans la discussion de cet après-midi. L'un d'eux est le rapport de l'écrivain avec les nouveaux media. A la question: "faut-il écrire pour la télévision ou faut-il la boycotter?" l'écrivain est libre de répondre comme il veut. L'autre problème traite de l'influence prédominante de l'électronique sur la sensibilité, la prise de conscience, le mode de vie, etc. A son avis, M. McLuhan a exagéré cette influence. Il est évident qu'elle est immense, mais le président en parle comme si nous étions en train d'assister "à une sorte de mutation non pas de la civilisation mais de l'espèce humaine". Il n'y croit pas, et il estime que cela n'est d'aucune conséquence quant à l'attitude des écrivains envers la xérographie ou la télévision. En fait, il croit que la xérographie contribuera à une plus grande diffusion du texte imprimé, et non pas le contraire. A part la question argent, rappelée par Mme Janeway, l'écrivain n'a rien à craindre; le défi s'adresse à la presse d'imprimerie et au typographe, pas à l'écrivain.

Mlle Nott, faisant allusion à la remarque de M. Tabori ("ce serait agréable si au cours d'un congrès du P.E.N. on parlait de l'écrivain en tant qu'écrivain") déclare que dans ce cas, la chose à faire serait de conseiller à l'écrivain de l'ère électronique d'ignorer l'ère électronique. Après tout, il ne s'agit ici que de moyens. Or, on n'apprend pas à marcher en comptant ses pas ni à respirer en comptant son souffle.

M. de Campos ne croit pas qu'un écrivain abandonne sa faculté morale de prendre des décisions en reconnaissant être un adepte des nouveaux media. A son avis, il n'y a pas de différence entre un ordinateur et son crayon. William Carlos Williams, le poète américain, écrivit un jour qu'un poème était une "machine faite de mots", et en faisant cette déclaration il n'avait pas jugé nécessaire de faire des élucubrations sentimentales au sujet de cette machine.

M. Gandon rappelant au président qu'il avait mentionné Mallarmé, cite les mots du poète selon lesquels "tout doit aboutir à un livre". Il semble à M. Gandon que dans une certaine mesure, on a parlé ici un peu dans le vide. On a donné l'impression que la télévision était un organe librement ouvert à tous les écrivains. Malheureusement ce n'est pas le cas en France où il y a, jusqu'à présent, deux sortes d'écrivains: ceux qui continuent à écrire des livres et qui voudraient, peut-être, écrire pour la télévision, et d'autre part les spécialistes qui semblent être les seuls écrivains auxquels la télévision soit ouverte. M. Gandon se demande s'il faut être un spécialiste pour être admis à la télévision. S'agit-il d'un nouveau moyen d'expression qui demande des qualités et des techniques nouvelles? Si oui, M. Gandon le regrette, mais il craint que l'on ait parlé pour rien à cette Table Ronde.

Voix d'homme, parlant anglais: une déclaration malencontreuse du programme implique que l'usage universel des nouveaux media pourrait conduire à une ère dans laquelle la conscience individuelle de l'être humain serait absorbée par une sorte de conscience cosmique". Le président se reconnaît-il responsable de cette déclaration? M. McLuhan ayant répondu "oui, mais seulement en tant que sondage", l'orateur proteste, estimant que ceci ne représentait pas un but valable pour un homme civilisé, et que ce n'était pas juste d'essayer de mobiliser tous les écrivains sous l'étendard d'une pareille idéologie. Il n'aime pas le mot "masse", et trouve que c'est un terme difficile à définir. A son avis, l'écrivain doit tout d'abord avoir un sens de son propre "fardeau humain", posséder un mode d'expression personnel. En employant des expressions comme "étendre nos informations conscientes" on risque de faire des fétiches avec des trucs techniques tout simples.

M. Darko Suvin (du P.E.N. yougoslave de Zagreb), parlant anglais, propose de se joindre à ceux qui font objection aux "idées effrontées, scintillantes, embryonnaires et parfois contradictoires" du président. Ce n'est pas parce que M. Suvin languit après le bon vieux temps, qui n'avait certainement pas que des bons ou que des mauvais côtés. Le président a rendu service à tous ceux qui ont assisté à cette Table Ronde en raison du fait qu'il a "identifié la situation dans laquelle les technologues constituent notre nouvel environnement, sont nos fenêtres sur le monde nouveau"; pour citer la phrase très Joycienne du président, "ils portent l'humanité comme une peau". M. Suvin désire également faire remarquer qu'information et signification ne sont pas la même chose. La chansonnette publicitaire qui ne transmet rien que de l'information force l'auditeur à être conscient du moyen électronique; tandis qu'en écoutant Mozart—ou Louis Armstrong, selon ce que l'on préfère—on est tout d'abord conscient de la musique. Par conséquent, la question est de savoir si les écrivains vont constituer une peau saine ou une peau malsaine (pour faire usage de la métaphore de M. McLuhan). Savoir si cette fenêtre s'ouvrira sur le monde de l'imagination ou sur le monde de l'irrévocable. La question de savoir si nous voyons l'avion en tant que triomphe de l'ingéniosité humaine ou transporteur de bombes peut également être posée au sujet des moyens discutés aujourd'hui. Bien que M. Suvin soit un marxiste, il estime que la situation est "indéterminable". La question, c'est de savoir si les nouveaux media vont dégrader l'oeuvre littéraire, ou au contraire permettre une plus grande puissance créatrice.

La littérature et les sciences humaines devant la condition de l'homme contemporain

mercredi 15 juin
PREMIÈRE SESSION

Louis Martin-Chauffier, PRÉSIDENT
Membre de l'Académie des Sciences morales et politiques, Paris

Sutan Takdir Alisjahbana
Indonésie

Leon Edel
New York University, New York

Ralph Ellison
New York

Heinz Kamnitzer
Berlin-Est

Cheik Hamidou Kané
Dakar

Rudolf Krämer-Badoni
Wiesbaden

Dr. Jost A. M. Meerloo
New York

Leda Mileva
Sofia

Maurice Nadeau
Paris

Dr. Ramon Parres
Mexico

jeudi 16 juin

DEUXIÈME SESSION

Louis Martin-Chauffier, PRÉSIDENT
Paris

Joseph W. Abruquah
principal de l'école Mfantsipim, Cape Coast, Ghana

Claude Arsac
Genève

Ralph Ellison
New York

Jean Follain
Paris

Sei Ito
Tokyo

Cheik Hamidou Kané
Dakar

Maurice Nadeau
Paris

Dr. Ramon Parres
Mexico-City

Mihail Petroveanu
Bucarest

La littérature et les sciences humaines devant la condition de l'homme contemporain

PREMIÈRE SÉANCE

M. Louis Martin-Chauffier ouvre la discussion en rappelant à ses collègues que, dans le large cadre du thème général du congrès, *l'écrivain en tant qu'esprit indépendant,* on leur avait demandé de limiter leurs déclarations au sujet particulier qu'ils avaient à traiter: *la littérature et les sciences humaines devant la condition de l'homme contemporain.* De l'avis du président, si quelques savants savent vraiment écrire, nombreux sont ceux qui n'en sont pas capables; s'il y a quelques écrivains qui connaissent à fond une science ou une autre, nombreux sont ceux qui n'ont aucune prétention à des connaissances scientifiques. En attendant, il est clair que les savants écrivent dans un langage qui leur est propre et les écrivains dans un autre. Le sujet à traiter devant cette Table est essentiellement l'écrivain en tant que tel, et on peut le décrire comme étant un homme ayant quelquechose à dire, l'exprimant dans un style personnel, sans se laisser influencer par les modes et capable de leur survivre. Son sujet peut être complexe, mais sa langue est finalement accessible à tous: Proust est mentionné comme exemple. On peut dire que l'écrivain est en fait indépendant des sciences sociales ou humaines en grande partie parce que les savants n'ont pas le don d'expression de l'écrivain.

L'écrivain est un artiste; et un artiste est un homme qui cherche d'abord son plaisir et ensuite à communiquer ce plaisir aux autres. Il en résulte que ce qu'il écrit est personnel, inimitable; on peut le pasticher; on ne peut pas le copier dans ses intentions.

Le Dr. Meerloo, parlant anglais, dit qu'on lui a demandé quelques points de départ pour la discussion. Il commencera donc en faisant remarquer que tous les hommes, sans omettre le poète et "l'artiste révolutionnaire", "sont nés dans un langage particulier", et tout au long de leur croissance ont été influencés par les concepts, les modes de pensée, et les styles que leur entourage leur impose. Ils sont en outre influencés, comme Charcot l'a remarqué il y a presque un siècle, par le jeu de la mémoire involontaire, de telle façon qu'ils sont poussés à reproduire, "plagier" leur expérience accumulée inconsciemment. Ceci également leur procure un style particulier. Parmi les influences plus récentes on constate celles des divers aspects de la technique, entre autres cette sorte d'hypnose exercée par la télévision ainsi que les effets de la production en masse des imprimés. Quand, en outre, on nous demande si l'homme est un "penseur indépendant", notre réponse doit tenir compte des mouvements suscités par "l'irrationnel", qui est "une façon de donner de nouvelles significations aux choses". C'est en considérant ces quatre éléments que l'on peut arriver à déterminer jusqu'à quel point l'écrivain est à même de créer dans un esprit d'indépendance—particulièrement en se libérant de l'influence des appareils électroniques.

Le président, avant de passer la parole à l'orateur suivant, définit à nouveau le sujet comme étant "l'écrivain menacé dans sa recherche de la nature de l'homme"—l'homme qui n'a pas changé alors que la société evoluait, les activités culturelles se sont élargies et multipliées, tandis que les media de masse tendent de plus en plus à abaisser l'être humain plutôt qu'à l'èlever.

M. Krämer-Badoni, parlant français, commence en citant des exemples de la tendance impliquée dans le suject et résume en disant que "le but de Freud n'a pas été d'offrir des modèles aux écrivains, mais de guérir des malades". Les malades figurent parmi les personnages les plus intéressants de la littérature. John Ford, auteur contemporain de Shakespeare, n'a pas fait dans "Dommage qu'elle soit une putain" une étude scientifique de l'inceste; sa pièce est une tragédie traitant de l'amour éperdu ravageant un frère et une soeur; ce n'est pas du tout l'étude d'un "cas" basée sur des "enquêtes".

L'être humain, continue M. Krämer-Badoni, est à la fois un individu et un être social, et pour être mieux à même de vivre dans la communauté humaine, l'homme a besoin d'être parfaitement renseigné sur la condition humaine. Mais l'artiste—même politiquement ou socialement engagé—souffre, se réjouit, subit le destin, est un anarchiste, crée des symboles de la réalité qu'aucune science n'est capable de créer, et l'artiste ou l'écrivain vivent dans un monde imperméable à la science, qui appartient entièrement à l'art.

M. Ellison, qui suit, attire l'attention sur le rôle "joué par la sociologie contemporaine qui tend à se substituer à l'art." Le sociologue, au lieu de se borner à réunir des données et les classifier, devient un "mani-pulateur de cette mythologie" qui est une création de la sociologie. Cela a eu pour résultat de persuader quelques écrivains, quelques artistes, d' abandonner leur croyance en "l'autonomie de l'art". De tels écrivains cessent de regarder en eux-mêmes, cessent de chercher dans les trésors de connaissance accumulés dans la littérature pour apprendre à connaître l'homme et la société. Ils se tournent au contraire vers les sociologues pour apprendre ce qu'est l'animal humain, ce que sont les valeurs hu-maines, dans quelle direction la littérature doit se diriger et quels doivent être les critères de la création artistique.

L'une des fonctions les plus sacrées de la littérature n'est-elle pas précisément de disséquer les rouages de l'expérience humaine, de re-vivre ce qui est éternellement humain, dans les chefs-d'oeuvre du passé, le rationnel et l'irrationnel, et de donner une forme et une signification nouvelles à l'éternel humain. Ceci est une tâche des plus importantes, l'art est en fait le moyen principal pour l'homme de préserver son humanité. Le sociologue ne peut participer à cette mission qu'à condi-tion d'écrire en artiste, ce qui se trouve de temps à autre. Il est à dé-plorer, ici aux Etats-Unis, que tant d'écrivains aient perdu courage face aux "données massives de la sociologie". L'homme ne peut se réaliser, se sentir faisant partie d'une fraternité et devenir conscient de la richesse de l'expérience humaine si poètes et éditeurs—M. Podhoretz, par exemple, qui prétend que le roman est mort—acceptent de confier la tâche de décrire la vie et de définir les valeurs humaines à des "ma-chines indifférentes".

Le Dr. Parres, parlant anglais, dit que beaucoup de gens semblent se sentir menacés par la machine à l'âge électronique. Il peut y avoir quelque vérité dans l'idée que l'écrivain se sent oppressé par la machine. Mais ne devrions-nous pas garder présent à l'esprit que, pour l'homme créateur—dans les sciences aussi bien que dans les arts—la chose im-portante est l'acte de créer. La machine elle-même a été le résultat d'un acte créateur de l'homme; et le but de sa création était sûrement de contribuer à une vie meilleure pour tous les hommes. Le Dr. Meerloo nous a cité Descartes: le Dr. Parres n'aime pas Descartes qui a divisé l'homme en un corps et une âme. Au lieu du "je pense, donc je suis" de Descartes, il suggère "je cherche donc je suis". Le Dr. Parres dénonce le danger de citer des donnés sociologiques hors de leur contexte. Selon lui, la tâche de l'artiste, de l'écrivain, consiste en une introspection qui lui donnera une certaine connaissance de l'homme: et son importance réside dans le fait qu'il exprimera cette connaissance de façon esthétique, tout en lui donnant une signification plus profonde. L'aggressivité est un phénomène psychologique, et pourtant Dostoïevski en a parlé dans ses romans de façon plus mémorable que n'importe quel savant. L'écrivain cependant, et nous tous avec lui, y compris les patients du psychiâtre, ne peut vivre en dehors des influences qui l'entourent.

Le président, avant de donner la parole à M. Nadeau, fait remarquer qu'il a entendu jusqu'à présent une succession de monologues très intéressants. Il demande cependant aux orateurs d'essayer, dans la mesure du possible, de commenter ce qu'ils ont déjà entendu, de façon que par cet échange de vues la discussion puisse y gagner en continuité et en forme.

M. Nadeau fait remarquer que Shakespeare et Balzac ont pratiqué la psychologie avant que la science psychologique n'existât. Les écrivains se sont occupés de la vie sentimentale et instinctive de l'homme longtemps avant que les spécialistes—qui naturellement ont leur place dans la société—n'apparaissent avec leurs instruments, leurs méthodes et leur jargon. Le savant cherche à communiquer une information dans son langage; l'écrivain, en tant qu'artiste, n'a rien à voir avec l'information; son but n'est pas d'augmenter les connaissances de l'homme; son domaine est différent parce qu'il utilise le langage d'une manière particulière; et quant à l'écrivain gardien des valeurs humaines, comme M. Ellison semblait le suggérer, M. Nadeau est partagé à ce sujet.

Le rôle de l'écrivain réside dans l'usage d'un langage, usage qui est à la fois gratuit et nécessaire, pour exprimer ce qu'il sent, ce qu'il pense, et pour manifester ces situations limites que les sciences ne peuvent exprimer. L'amour par exemple. La science s'occupe beaucoup de l'amour, analysant, classant, allant même jusqu'à mesurer la durée de l'orgasme; cependant que peut-elle nous dire des sentiments qu'éprouve l'amoureux? Ou la mort. Qui, si ce n'est l'écrivain, peut dire ce sentiment de la mort qu'éprouve un individu particulier à un moment donné? La seule chose qu'on puisse espérer voir résulter d'une confrontation d'écrivains et de savants est peut-être une nouvelle définition de la littérature. On pourra alors différencier les savants et les littérateurs. Tous deux ont leur place et doivent être reconnus; il n'y a, ni d'un côté ni de l'autre, à avoir de l'admiration ou du mépris.

M. Edel relève une remarque de M. Krämer-Badoni selon laquelle l'artiste est libre d'exprimer son inspiration créatrice et sa vision du monde. "Mais", demande M. Edel, "que dire des inventions de notre temps qui sournoisement harcèlent l'artiste?" Il a visité le Walden Pond de Thoreau, espérant communier tranquillement avec la nature: il y a trouvé des remorques de camping et entendu la clameur des télévisions. Il a visité la Villa d'Adrien en Italie seulement pour se trouver entouré de charmants jeunes Italiens munis de transistors retentissants. Voilà, dit M. Edel, quelles sont les puissances liguées contre nous.

Pour éviter de voir un film de guerre à la télévision, il a changé de station—et il est tombé sur un documentaire sur la guerre. Serait-ce trop s'avancer que de dire que le public, cette grosse éponge, finira par perdre le pouvoir de distinguer entre la réalité et la fiction? Qu'à cause de cela peut-être, les gens de New York avaient tout récemment assisté de leurs fenêtres au meurtre d'une femme et n'avaient pas appelé la police? Tout ceci est certainement pertinent pour l'écrivain. Il écrit pour un public. Le public change. On le désensibilise, le dissocie. "Je pense que M. Ellison a raison de dire que la sociologie nous donne de l'homme une image toute faite et conventionnelle". M. Edel attribue ceci particulièrement à l'influence qu'exerce la publicité qu'il estime infiniment plus dangereuse que le fait que les intellectuels académiques tuent la littérature à force d'en parler, ainsi que s'en plaint M. Bellow.

Quelle est la réponse? Le Dr. Meerloo a insinué que les écrivains n'étaient pas véritablement indépendants: "Je dis que nous avons seulement l'illusion de l'indépendance". Ce ne sont pas les lecteurs qui aideront les écrivains à faire de cette illusion une réalité: et ceci implique peut-être que le critique a une tâche et un devoir aujourd'hui plus grands que jamais. Cela signifie peut-être également qu'une "part de l'engagement de l'écrivain consiste à être aussi un critique, critique de toutes ces conventions et de toutes ces horreurs de notre temps".

Puis, M. Edel donne son appui à M. Martin-Chauffier qui recommande une recherche constante de la perfection du style et de la pureté du langage, ainsi qu'un engagement dans la lutte contre l'influence exercée par le langage semi-lettré, extravagant et sans forme, du journalisme et de la publicité. De réels dangers existent, et le plus menaçant est la désensibilisation de l'individu, qui devient un simple spectateur de la réalité au lieu d'y participer.

M. Hamidou Kané, qui parle français, dit qu'en tant que Sénégalais il représente une "civilisation orale plutôt qu'écrite", vivant dans un monde avançant vers la "totalisation". Pour une telle civilisation, dans un tel monde, la mission de l'écrivain est particulièrement importante. La plupart de ceux qui ont étudié les peuples de l'Afrique noire étaient des ethnologues et des anthropologues étrangers à ce continent, alors que la sensibilité africaine, les valeurs traditionnelles africaines ne peuvent être bien exprimées et interprétées que par les poètes et les artistes de l'Afrique elle-même. C'est en ceci que réside l'importance des artistes pour leur propre peuple.

Mme Mileva parle anglais. Partageant ce qu'elle apelle le point de vue optimiste—peut-être même réaliste—qu'aucun effort de la psychologie ni des sciences sociales ne peut transformer la littérature en un simple sous-produit, elle dit qu'elle perçoit néanmoins un pessimisme larvé, particulièrement chez ses collègues américains. Ils semblent déroutés par l'électronique, la cybernétique, la nouvelle psychologie et tout le reste. Les meilleurs écrivains bulgares, eux, ont été prêts à endurer la pauvreté, la souffrance, et même la mort, pour transmettre leur message à leur peuple. Ne vaudrait-il pas mieux accepter le défi et créer une littérature encore plus élevée et plus significative?

Aujourd'hui nous pouvons changer des déserts en palmeraies, mais nous sommes également capables de créer de vastes et terribles déserts. Nous sommes les témoins de réalisations scientifiques, mais le mot "guerre" reste dans nos dictionnaires. La psychologie peut expliquer les réflexes intérieurs les plus subtils, mais elle est incapable de lutter contre les égarements de l'esprit, l'avidité et l'indifférence de l'homme, ainsi que l'a fort bien souligné M. Edel. Manifestement ceci n'est pas suffisant.

Puis, Mme Mileva aborde un point qui n'a pas encore été discuté jusque là—l'écrivain qui prend comme sujet la société plutôt que l'être humain renonce-t-il de ce fait à une partie de son indépendance? Il lui semble que l'écrivain qui choisit de traiter de l'âme humaine seulement, traite malgré lui de la société par la même occasion. Ceci est vrai en ce qui concerne Gogol, par exemple, ou Tchékhov; vrais egalement, en d'autres temps et d'autres circonstances, pour Kafka. "Ni l'érivain en tant qu'individu, ni les personnages qu'il crée ne peuvent échapper à la société". Quant au choix entre s'enfermer pour écrire "uniquement" de l'âme, ou s'ouvrir à l'extérieur pour examiner tout l'horizon des relations humaines, Mme Mileva dirait qu'il y a, dans la littérature moderne, de nombreux exemples de la première sorte d'écrivains produisant des fantômes sans chair ni os. Sans foi en l'homme, sans la volonté de construire un monde meilleur, la littérature lui semble n'être qu'un cri de désespoir. C'est une sorte de maladie que d'écrire des cris de désespoir, mais une maladie dont on ne peut dire que souffrent les écrivains qui ont traversé les océans et les continents pour participer à un Congrès du P.E.N.

M. Alisjahbana, parlant anglais, dit que les progrès accélérés de la science depuis la Renaissance ont atteint un état de crise aigu, dans lequel la technologie est l'élément le plus important. Nous devons comprendre tout ce que cette crise implique avant de chercher à définir la place de l'écrivain. "L'expansion de l'homme dans le temps et l'espace" qui en résulte a été accompagnée d'une diminution du sens religieux, du sens de la conscience, de la force intégrante de la personnalité humaine à tel point que nous pouvons dire que l'homme contemporain a été "vidé par l'intérieur". Il n'est pas étonnant que les maladies mentales soient aujourd'hui les maladies les plus courantes, se répandant dès que la société industrielle prend racine, même dans le pays "sous-développés". Et avec la croissance de nombreux nouveaux États nationaux, de nouvelles tensions entrent dans le champ de la politique. Tout ceci a été perçu par des philosophes sociaux tels que Spengler en Allemagne et Ortega y Gasset en Espagne.

De nombreux écrivains se sont par conséquent réfugiés dans le monde des émotions et des rêveries poétiques. D'autres se sentent les victimes de la société industrielle, et ici il semblerait que ce sont les écrivains des Etats Unis qui sont les moins aptes à faire face à leur situation. Nous nous souvenons comment une génération précédente, la génération "perdue", s'échappa vers Paris dans les années vingt. Nous avons vu Nelson Algren et Norman Mailer rejeter la civilisation industrielle. Il est caractéristique que quelques écrivains américains envient maintenant les sociologues.

Mais, de l'avis de M. Alisjahbana, les sociologues eux-mêmes n'ont pas su relever ce même défi. Les psychologues, les sociologues et les anthropologues ne peuvent plus se parler, si profond est le bourbier de terminologie dans lequel ils sont enlisés respectivement. D'autre part, les savants "purs" n'ont pas de langage par lequel ils peuvent communiquer avec nous autres.

Il apparaît au *Dr. Kamnitzer* (parlant anglais) que quelques orateurs précédents considèrent qu'ignorer le monde contemporain, ou rester indifférent à son endroit serait "presque comme l'estampille du poète". Cesi l'amène à se demander comment un aveugle trouve son chemin. Etant lui-même sociologue, il est apparemment l'un des terribles manipulateurs de M. Ellison. Mais, à son avis, ce n'est pas le sociologue qui pose le problème, c'est le poète, le dramaturge, l'artiste. S'il est vrai, comme le fait remarquer le programme, que "l'écrivain n'éclaire plus l'homme sur sa nature et son esprit" et que "la littérature peut être maintenant une ressource technique", alors c'est l'écrivain lui-même qui est à la source de son propre dilemme: aujourd'hui ce n'est pas Hamlet, mais l'espèce humaine qui pose la question "être ou ne pas être"; ce n'est pas le poète, ou le mieux adapté, dont la survivance est en question, mais nos institutions. Pour adapter le vers de T. S. Eliot: "Voici comment finit le monde, non pas avec des gémissements, mais avec fracas". Si l'écrivain doit influencer son semblable, it doit s'engager et "je demande instamment qu'il s'engage". De plus en plus souvent on manque d'idéal et de visions amples dans certains écrits d'aujourd'hui. Certains pensent qu'il est presque blasphématoire de s'occuper des souffrances qui existent. Brecht, qui était marxiste—ce qui était sa prérogative—disait que c'était presque un crime d'écrire au sujet des arbres alors que des méfaits étaient commis constamment; pourtant il a écrit lui-même un merveilleux petit poème au sujet d'un peuplier planté au milieu d'un square dévasté de Berlin. A vrai dire, il traitait en même temps de la nature et de l'humanité.

Le Dr. Kamnitzer fait remarquer que le programme mentionne l'existence d'un véritable avidité de documentation; il y a cependant aussi une aspiration à la poésie, plus grande que jamais, du moins dans son pays. "L'homme a faim de pain et de roses, et il se détournera avec dédain et chagrin si on lui offre des pierres à la place".

M. John Coutsoheras, président du P.E.N. grec, parlant de la salle en français, fait objection à quelques commentaires du programme qui disent qu'à la source des oeuvres littéraires du passé il n'y avait ni jaugeage, ni analyse, ni enquête sociale, mais bien contemplation, connaissance de soi, et imagination créatrice. A son avis, les uns n'excluent pas les autres. Le programme mentionne aussi une tendance des lecteurs contemporains à se détourner de la littérature pour s'adresser aux écrits des sociologues et des psychologues afin de trouver la lumière sur la nature de l'homme contemporain. M. Coutsoheras demande la permission de résumer les vues d'Aristote à ce sujet.

L'assistance se rappelle qu'Aristote trouve la source de la littérature dans la *mimesis,* l'imitation de la vie; mais pas de la vie extérieure seulement, de la vie intérieure également; cruauté, pitié (Ελησς) et catharsis, ou purification des passions. Aristote ne s'arrête pas là; l'homme est aussi un animal social. D'où on devrait conclure qu'il n'y a pas lieu de craindre que la littérature contemporaine ne devienne secondaire simplement parce qu'elle se préoccupe de la société. Comme le président l'a dit si bien tout à l'heure, le poète et le romancier créent par leur imagination, dans un style, dans un langage qui n'appartient pas aux sociologues.

DEUXIÈME SÉANCE

M. Louis Martin-Chauffier prie instamment les délégués de la Table Ronde d'essayer d'établir des dialogues et d'éviter de prononcer des monologues. Puisque le temps a manqué lors de la première session pour entendre les commentaires de la salle, il commencera par leur consacrer vingt minutes.

M. den Doolaard dit qu'un écrivain n'a pas à craindre que les sciences ne l'emportent sur son indépendance d'esprit tant qu'il sera capable de "maitriser les choses nouvelles". Il pense que les sciences sociales sont utiles au romancier. Zola, qui prenait des notes volumineuses en est un exemple frappant. Il est d'accord avec Mme Mileva que les écrivains sont des membres de la société, et avec la citation d'Aristote de M. Coutsoheras—l'homme est un animal politique. Pour les écrivains, l'univers est leur sac à provisions; ils n'ont qu'à y prendre ce dont ils ont besoin et ignorer le reste.

M. Follain (du P.E.N. français) approuve cette phrase de Victor Hugo: "la forme c'est le fond qui remonte à la surface". La forme et le fond sont indissociables et la littérature ne peut être remplacée par aucune autre forme d'art. Certes l'humanisme traditionnel semble être en recul. Les écrivains se sont aperçus que le raisonnement socratique n'était pas suffisant; qu'ils dépendaient plus qu'ils ne le croyaient du cosmos et du social; mais cela constitue un enrichissement plus qu'une déperdition. De même, une certaine psychologie traditionnelle se trouve entamée par une psychologie plus fluide, plus mystérieuse, moins assurée. La nouvelle sociologie révèle une communion humaine dont le totalitarisme est une caricature grossière. Malgré tout, la personnalité individuelle demeure irremplaçable. Beaucoup d'écrivains ont tendance à renoncer trop facilement à leur indépendance et manifestent ce que Jean Paulhan appelle une "terreur" dans les lettres, qui les amène à répudier des mots tels que "art" et "inspiration", et à adopter un jargon désincarné. Mais les autres, conscients de leur communion et de leur communication avec l'univers, sont fortifiés par un sentiment d'indépendance aux racines plus profondes.

M. Mansukhlal Jhaveri (du P.E.N. All-India) parlant anglais, résume certains faits fondamentaux: un certain degré d'échange entre l'écrivain et la société est inéluctable: néanmoins l'écrivain doit garder une totale liberté d'expression; il devrait avoir cette étincelle que nous appelons génie, et pour tirer la lumière de cette étincelle il lui faut rester en contact avec la vie et l'étudier. Il ne perdra pas son indépendance d'esprit en choisissant de faire usage des techniques et disciplines les plus récentes pour arriver à mieux déterminer la place de l'homme dans l'ordre des choses—à condition que l'homme lui-même reste l'objet de son étude.

M. Tome Momirovski (du P.E.N. yougoslave de Skopje), parlant anglais, observe que l'indépendance d'esprit de l'écrivain créateur est en danger d'être vulgarisée par les sujets qui lui sont offerts sur une "planète limitée et contradictoire". Qu'est-ce qui limite cette indépendance? Les clameurs et les discordes du monde? Doit-on trouver la solution dans une "théorie synthétique ou analytique de la totalité humaine"? Dans la longue histoire de l'émancipation de l'homme il semble que nous ayons atteint maintenant un point où la personnalité de l'artiste se sépare de la réalité sociale. Un processus d'aliénation est en cours; l'écrivain peut essayer soit de le dominer, soit d'y échapper en cherchant refuge dans une "névrose illusoire".

M. Czeslaw Milosz (du P.E.N. des écrivains en exil) parlant anglais, propose de poursuivre un dialogue avec Monsieur Nadeau, le Dr. Kamnitzer et M. Edel. Il y a des gens, dit-il, qui épluchent les préoccupations de Tolstoï dans *Guerre et Paix* en partant de conceptions abstraites telles que liberté et nécessité, masse et individu, etc. Il a un ami, un jeune poète polonais, qui estime que la poésie ne devrait pas être "emprisonnée", et dont l'idéal se situe dans les temps pré-socratiques "quand la poésie et la philosophie ne faisaient qu'un". M. Milosz opte pour la zone située entre la connaissance et la littérature; cette zone, bien qu'elle se déplace d'âge en âge, est un lieu de refuge à l'abri de ces savants en sciences sociales et politiques dont les précurseurs s'appelaient publicistes et qui sont aujourd'hui des journalites employant un jargon compliqué et jouissant du prestige des chaires d'université. Il est surprenant de voir des écrivains s'humilier devant des soi-disant savants, car une littérature—le théâtre de l'absurde par exemple—qui tourne à la parabole philosophique et à l'investigation, n'a aucune raison de mettre l'écrivain en déroute. La cause de ce sentiment de défaite n'est-elle pas due à une crise de la philosophie elle-même, comme un professeur l'a écrit dans un récent article intitulé "La Philosophie américaine est morte"?

M. Dragomir Nenoff (P.E.N. des écrivains en exil), parlant anglais, dit que nous nous trouvons en présence de deux écoles, l'une qui prend la défense de "la reproduction électronique de la littérature", alors que l'autre cherche à "augmenter la source d'idées originales". Il croit qu'elles finiront par former un tout; il ajoute encore que le danger pour l'esprit libre ne pourrait venir que de l'importance excessive accordée à la première par cette Table Ronde, alors que la seconde est passée sous silence.

M. Abruquah, du Ghana, parlant anglais, se présente en tant que sociologue et directeur de collége. Les sociologues présents, dit-il, ont "tendance à nous éblouir par leurs excursions dans les technicités". Les écrivains ont essayé vaillamment de défendre leur indépendance, oubliant néanmoins qu'ils sont eux-mêmes, en tant qu'écrivains, les pourvoyeurs de matière première pour les media de masse. Le fait est qu'on ne peut revenir à un âge pré-scientifique. On ne peut dire que la science est "complètement fausse", parce que la Bible affirme que l'univers a été créé en six jours. Ce que l'on veut dire, probablement, c'est que le rôle de la littérature est d'insuffler la vie à l'argile de la science.

Autrefois les écrivains étaient une aristocratie; ils étaient les philosophes de leur époque. Les écrivains d'aujourd'hui devraient s'inspirer de leurs prédécesseurs. "Je suis sûr", dit M. Abruquah, "que les écrivains modernes sont plus aptes à scruter la vérité de la nature de l'homme" précisément à cause de l'apport des sociologues à leurs connaissances (même si c'est en disséquant l'homme en de petites entités classifiées). C'est pourquoi il ne voit pas la nécessité de cette controverse. Les oeuvres de littérature qui dureront restent celles qui insufflent âme et vie dans l'homme.

Mme Claude Arsac (du P.E.N. suisse de Genève) qui est sociologue et l'auteur de trois romans, se réfère tout d'abord à la déclaration que M. Edel a faite le jour précédant, disant que, si la culture s'élargit, elle n'élève pas l'homme pour autant, et qu'on désensibilise l'être humain. Ceci est, à son avis, particulièrement le cas aux Etats-Unis dont la télévision, avec sa violence, ses meurtres et ses rixes, est nettement inférieure à la télévision européenne. Certes l'écrivain ne peut plus s'enfermer dans une tour d'ivoire, ne pas se préoccuper du tout du contexte social et politique dans lequel il vit. Mais le marxisme "avec son contexte de haine et de violence", lui paraît un source bien maigre d'inspiration. Cependant, elle donne raison au Dr. Kamnitzer qui a dit qu'un écrivain de notre temps doit être *engagé*, ne serait-ce que dans une lutte pour la sauvegarde de la vraie beauté dans un monde sans âme. La mission de l'écrivain est de créer la beauté, de veiller à ce que les hommes demeurent réceptifs à l'art véritable. Elle réfute la notion exprimée lors de la première session, à savoir que l'écrivain comme personnage social se différencie absolument de l'écrivain en tant qu'individu forcément anarchiste. Ce n'est pas "anarchiste" qu'il faut dire, mais "non-conformiste", et par non-conformiste elle entend "cet homme dont les actes sont le produit de sa nature profonde". Avec C. G. Jung et Bernanos elle s'insurge contre le robot. Et elle cite l'avertissement du professeur Gourvitch qui dit que lorsqu'on exalte la vie intérieure de la personne, qu'on l'oppose à l'extériorité du social, on ne doit pas identifier arbitrairement la vie sociale toute entière avec la masse anonyme, qui ignore ce qu'est la vraie communauté. Le vrai sentiment social est intense; il est une forme de communion intime avec les autres. Le P.E.N. lui-même en est un exemple—les écrivains n'ont aucune raison de craidre la concurrence des sciences, précisément parce que la littérature est un art.

M. Ito (du P.E.N. japonais) parlant anglais, dit qu'un psychologue japonais lui a affirmé que "de nos jours, nous n'avons pas besoin de romanciers dans la société. Le psychologue fera tout ce qu'ils ont fait jusqu'à présent". Cette remarque l'a plongé dans de profondes réflexions. Le problème de la littérature lui paraît assez compliqué; de même que celui de la peinture qui semble avoir "perdu son caractère religieux depuis que l'art photographique entreprend de dépeindre des "choses idéales". Le roman a été à certains égards remplacé par le document, la "non-fiction". Sans aucun doute certains livres de psychologie intéressent les lecteurs plus que le roman ordinaire. Dans le monde occidental, certes, la roman réaliste a traité l'analyse des rapports entre êtres humains, en tous cas jusqu'à ce que Freud apparaisse, donnant lieu à des changements. La psychanalyse a mis à jour des rapports nouveaux, entre mère et fils, père et fille, par exemple; rapports qui sont inhérents à la nature. Le but de la littérature est de décrire l'homme tout entier. Néanmoins peut-on nier que, dans un certain sens, les oeuvres scientifiques ont pris la relève du romancier?

En résumé, dit M. Ito, on ne peut nier la valeur ni des sciences, ni de la littérature.

M. Paolo Milano (du P.E.N. italien), parlant anglais, s'insurge contre la tendance qu'on a de décrire la science comme étant une étude "d'aspects isolés de la réalité" et l'art comme "la puissance divine qui affronte l'homme dans son universalité, et la réalité dans sa totalité". Il doute fort que les écrivains, passant tour à tour de la réalité cosmique à cet individu, l'homme "total", sachent ce qu'est l'universalité. Deuxièmement, la notion de "l'influence des sciences sur l'art" lui paraît une formule défectueuse. D'une part l'écrivain est libre, il n'est pas obligé de puiser dans les sciences pour sa compréhension de la réalité. D'autre part le monde des lettres et de l'art contemporains a de lui-même une approche scientifique de son travail. On parle d'art symbolique, d'art structural, d'anti-roman, de "roman-document". Qu'est-ce que cela prouve si ce n'est que l'artiste se demande s'il est vraiment possible de saisir la réalité par une conception scientifique, tandis que le savant, lui, qui affronte un aspect isolé de la réalité qu'il sait multiple, doute de la validité de sa propre recherche qui est limitée.

M. Petroveanu (du P.E.N. roumain) parlant français, se demande si le problème posé à la Table Ronde est vraiment aussi crucial qu'on ne le fait paraître. Il y a plus de quarante ans, le poète et philosophe roumain Lucien Blaga a relevé les correspondances unissant la vision de Picasso et les géométries non-euclidiennes, ainsi que l'expressionnisme, à la "psychologie abyssale". A la Renaissance, l'artiste et le savant ne faisaient qu'un. Au XIXe siècle la thermodynamique associée à la philosophie du positivisme d'Auguste Comte donna naissance à la théorie de la volonté, force motrice de la comédie humaine. Le Romantisme lui-même a produit les "hallucinations lucides" d'Edgar Poë et le "naïf optimisme scientiste" de Victor Hugo. Aujourd'hui nous voyons la psychanalyse influencer les pièces des surréalistes, d'Arthur Miller, de Tennessee Williams, et le marxisme les pièces de Brecht et son école. A ce point, M. Petroveanu s'insurge contre la haine et la violence imputées au marxisme par Mme Arsac, disant que le marxisme est un instrument de libération de l'homme et que même les critiques catholiques reconnaissent qu'il a un but humanitaire visant à fusionner essence et existence, ce qui est justement le but même de la littérature. Qu'on puisse en mésuser est incontestable; mais personne ne blâme le catholicisme parce que les Jésuites en ont fait un instrument de terreur à un certain moment.

Pour en revenir au sujet de la Table Ronde, quelle que soit la matière utilisée par l'écrivain ou l'artiste, c'est ce qu'il en fait qui importe; et la question essentielle est: quels sont la fin et les moyens de l'art et de la science respectivement? Le poète américain Emily Dickinson a écrit: "Il y a une couleur là-bas, sur les cimes de collines solitaires, que jamais la science ne recomposera, mais qui à jamais bouleversera l'homme".*

Mais le sujet de l'artiste ne se réduit pas au domaine de l'ineffable, il s'étend également à celui de la nature humaine, et c'est là que la littérature rencontre les sciences. Les méthodes de la science ne sont pas celles de la littérature, elles tendent à l'objectivité, ou pour citer le critique hongrois Lukács, elles tendent à "désanthropomorphiser le monde". L'art au contraire, est une forme subjective d'accès à la réalité, saturée d'humanité et créant un monde pleinement anthropomorphique. De plus, le langage de l'écrivain est ambivalent: il est d'une part un moyen de communication, d'autre part un moyen de création, d'invention de nouveaux univers et en même temps le soutien des valeurs esthétiques.

En tant que moyen de communication, il n'en est qu'un parmi d'autres pour informer l'humanité. Même quand la littérature essaie d'être purement impersonnelle et analytique—comme dans Flaubert, ou le "nouveau roman" français contemporain—et qu'elle est fascinée par les procédés objectifs de la science, elle reste un produit de la conscience individuelle. C'est pourquoi, même si l'écrivain proclame que son point de départ est le marxisme, la psychanalyse ou toute autre théorie ou science, ses implications humaines survivent aux théories scientifiques sur lesquelles il a fondé ses concepts littéraires.

En résumé, la littérature transforme les idées scientifiques en des éléments de mythe; la propre volonté de Balzac dote ses personnages d'une énergie qui leur donne la dimension de figures mythiques. L'écri-

---

* A color stands abroad/ On solitary hills
That science cannot overtake/ But human nature *feels*.

vain qui soumet la science à l'art est un conquérant, tandis que l'écrivain qui assujettit l'art à la science assure sa propre défaite. La littérature atteint son but par des voies détournées qui ne sont pas celles de la science. En se battant sur son propre terrain, avec ses propres armes, ou même aidée par des moyens empruntés à la science, elle nous offre le spectacle fascinant de la conscience humain se débattant avec les problèmes de la vie et de la mort de l'individu et de la société, réussissant, selon l'expression de Huxley, "à dévoiler ce qu'il y a de bas dans le haut, et de haut dans le bas de la condition humaine".

Mme Arsac intervient pour expliquer que M. Petroveanu l'a mal comprise. Elle n'a pas voulu attribuer les défauts de la télévision des Etats-Unis aux marxistes, et bien qu'elle n'ait aucun désir de se lancer dans une controverse, elle veut exprimer l'espoir qu'il nous est permis de croire qu'il existe des moyens plus adéquats et plus fructueux que le marxisme pour essayer de concilier l'essence de l'homme avec son existence.

Le président annonce une pause d'un quart d'heure, après quoi sept orateurs de la salle prendront la parole, chacun étant prié de ne pas parler plus de cinq minutes.

A la reprise de la session, le *Dr. David Abrahamsen,* (du **P.E.N.** américain), s'insurge contre la déclaration métaphorique de M. Abruquah qui dit que la "science c'est l'argile dans laquelle la littérature insuffle la vie". Il dit à M. Ito qu'il pourrait présenter à ce collègue qui n'a plus besoin de romanciers cent ou mille psychologues qui pensent encore qu'écrire un roman est une entreprise justifiée. En tant que psychanalyste il voudrait dire que les influences environnantes (y compris celles produites par les moyens électroniques) qui agissent sur l'esprit humain, varient selon la personnalité de l'individu en cause, celle des écrivains comprise. La soif de gain matériel fait parfois partie du caractère de l'écrivain; mais nous ne devrions pas oublier non plus que pour un écrivain qui gagne de grosses sommes, il y en a un nombre incalculable qui écrivent sans se préoccuper d'argent.

Quant aux écrivains affrontant les sciences, le Dr. Abrahamsen affirme que "si vous êtes un bon écrivain, vous n'avez rien à craindre". Il y a eu de grands poètes avant et après Freud; ce dernier a simplement systématisé notre connaissance de tous les intérêts, idées et instincts, décrits par les poètes. C'est l'intégrité personnelle du poète qui compte.

Voix d'homme parlant anglais: critique une phrase des remarques du programme qui dit: "Aujourd'hui, nous dit-on, l'homme se détourne de la littérature pour s'adresser au sociologue et au psychologue afin de savoir où se trouve l'essence de l'homme—ou du moins celle de l'homme contemporain". Et il dit: "J'estime qu'il est faux d'affirmer qu'en tant que source d'information la littérature ait une valeur égale". Après avoir fait remarquer que la littérature et la science peuvent parfaitement bien être le complément l'une de l'autre, l'orateur déclare que "très peu d'écrivains ont été de grands penseurs à l'état pur; l'écrivain a toujours pris des idées dans l'atmosphère qui l'entoure"; en fait "idées" est encore un terme mal choisi, car l'écrivain s'est toujours appuyé sur l'expérience. A la vérité aucun écrivain ne s'adresse à des livres de science pour trouver des idées; "il n'est jamais à ce point mécanique".

Le président, exprimant son accord avec le commentaire du Dr. Abrahamsen sur la "systématisation" des pensées et des instincts des poètes par Freud, ajoute que les écrivains ont beaucoup de choses à apprendre de Freud, mais qu'il s'en servent d'une autre façon qu'il ne l'aurait fait.

Le Dr. Henri-Jean Barraud (du P.E.N. français) note que les remarques du programme ont omis de mentionner une catégorie d'écrivains: les philosophes. L'écrivain n'est pas seulement un artiste, il est aussi, à sa manière, un philosophe. Cela est inévitable, quoique l'écrivain s'exprime "en images" et le philosophe professionnel en concepts. L'écrivain, cependant, ne s'explique pas, il suggère simplement; il est "libre d'évoluer entre le rêve et la réalité". Mais si leurs modes d'expression diffèrent, tous deux, écrivain et philosophe, ont les mêmes sources d'information qui, pour la littérature aussi bien que pour la science, sont universelles. Tous deux aussi doivent rejeter une attitude préordonnée et, en outre, leur but est le même: la connaissance de l'homme.

Le second point du Dr. Barraud est amené par la remarque faite par M. McLuhan au cours de la première Table Ronde disant que "l'histoire est le royaume de la nostalgie". Pour nous, c'est une erreur fondamentale; l'histoire est en quelque sorte la matrice de l'avenir. La pensée européenne a été imprégnée des idées d'Aristote jusqu'à la naissance de l'esprit scientifique au XVIIe siècle, qui a mis fin à la communion qui avait régné jusque là entre le philosophe, l'artiste et l'écrivain. Ce point, dit le Dr. Barraud, a été décisif, car dès lors la science a cherché à imposer la mesure et la quantité à ceux—l'écrivain, le philosophe, l'artiste—dont le domaine était la qualité. Etant donné la prodigieuse efficacité de la science expérimentale d'une part et l'idéal de qualité qui anime l'écrivain d'autre part, nous nous trouvons devant "deux mondes absolument séparés". Le Dr. Barraud croit qu'en maintenant la primauté de la qualité sur la quantité, l'écrivain a devant lui un avenir splendide.

Le président, tout en appréciant la défense de la philosophie du Dr. Barraud, fait remarquer que la philosophie contemporaine s'exprime souvent en un jargon emprunté, en fait, au vocabulaire scientifique. Il voudrait qu'on fasse la distinction entre les philosophes professionnels et ceux qui ont été d'abord des écrivains—en France, un Montaigne, un Alain. Un homme se préoccupe-t-il ou ne se préoccupe-t-il pas de bien écrire, voilà la question. Le Dr. Barraud a parlé d'histoire. M. Martin-Chauffier est lui-même un chartiste et un archiviste paléographe par sa formation; il croit aux documents historiques, mais beaucoup moins à l'interprétation de l'histoire qui lui paraît n'avoir de valeur que dans la mesure où l'historien est un écrivain et un penseur, puisque les interprétations des historiens sont toujours le produit de leurs conceptions personnelles. La valeur de Michelet, par exemple, réside dans les vérités qu'il découvre par son intuition, par l'esprit qui brûle en lui. En parlant ainsi, ajoute le président, c'est un avis d'historien qu'il donne.

M. Pham Viet Tuyen (du P.E.N. du Viet Nam) parlant français, examine premièrement le public de la littérature. Il prend comme exemples une jeune fille dans une rizière vietnamienne chantant des vers folkloriques, une ménagère de Hong-Kong se passionnant pour un ancien roman chevaleresque, un professeur américain en train de lire un essai sur l'esprit indépendant à l'âge électronique. Aucun d'eux ne demande à son auteur de lui donner des éclaircissements sur la nature de l'homme; c'est une question que se pose une petite minorité seulement. Ils demandent de la littérature qu'elle leur procure un plaisir comme le vin ou le thé et qu'elle leur permette de s'évader des réalités terrestres.

Deuxièmement l'orateur parle des connaissances scientifiques et littéraires. Les éclaircissements apportés sur l'essence de l'homme par la psychologie ou la sociologie sont le produit d'un regroupement méthodique de connaissances disparates; ces connaissances sont plus ou moins fidèles à la réalité, à la vie, cette vie même que le poète, le romancier ou le dramaturge s'efforce de saisir au vol. Pour comprendre, par exemple, l'idéalisme du mouvement actuel contre la guerre, aux Etats-Unis, on devrait venir vivre ici quelque temps. Et pour pouvoir communiquer les aspirations de liberté et de paix du peuple vietnamien on devrait avoir vécu les cruautés endurées par ce peuple depuis 1959.

M. Pham Viet Tuyen aborde troisièmement la question des oeuvres littéraires et et des ouvrages scientifiques. C'est un fait que les oeuvres d'Homère nous éclairent sur l'essence de l'humanité et nous émeuvent encore; une oeuvre littéraire peut encore produire un effet plus profond qu'un ouvrage scientifique quoi qu'en dise un psychologue ou un sociologue.

Quant aux écrivassiers et aux vrais écrivains, il se peut que l'étude des disciplines nouvelles nuise à l'écrivassier et le submerge, alors qu'elle favorisera l'écrivain de talent. Ayant à leur disposition de plus amples moyens pour comprendre l'homme et la société, les génies créeront des personnages plus originaux et peut-être même immortels.

Mme Jean Durtal (du P.E.N. français), après avoir salué le congrès au nom du Comité de la Société des Gens de Lettres de France, dit que les écrivains du XVIIIe siècle sont à la source des idées de liberté, et que les écrivains romantiques et réalistes du XIXe sont les inspirateurs de la sociologie. A notre époque, dit-elle, "un certain déséquilibre" est né de la divergence des voies suivies par la science et par la littérature. Le développement extraordinaire de la science remplit l'homme à la fois d'une peur et d'un espoir immenses. Or c'est entre ces deux émotions que Mme Durtal voit "la place du véritable rôle de l'écrivain". Son rôle est "d'édicter cette loi d'amour sans laquelle l'évolution du monde ne sera pas possible", loi qui est l'espoir de l'homme et la clef de l'humanité. Mme Durtal met en garde les savants contre le danger de tout effort visant à prendre en mains la direction du monde, "alors que cette direction revient aux penseurs et aux écrivains que nous sommes". Elle insiste sur le fait qu'il n'existe qu'un problème, celui de "l'évolution harmonieuse du monde".

M. Nadeau, interpellé par le président pour dire ce qu'il pense de cette loi d'amour dont les écrivains seraient les propagateurs, dit: "Eh bien, bien sûr, je suis pour l'amour, mais enfin. . .". Un des sujets proposés par la Table Ronde devrait être examiné: l'habitude d'emprunter un moyen scientifique dans des buts artistiques. Un américain, Oscar Lewis, a enregistré au Mexique, à l'aide d'un magnétophone, l'histoire de la vie d'une famille du nom de Sanchez, vivant en ville, puis de celle d'une famille paysanne, les Martinez. Voilà le cas d'un sociologue que les écrivains feraient bien d'examiner. Lewis n'est pas un écrivain professionnel; il use d'un moyen électronique, et fait pourtant une oeuvre d'art. Un second exemple, dû peut-être à l'air raréfié dans lequel travaille le nouveau roman, est celui des écrivains en France qui cherchent le retour à la réalité en enregistrant simplement les conversations des gens qu'ils ne décrivent même pas. M. Nadeau voudrait poser la question à laquelle il ne peut répondre lui-même: comment le résultat de ces efforts peut-il atteindre la qualité d'une oeuvre d'art?

Voix d'homme parlant anglais: dit que la question "est bien ardue". Le travail de découpage de bande magnétique—une sorte de montage —que Lewis a accompli pour la composition de ses livres est analogue, en forme, au travail du cinéaste. Il y a, pourrait-on dire, une intervention intellectuelle et même artistique. Il y a également l'intervention des traducteurs, car, si M. Nadeau a lu *Les Enfants de Sanchez* en français, il a lu la traduction du texte anglais d'Oscar Lewis, qui lui-même l'a composé d'après l'espagnol parlé qu'il avait enregistré—et pas de l'espagnol simplement, mais d'un dialecte mexicain de l'espagnol.

L'écrivain en tant que collaborateur aux desseins d'autrui

mercredi 15 juin
PREMIÈRE SESSION

Robert Goffin, PRÉSIDENT
membre de l'Académie Royale de la Langue et de la Littérature
Françaises, Bruxelles

Jean Bloch-Michel
Paris

Philip A. Hope-Wallace
Londres

William Jovanovich
président de Harcourt, Brace & World, New York

Melvin Lasky
directeur de *Encounter,* Londres

Paolo Milano
Rome

Victoria Ocampo
fondatrice et directrice de *Sur,* Buenos Aires

Bogdan Pogačnik
Ljubljana

Elmer Rice
New York

Dolf Sternberger
Frankfurt-am-Main

jeudi 16 juin

DEUXIÉME SESSION

Robert Goffin, PRÉSIDENT
Bruxelles

Piero Chiara
Varese, Italie

Marchette Chute
New York

Alberto S. Florentino
éditeur de 'Peso Books,' Quezon City, Philippines

Philip A. Hope-Wallace
Londres

William Jovanovich
New York

Donald Keene
Columbia University, New York

Edward Lucie-Smith
Londres

Victoria Ocampo
Buenos Aires

Dolf Sternberger
Frankfurt-am-Main

L'écrivain en tant que collaborateur dans les desseins d'autrui

PREMIÉRE SÉANCE

M. Goffin ouvre la séance en déclarant qu'il a accepté l'invitation à présider cette discussion avec plaisir et quelques réticences. Les notes du programme définissant leur thème ne lui pasaissent pas tout à fait claires. Il voudrait l'opinion des participants à cette Table Ronde et commence par demander à M. Elmer Rice quelle serait sa définition du thème.

M. Rice est d'avis que cette table ronde doit discuter des effets que peuvent avoir les nouveaux arts mécanisés sur les écrivains qui sont appelés à y collaborer dans les formes les plus diverses. Il a lui-même écrit, il y a quatorze ans, un article intitulé "L'écrivain industrialisé" qui traite de ce sujet, et il espère avoir la permission d'en lire quelques extraits.

M. Pogačnik, parlant anglais, craint que le genre de littérature qu'on leur demande d'examiner ne soit pas le produit de génies, mais bien plutôt l'oeuvre de ceux qui travaillent dans le domaine des communications de masse. La question reste néanmoins de savoir comment ces écrivains, dont le nombre est considérable, peuvent, quel que soit leur talent, garder leur "moralité" et rester des écrivains vraiment honnêtes et indépendants.

M. Sternberger qui suit, parle aussi anglais. Le sujet lui paraît plus vaste que M. Rice l'a esquissé, car il a l'impression qu'il s'agit ici non seulement des media, mais aussi et surtout des patrons! L'écrivain au service d'un gouvernement, d'une doctrine, d'un éditeur commercial, de l'administration d'un théâtre.

M. Jovanovich estime que le sujet, tel qu'il est défini dans le programme, implique que l'écrivain est constamment "violé." Pourquoi

d'ailleurs faire une distinction entre les écrivains et les autres hommes?
Pour le moment il voudrait que l'écrivain cesse "d'être sentimental à
son propre sujet".

Mme Ocampo, parlant français, est d'avis que les ressources nouvelles
ont en effet mis les écrivains devant un problème de conscience, un
problème moral. Il est clair que ces "terribles moyens de communication" peuvent être employés pour le mieux ou pour le pire. Sur ce
point elle est d'accord avec M. Sternberger.

M. Bloch-Michel commence par approuver les déclarations de M.
Jovanovich: qui sont ces "autres hommes" auxquels on oppose les
écrivains? Le thème tel qu'il leur est proposé peut être cependant défini
de deux façons. Premièrement est-il vrai que les conditions dans lesquelles l'écrivain écrit et publie sont maintenant si différentes qu'elles
menacent son indépendance spirituelle? Par exemple les éditeurs ont
toujours commandé des livres. Deuxièmement, est-il vrai que le fait
d'avoir eu à se plier aux exigences des nouveaux moyens techniques—
le cinéma, la radio, la télévision—ait privé l'écrivain de son indépendance?

M. Hope-Wallace voit tout d'abord une différence bien simple entre
écrire sur le plan journalistique et écrire sur le plan artistique. Lorsqu'on écrit en tant que journaliste, on s'engage au service de quelqu'un
et on accepte les servitudes que cela implique, même les "corrections des
rédacteurs en chef". Un bon journal, cependant, n'interviendra pas trop
sérieusement dans votre travail. La seule forme grave de correction
réside, selon son expérience, dans les coupures de texte. L'oeuvre littéraire pure, par contre, qui est pour l'écrivain un moyen de se faire
plaisir à lui-même, devrait rester "inviolable dans la plus grande
mesure du possible". Les servitudes du journalisme doivent être ac-
ceptées, même lorsque les coupures du rédacteur en chef, dans la critique d'une pièce par exemple, nuisent à l'écrivain, à la pièce, et à l'acteur
dont le nom a peut-être été biffé. Mais il existe différentes formes de corrections. Les notes du programme mentionnent par exemple un "style
maison". M. Hope-Wallace connaît un magazine dont les éditeurs trans-
forment et condensent régulièrement les "morceaux personnels" de
nombreux journalistes pour produire un article qui falsifie toutes les
contributions originales. Cette pratique va s'accroissant et elle représente un danger réel pour l'indépendance de l'écrivain.

M. Lasky admet que la distinction faite par M. Hope-Wallace est importante, il ajouterait cependant qu'une "certaine forme de journalisme élevé vaut mieux qu'un art de basse catégorie". Il demande qu'en
corrigeant les manuscrits des poètes et autres écrivains créateurs on ne

tombe pas dans les fâcheuses habitudes du journalisme de masse qui tend à "tripoter, couper, censurer, tordre et récrire". Il a l'impression que cette tendance n'est pas accidentelle, mais qu'elle correspond à un manque de respect pour la parole et pour l'indépendance de l'écrivain.

M. Milano, parlant anglais, suggère qu'il faut trouver si la liberté d'expression de l'écrivain est entravée par quoi que ce soit d'inhérent aux media de masse. Voilà, selon lui, le fond du problème. Il se demande si les participants à cette table ne devraient pas examiner des questions telles que: "Qu'est-ce qu'un spectacle de télévision? Qu'est-ce qu'une émission de radio dans l'état présent de la civilisation? Qu'est-ce que la publication de masse?" Certain disent qu'une représentation d'Antigone de Sophocle à la télévision ne peut être qu'une trahison en vertu de la nature même du moyen employé, et qu'aucun idéalisme, aucun degré d'intelligence ne pourront l'empêcher.

M. Hope-Wallace cite le vieux dicton italien: *traduttore traditore.* Pourquoi, demande-t-il, une représentation d'Antigone à la télévision serait-elle nécessairement plus mauvaise qu'une traduction anglaise du grec? Dante, par exemple, est probablement intraduisible en bantou. On doit faire des concessions, quel que soit le moyen de communication. Le producteur de télévision peut parfaitement bien dire à l'écrivain: "Vous écrivez pour des gens qui ne sont par en train de lire, mais qui regardent et écoutent; c'est pourquoi vous devez 'mettre le nom ici et le verbe là'." Cette restriction de la liberté de l'écrivain est nécessaire pour assurer la valeur artistique de la production télévisée. La télévision n'est pas le seul moyen dont les limitations gênent la transcription ou la traduction d'une complexité reconnue comme étant "un chef d'oeuvre".

M. Sternberger insiste premièrement sur le fait que les oeuvres produites par ces media sont le plus souvent le résultat d'un travail d'équipe et non pas d'un travail individuel, et deuxièmement que "l'affaire de l'écrivain"—qu'il soit confesseur, amuseur ou conteur—c'est "l'affaire de tous les hommes" et non pas l'affaire des media de masse seulement.

Le président prie les orateurs d'être brefs s'ils désirent que la discussion progresse et il leur rappelle que leur sujet est "la confrontation de l'écrivain avec les difficultés qu'il rencontre". A son avis, la question la plus importante est de savoir si l'écrivain doit répondre aux désirs du public ou s'il doit écrire dans une forme que le public ne saisira que plus tard. Il prend comme exemple le poète Emily Dickinson, une femme qui ne réussit à convaincre ses éditeurs de publier que six poèmes de son vivant, alors que cinquante ans après sa mort on avait déjà écrit cinquante livres à son sujet. Mallarmé a écrit: "Nous sommes l'opacité mélancolique de nos futurs fantômes"; et en dédiant un poème à Théophile Gautier il a écrit: "Le poète est le héros des espérances posthumes". Voilà pour l'écrivain et le public.

M. *Rice* pense que les idées qu'il a publiées en 1942 sont encore valables, et il en citera quelques unes au cours de sa déclaration. Lorsqu'il s'y est inscrit en 1914, la Ligue des auteurs américains était composée de romanciers, de dramaturges et de poètes. Plus tard apparurent la Guilde des écrivains du cinéma puis la Guilde des écrivains de la télévision. La première préoccupation de la Ligue était de s'occuper de tous les problèmes touchant à la protection des droits d'auteurs. Avec l'avènement du cinéma et, plus tard, de la radio et de la télévision, elle s'occupa des problèmes de syndicats, de conditions d'emploi et de "listes noires" (exclusion d'écrivains sous prétexte, vrai ou faux, d'appartenances idéologiques). Les importantes préoccupations matérielles des écrivains travaillant pour le cinéma et la radio-télévision les amenèrent à se retirer de la Ligue des auteurs et à fonder leurs propres associations professionnelles. La signification de ce mouvement est claire: elle reflète le glissement rapide de l'écrivain de la position de créateur indépendant à celle de salarié. Aujourd'hui la Ligue des auteurs ne s'étend pas aux dizaines de milliers d'écrivains qui gagnent leur vie en tant qu'écrivains salariés travaillant pour des journaux, des publications commerciales, la publicité et les *public relations*. C'est seulement dans le domaine de l'édition et du théâtre, et jusqu'à un certain point dans celui des magazines, que l'écrivain américain reste réellement un écrivain indépendant. Sous l'influence des pressions exercées par la mécanisation et la standardisation, écrire a cessé d'être une "occupation personnelle et librement choisie". Même le certain degré d'indépendance dont jouit encore l'écrivain est précaire en raison des changements bien connus survenus dans le monde de l'édition. Quant au théâtre new-yorkais, il a passé de 280 pièces jouées dans 70 théâtre en 1926, a 60 pièces dans 30 théâtres lors de la saison 1965–1966.

Pour laisser du temps à d'autres orateurs M. Rice dit qu'il s'en tiendra là et demande à l'assistance de bien vouloir réfléchir à ces faits.

M. *Bloch-Michel* se permet de dire qu'il ne croit pas que la citation de Mallarmé faite par le président soit une définition valable pour la littérature en général. On ne peut dire que l'écrivain écrit pour lui seul et sans occuper de l'accueil qui sera fait à son travail. M. Bloch-Michel cite Dickens comme étant un auteur qui écrivait pour son public. On peut dire qu'il y a deux sortes d'écrivains, ceux qui écrivent pour eux-mêmes (tout en pensant ou ne pensant pas à l'avenir) et ceux qui ont un contact immédiat avec le public.

Dickens—sans parler d'Eugène Sue (tombé dans un oubli immérité), qui a influencé Dostoïevski entre autres—Dickens donc, a pu exercer une influence sur un large public au moyen du *feuilleton,* qui paraissait fragment par fragment. Ceci n'est plus possible de nos jours, car le feuilleton a été remplacé maintenant par la télévision et la radio, pour lesquelles Dickens et Sue travailleraient s'ils étaient encore en vie. Est-ce que cela diminurait leur indépendance d'esprit? M. Bloch-Michel pense que non; pour lui le noeud du problème réside dans le fait important qu'aucun écrivain n'est forcé de travailler pour ces moyens de communication. Les Mallarmé de notre époque écrivent dans leur cabinet de travail alors que d'autres, avides de contacts et d'influence sur le public, se soumettent aux exigences de la télévision.

M. Jovanovich commence par se présenter comme étant non seulement un écrivain mais aussi un éditeur. Lors de sa première déclaration il avait parlé de sentimentalité; on en a beaucoup discuté autour de la table ronde sur l'âge électronique. M. Podhoretz avait relevé la difficulté qu'avait M. McLuhan à faire fonctionner ses machines électroniques. Difficulté qui n'était pas due à une faillite de la technique mais plutôt à un échec des êtres humains et même de l'humanisme. Lors d'une réunion récente des écrivains allemands, la *Gruppe 47* bien connue, M. Jovanovich a entendu une discussion traitant de ce sujet sous le titre "L'écrivain souffre-t-il de la technologie et de l'opulence?" A cette réunion là, tout comme à celle-ci, on a suggéré que l'écrivain avait un rôle à jouer en tant que modèle et guide. A son avis, l'écrivain n'a jamais eu ce rôle et ne l'a pas non plus de nos jours. C'est une notion sentimentale à laquelle tous les écrivains semblent être enclins. L'inquiétude de M. Milano au sujet de la télévision semble excessive à M. Jovanovich. Quiconque a lu les mystères, moralités et soties du Moyen-Age—qui font partie de l'enseignement universitaire, non pas en tant que littérature mais en tant qu'histoire culturelle—remarque deux choses: ils étaient écrits et joués pour les masses, et la plupart étaient "pires que les scénarios de télévision d'aujourd'hui".

Il est bien connu que les gens lisent aujourd'hui plus de livres que jamais; il est moins connu que ceux qui passent tout leur temps libre à regarder la télévision n'ont jamais lu de livres avant qu'elle n'apparaisse. M. Jovanovich croit que rien ne devrait survivre qui ne soit plausible et viable. La disparition de formes littéraires—le poème épique par exemple—n'est pas un fait nouveau. Si le roman venait à disparaître, la cause n'en serait pas "les desseins d'autrui". Si l'essai meurt (M. Jovanovich est un essayiste) ce sera parce qu'il ne trouve plus de public. Contrairement à M. Rice, il croit qu'il y a en Amérique probablement plus de bons écrivains aujourd' hui qu'il y a cinquante ans; l'accroissement de la lecture des livres en témoigne. Il n'est pas d'accord non plus avec l'affirmation que la littérature est mise en péril par le fait que des rédacteurs "récrivent" des textes; il y a un "nombre énorme" de mauvais écrivains dans le monde. Il est de première nécessité que l'écrivain soit exigeant vis-à-vis de son propre art. Les écrivains qui désirent être des "modèles et des guides" pour autrui devraient prendre garde à ne pas être confus.

Mme Ocampo dit qu'ils ont en Argentine un grand écrivain du nom de Jose Hernandez qui est intraduisible. Son livre, *Martin Fierro*, a été lu par tout argentin capable de lire; ses poèmes s'apprennent par coeur, même par ceux qui ne savent pas lire. Il y a aussi Jorge Luis Borges qui est reconnu depuis trente ans—pas par les masses cependant—comme un écrivain de grand talent. Voilà deux exemples de la diversité des voies empruntées par les écrivains pour s'adresser aux hommes. En ce qui concerne les moyens mécaniques, Mme Ocampo veut mentionner seulement *Under Milk Wood* de Dylan Thomas qu'il a désignée comme "pièce écrite pour des voix". Elle l'a traduite en espagnol avec un collaborateur, l'a lue à une troupe d'acteurs et l'a travaillée avec eux pendant quinze jours. Au début ils ont été déconcertés; à la fin ils étaient enthousiastes. Bien sûr il a été difficile aux masses de comprendre, de saisir les intentions de l'auteur, et par "masses" Mme Ocampo n'entend pas illettrés, mais gens qui peuvent lire et qu'on estime capables de comprendre ce qu'ils lisent. *Under Milk Wood*, une pièce magnifique, a été écrite spécialement pour la radio.

Le président demande si la salle a des commentaires à faire.

M. James Ngugi (du Kenya) parlant anglais, se reporte à une remarque faite en passant par M. Hope-Wallace, et dit qu'il n'existe pas de langue bantoue à proprement parler, mais qu'il y a les langues bantoues. Le swahili par exemple en est une. Quant aux limitations de vocabulaire, il ne faut pas oublier que les livres anglais et français ont été traduits dans certaines de ces langues. M. Ngugi continue en disant que "nous, en Afrique, nous ne pensons pas que l'art soit sacré . . . et notre but est d'employer tous les moyens en notre pouvoir pour atteindre notre peuple". Quant à lui, il est prêt à récrire n'importe quel poème pour pouvoir atteindre son public.

Mme Claire Sainte-Soline (du P.E.N. français) dit que, ayant été récemment dans l'obligation de lire un grand nombre de romans, elle a remarqué que, dans le roman contemporain, l'action semble avoir diminué d'importance, que l'espace du temps a été progressivement écourté, que le décor s'est aménuisé (se limitant parfois à un simple lit) et que le nombre des personnages est réduit. C'est pourquoi le roman en tant que source d'information ne semble plus être ce qu'il a été. C'est la télévision maintenant qui nous ouvre le monde. Zola, dans *Le ventre de Paris,* a décrit les Grandes Halles de Paris: aujourd'hui c'est la télévision qui le fait. Puisqu'il en est ainsi, quel est donc de nos jours le but du roman? D'étudier l'individu—et elle n'entend pas *un* individu —dans toute sa complexité. Pour ce faire, le romancier emploie un style trés méticuleux, très précis. Madame de Sainte-Soline ne peut donc approuver la déclaration du programme qui dit que "l'oeuvre bien écrite cède la place au travail bâclé". A son avis, c'est le long roman démodé qui est hâtivement et mal écrit, et où les incidents comptent beaucoup plus que la beauté du langage. Elle ajoute finalement que certaines "prérogatives" entravent bel et bien l'indépendance de l'écrivain. Les clubs du livres, les éditeurs de séries proposent que les auteurs écrivent sur commande. Les auteurs ont des réticences, se plaignent à leurs amis qu'ils vont écrire un livre qui ne leur dit rien, et une semaine plus tard ils se sont persuadés qui'ils ont choisi le sujet eux-mêmes. Naturellement, cela n'est pas vrai pour les romans, qu'aucun éditeur ne peut commander à son idée.

Mlle Rosamond Lehmann (du P.E.N. anglais) approuve tout ce que M. Hope-Wallace a dit, ainsi qu'une grande partie des déclarations de M. Jovanovich, excepté son mot "sentimentalité" qu'elle remplacerait par "conscience de soi-même". Si elle a bien compris ce qui a été dit, l'idée serait que les écrivain avaient écrit ou devaient écrire en gardant un oeil sur le public. Cela ne lui paraît pas exact pour les écrivains créateurs qui écrivent sous "une sorte de pression imaginative qui leur procure un certain plaisir" et dont le but est de transmettre ce plaisir aux lecteurs. Ce que le lecteur pensera leur importe peu pendant qu'ils sont occupés à écrire; ils ont à faire ce qu'ils sont en train de faire. Dickens et Shakespeare aussi écrivaient sous l'influence de cette "pression imaginative colossale", et tous deux sont universels car tous deux donnent du plaisir.

M. Sternberger pense "qu'au point où nous en sommes, il serait utile de décider de quoi nous parlons." On a discuté de l'écrivain face aux media de masse, des rapports entre écrivain et éditeur, de catégories d'écrivains, des journalistes opposés aux artistes. Il propose de revenir au sujet qui leur a été proposé, aussi mystérieux soit-il: l'Ecrivain en tant que collaborateur aux desseins d'autrui. En rapport avec leur sujet, qui est "les desseins d'autrui", M. Sternberger veut attirer l'attention sur un champ de la littérature qui est plus vaste que celui de l'art et du journalisme réunis. Il comprend la littérature d'érudition, le pamphlet, l'essai sur des sujets non littéraires, sociaux, politiques et autres. En examinant ces matières, on voit que certains sont plus "exposés" que d'autres au phénomène de la collaboration. Un grand exemple à ce sujet est le philosophe et théoricien politique du XVIIe siècle, John Locke. C'était un idéologue et il servit délibérement la cause de la "Glorieuse Révolution" de 1688 en Angleterre. Elle *l'inspira*. Un autre exemple: Dante. Il vénerait Henry VII, empereur du Saint Empire romain, et chercha à l'aider à unifier l'Empire contre le Pape. Ces exemples amènent une question importante: l'écrivain sympathise-t-il ou non avec le but auquel il collabore. C'est cela qui importe.

M. *Lasky* commence par l'anecdote d'un éditeur sur Sinclair Lewis parlant aux étudiants d'un cours sur l'art d'écrire. Lewis avait demandé que tous ceux qui aspiraient à devenir écrivains lèvent la main. Tous levèrent la main; en suite de quoi Lewis demanda: "pourquoi n'êtes-vous pas à la maison en train d'écrire?"

Les membres qui sont réunis à cette table sont là pour "collaborer aux desseins" de l'auteur de ce thème et des trois questions "dramatiques" qui cherchent à le rendre plus compréhensible. M. Lasky se propose de répondre à ces trois questions. En y réfléchissant la nuit passée, il y avait répondu par l'affirmative. Aujourd'hui, un peu plus perplexe, il répond non. Il peut résumer sa position en un mot qu'il a appris d'un professeur de Heidelberg: *Janein;* en d'autres termes oui et non à la fois.

La première question se réfère au grand intérêt que le public porte à l'information, au "document". Elle demande si le domaine de la littérature est maintenant plus vaste que lorsque Sainte-Beuve écrivait il y a un siècle. En prenant le critique et essayiste américain Edmund Wilson comme exemple d'écrivain de même envergure, M. Lasky répondrait qu'il n'y a pas de changement notable: on trouve cependant des différences dans la substance et le style des oeuvres de ces deux époques. On pourrait se permettre d'ajouter que tout comme Truman Capote qui a été inspiré par une coupure de journal pour écrire *De sang froid,* Dostoïevski a peut-être été inspiré lui aussi par un fait divers pour écrire *Crime et châtiment.* Mais, si on se souvient que lors de la séance inaugurale Saul Bellow a fait allusion à "une transcription imaginative d'un problème de la vie", et qu'on constate que Capote l'a réduite à une transcription documentaire et journalistique—hautement journalistique—on peut répondre oui, tout a changé.

M. Lasky est tenté de répondre non à la deuxième question qui demande si les directeurs de journaux et les éditeurs se sont attribué des prérogatives au-dessus de l'ordinaire; les frottements entre auteurs et éditeurs ont toujours existé. M. Lasky cite les noms de Thomas More, Spinoza, Diderot et Voltaire. Ce matin encore il a reçu un télégramme du romancier anglais Colin MacInnes dont il avait légèrement corrigé le manuscrit peu avant son départ de Londres. Le télégramme disait:

"Eliminez vos flasques points-virgule et rétablissez mes superbes tirets".

La troisième question est plus importante: elle demande si de nos jours, oui ou non, le travail bâclé prend la place de l'oeuvre bien écrite. Les oeuvres bien écrites ont toujours été rares, et les mal écrites courantes. Mais les éditeurs de publications à grand tirage plongent bel et bien leurs collaborateurs dans l'embarras. Un ami lui a raconté l'histoire suivante. De retour à New York après plusieurs années en tant que correspondant à l'étranger, cet ami avait soumis à son rédacteur en chef quelques idées au sujet d'un article qu'il désirait écrire. "Formidable" dit celui-ci. "Nous allons en faire une grande histoire qui figurera en première page", et de commander une couverture de magazine au peintre Artzybashev. Quatre semaines plus tard, après avoir lu la grande histoire, on décide que le sujet ne vaut qu'un petit article composé de quelques anecdotes. Puis nouveau changement d'avis. On arrête qu'il sera de longueur moyenne, accompagné de deux photos. En ayant déjà écrit deux versions, ce fut un cauchemar pour l'écrivain que d'écrire la troisième. "C'est très simple", dit le rédacteur en chef à qui il se plaignait; "l'histoire devrait aller ainsi: da *dat* a *ta* da *dat;* da *dat* a *ta* da *dat*". M. Lasky n'ira pas jusqu'à dire si ce rythme représentait un bon ou un mauvais style; il décrit cependant un style ayant sa fonction. L'orateur cite l'exemple d'un style journalistique parmi tant d'autres:

". . . Et ainsi, tandis que la guerre va son chemin et que les nuages de la mousson s'élèvent au-dessus de nos têtes tels des champignons de plomb, le train-train politique nous met sur la forme".

Ce passage n'est pas simplement un lapsus littéraire. Il est représentatif d'un "langage sans signification, d'une sorte de laisser-aller systématique qui obscurcit tout effort de réflexion sur des questions graves". C'est un produit de la médiocrité alliée à l'arrogance et à l'ignorance, et ce phénomène ne doit pas se borner à provoquer un froncement de sourcil dédaigneux chez un mandarin dont la spécialité est le langage du XVIIe ou XVIIIe siècle, mais il devrait éveiller en nous une véritable préoccupation pour travailler aux côtés de ceux que les européens appellent des "paysans", les humbles. "Qu'est-ce qui mijote au quartier général du *Peace Corps* à Washington?" demande l'article. "La *hot line* nous révèle que le monde entier réclame de la révolution; que ces bons vieux États-Unis devraient commencer à en exporter. Quelle belle occasion pour nos jeunes missionnaires du *Peace Corps!*" "Amour égale engagement", dit une personnalité de Washington. Un tel langage est non seulement déprimant, dit M. Lasky, mais en outre il rend impossible toute réflexion et toute décision concernant des problèmes graves. Qui niera que les grandes questions politiques ne peuvent être résolues que dans la forme de langage employée par Aristote, Machiavel, John Locke? Aujourd'hui la drogue nous préoccupe: la marijuana, le LSD; nous devrions aussi nous préoccuper d'une langue devenue stupéfiante et dégénérée.

M. Pogačnik félicite M. Ngugi pour ses éclaircissements concernant les langues bantoues, et, tout en mentionnant qu'il vient d'un pays de 1.500.000 habitants seulement—la République de Slovénie—il met l'accent sur l'importance de la langue, de la littérature, et des arts pour maintenir l'existence nationale d'un peuple.

Se référant aux observations de M. Lasky sur les formes d'expression, *M. Jovanovich* demande ce que cela a à voir avec les desseins d'autrui; *M. Lasky* répond que l'écrivain ne crée pas un style rien que pour lui-même. Si Truman Capote a écrit un reportage réaliste et non un roman, c'est parce qu'il "a écouté son éditeur"—et ceci non pas dans un but vulgaire et commercial; il a simultanément prêté l'oreille au *Zeitgeist*.

M. Jovanovich rétorque que Capote "n'a été contraint en aucune sorte" et *M. Lasky* répond que Capote, comme tout écrivain, "collaborait à des desseins institutionnels."

M. Jovanovich enchaîne à nouveau: "Je ne crois pas qu'il aurait pu écrire ce livre sous forme de roman", à quoi *M. Lasky* répond "Eh bien, c'est possible", bien qu'il estime que "la force des tendances est souvent telle qu'elle incite un homme à adopter une forme, ou un sujet, ou un style qui normalement n'aurait pas été son choix". Quant à son rapport avec les desseins d'autrui, la communication entre êtres humains est en elle-même une communication de desseins. Quand le Président des Etats-Unis doit communiquer avec l'ensemble de l'opinion publique démocratique, il est obligé de tenir compte du langage auquel ils sont habitués, langage requis pour communiquer avec les masses. S'il s'abandonne entièrement à ce "langage LSD" cependant, il n' entrera pas en communication avec les gens qui ne sont pas victimes de ce jargon.

M. Jovanovich ne voit pas dans la presse et le langage actuels des marques évidentes de vulgarisation et de brutalisation qui aillent au-delà de ce que les Etats-Unis ont connu dans le passé; il croit en vérité que le langage des Américains est "meilleur" que jamais, et que la presse est plus sérieuse, moins vulgaire, qu'en 1910. Si Burke dans l'Angleterre du dix-huitième siècle, ou les pères fondateurs des Etats-Unis en 1776, parlaient et écrivaient comme ils le faisaient, la raison en est qu'ils "écrivaient de la prose destinée à 2.000 ou 5.000 personnes". Et si aujourd'hui le langage du public est "épouvantablement dégénéré", ce n'est pas un phénomène particulier aux Etats-Unis. Son collègue Sternberger a écrit un opuscule sur le "vocabulaire de l'inhumanité" qui montre ce qu'est devenue la langue allemande de nos jours.

A ce moment *le président* demande si la salle a des commentaires à faire.

Mme Barbara Tuchman (du P.E.N. américain) s'élève avec véhémence contre la notion que tout écrivain est obligé d'employer ce langage que M. Lasky appelle dégénéré; ou de choisir un sujet par contrainte—ce qui n'est pas concevable lorsque c'est dans le but d'écrire un livre. Un écrivain qui fait un compromis, qui renonce à son indépendance d'esprit, ferait mieux de devenir employé de banque. Il n'est pas non plus nécessaire qu'un homme politique américain se serve d'un tel langage; Adlai Stevenson ne l'a pas fait, Woodrow Wilson non plus.

Voix d'homme parlant anglais: offre un autre exemple de collaboration aux desseins d'autrui. Luther a dit dans l'un de ses opuscules que le langage dans lequel il était écrit était celui qu'il avait appris en écoutant attentivement les conversations des paysannes sur le place du marché. C'est ce langage que Luther a sublimé dans sa version de la Bible. L'orateur a l'impression que lorsqu'ils écrivent pour des illettrés, les écrivains deviennent l'instrument qui transforme le mauvais langage en bon langage. Les banalités manipulées par Robert Frost en sont un exemple. William Carlos Williams en offre un autre. Le passage de Dante du latin au patois italien en est un troisième. Leurs intentions se résument en un mot clef: communiquer. Au cours de leur carrière, même Dante (*Inferno,* Canto XXII) et Goethe ont passé ici et là par des "périodes *hip* et LSD".

DEUXIÈME SÉANCE

M. Goffin demande à M. Hope-Wallace de dire en quelques mots où l'on en était arrivé à la fin de la première session. *M. Hope-Wallace* répète en substance la réponse de M. Lasky aux trois questions posées par le programme: (1) malgré les demandes accrues d'information, le champ de la littérature ne s'est pas élargi de façon notable par rapport au siècle passé; (2) les auteurs d'oeuvres d'imagination peuvent en effet avoir quelque ressentiment à l'égard des prérogatives que se sont arrogées les directeurs de journaux et de revues. Quant aux écrivains "salariés", ils n'ont plus la même liberté; (3) en général les oeuvres mal écrites prennent le dessus. Etant d'accord avec M. Lasky sur ces trois points, M. Hope-Wallace ajoute qu'en ce qui concerne le troisième, les diverses pressions sociales, de même que la façon de penser stérile et la fausseté d'une certaine catégorie de journalisme sont responsables d'ouvrages pauvrement écrits.

M. Wieland Herzfelde (du Centre du P.E.N. de la République Démocratique Allemande), parlant anglais, dit qu'écrire est un métier aussi bien qu'un art. Certains problèmes qui ne touchent pas l'homme de métier se posent cependant à l'artiste. La difficulté surgit lorsque l'écrivain doit faire le choix entre écrire sur un sujet qui n'exprime pas ses convictions personnelles, ou lutter afin d'écrire ce qu'il ressent profondément, mais qu'il a de la peine à exprimer spontanément.

Coopérer avec autrui n'offre aucune difficulté pour autant que les participants partagent les mêmes convictions. Celui qui compose des textes publicitaires pourra admettre que le but n'est pas de juger de la qualité d'une pâte dentifrice, mais de persuader le public d'en acheter. Des relations d'une autre ordre s'établissent quand un homme écrit et qu'un autre—critique ou rédacteur en chef—le juge. Il est difficile de généraliser en ce cas: le rédacteur en chef est souvent utile par sa critique. Peut-être peut-on seulement dire que l'écrivain honnête rejettera les corrections éditoriales qu'il ne peut admettre.

M. Lucie-Smith fait remarquer premièrement que le mot publicité signifie "vente mécanisée", et deuxièmement, que dans ce domaine les mots sont des facteurs d'ordre secondaire, celui qui écrit le texte et le graphiste forment une équipe d' "inventeurs d'images". Il est très difficile à quiconque de faire honnêtement de la morale au sujet de la publicité quand il accepte de vivre dans une société qui en est imprégnée. Le professeur Herzfelde a parlé en fait de plume et de papier. Quant à M. McLuhan, M. Lucie-Smith qui n'a pas beaucoup apprécié son exposé, estime qu'il a eu raison de parler des nouveaux moyens de communication. De nos jours un grand nombre d'auteurs à succès emploient des magnétophones; pourquoi le résultat de leurs travaux ne s'appellerait-il pas littérature? Si cette Table Ronde veut analyser ces questions sous un angle moral, M. Lucie-Smith pense qu'il serait préférable de décider "de quelle morale il s'agira".

M. Keene commence par objecter que jusqu'à présent on a parlé de l'écrivain en tant que victime plutôt qu'en tant que collaborateur. Beaucoup d'écrivains—pas tous naturellement—sont collaborateurs de plein gré. M. Auden a dû être très heureux de collaborer avec Stravinsky à *The Rake's Progress*. Les *Exercices de Style* de Queneau, publiés par Gallimard, réprésentent un triomphe de la virtuosité que peut atteindre la collaboration entre auteur et maquettiste; les oeuvres publiées récemment par Michel Butor montrent combien l'écrivain peut tirer profit d'une collaboration avec les arts graphiques. Il y a également le cas de l'écrivain en tant que professeur dont la collaboration avec ses étudiants n'est pas à mépriser. Saul Bellow a parlé avec une certaine ironie de l'écrivain à l'Université: et pourtant il a lui-même profité de cette situation bien plus que grand nombre d'auteurs, que cela ait été intentionnel ou non.

On a souvent considéré que la situation des "poètes en résidence" dans de nombreuses universités américaines limitait leur liberté d'expression; c'est absurde. Dans toute société les poètes ont toujours discuté la poésie ensemble, pourquoi ce "professeur" ne lirait-il pas celle de ses étudiants? Au Japon, des siècles durant, les poètes ont gagné leur vie en lisant à haute voix des poèmes écrits par d'autres et en les aidant à écrire de la meilleure poésie.

Et puis il y a l'écrivain en tant que traducteur. M. Keene, comme membre du Comité de traduction du P.E.N. américain, a récemment fait partie du jury chargé de décerner son Prix annuel de la traduction. Ils ont lu cinquante oeuvres de traducteurs américains et anglais, traduites de nombreuses langues différentes. La qualité des traductions était déplorablement médiocre. Le jury a eu de la peine à en trouver une valant la récompense de mille dollars.

Un éditeur parisien lui a parlé d'une traduction du japonais qui était si mauvaise qu'il ne pouvait la publier: "Ce n'était même pas du français". Cela lui a donné l'idée de la possibilité de traduction en coopération. "Idéalement, nous devrions tous apprendre les langues étrangères et faire un peu de traduction, car, comme écrivains, il nous est plus facile qu'à d'autres d'écrire dans notre propre langue!" Il y a aujourd'hui moins de gens capables de traduire du japonais en anglais que lorsqu'il s'était plaint du manque de ces traducteurs en 1957 au Congrès du P.E.N. à Tokyo. Il y a peut-être trois ou quatre traducteurs seulement qui peuvent traduire du chinois en bon anglais. On ne peut attendre d'écrivains déjà éminents qu'ils consacrent cinq ans à apprendre une langue orientale difficile; mais il y a "d'immenses possibilités de collaboration, particulièrement dans la poésie". Le plaisir et l'inspiration que les écrivains, pour ne pas dire les lecteurs, retireront d'une traduction faite de la sorte ne doit pas être dédaignée. Le P.E.N. ferait bien d'encourager la collaboration dans ce domaine.

Pour finir, la tendance, hier, a été de parler de l'écrivain et de l'éditeur comme s'ils étaient ennemis. A vrai dire nous sommes partout en présence de l'écrivain en tant qu'éditeur, comme le prouve un certain nombre de revues littéraires trimestrielles. Ces éditeurs-rédacteurs-écrivains ont une certaine responsabilité: celle d'encourager (ou peut-être de décourager) les écrivains asiatiques et africains qui sont en train de créer des littératures nouvelles et qu'on devrait aider dans leur tâche. Mais c'est une erreur de publier des numéros spéciaux consacrés à la littérature japonaise, philippine ou thaïlandaise: les histoires et poèmes provenant de tels pays ne devraient pas être réunis en bloc dans un numéro national, comme si on voulait les patronner et faire une sorte de "bonne action". Qui voudrait aller à un concert composé uniquement de musique américaine? Les traductions des oeuvres des pays sus-mentionnés devraient être publiées en tant que littérature dans des éditions normales et devraient être capables de résister à une comparaison avec des oeuvres d'autres langues.

Il a été dit qu'un écrivain est aussi un lecteur. Qui d'entre nous lit l'excellent magazine "Transition" publié en Uganda? Ou l'excellent recueil de morceaux choisis sorti à Calcutta? Ils valent beaucoup plus la peine d'être lus que les livres de troisième ordre qu'on analyse dans notre presse. M. Keene mentionne deux grands écrivains de notre temps qui lisent la littérature orientale: Borges, en Argentine, et un ami de M. Keene, Octavio Paz, le grand poète mexicain (ambassadeur en Inde en ce moment) qui ont su adapter les formes poétiques japonaises et chinoises. "De tels écrivains sont des lecteurs de la meilleure sorte, de ceux qui donnent à la littérature toute sa valeur".

Mlle Chute dit qu'elle ne peut se poser en victime. Etant ce qu'on appelle un érudit, elle n'a pas de moyens pour collaborer aux buts d'autrui. Elle ne peut le faire qu'en tant que lectrice. Il est exclu pour un érudit d'écouter d'autres voix que celles de ses documents; et une principale raison d'existence des universités est qu'elles procurent un refuge où le savant peut être à l'abri pour réaliser ses ambitions.

De temps en temps il arrive qu'un érudit découvre qu'il a choisi un sujet intéressant le public. La vie de Shakespeare, qu'elle a écrite, en est un exemple. L'intérêt que le public a manifesté à l'égard de son livre a rendu possible son premier voyage en Angleterre; là elle a découvert qu'il lui avait été plus aisé d'écrire sur l'Angleterre à partir de documents qu'elle n'aurait pu le faire en la visitant. Ses écrits ont porté principalement sur les poètes, surtout parce qu' elle s'intéressait à "un certain grand talent que le manque d'argent avait éprouvé". Shakespeare avait un métier—il était acteur—qui lui permettait de gagner sa vie et d'être libre d'écrire comme il lui plaisait; la preuve en est qu'après le grand succès de *Hamlet,* il n'a pas jugé nécessaire d'écrire à nouveau une pièce du même genre. Son ami Ben Jonson qui avait raté sa carrière d'acteur n'avait pas d'autre métier que celui d'écrivain. Les quatre grandes pièces de Jonson ont été écrites pour la compagnie de Shakespeare; après cela il passa le reste de sa vie à chercher des Mécènes et son talent s'effrita petit à petit.

L'écrivain qui a un métier n'a pas tort. Deux des grands poètes américains de ce siècle ont travaillé pour des compagnies d'assurances. T. S. Eliot, après avoir lu pendant des années la presse européenne pour une banque de Londres, est devenu directeur de revue littéraire. Un autre des écrivains qui ont fait l'objet des études de Mlle Chute, Geoffrey Chaucer, le plus grand poète anglais après Shakespeare, était fonctionnaire. D'avoir un métier ne peut changer le fait qu'écrire (pour elle en tous cas) est la plus grande joie au monde. On a de la chance, bien sûr, si on n'as pas besoin de faire autre chose; mais il est évident que de gagner sa vie dans un autre domaine ne limite pas le privilège, ni ne diminue le plaisir d'écrire.

M. Florentino, parlant anglais, dit qu'il représente une jeune nation, la République philippine, qui est une république démocratique depuis vingt ans, après 46 ans d'hégémonie américain et 350 ans de domination espagnole; un pays de 7.000 îles et de 27 millions d'habitants. On peut considérer peut-être qu'il "représente" n'importe quelle jeune nation africaine ou asiatique, car cela a été un choc pour lui que d'être "projeté dans une conférence où le sujet, le point de vue, et la plupart des participants" sont européens et américains. L'âge électronique ne préoccupe pas les Philippins; leur problème est le manque de lampes électriques pour lire, plutôt que la menace des media de masse, la question de servir aux buts d'autrui, ou l'avilissement de leur langue.

Au contraire, leurs problèmes résident dans un manque de débouchés et la quête d'un langage littéraire: il y a de nombreuses nations (d'anciennes colonies) qui n'ont pas encore décidé quel serait le leur. Quant à la sujétion aux éditeurs, le problème serait plutôt d'établir ses propres maisons d'édition face à l'avalanche de livres et de magazines (et de télévision) que l'étranger déverse sur eux. Leur problème n'est pas la fin de l'ère de Gutenberg, mais bien plutôt leur entrée dans cette ère.

M. Florentino espère que sa prise de position encouragera l'organisation d'une future conférence, ou d'un colloque, sur les problèmes des arts et des lettres en Asie, en Afrique et aussi peut-être en certains pays d'Amérique latine.

M. Lasky relève que les formes de collaboration qui ont été citées sont moins simples qu'elles ne le paraissent. C'est de la sentimentalité que de croire qu'il suffit de sincérité pour créer des oeuvres valables. M. Herzfelde, si M. Lasky se rappelle bien, a dit, en résumé, qu'une oeuvre mal écrite est en quelque sort la conséquence d'une mauvaise cause, et que les dieux de la littérature garantissaient qu'une bonne cause engendrait une oeuvre de valeur.

Cela est une apparence trompeuse. Hier, M. Sternberger a mentionné deux grands écrivains "engagés": Milton et John Locke; tous deux ont parlé pour des causes diamétralement opposées. On peut dire la même chose de ces deux hommes au style brillant et raffiné, Marat et Robespierre. On pourrait comparer Trotsky, cet historien-génie de la phrase, avec Staline "ce presque illetré au style de plomb"; dans leur lutte, c'est le génie qui a eu le dessous.

On a longtemps considéré que New York était gouvernée par trois rues haïssables: "Wall Street qui nous exploite, Broadway qui nous manipule, Madison Avenue qui nous fait subir un lavage de cerveau". M. Lasky s'est demandé comme enfant si la publicité était réellement nécessaire, si ce mauvais goût n'était pas en fait gratuit. Les spécialistes en sciences politiques nous disent que non, que c'est un mécanisme social essentiel. M. Lasky n'aimerait pas écrire des annonces publicitaires, mais s'il avait à le faire, son but serait d'accomplir "un travail professionnel qui aurait certaines conséquences sociales". Des années durant il a vu des annonces publicitaires—dans l'hebdomadaire *New Yorker* par exemple—dont les idées et les images sont, à certains égards, plus spirituelles, plus vivantes, et plus amusantes que les textes qui les accompagnent. La composition de textes de publicité a certainement pris une tournure plus professionnelle, plus sophistiquée. Le texte écrit pour la compagnie américaine de location de voitures qui s'avoue elle-même être la "seconde plus grande compagnie" en est un exemple. Si celui qui l'a écrit fait partie des écrivains exerçant un métier pour vivre, et s'il écrit aussi "pour lui-même" (condition que Mlle Chute a approuvée), il est alors, de l'avis de M. Lasky, potentiellement capable de produire des romans comiques excellents. Cet écrivain perd peut-être son temps, mais il démontre qu'écrire des annonces publicitaires peut contribuer à la gaieté des nations.

M. Bloch-Michel revient à la question de savoir si la mauvaise littérature chasse la bonne. Il est évident que ceux qui écrivent pour la radio, le cinéma ou la télévision sont forcés de se plier à certaines règles de ces techniques. Cependant ces techniques sont créatrices de formes, de formes esthétiques qui sont absolument nouvelles. Il existe un art de la radio, de la télévision et du cinéma qui n'ont de rapport ni avec le théâtre, ni avec la photographie, ni avec le simple usage de la parole. Et inévitablement ces formes nouvelles influencent une certaine littérature, pas du tout en imposant un mauvais style, mais en l'amenant elle-même à rechercher ses propres formes nouvelles qui correspondraient à une transposition de celles nées des nouveaux moyens de communication. Nous voyons en France toute une école romanesque qui, délibérément ou pas, transfère dans la littérature certains procédés qui sont nés soit de la radio, soit du cinéma. Les romans de Robbe-Grillet, par exemple, sont inspirés par ce qu'on peut appeler "le récit en images", une sorte de récit cinématographique entièrement différent du récit littéraire traditionnel. Un écrivain comme Michel Butor a essayé dans ses dernières oeuvres, d'une réussite contestable, de transposer sur le plan littéraire les possibilités que donne la multiplicité des "canaux" employés dans les oeuvres radiophoniques ou stéréophoniques.

Ces moyens de communication, par conséquent, exercent d'autres influences que celle, unique, dénoncée par M. Lasky. Il est certain que leur influence sur le journalisme est désastreuse. Mais plus d'ecrivains qu'on ne croit se sont engagés dans des recherches de style purement formelles. Une sorte de revirement a lieu; et des formes qui, dans une certaine mesure, sont contraires à la littérature, ont amené certains écrivains à des recherches purement littéraires. A ce point de vue M. Bloch-Michel dirait: Non, la mauvaise littérature ne chasse pas la bonne. On peut aimer ou ne pas aimer la littérature extrêmement sophistiquée et savante qui résulte des ces expériences; on ne peut nier que c'est une excellent littérature.

M. Goffin demande la permission de répondre aux déclarations de M. Bloch-Michel et dit qu'il est d'un avis contraire. Le public est attiré par "des formes plus faciles". Une certaine "loi de la littérature" veut, il est vrai, que les poètes passent par une période de purgatoire avant d'être lus. Et pourtant il est vrai aussi que, de siècle en siècle, ce sont les poètes qui forment et représentent les pays—les poètes et non les politiciens. Verlaine a été condamné à deux ans de prison par un ministre belge: qui se souvient du ministre? Mais qui ne connaît Verlaine? Victor Hugo s'est attaqué à Napoléon III et s'exila en Belgique. Là, en deux lignes il immortalisa un homme qui, autrement, serait tombé dans l'oubli, le ministre qui posa cette question à la Chambre des Députés: "Est-ce qu'on va bientôt expulser cet individu, Victor Hugo?" Hugo a écrit:

> Pour comble de malheur, les animaux parlèrent:
> Un certain Ribaucourt m'appelle "individu".

M. Lucie-Smith dit qu'il va essayer de rassembler différentes choses énoncées par les trois derniers orateurs. Premièrement, comme le langage est le "baromètre d'une société", on ne peut dire qu'un langage est malade sans dire que la société est malade. Les critiques littéraires moralisateurs se servent du langage pour fustiger la société. Deuxièmement, la collaboration peut être soit une pierre d'achoppement soit un tremplin: la première force l'écrivain à sortir de sa voie naturelle, la deuxième l'amène à un point où il ne serait parvenu de lui-même. Quant à la publicité, M. Lucie-Smith répète que le compositeur de textes publicitaires "s'occupe moins de mots" qu'on ne le pense, et que la publicité représente un aspect de la culture contemporaine, une mixture de vu et d'entendu, de mot (imprimé ou dit) et d'image. Dans un monde où tout est synthétisé, on ne peut être sûr que la littérature ne soit pas "aussi bien une séquence d'images qu'une séquence de mots sur une page". C'est cela le problème de l'écrivain de télévision.

M. Lucie-Smith estime que la littérature ne remplit pas toujours la même fonction dans chaque société. Le rôle du poète que le Président a vanté n'est plus le même qu'autrefois. En Russie Voznesensky et Evtushenko, en Amérique Allen Ginsberg, ont écrit des poèmes destinés à être lus à haute voix en public. C'est pourquoi M. Lucie-Smith se demande si cette table ronde n'attribue pas à l'écrivain un rôle qui n'est plus le sien depuis longtemps.

M. Chiara, parlant français, remarque que ses collègues français, qui représentent probablement "la partie la plus vivante de la culture européenne" peuvent parfaitement bien exposer les "points de vue méditerranéens". Les écrivains italiens regardent toujours vers la littérature française, et, dans l'ensemble, partagent ses idées sur les relations entre les écrivains et la société contemporaine. A son point de vue, les problèmes sociaux ne représentent qu'un "moment dans le développement de la communauté humaine, une abstraction en quelque sorte, tandis que l'homme est quelque chose de réel, d'unique, l'objet de chaque philosophie, de la littérature et de l'art". Pour lui donc, les problèmes sociaux sont d'un caractère un peu extérieur, différent de l'expérience individuelle, personnelle de l'écrivain.

M. Sternberger voudrait dire un mot au sujet d'un "domaine de collaboration qui est favorisé", celui de l'écrivain et du politicien dans la République fédérale allemande. Pendant les élections générales de 1965, un groupe d'éminents écrivains professionnels a décidé de soutenir le Parti social démocratique, malgré certains fonctionnaires du parti qui craignaient que leur contact avec les électeurs ne soit empreint d'un intellectualisme excessif. Dans la République fédérale allemande où "les politiciens et les écrivains sont pour ainsi dire divisés en deux classes, et où la politique ne dispose pas d'écrivains tels que Churchill et de Gaulle", le résultat a été particulièrement heureux. Les Etats-Unis ont également leurs exemples dans les personnes du Président Kennedy, d'Arthur Schlesinger et d'autres. Quant à la publicité, M. Sternberger attire l'attention sur les slogans américains: *New Deal*,

Fair Deal, New Frontier, Great Society et autres. Il approuverait que les écrivains collaborent à des inventions verbales de ce genre.

M. Keene dit qu'on a laissé entendre que la littérature de qualité supérieure est de vente plus restreinte que la littérature de mauvaise qualité, et qu'elle jouit de moins d'estime dans le grand public. Ce n'est pas le cas au Japon où environ "mille fois plus d'écrivains qu'aux Etats-Unis" peuvent vivre—certains extrêment bien—de leurs oeuvres.

Vers la fin des années quarante, l'écrivain qui gagnait le plus, le romancier Tanizaki, fut proposé pour le Prix Nobel, qui ne lui fut finalement pas décerné. Au Japon les poètes sont grandement respectés et on y publie 200 revues de poésie. A l'opposé de ce qui semble se passer à l'Ouest, c'est le meilleur journal de Tokyo qui a le plus grand tirage et non pas le plus mauvais. Le P.E.N. ferait bien d'examiner ce qui se passe au Japon.

Le président a l'impression qu'aux Etats-Unis on néglige peut-être quelque peu les littératures mineures d'Europe. La Belgique a deux centres du P.E.N.: un P.E.N. français et un P.E.N. flamand. Les Hongrois sont sur le point de publier une anthologie de poésie belge, ainsi que l'ont déjà fait les russes. Des groupes tchécoslovaques et yougoslaves ont proposé des échanges d'anthologies au P.E.N. de Belgique. M. Goffin demande instamment aux P.E.N. de langue anglaise qu'ils encouragent la traduction de poésies de langues moins favorisées.

M. Hope-Wallace dit qu'ils ont "un problème très étrange en Angleterre". La langue de Shakespeare devient archaïque au point d'être inintelligible au grand public. Ce n'est pas le cas de Shakespeare en Allemagne, grâce à la traduction Tieck-Schlegel datant d'un siècle et demi; le grand public russe aussi, est beaucoup plus "conscient de Shakespeare" que les propres compatriotes du poète. Devrait-on "moderniser" Shakespeare comme on a modernisé la Bible "du Roi James"? Cela est-il dangereux ou utile?

M. Sulaksana Sivaraksa (du P.E.N. thaïlandais) parlant anglais, pense que la cause de bien des difficultés réside dans le contrôle des media de masse par des "groupes d'intérêts faisant pression", dans les pays démocratiques, et par les autorités du Parti dans les pays communistes. "Des groupes ayant des partis pris et des préjuges contrôlent et manipulent de plus en plus la presse occidentale extrêmement concentrée, dans laquelle s'infiltrent en même temps des éléments pro-communistes sous le couvert de libéralisme". La purge culturelle qui sévit en République populaire de Chine est la cinquième depuis 1951. M. Sivaraksa exprime le voeu que le Congrès proteste contre "la suppression de l'impulsion créatrice dans un pays qui a grandement contribué dans le passé" à tous les arts créateurs. Le P.E.N. chinois du Tibet [sic] a publié un rapport sur la purge actuelle; une copie en a été envoyée au Secrétariat International du P.E.N.*

Mme Ocampo trouve que M. Lasky a raison de dire que la sincérité en elle-même ne suffit pas. "La sincérité n'a qu'un seul traducteur en littérature: le talent", dit-elle. Mais le talent lui-même, s'il n'est accompagné de conscience, peut servir lamentablement la propagande et le mensonge.

M. Matej Bor, ancien président du P.E.N. slovène, et président du 33e Congrès international du P.E.N. (Bled, juillet 1965), parlant anglais, est convaincu que des déclarations très utiles ont été faites à cette séance. Il avoue cependant que la façon dont leur thème a été formulé lui a paru peu claire.

Sur la question de la "distortion" du langage, il pense que si les écrivains cessent de produire "des oeuvres de qualité supérieure", c'est parce qu'ils ne fournissent bien souvent que de "la matière première aux autres arts" comme la télévision et le cinéma. Il trouve, tout comme M. Bloch-Michel, que ces arts nouveaux influencent la littérature contemporaine, mais cependant il ne peut admettre que leur influence soit toujours bonne. Les techniques de l'écran abaissent le niveau de l'oeuvre de l'écrivain qui les adopte, car elles l'incitent à produire des séquences d'images et à négliger la "méditation".

A ceci, M. Bor veut ajouter son regret que les remarques de son collègue, M. Pogačnik sur "l'engagement" n'aient pas engendré plus de commentaires, et que la requête de M. Coutsoheras pour une résolution sur le danger d'une catastrophe atomique ait été repoussée par le Comité exécutif international comme étant d'ordre politique et non littéraire.

Voix de femme, parlant anglais, se fait entendre sur deux points. Le premier concerne les écrivains qui gagnent leur vie avec un autre métier. Elle est elle-même dans l'enseignment et trouve qu'il n'y a pas de "dichotomie" entre "les recherches auxquelles s'adonnent les professeurs et les sujets qu'ils traitent dans leurs écrits". Mais l'écrivain qui "déprécie sa marchandise" dans une agence de publicité pourra trouver que cette façon de gagner sa vie ne l'aide pas et qu'elle est plutôt une entrave à son métier d'écrivain. A son avis, si un écrivain doit vivre d'un autre métier, il ferait mieux de le choisir sans relation aucune avec le fait d'écrire, mais enrichissant cependant son expérience et l'aidant à écrire de façon plus objective.

---

* Il n'y a pas de Centre tibétain du P.E.N. (ni en République populaire de Chine). Le rapport auquel il est fait allusion n'a pas été reçu par le Secrétaire Général du P.E.N. International. (*Note du rapporteur.*)

Son second point concerne les réfugiés qui ont appris une deuxième langue. Ne pourraient-ils pas se mettre à la traduction, et cela ne serait-il pas une idée dont le P.E.N. devrait s'occuper?

Mlle Chute est d'accord avec l'idée qu'il vaut mieux que le gagne-pain d'un écrivain consiste en un travail "qu'il aime faire, qui rapporte et qui ne soit pas écrire".

M. Alexandron Balaci (du P.E.N. roumain) parlant français, remercie le président d'avoir mentionné les traductions roumaines de poètes belges, qu'ils soient de langue française ou flamande. Au sujet du duel entre la grande littérature d'imagination et le document sur le vif actuellement si populaire, il ne croit pas que ce dernier remplacera le premier, pas plus que la machine ne remplacera l'écrivain. Il y a une anecdote à ce sujet, racontant qu'une machine à traduire électronique, ayant produit deux versions différentes d'un fragment de Shakespeare, avait déclaré "Je ne sais laquelle choisir!" et fait explosion.

A la question les éditeurs et directeurs de revues empiètent-ils sur la liberté créatrice de l'écrivain, M. Balaci répond qu'aucun vrai poète n'écrira des bouts rimés, qu'aucun vrai romancier ne deviendra un simple reporter, de même qu'aucun vrai dramaturge ne renoncera au théâtre pour le music-hall. La loi de Gresham, qui dit que le mauvais argent chasse le bon, ne s'applique pas à la littérature.

M. Anoma Kanie (du P.E.N. de Côte d'Ivoire) résume ses impressions sur ce qui a été dit jusque-là: "Si de nos jours l'écrivain se sent lui-même menacé, c'est que l'homme en tant qu'homme se sent menacé par ce que la science et la technique lui offrent". Nous avons donné naissance à un monstre que nous sommes incapables de comprendre et avec lequel nous ne savons comment vivre. La faute n'en incombe pas à la technique, mais à l'homme lui-même qui s'est endormi sur ses réalisations passées. La mission de l'homme est de se rappeler qu'il est, ainsi que le dit le christianisme, créé à l'image de Dieu, et qu'il doit chercher la vérité et dominer sa condition. La tâche de l'écrivain est, somme toute, semblable à celle de l'homme: ne jamais se contenter de solutions temporaires et lutter pour tenter d'accomplir des réformes. La même tâche attend tous ceux qui sont présents à ce Congrès.

Le président dit qu'avant de passer la parole à M. Lasky il a une histoire à raconter. A New York en 1940, il travaillait à une pièce de théâtre avec le grand poète Maeterlinck. Le poète venait de vendre un article à *Liberty* Magazine pour $2,500. M. Goffin était présent lors-qu'un représentant du magazine arriva pour demander à Maeterlinck son accord sur certaines modifications de l'article. La réponse de Maeter-linck fut qu'il ne pouvait être question de changements, "car je sais ce que je veux écrire, et c'est ça que je veux dire"; le représentant du magazine répondit: "Vous savez peut-être ce que vous voulez dire, M. Maeterlinck, mais notre magazine, lui, sait ce que ses lecteurs veulent lire".

M. Lasky reprend le problème de M. Sternberger au sujet des services qu'un écrivain peut rendre à des groupes politiques, que ce soient des groupes partageant ses propres convictions (en ce cas nous avons parlé "d'engagement" et de "sincérité") ou de groupes qui le paient bien ou qu'il trouve amusant de servir passagèrement (ce que nous avons appelé "irresponsabilité"). Lorsqu'il s'agit d'une composition purement littéraire, l'ingéniosité de l'écrivain, alliée à son irresponsabilité, peut donner un résultat inoffensif et badin; mais il en est tout autrement lorsqu'il est question de formules politiques.

Il y a trente ans, alors qu'il était étudiant, M. Lasky a entendu Earl Browder, alors chef du Parti communiste américain, lancer un slogan qu'il désapprouvait entièrement mais "qu'il aurait aimé avoir trouvé lui-même"—tout comme Oscar Wilde lorsqu'il avait entendu un bon mot dit par Whistler, le peintre américain. Le slogan disait: "le communisme est l'américanisme du vingtième siècle". En ce temps-là Paul Robeson chantait d'anciens chants populaires américains. Browder et Robeson manifestaient leur dévotion culturelle d'une façon qui leur paraissait conforme au communisme et à l'américanisme à la fois. M. Lasky avait admiré la dextérité avec laquelle Browder avait fusionné ingéniosité et irresponsabilité. Le tragique avait été que beaucoup d'américains avaient cru ce que Browder leur disait. Un exemple du même genre est le "Nous n'avons rien à craindre que la crainte elle-même" de Franklin Roosevelt, proclamé à un moment où la guerre, le fascisme, et la désintégration sociale étaient à craindre . . . Les slogans servent un but, mais il faut toujours en examiner attentivement la fonction et les conséquences. Un très bon poète a forgé le mot "Négritude", qui exprime un aspect de la personnalité africaine; mais les conséquences sociales et politiques qui en résultèrent ne furent pas toujours constructives. En résumé, quand "l'ingéniosité devient une prison et l'irresponsabilité une tromperie", on préférerait que la politique s'exprime d'une manière peut-être plus terne, mais en se passant de slogans.

M. Lucie-Smith a été agréablement surpris que les orateurs précédents aient rappelé "jusqu'à quel point les écrivains de littératures "mineures" étaient restés les gardiens de l'identité et de l'âme nationales". Il a souvent remarqué dans des traductions d'oeuvres de ces littératures "une sorte de richesse d'identité sociale" qu'on ne trouve plus dans les romans anglais. Il suppose que ces écrivains sont attentifs à ne pas trahir leur pays, car ils savent qu'un "dépôt" leur a été confié. Un écrivain qui écrit dans une langue quasi-universelle—l'anglais—est conscient d'être "repoussé en marge de la société"; il a moins d'importance aux yeux de sa propre société. C'est pourquoi il se sent plus libre de se laisser aller à écrire dans des formes qui pourraient l'amener à des compromis (les media de masse, etc.). Cependant, M. Lucie-Smith "tiendrait bon" à la distinction que Mme Ocampo fait entre une oeuvre bien écrite et une bonne conscience. Il est peut-être aussi plus aisé de maintenir l'une et l'autre dans une littérature "mineure" où elles ont une réelle signification; en cela il envie M. Florentino.

M. Combs pense que l'aptitude à formuler des slogans est "l'une des plus grandes forces sociales de l'écrivain" qui mérite qu'on y réfléchisse. Dans le monde d'aujourd'hui il existe deux hommes qui se considèrent des poètes et qui ont une emprise extraordinaire sur leurs sociétés, les entraînant et excitant leur zèle par leurs paroles. L'un est Mao Tsetung, l'autre est Luis Muñoz Marin, de Porto Rico, dont l'autorité est due en partie à son habileté à créer des slogans. Dans cet ordre d'idées, M. Combs recommande aux poètes l'usage de la forme brève lorsqu'ils écrivent—comme le *haiku* japonais par exemple—car si les poèmes peuvent être retenus aisément, la vie des hommes s'en trouvera enrichie.

M. Leslie Konnyu (du P.E.N. des écrivains en exil) remarque qu'on a soulevé la question des réfugiés écrivant des traductions en anglais. Un programme de ce genre existe en Europe et ici en Amérique; la Revue américano-hongroise, par exemple, publie de la littérature hongroise en anglais aussi bien que de la littérature anglaise et américaine en hongrois. Elle a fait paraître un livre sur la littérature hongroise moderne, et une histoire de la littérature américano-hongroise.

Mme Vera Blackwell (du P.E.N. anglais) est une traductrice du tchèque se spécialisant dans la littérature théâtrale; elle a récemment traduit les pièces de Vaclas Havel qui, avec deux autres écrivains, s'est vu refuser un passeport par le Gouvernement tchécoslovaque pour assister à ce congrès. Elle s'est trouvée face à la difficulté suivante: les directeurs de théâtre anglais ne demandent pas une traduction, mais une adaptation des pièces, afin qu'elles soient plus facilement accessibles au public britannique. Ces textes contiennent toujours des allusions d'ordre politique ou local qui sont difficiles à transposer. Dans le cas des deux pièces de Havel, ce problème n'a pas été résolu. Où se trouve la réponse, demande Mme Blackwell? On a joué Havel dans 18 théâtres allemands, en Suède, en Finlande, et deux fois à Vienne. Pourquoi ne peut-il être joué en Angleterre et en Amérique?

Le président regrette que le temps manque pour discuter cette question intéressante et se trouve obligé de clore cette séance en remerciant tous ceux qui y ont participé.

TABLE RONDE IV

L'écrivain en tant que personnalité publique

vendredi 17 juin
PREMIÉRE SESSION

Douglas Young, PRÉSIDENT
University of St. Andrews, St. Andrews, Ecosse

Daniel Bell
Columbia University, New York

Chang Ho Choi
Séoul

A. den Doolaard
Hoenderloo, Hollande

Gyula Illyés
Budapest

Rosamond Lehmann
Londres

Arthur Miller
New York

Pablo Neruda
Valparaiso

Ignazio Silone
Rome

Hsu-pai Tseng
Taipei

DEUXIÈME SESSION

Douglas Young, PRÉSIDENT
St. Andrews

Daniel Bell
New York

A. den Doolaard
Hoenderloo

Jean Follain
Paris

Rosamond Lehmann
Londres

Horia Lovinescu
Bucarest

Arthur Miller
New York

Pablo Neruda
Valparaiso

Ignazio Silone
Rome

L'écrivain en tant que personnalité publique

PREMIÈRE SÉANCE

Le président dit en quelques mots comment il va procéder et cite quelques extraits du programme concernant le thème qui va être discuté par les participants à la Table Ronde, puis par les membres présents dans l'audience qui se sont inscrits à l'avance à cet effet. Puis, M. Young constate que dans une certaine mesure tous les écrivains sont des personnalités publiques puisque les lecteurs se forgent une idée plus ou moins vague de leur personnalité. Mais en fait l'écrivain est un individu qui écrit pour lui-même, le lecteur également lit en tant qu'individu et n'est pas conscient de faire partie du "public lisant". Au théâtre la situation est quelque peu différente: le dramaturge écrit en pensant à son public, et les réactions du spectateur sont influencées par celles des autres spectateurs. Pour ces raisons, M. Young tend à ne pas être d'accord avec la suggestion du programme prétendant que l'écrivain adoptait consciemment une *persona*.

M. Illyés, parlant français, dit que selon sa propre expérience les lettres adressées à un auteur par ses lecteurs, lettres parfois surprenantes et qui relèvent souvent de la psychiâtrie, sont extrèmement révélatrices quant au rôle de l'écrivain dans la société. Entre les deux guerres il avait publié un journal sur un voyage en Russie. Un pépiniériste russe lui avait alors écrit pour lui demander de lui faire parvenir secrètement et en cadeau—car à ce moment il n'y avait pas de relations diplomatiques entre la Hongrie et Moscou—500 plantes de pêchers sibériens résistants au gel. Tous les auteurs ont une fois ou l'autre eu affaire avec la jeune lectrice qui exige une lettre personnelle et détaillée justifiant la conduite du héros qu'elle réprouve; également avec la dame d'un certain âge qui a cru découvrir en vous une âme sœur et vous propose un échange de lettres hebdomadaire.

Un de ses éminents confrères lui a une fois décrit le comportement d'un lecteur-aristocrate, qui considérait que le livre qu'il était en train de lire au coin du feu était une communication personnelle: comme il n'est pas de bon ton de garder une lettre, l'honneur exigeait qu'il arrachât chaque page après lecture et qu'il la jetât au feu.

Dante n'a pas écrit pour gagner sa vie, mais pour renseigner . . . pour enseigner. Comment un auteur pourrait-il enseigner d'une manière impartiale s'il dépendait de son élève, le lecteur? Et si l'on demandait à M. Illyés: "l'écrivain de notre époque a-t-il le droit de faire la leçon?" il répondrait "oui" sans hésitation, car sans ce droit il n'y aurait pas de littérature, pas d'écrivains et pas de lecteurs.

Quelle est la situation aujourd'hui? L'auteur est-il libre de parler à son élève? Il y en a—des éditeurs, des hommes d'argent—qui prétendent que les auteurs et les lecteurs forment deux camps opposés. M. Illyés n'y croit pas, pour lui ils sont fonction l'un de l'autre. Toute littérature est le produit de son époque. Nous vivons dans un monde commercialisé, plein de troubles et d'espérances, où les yeux lucides et les coeurs purs se font rares. Les éditeurs sont exigeants, mais les muses sont plus exigeantes encore. Nous n'écrivons pas pour des lecteurs qui s'ennuient dans leurs grands fauteuils, nous écrivons pour ceux qui souffrent comme nous avons souffert, ceux pour qui la beauté et la vérité, à tout prix, sont les meilleurs remèdes.

M. Silone, parlant français, évoque pour commencer l'oeuvre d'un jeune essayiste italien intitulé *L'éclipse des intellectuels.* Dans ce texte l'éclipse—qui en astronomie est un phénomène de courte durée—est considérée comme un obscurcissement durable, voire permanent. Ce paradoxe rejoint une sociologie déjà périmée qui affirmait que dans la société industrielle la question sociale, c'est-à-dire les rapports entre Etat, capital et ouvriers, avait relégué les intellectuels dans un rôle secondaire, au service de l'une ou l'autre des forces en présence: au service de l'Etat, des grands trusts ou de l'organisation révolutionnaire.

Historiquement parlant, les intellectuels ont déjà été détrônés en 1848 et réduits à l'état de "simples ornements de la société, d'instruments utilisés pour des fins d'autrui". Bismark a dit qu'il suffisait d'un peu d'argent pour acheter un poète ou une prostituée. Le Chancelier de Fer a peut-être exagéré, mais il faut admettre que la psychologie des intellectuels—qui est un produit du genre de vie que beaucoup de nous menons, qui mène facilement au narcissisme et à la servitude, tout au moins extérieure—semble parfois lui donner raison.

A notre époque nous vivons avec le phénomène du totalitarisme. Si nous prenons ce terme non dans son sens injurieux et polémique, mais strictement dans son sens historique et scientifique, c'est-à-dire comme une conception de la société dans laquelle la politique prédomine, et où tout est subordonné aux fins politiques de l'Etat, nous pouvons constater que la théorie citée plus haut de l'intellectuel au service d'une puissance supérieure, trouve sa perfection définitive dans l'Etat totalitaire. Matériellement les écrivains et poètes y sont bien traités en échange de leurs services comme instruments de la propagande; on les organise en brigades de choc pour encourager les récoltes dans les kolkhozes ou assister à l'inauguration d'un nouveau plan quiquennal. On les envoie aussi à l'étranger, ce qui est moins fatigant, mais du travail de propagande quand même: s'afficher publiquement avec l'avant-garde révolutionnaire, signer des manifestes sans toujours savoir de quoi il s'agit et jouer les mouches du coche de la nouvelle histoire. Mais l'art et la littérature qui s'expriment ainsi restent des pâles reflets de la réalité, sont des mots d'ordre élaborés au ministère de la propagande.

De nos jours il s'est tout de même présenté des occasions où des intellectuels indépendants, s'exprimant au nom de l'intérêt général, se sont attaqués à certains problèmes sociaux—liberté de l'individu, indépendance nationale—et ceci chaque fois que les grands organismes qui représentent les classes restaient muets. Dans les dernières décennies il y a eu des épisodes dans lesquels la scène politique a été dominée par l'initiative de groupes intellectuels ou même d'intellectuels isolés. Ceci a été particulièrement visible dans des pays coloniaux où l'organisation tribale était rudimentaire et où quelques intellectuels, instruits à l'étranger mais restés fidèles à leur peuple d'origine, ont mené la lutte contre les puissances colonisatrices. La "Négritude" est une invention d'intellectuels.

Ce sont eux qui sont également à la base de la lutte contre l'Etat totalitaire, dont la bureaucratisation abolit toute spontanéité créatrice. Dans tous les pays ce sont la paysannerie, les communautés religieuses, les groupes culturels ou même des intellectuels isolés, qui se sont révélés être les maillons les plus faibles de la chaîne totalitaire; c'est ainsi que nous avons vu la *Rose blanche* en Allemagne nazie, le groupe *Non mollare* à Florence et la personnalité de Croce en Italie fasciste. Nous n'oublierons jamais les clubs *Petoefi* en Hongrie et les petits cercles *Propostu* de Pologne en 1956. Aujourd'hui c'est sur les universités et la masse estudiantine d'Espagne que nous comptons. Il y a aussi des livres qui one gagné des batailles sur le front antitotalitaire, tel le *Dr. Jivago*.

Seul celui qui l'a éprouvé peut savoir ce que cela coûte d'angoisse et de doute de résister au bourrage de crâne, de suivre l'appel de sa conscience, de rompre avec un régime auquel on est lié par toutes les fibres de son âme. Mais le pire n'est pas la persécution policière, ni la faim, ni la calomnie, c'est l'accusation de trahison portée contre vous par des esprits simples et honnêtes et parmi eux vos propres amis.

Mais de ce côté-ci du monde, dans les pays aux traditions démocratiques, des conditions peuvent se présenter qui exigent l'intervention des intellectuels, même de ceux qui d'habitude restent à l'écart des agitations politiques. Ceci lorsque la conscience nationale est confrontée par des problèmes graves, et que les organismes politiques existants ne les ont pas analysés sérieusement, ni pris les mesures qui s'imposaient; les partis traditionnels semblent frappés de sclérose et font l'impression d'attendre que les esprits s'apaisent d'eux-mêmes et que la routine reprenne le dessus. C'est ce qui a conduit à sa perte la 4ème République française. Rappelons-nous que pendant la guerre d'Algérie, devant l'incurie des partis et des organismes démocratiques, ce sont les intellectuels qui ont sauvé l'honneur de la France.

Ici aux Etats-Unis, dans un contexte social et politique différent, nous voyons un malaise analogue se répandre parmi les étudiants et les intellectuels au sujet du conflit vietnamien. On pourrait naturellement rétorquer que le problème est plus complexe que ceux-ci ne l'imaginent, et qu'on ne peut pas résoudre les affaires du monde et les contradictions de notre temps en invoquant des valeurs morales et intellectuelles. Mais la liberté qui leur permet de protester est en elle-même une des conditions du débat, et c'est elle qui rend possible la réfutation d'affirmations éventuellement fausses. Et M. Silone, constatant qu'il est en train de parler de guerre et de paix, termine sur le mot de Clemenceau qui disait que la guerre est une chose trop sérieuse pour qu'on la laisse aux généraux.

M. den Doolaard annonce qu'il a l'intention d'être polémique et concret. Concernant la question de savoir si l'écrivain adopte une *persona* il s'oppose, comme l'avait fait le président avant lui, à la notion que l'écrivain engagé joue consciemment un rôle. "L'engagement et l'oeuvre littéraire sont fréquemment les deux faces de la même personalité". Ce n'est pas parce que Zola était un écrivain "engagé", pas non plus parce qu'il avait eu le courage de prendre la défense de Dreyfus devant la populace, que M. den Doolaard admire les meilleurs romans de Zola. D'autre part il ne croit pas que Zola jouait un rôle, avait volontairement adopté une *persona*. Il était engagé de par sa nature même, "il ne pouvait faire autrement". Un autre exemple est M. Romain Gary qui a symboliquement défendu l'humanité dans *"Les racines du ciel"*, tout en prétendant défendre les éléphants d'Afrique.

M. den Doolaard n'est pas satisfait non plus de ce que le programme impliquât "qu'il n'était pas souhaitable que l'écrivain fût engagé". La Charte du P.E.N.—qu'il a lui-même traduite en hollandais—n'engage-t-elle pas tous les membres du P.E.N. à faire leur possible pour bannir la haine entre races, classes et peuples? C'est une décision purement personnelle que d'accepter un engagement ou non; on est un "lutteur" ou on ne l'est pas, et la décision n'est pas l'affaire d'un sentiment ou d'une conviction intellectuelle—comme le programme le laisse entendre— mais avant tout fonction de cet élément mystérieux appelé "conscience". Elle peut dépendre aussi de l'éducation ou des traditions, ce qui fut probablement la raison de la position très prudente que le grand Faulkner avait adoptée face au problème de la déségrégation. M. den Doolaard a été lui-même un anti-fasciste "engagé", ce qui lui a valu d'être expulsé de quatre pays avant la guerre. Depuis la guerre, depuis Hiroshima, il lutte contre l'armement nucléaire, et il termine en ces termes: "vous ne le trouverez pas en toutes lettres dans mes écrits, mais c'est la base de toute mon oeuvre. Nous sommes menacés d'anéantissement et c'est pour cela que je suis un écrivain engagé".

Mlle Lehmann nous confie qu'elle a été toute la semaine poursuivie par une phrase de W. H. Auden: "des visages privés dans les lieux publics sont plus agréables et plus sensés que des visages publics dans des lieux privés". C'est là que réside le problème. Elevée comme elle l'a été dans un milieu aux traditions littéraires et musicales, ayant pris comme modèle de ses ambitions juvéniles des auteurs anglais tels que Jane Austen, Mrs. Gaskell et George Eliot, son rêve était d'écrire des livres tout en restant "extrêmement privée", anonyme en fait, comme l'avaient faite ses idoles. Le fait qu'un écrivain pouvait signer ses oeuvres d'un pseudonyme lui semblait une "libération", et elle le croit encore.

Mais quand le roman *Dusty Answer,* qu'elle avait publié fort jeune et sous son propre nom, se révéla être un *best-seller,* elle fut terrifiée. Depuis, elle n'a pas réussi à concilier son désir d'introspection avec ce qui était devenu sa personnalité publique—la personne que les éditeurs envoyaient faire des tournées de conférences, qu'on suppliait de parler à la radio, et tout le reste. Selon Mlle Lehmann, la raison d'être d'un écrivain c'est d'écrire, et de continuer à écrire aussi honnêtement que possible. Henry James a dit que "la véritable initiation commençait au moment où l'on savait gaspiller son temps, ses passions, ses curiosités". Flâner, absorber sans avoir à produire—ce que Keats appelle la "capacité négative" du poète—voilà la vraie vie pour un écrivain.

Il est vrai que James a aussi dit: "il faut se jeter la tête la première dans l'élément destructif", peut-être même monter sur le podium et parler! Mais voilà que se présente le danger de croire à nos propres opinions; on finit par être tenté d'admirer sa propre image, de la fabriquer soi-même! Mlle Lehmann suggère un bon thème—ou sous-thème—pour un congrès futur: "l'écrivain en tant qu'esprit silencieux". Marianne Moore a dit qu'on devrait apprendre avant tout à garder le silence, à écouter, à être prêt à recevoir "l'inspiration d'en haut". Pour Mlle Lehmann, "en haut" veut dire "de l'intérieur". Et c'est pourquoi elle imagine un futur congrès sous la forme d'une quantité de petites chambres avec des petites tables rondes, autour de chacune d'elles une douzaine d'écrivains assis dans le silence le plus complet pendant 20–30 minutes, après quoi chacun aurait la permission de prononcer une seule phrase. "Je pense qu'ainsi nous trouverions quelques idées formidables, on peut-être même rien qu'une seule".

M. Choi, parlant anglais, déclare pour commencer que l'écrivain coréen n'écrivait pas pour distraire la classe dirigeante, ni pour faire la propagande du parti au pouvoir, mais comme porte-parole de son peuple, un peuple qui avait dans le passé connu la pauvreté et l'oppression. Avant l'ère de domination japonaise (1910–1945) la cour royale avait imposé la culture chinoise, et la littérature chinoise était la seule admise. Sous le régime colonial japonais, la langue et la littérature japonaises furent seules enseignées, et pendant les années de guerre la liberté d'expression fut réprimée sans ménagements. C'est la raison pour laquelle—à part un certain grand poète des temps reculés qui avait écrit en patois coréen—ce n'est que depuis 1945 que l'écrivain coréen a été à même de penser, sentir et parler pour son peuple.

Si cela correspond à un "engagement", il est inconscient et instinctif, pas voulu. M. Choi est d'avis qu'un engagement conscient est dangereux, il fait perdre à l'artiste créateur son indépendance. Il a l'impression que les jeunes écrivains coréens ont tendance à s'éloigner de cette attitude de communion avec le peuple. Ce n'est qu'en vivant avec son peuple que l'écrivain peut se considérer comme engagé sans courir le danger de perdre son indépendance spirituelle.

Le président annonce que les chaînes de radio ont exprimé le désir d'interviewer un certain nombre de membres présents, y compris Messieurs Nasciamento (Brésil), Ngugi (Kenya), Kané (Sénégal), Abruquah (Ghana), Mme Ocampo (Argentine), puis il donne la parole à M. Pablo Neruda.

M. Neruda, parlant français, avoue qu'en écoutant les discussions—si intéressantes et touchantes—qui viennent d'avoir lieu, il a eu une petite surprise. Il croyait qu'on avait fini la guerre froide, qui avait été si terrible pour les écrivains des deux côtés. Apparemment il avait rêvé, car il y avait ici des collègues illustres pour lesquels la guerre froide continuait. Il ne dirait qu'une seule chose au sujet de cette guerre froide entre écrivains: il a visité tous les pays socialistes que les capitalistes appellent totalitaires, il a visité tous les pays capitalistes, il a partout parlé avec les écrivains, et sous tous les régimes il a trouvé des écrivains heureux et des écrivains malheureux, et en toute sincérité, il en a trouvé plus de malheureux dans la société capitaliste. Son grand désir est que tous les écrivains, quels que soient leur rôle, leur célébrité ou leur anonymat, soient heureux et créateurs.

Le Chili, patrie de M. Neruda, a été "inventé" par un poète du 16ème siècle, Ercilla, qui était venu avec les conquistadores sanglants de l'empire espagnol. Homme de la Renaissance dont la mission était de chanter les conquêtes impérialistes, il a assisté au sort tragique des Indiens araucaniens, a été témoin de l'héroïque défense de leur terri-toire, de leurs privilèges, de leurs croyances, et il a écrit une longue et merveilleuse épopée: *la Araucana*. Le Chili est donc né d'un poème écrit par un héros qui venait pour célébrer les héros de son propre pays et qui a fini par exalter la fierté et les prouesses de ceux que la conquête allait anéantir. Depuis, les écrivains chiliens n'ont jamais cessé d'avoir un esprit d'indépendance.

Si l'on étudiait la poésie de Rimbaud ou de Whitman sans penser à leurs opinions politiques ou sociales, on pourrait imaginer qu'elle est libre de toute préoccupation politique et sociale. Rimbaud a pourtant été marqué au plus profond de son être par son désaccord avec la société, la personnalité de Whitman a été pénétrée par le tragique de son époque et par la ferveur qu'il portait à la cause de Lincoln. Sans cette grande commotion il n'aurait pas existé, et Rimbaud non plus, s'il n'avait été la créature du conflit intérieur entre la société et sa per-sonne.

M. Neruda a parcouru tous les villages, toutes les mines de son vaste pays qui s'étend presque de l'Equateur au Pôle Sud. Le peuple est venu à lui, l'a écouté, lui a posé des questions—parfois rien que du re-gard—et ce qu'il demandait était: "parle au nom de ceux qui ne peuvent pas parler, écris au nom de ceux qui ne peuvent pas écrire". Il accomplit cette mission avec humilité et avec orgueil; sa poésie a été écrite avec angoisse mais dans l'espoir qu'en luttant contre la guerre et l'injustice il contribuerait à changer la condition des peuples de l'Amérique latine, et il ne veut poser qu'une seule question: "si l'écrivain ne se fait pas le porte-parole de la condition humaine, que peut-il faire?"

En somme, M. Neruda est le "poète totalement engagé", convaincu que l'avenir de l'humanité est un avenir de liberté, de création, de dignité et de justice, et si on le qualifiait de propagandiste il l'accep-terait avec fierté; Whitman et Hugo n'étaient-ils pas aussi des propa-gandistes? Il a connu un poète qu'il a aimé comme aucun autre—Federico García Lorca—un homme fier qui n'avait pas voulu s'engager;

il était son ami. Pendant la guerre d'Espagne Lorca a été sacrifié par ce qu'on appelait alors le "totalitarisme socialiste". Cette blessure, Neruda la porte encore dans sa littérature, dans sa poésie, dans sa conscience et il s'est dit: "Il n'était pas engagé, mais moi je le serai, je lutterai un peu pour que ces choses ne se répètent pas".

M. Bell annonce qu'il va parler des auteurs d'oeuvres d'imagination et de sensibilité, au risque de blesser les uns ou les autres. Il parlera surtout en tant que sociologue et fait remarquer que "ce qu'on appelle de nos jours un écrivain est un personnage dont l'apparition sur la scène sociale est récente". Ceux qui cherchaient jadis à symboliser les sentiments étaient soit des prêtres qui utilisaient un rituel, soit les bardes qui se servaient de mythes, de légendes et des thèmes éternels de la tragédie. L'écrivain moderne est le produit de deux tendances. La première est celle qui insiste sur l'expérience et sur l'immédiat, en contraste avec le passé où on se préoccupait de révélation, d'autorité, de tradition et même de raison. La seconde est celle qui met l'accent sur l'individu en opposition au groupe, sur le "moi" qui se rapproche le plus de la vérité.

L'écrivain n'est toutefois pas un être isolé, il vit dans un milieu social, fait partie d'une coterie, rencontre les autres. Rien de ce qui le concerne, son imagination, son art, son style de vie, ne sert de modèle aux autres hommes.

Etant donné qu'il existe toujours une tension entre le "moi" et la société, les écrivains jouent un rôle social, non pas dans le sens de se donner en spectacle, mais dans celui d'une obligation envers eux-mêmes et envers les autres. En jouant ce rôle, l'écrivain est exposé à certaines tentations—le "moi" est un aimant puissant—il est souvent séduit par l'idée du pouvoir, il devient un idéaliste, un apologiste, un moralisateur imbu de sa propre vertu. Une bonne partie de ces choses—même les meilleures—il les rationalise et appelle cela "être engagé". Dès ce moment, l'engagement devient une mystique. "Engagement", cette notion reste abstraite, elle est rarement l'expression d'une intention simple et définie, au pire elle peut dégénérer en attitude, devenir ce que le philosophe américain Williams James apelle "l'ascension de l'échelle de la foi", au cours de laquelle les possibilités ne se distinguent pas des probabilités, et l'échelle elle-même devient une certitude. Une définition de l'écrivain idéologue: "l'homme qui court dans la rue en criant: "J'ai une réponse! Quelqu'un a-t-il une question?"

Dans les sociétés industrielles avancées, la situation est un peu meilleure, car là on peut au moins affirmer que l'écrivain se trouve aux prises avec un problème important: ses rapports avec les hommes politiques, avec le pouvoir, avec l'intelligentsia technologique.

Dans le domaine des rapports avec la politique, on court le risque de voir son "moi" anéanti. Et là M. Bell voudrait rappeler que le problème n'est plus: "l'écrivain est-il heureux ou malheureux?"—car il peut l'être pour bien des raisons—mais que la question ultime est: 'l'écrivain est-il libre ou asservi, est-il pur ou souillé, est-il en prison ou est-il en liberté?"

Dans le domaine des relations avec l'intelligentsia technologique la situation est plus compliquée, car les questions essentielles que se pose l'écrivain sur la vie sont liées à de nombreux problèmes de détail, qu'il n'est pas en mesure de résoudre par ses propres moyens. Prenons par exemple le problème complexe de la vie dans les grandes cités, qui est bien au-delà de sa compétence. Et pourtant l'écrivain en parle sans être le moins du monde conscient des lacunes de ses connaissances.

Tous les hommes sont plus ou moins dans le même panier et M. Bell suggère que si l'écrivain avait un rôle, ce serait celui de porter l'accent sur le doute plutôt que d'insister sur l'engagement. L' "aliénation", ce mot employé aujourd'hui à toutes sauces, pourrait être un élément positif, car il signifie en fait "se distancer d'un événement". Avec un certain recul on prend mieux conscience de soi-même, et on découvre que les exigences du doute prennent le dessus sur celles de la foi. Mlle Lehmann a cité la "capacité négative" de Keats, le même qui avait dit que Shakespeare avait eu le don de demeurer dans l'incertitude sans toujours vouloir absolument atteindre la foi ou la raison. Goethe a dit: "le doute ne me plaît pas moins que la certitude". D'après M. Bell, le rôle de l'écrivain en tant que personnalité publique serait peut-être de "demeurer en état de doute".

Le président fait alors appel aux opinions venant de l'assistance.

M. Aleksis Rannit (président du P.E.N. des écrivains en exil, membre du P.E.N. américain et du P.E.N. esthonien) tient à souligner que parmi les personnalités publiques il existait des écrivains qu'on pouvait qualifier de "porte-parole exprimant des opinions politiques". Beaucoup d'écrivains de notre époque ont courageusement résisté aux forces sinistres de la politique, mais d'autres ne se sont opposés à Hitler que pour succomber à Staline, abhorrant un gangster et vénérant l'autre. Il propose que de tels écrivains soient tout simplement ignorés en tant que personnalités publiques. Peu ont fait preuve du courage civique et moral de M. Silone qui a rejeté toute dictature. En général l'écrivain personnalité publique a trahi le peuple.

M. Coutsoheras déclare en tant que poète et membre du Parlement grec, qu'il est persuadé que l'écrivain est intimément lié au cadre de son pays et du monde entier. L'histoire nous enseigne que la mythologie et le folklore sont nés dans un société dominée par l'idée de Dieu. La littérature grecque s'adressait à l'homme et en même temps au citoyen: l'homme, disait Protagoras, est la mesure de toute chose. La littérature romaine porte l'emblême du *res publica romana,* et cette analyse historique pourrait se poursuivre si la clepsydre du président ne l'obligeait d'arriver à notre temps où nous admettons que la loi naturelle, le quasi-contrat social entre le bourgeois et son milieu, ont été l'influence déterminante sur la littérature créatrice. Ceci est la preuve que la littérature, bien loin d'y perdre, a beaucoup gagné à être le fruit du climat social, et que le poète également ne peut que gagner à être une personnalité publique.

Eschyle aurait-il écrit *les Perses* s'il n'avait pas été à Marathon et à Salamine? Sophocle et Euripide auraient-ils su nous communiquer leur idée de l'homme et de l'humanité s'ils s'étaient tenus à l'écart de la vie publique? Dante n'a-t-il pas écrit la Divine Comédie parce qu'il était un homme politique? L'écrivain ne peut échapper à une participation à la vie de sa société, car c'est son milieu social qui a guidé sa sensibilité, son humanité, son lyrisme. Ceci est le credo d'un poète qui est également député d'Athènes.

Mme Hilda Domin cite trois poètes qui ont chanté la beauté et le pouvoir consolateur des arbres, puis Confucius qui a dit que "les arts ne peuvent pas prospérer tant que le langage est incorrect". Quand ceci est le cas, les lois sont inefficaces et il s'ensuit la confusion des peuples. Elle ajoute qu'un écrivain peut être engagé et tout de même faire de la poésie pure. Chaque écrivain "devrait se constituer contrôleur de la pureté de la langue de son pays, gardien du vrai sens de la réalité". En outre elle demande instamment qu'on prenne la défense des écrivains contre les Etats qui les mettent en prison.

M. Tseng affirme que l'écrivain est un individu intégré dans une communauté et que tout ce qu'il écrit agit sur sa communauté. Dans ce sens il est inévitablement une personnalité publique. Cela dépendra de sa force de caractère et de ses convictions si sa *persona* publique parvient à le détourner d'une activité créatrice artistique indépendante. Au cours des 120 siècles d'histoire de la Chine une figure se détache, Confucius, un grand écrivain qui fut aussi une grande personnalité publique, un maître qui avait attiré 3000 étudiants. Il n'avait pas désiré devenir une personnalité publique, mais il l'était devenu par la force de ses écrits, et personne n'oserait prétendre que cela l'avait amené à renoncer à son indépendance.

M. Tseng se permet de mentionner que dans sa propre famille avait existé, au cours de la dynastie Chiu, un philosophe et écrivain—en même temps général en chef—qui avait été une personnalité publique incorruptible. Aujourd'hui la science essaye de contester ou de supprimer l'impulsion créatrice en "computérisant" l'esprit humain, l'idéologie a l'ambition de "refaire" les esprits. En Russie, Sinyavsky et Daniel sont en prison. En Chine communiste la littérature devient un instrument de contrôle politique, L'honnêteté intellectuelle "ne peut être garantie tant que ces forces fascistes continuent d'exister," et les écrivains doivent sortir de leur tour d'ivoire pour lutter contre elles. M. Tseng a rédigé un rapport sur la situation en Chine qu'il tient à la disposition de ses confrères.

Le président Miller, prié de prendre la parole, désire se limiter à sa propre expérience, et essayer de ne pas formuler des dogmes; il croit néanmoins que c'est une erreur de prétendre que l'engagement de l'écrivain met nécessairement son art en péril, ou que le fait qu'un écrivain soit non-engagé (quoi que cela veuille dire) ait une influence positive ou négative sur son art.

D'une part nous avons des exemples d'écrivains engagés—un Neruda, un Brecht—dont on ne peut mettre en doute la qualité artistique. D'autre part il existe de grands écrivains pour qui "l'engagement est une prison". La question semble par conséquent mal posée. Aux Etats-Unis l'attitude des écrivains face à l'engagement a subi une profonde modification. Pendant la dépression économique des années 30, les écrivains américains—ou du moins une bruyante minorité—se déclaraient en général engagés à l'une ou l'autre forme de l'idéologie socialiste. A ce propos, il faut se rendre compe que par tradition le public américain ignorait ses écrivains. L'auteur en tant que personnalité publique était un phénomène rarissime il y a peu de temps encore. Par "personnalité publique" M. Miller n'entend pas un écrivain célèbre, mais celui "dont l'opinion sur les affaires publiques peut avoir une influence politique".

Le poète Robert Lowell s'est exprimé sans retenue su sujet du conflit vietnamien. Tous les citoyens ont réagi à ses affirmations, soit en les rejetant avec dégoût, soit en les applaudissant—suivant leur point de vue personnel; ce phénomène mérite d'être remarqué dans un pays où jusqu'alors un écrivain qui prenait position sur un problème politique était ridiculisé ou tout simplement ignoré.

M. Miller a connu des écrivains américains qui parlaient en public et signaient des manifestes, dont les oeuvres ne révélaient aucun engagement spirituel à quoi que ce soit. Il en a aussi connu qui n'avaient jamais fait de déclarations, signé aucune pétition, mais dont l'oeuvre était l'évidence d'un engagement sans ambiguïté à l'une ou l'autre conception de la société humaine. C'est pourquoi il lui paraît être une entreprise stérile que de vouloir à tout prix établir un rapport entre l'oeuvre d'un écrivain et le degré de son engagement—ceci tout en respectant les deux points de vue, et en admettant que les deux espèces d'écrivains sont de bonne foi. Lui-même s'est engagé publiquement de temps à autre, et a exprimé cet engagement dans ses écrits, "cela faisait partie du sang et de la chair de ce que j'écrivais", mais il ne croit pas que ces oeuvres en aient été rendues meilleures ou moins bonnes, ni qu'un ecrivain choisisse de propos délibéré d'être engagé ou non.

Certains sont "emportés par leur vision de ce qui ne va pas dans le monde", ce qui les pousse à attaquer ou à défendre. Quoi qu'il en soit, ce problème n'appartient pas au domaine du "soit l'un soit l'autre", il n'a rien d'impératif, mais M. Miller est persuadé—si contradictoire que cela puisse paraître—que le lecteur et le spectateur sont particulièrement sensibles aux problèmes qui se rapprochent le plus de leurs propres problèmes personnels ou sociaux. Cela revient à dire que quand un écrivain se penche sur les réalités de son temps, son "engagement" a une influence sur les réactions du public à son oeuvre. Une pièce de théâtre qui traite les problèmes de la vie quotidienne de manière vivante stimule plus les spectateurs, reçoit plus d'attention de la part de la critique, qu'une oeuvre, si bien écrite soit elle, qui n'a aucun point commun avec ce qui préoccupe l'homme dans la rue, à l'usine ou au lit. M. Miller croit que la littérature subit "une pression implacable, qui l'oblige à se préoccuper de ce qui est pertinent", et que l'engagement de l'écrivain consiste à "être l'oeil qui voit la réalité du moment".

En ce qui concerne ses opinions politiques, l'écrivain peut être "aussi stupide et naïf que n'importe qui d'autre". Il est naturel que "tout ce qu'on écrit soit personnel, puisqu'on écrit ce qu'on a envie de lire, ce qui nous envahit et nous donne envie de continuer". L'engagement est un auxiliaire puissant pour l'écrivain à qui il a permis de se trouver lui-même, il est néfaste à celui qu'il a entraîné loin de son "moi".

M. Silone tient à clarifier certains points de sa précédente intervention. Il a parlé avec admiration des intellectuels qui s'étaient opposés au nazisme, au fascisme, au colonialisme, à la guerre d'Algérie et à celle du Vietnam, et des Polonais et des Hongrois qui ont gardé leur amour de la liberté, et de Pasternak, Sinyavsky et Daniel, sans avoir le sentiment de retomber "dans la mentalité de la guerre froide". Celui qui pense à la guerre froide sitôt qu'on prononce le nom de Pasternak est lui-même le prisonnier de cette mentalité.

Deuxièmement, M. Silone avait insisté sur le fait qu'il utilisait le terme "totalitaire" non dans son sens péjoratif vulgaire, mais dans son sens objectif, juridique et historique—un régime où l'autorité politique a un pouvoir absolu sur l'homme et la société, où elle décide ce qui est beau et ce qui est laid, ce qui est vrai et ce qui est faux. Nous avons heureusement pu être témoins d'une évolution de cette forme extrême dans plusieurs démocraties populaires et même en Russie, et nous espérons que cela aura le résultat d'une transformation du socialisme totalitaire en socialisme démocratique.

En ce qui concerne l'élargissement des rangs du P.E.N. international, M. Silone verrait favorablement la cooptation de nos confrères russes ou même chinois dans cette association libre, qui librement et franchement discute tout ce qui touche la vie littéraire et artistique sans réserve mentale et avec un respect mutuel. Son respect à lui est complet envers tout le monde et—si M. Neruda le permet—également envers lui.

M. Bell partage la plupart des vues de M. Miller, mais aimerait faire une distinction. Il est certainement important qu'un écrivain dise: "je sens la vérité, je la vois, il faut que je l'exprime". Mais au moment où il donne "une réponse naïve à la réalité", il fait deux choses: il exprime et il affirme. Son expression est peut-être naïve, mais son affirmation est une sorte de jugement. C'est la même différence que celle qui existe entre la connaissance et l'opinion. Les opinions ne s'appuient pas toujours sur des connaissances, et les écrivains bien souvent affirment en croyant qu'ils ne font que s'exprimer. On pourrait se demander s'ils disposent toujours du degré de connaissance, du degré de jugement, ou de la "disposition d'esprit" qui sont nécessaires au jugement porté dans son affirmation. Quand ils ne sont pas en possession de ces attributs, leur engagement risque de devenir une mystique qui leur servira à justifier la croyance que tout ce qu'ils affirment est la vérité.

M. Franz Theodor Csokor (président du P.E.N. autrichien) parlant anglais, exprime sa joie à se trouver pour la première fois dans le pays de la Déclaration de l'Indépendance, le pays du regretté "jeune et merveilleux" président Kennedy. Au sujet du thème du congrès, il fait remarquer que la littérature connaît trois formes, "art pur, art engagé, art dirigé". Concernant la première, c'est dans la poésie que nous cherchons le plus souvent une expression libre et indépendante, et pourtant les plus profondes impressions poétiques que nous avons ressenties ces dernières années proviennent de la poésie engagée, par exemple la *Fugue de la Mort* de Celan ou *Hauspostille* de Brecht, oeuvres qui ont même été plus durables que les *Elégies de Duino* de Rilke, qui pourtant comprenait un des vers les plus profonds qui existent: *Alles Volkommene fällt zum Uralten*—"tout ce qui est parfait devient une partie de ce qui est vieux comme le monde". Là le poète est son propre patron, le musicien se paie lui-même et choisit son morceau.

En ce qui concerne les oeuvres engagées, il suffit de rappeler la phrase de Gide selon laquelle "chaque écrivain a un facteur—la conscience—

qui est réveillé et stimulé par les événements". Quant à l'art dirigé, on peut admettre que ce n'est que dans ce domaine que l'écrivain produit en obéissant à un dessein "en dehors de sa propre sphère". M. Csokor rappelle que les arts visuels ont toujours été influencés—voire dirigés— par des institutions religieuses et sociales, sans que pour cela leur qualité en eût souffert.

Le facteur décisif est toujours la personnalité du patron, et quand celui-ci est une collectivité, il est plus probable que la qualité du résultat sera moins bonne. Pourtant même là des progrès ont été faits, il s'est produit une sorte d'éducation des adultes. Aujourd'hui plus de gens ont quelques notions sur l'évolution de l'art, et ont pris l'habitude de se préoccuper d'art. L'art a une fonction sociale, est en quelque sorte une science sociale, et a été "engendré par les forces prédominantes de son époque". Ceci donne un sens à des choses restées jusqu' ici sans explication. Il procure aux hommes un "centre d'intérêt" sans lequel leur vie serait vide. En ce sens seulement "un art authentique est, et sera toujours, engagé".

M. den Doolaard, qui parle en tant qu' écrivain profondément engagé désire—dans l'intérêt de la tolérance—ajouter une catégorie d'écrivains à celles énumérées par M. Miller. Pendant l'occupation allemande aux Pays-Bas, un jeune poète hollandais avait quitté Amsterdam où régnait la famine pour vivre dans une ferme. Là, bien nourri et sans soucis, il avait écrit "le plus merveilleux poème de la littérature hollandaise contemporaine". Des écrivains de ce genre ne sont peut-être pas le sel de la terre, mais ils sont des anges qui nous restent invisibles, et si leur race s'éteignait, le monde serait perdu.

DEUXIÈME SÉANCE

M. Lovinescu, parlant français, félicite le P.E.N. américain et le comité du programme pour le "choix intelligent d'un sujet qui suscite un intérêt universel". Il a été impressionné par le soin consacré à expliquer la préoccupation de tous face aux "forces plus insideuses encore que la censure et le dogmatisme, qui semblent menacer la réalisation des conceptions de l'écrivain quant à sa fonction et à sa raison d'être". M. Lovinescu se trouve cependant dans un dilemme au sujet de la déclaration du comité: "l'écrivain cherche à discerner un ordre cohérent dans le monde actuel". C'est vrai et ce n'est pas vrai. De grands artistes se sont tenus à l'écart de la recherche de cet ordre cohérent qui a toujours été le "fruit suprême" du travail de l'artiste, et la plus haute expression de sa dignité. Toutes les civilisations sont le résultat de la lutte acharnée de l'homme pour introduire un ordre à lui, humain, dans le mystère d'un monde impersonnel. Cette entreprise précaire et pathétique de recréer le monde à son image a amené l'homme a créer "l'artificiel" dans son sens étymologique, car l'homme est un *artifex* et c'est là sa suprême dignité.

Or il semble qu'aujourd'hui des écrivains parmi les plus grands, fascinés par le non-humain, l'irrationnel, ou, pour employer un mot à la mode, l' "absurde"—"je veux remarquer entre parenthèses", dit M. Lovinescu, "que ce qui est absurde, c'est de qualifier d'absurde un monde étranger à l'homme. Sans l'homme le monde n'est ni bon ni mauvais, ni absurde ni raisonnable, il est ce qu'il est"—ont abandonné, soit par manque de foi, soit par une sorte de fascination du vide, ce qui constituait la raison d'être de leurs prédécesseurs, et se complaisent dans l'entreprise terrible et dangereuse d'évoquer l'irrévocable, le monde étranger à l'homme.

Ce serait lamentablement sot de porter des jugements moraux ou esthétiques sur ce phénomène si caratéristique de notre siècle souffrant. Mais ces constatations nous permettent d'envisager sous un aspect plus sérieux le problème de l'écrivain en tant que personnalité publique, le problème de l'engagement de l'artiste. M. Lovinescu considère comme non-engagé l'écrivain qui refuse de croire à la possibilité d'un ordre humain; et comme engagé l'écrivain qui, soit qu'il embrasse une idéologie politique ou une religion, soit qu'il professe un humanitarisme instinctif, n'a pas perdu sa foi dans l'homme et désire donner un visage humain au grand Tout impersonnel. La confrontation n'est pas une querelle des anciens et des modernes, ni une lutte entre écoles, mais une confrontation de structures mentales et spirituelles différentes. De ce point du vue, un écrivain marxiste a plus d'affinités avec un écrivain catholique, qu'un écrivain catholique avec un écrivain hostile au marxisme, mais non-engagé.

En prononçant des termes comme "foi dans l'homme, dignité humaine, responsabilité de l'artiste", M. Lovinescu ne peut s'empêcher de ressentir une certaine gêne, tant ces valeurs—qui avaient encore cours au XIXème siècle qui, quoique méprisable, appartenait encore à l'homme—ont été discréditées par les faits et la mauvaise littérature politique. C'est pour cela qu'il insiste sur le fait que l'engagement ne suppose pas, selon lui, un optimisme béat et grandiloquent, mais au contraire une discipline sévère, virile, amère parfois, souvent sans espoir, mais d'une noblesse incontestable—encore un de ces mots qui accrochent la langue.

Qui a raison? L'écrivain engagé, ou le non-engagé qu'on appelle indépendant (s'il est permis d'appeler indépendance le fait d'être passif face au monde)?

M. Lovinescu pose la question, mais pour lui elle est une argutie. Lui-même est un écrivain engagé, mais il reconnaît qu'aujourd'hui les plus déchirants cris humains, les plus authentiques images de la faiblesse humaine confrontée pour la première fois avec un monde sans nom et sans visage, ont été produits grâce à ces artistes qui ont perdu la foi en Dieu, en l'homme et même en l'art. Est-ce là l'art de l'avenir ou la dernière manifestation d'un cycle presque révolu? Il n'aura pas l'audace de répondre mais désire laisser aux auditeurs l'image d'une statuette "pas plus grande que ça", découverte en Roumanie dans une contrée étrange où l'on peut contempler la succession ininterrompue des civilisations de la préhistoire à nos jours, et que artistes et archéologues ont baptisée d'un commun accord *le Penseur*. Cette idole accroupie appuie les coudes sur ses genoux, les mains soutiennent une tête encore bestiale, mais sous le front fuyant, sous l'arcade immense des sourcils, les trous des yeux suggèrent un regard pathétique qui contemple avec terreur un monde inconnu et hostile; mais plus forte que la terreur est la curiosité, le désir de savoir et de comprendre, qui font de cet être, qui nous est fraternel, un symbole toujours vivant de l'homme.

M. *Won Ko* (du P.E.N. coréen), parlant anglais, avoue qu'il est incapable de trouver une définition pour le terme "personnalité publique" et que le sujet discuté ne lui semble "pas avoir beaucoup de sens". En Chine et en Corée l'homme de lettres, et plus spécialement le poète, a toujours passé des examens afin de servir son pays. Par conséquent il est un chef, admiré par le peuple pour sa culture, sa sagesse, sa capacité créatrice et sa pureté d'esprit. De nos jours il existe deux littératures coréennes, celle du Nord et celle du Sud, écrites dans la même langue. Les livres qu'il a pu compulser dans la Bibliothèque du Congrès à Washington lui ont révélé que la littérature contemporaine de la Corée du Nord était de la pure propagande. Les nouvelles et les poèmes sont pleins de louanges sur les chefs du gouvernement, le parti au pouvoir et l'allié soviétique, et d'expressions hostiles à ce qu'ils appellent "l'ennemi des peuples pacifiques". Les écrivains nord-coréens sont contrôlés par leur parti, ont l'obligation de tromper le peuple, et depuis 1945 beaucoup d'entre eux ont trouvé la mort pour avoir refusé de le faire. Des écrivains officiels de ce genre peuvent-ils être appelés "personnalités publiques?" En Corée du Sud "tout est différent, sauf la langue".

Pour M. Won Ko, l'écrivain est une sorte de messager, apportant à chaque homme un message nouveau. Il vit dans la république universelle de la compréhension et de l'amitié. Il n'exerce pas d'influence politique, et même quand il écrit un poème contre la guerre il reste un poéte. Paul Valéry a dit: "la poésie est l'esprit de nos vacances".

Mlle Henriette Drake-Brockmann (du P.E.N. australien de Melbourne) a été spécialement intéressée par les remarques faites par les délégués venant de pays en voie de développement. L'Australie est "la dernière voix de la civilisation de l'Occident". Elle n'a de littérature propre que depuis une vingtaine d'années. Les écrivains australiens sont pénétrés de l'esprit d'indépendance—serait-ce parce qu'ils ont dû, quoique de coeur et d'esprit avec l'Angleterre et la culture occidentale, se défendre de l'influence de la tradition britannique? Mais ils subissent la concurrence de livres venant du dehors, et ils souffrent de ce que la littérature australienne ne soit pas enseignée dans les universités. Elle-même a une fois donné un cours de grammaire australienne, il y a plus de 25 ans. Quoiqu'elle et ses confrères préféreraient, comme Mlle Lehmann, être des personnes privées, ils doivent faire tout le contraire, utiliser la TV, les conférences et la presse pour le bien de la littérature de leur pays. Leur engagement est en faveur de leur patrie, et sur ce point leurs capitalistes et leurs communistes sont parfaitement d'accord. La majorité se rallie toutefois à ce que l'on pourrait appeler "le point de vue du travail", et beaucoup prennent à l'occasion la défense des aborigènes. Ce n'est que tout récemment qu'ils ont commencé à devenir des personnalités publiques dans le sens défini par M. Miller.

Mme Anna Kamenova (du P.E.N. bulgare) parlant anglais, est heureuse de penser que ce problème était mis en lumière dans ce lieu où l'on peut entendre et comparer l'opinion d'une si grande variété de délégués. Il lui semble que le sentiment général est "que l'écrivain ne devrait pas s'aliéner de son public". Elle a l'impression que l'influence publique, sinon privée, de l'écrivain est en progrès—de ses oeuvres, veut-elle dire, car en tant que personne il laisse parfois à désirer.

Aujourd'hui, comme cela est symbolisé sur l'emblème du P.E.N. américain, la plume a brisé l'épée. L'écrivain joue un rôle en tant qu'interprète spirituel de son peuple. Il n'est plus le contemplateur solitaire, l'observateur sans préjugés, mais un guerrier sur le champ social, et c'est dans cette mesure qu'on peut l'appeler une personnalité publique. On ne peut cependant pas prétendre qu'il soit absolument indépendant, car il est responsable envers ses lecteurs et son pays. Mme

Kamenova insiste cependant sur le fait que les écrivains qui ne créent que des personnages incapables de surmonter les difficultés inhérentes à la vie de notre temps, et les pessimistes qui ne voient que les côtés sordides de l'existence, ne sont pas dignes de jouer le rôle de guerrier et de prophète. L'écrivain doit savoir mettre en valeur des forces latentes, inventer des personnages positifs et montrer le chemin qui mène vers un avenir lumineux.

M. *Follain* déclare que l'engagement inconditionné de l'écrivain est pour lui aussi répréhensible que le régime de l'indifférentisme ou de la tour d'ivoire. Maurice Barrès s'est déshonoré en écrivant des articles sur *Rosalie*—comme il avait baptisé la baïonnette en 1914—où il disait: "la joyeuse Rosalie doit pourfendre le ventre de l'ennemi, et le pourfendre joyeusement". M. Follain réprouve aussi Vallette, directeur du *Mercure de France,* qui pendant la guerre, alors que Paul Léautaud lui reprochait de bêtifier par pseudopatriotisme, lui répondit: "je ne peux pas être intelligent pendant la guerre. Je serai intelligent après", et il n'accepte pas qu'un écrivain ait les mains sales au nom de la discipline d'un parti. Il répudie aussi l'indifférence coupable, comme elle s'est manifestée chez Flaubert, un des écrivains du XIXème siècle que M. Follain aime le mieux, qui était Normand comme lui, et qui n'a jamais rien vu de ce qui se passait, n'a pas compris la portée de 1848, ni celle de la Commune de 70. Hugo ne l'avait pas compris non plus, mais avait au moins vu que cela existait, ce qui est déjà quelque chose. "A bas l'engagement inconditionnel, mais à bas aussi l'indifférence!"

M. *Valery Tarsis* (P.E.N. des écrivains en exil, Londres), parlant anglais, souligne qu'il porte une lourde responsabilité morale, car c'est lui qui plaide la cause de Sinyavsky, Daniel et autres écrivains russes. De cette déclaration il voudrait exclure les six "soi disant" observateurs qui sont censés apparaître au nom de l'Union des écrivains soviétiques. Il a appris avec une "grande indignation" que l'Union des écrivains avait eu le "toupet" de prétendre qu'en approuvant la condamnation de Sinyavsky et de Daniel, elle parlait au nom de tous les membres de l'Union. Même des écrivains communistes occidentaux— Aragon et d'autres—ont été choqués.

M. Tarsis se demande s'il peut y avoir une place dans le P.E.N. pour les représentants d'un organisme dont la raison d'être est de servir d'instrument à un gouvernement totalitaire, pour faire la police parmi les écrivains. Lui-même est un poète, la politique est pour lui un monde étrange et étranger, mais derrière le "rideau de fer" les écrivains sont forcés de s'occuper de politique. La politique communiste a expliqué pourquoi le prix Nobel 1965 avait été attribué à M. Sholokhov, l'écrivain qui avait publiquement demandé que Sinyavsky et Daniel fussent fusillés. M. Tarsis est "honteux" de ce prix Nobel, il est "honteux" aussi du discours de M. Pablo Neruda, mais il est "fier" de l'intervention de M. Silone.

"Je tiens à dire à M. Neruda", poursuit M. Tarsis, "que nous devrions proclamer non la guerre froide, mais la guerre chaude aux pays communistes. Nous devons cela au peuple russe—une guerre chaude!" En lisant un document plein d'inspiration dû au courageux jeune auteur yougoslave Mihajlov, M. Tarsis a pensé à ses jeunes amis de Russie. Ceux qui vivent dans un monde libre et appartiennent à "cette illustre organisation", pourraient se servir de la "formidable puissance de l'opinion publique", et les communistes au pouvoir ne pourraient pas l'ignorer plus longtemps.

M. Sandor Weöres (du P.E.N. hongrois—message traduit en anglais par Mme Amy Weöres). En ce qui concerne la célébrité de l'écrivain, certains auteurs excellents ne peuvent devenir des personnalités publiques connues que par l'entremise de traducteurs doués, parce qu'ils écrivent dans des langues qui ne sont parlées qu'à l'intérieur de leurs frontières. Beaucoup de poètes yougoslaves, russes, chinois ou japonais, vivants et morts, seraient devenus des personnalités publiques dans le meilleur sens du terme si des traducteurs étaient venus à leur aide; cela aurait également apporté une "nouvelle dimension" à la littérature mondiale et à nos "conceptions spirituelles". Dans l'état actuel des choses ils ne sont pas connus en-dehors de leur pays d'origine.

Mlle Hilde Spiel (du P.E.N. autrichien) parlant anglais, fait remarquer que plusieurs délégués ont semblé encourager les auditeurs à prendre part à des activités politiques non seulement en tant que citoyens, mais en raison de leurs talents, et même pour obéir à certaines traditions. Ceci exigerait de l'écrivain qu'il soit prêt à adopter des points de vues qui ne sont pas les siens—ce qui porterait préjudice à son métier —et qu'il assume des responsabilités qui appartiennent à d'autres—ce qui est souvent contraire à sa nature.

Mlle Spiel désire parler en faveur de l'écrivain qui ne recule devant aucun risque pour résister à l'engagement qu'on exige de lui, mais seulement s'il s'appuie pour cela sur un code moral. Elle ne veut pas se faire l'avocat de certaines exentricités, même de la part du poète que Conor Cruise O'Brien a intitulé "le plus grand poète de notre époque" dans un article récent. Pour elle, Günter Grass par exemple a parfaitement le droit de battre son petit tambour en faveur du parti socialiste pendant l'actuelle campagne électorale, elle admire tout écrivain qui, politiquement, prend position sans ambiguïté, mais là où Grass est dans l'erreur, c'est quand il attaque les écrivains de la République de Weimar pour ne pas s'être accordés sur les questions sociales et politiques. Le devoir de l'écrivain n'est-il pas de penser dangereusement (comme Koestler et Sartre) et d'une manière indépendante? Pour terminer, elle cite Emerson qui a dit que chaque réforme avait été d'abord une opinion privée, et que ce n'était qu'au moyen d'opinions privées que les problèmes étaient jamais résolus.

M. Edgar Johnson (ancien président du P.E.N. américain) a écouté ces débats pendant trois jours jamais avec indifférence, mais parfois avec impatience et rébellion. Il a entendu des prophètes pseudo-scientifiques "coassant un jargon abracadabrant, selon lequel les auditeurs devraient être terrifiés par la technologie, réduits au silence par la sociologie, écrasés par des connaissances computérisées, immolés sur l'autel des media de masse". Certaines voix se sont élevées pour protester ou pour défier, mais la majorité a respectueusement exprimé ses soucis et ses angoisses. Il y a plus de 50 ans, Henry Adams, homme de lettres et écrivain américain, a inventé une "loi de l'histoire" avec laquelle il s'est fait peur à lui-même. Il y a 20 ans, H. G. Wells déclarait que l'esprit humain avait atteint ses limites, et il n'a probablement pas été consolé par le télégramme de Bernard Shaw: "ne vous en faites pas, si l'homme se détruisait lui-même, Dieu le remplacerait par quelquechose de mieux". Aujourd'hui, Samuel Beckett voit la race humaine vivant dans des poubelles, ou enterrée dans le sable jusqu'au cou. M. Johnson, lui, n'attend pas un Godot qui n'arrive jamais, et il ne croit pas que beaucoup d'écrivains l'attendent encore.

Le professeur McLuhan a proposé le rétroviseur de l'automobile comme symbole de la littérature et de l'histoire du passé, il n'a pas tenu compte du fait que la connaissance du passé était indispensable pour comprendre le présent et préparer l'avenir. Pour McLuhan le passé est statique, pour M. Johnson il change constamment, certains éléments reculent, d'autres avancent, et c'est parce qu'il est dans le siège du chauffeur, regardant en avant, et sachant où il va.

Il est bien évident que la connaissance est devenue plus complexe, les ordinateurs sont bien entendu des machines extraordinaires, mais les problèmes qu'ils résolvent leur sont posés par des esprits humains. Il n'a lui-même rien contre les ordinateurs mais il se refuse à croire ceux qui prétendent que l'homme n'est pas capable de les mettre à son service pour en obtenir des renseignements, et qu'il sera forcément asservi par eux.

Quelle dérision de prétendre que l'art ne fait pas de progrès, que la science seule en fait, alors qu'en vérité la compréhension intuitive et la vision des grands écrivains nous ont depuis longtemps enseigné des choses que les psychologues découvrent maintenant à tâtons. Proust, Thomas Mann, Eliot et Joyce ont dit des choses que ni Cervantès ni

Wordsworth n'avaient dites, mais ceci parce que chacun est suprême dans son domaine propre. La littérature n'a pas besoin, comme c'est le cas pour la science, d'être constamment révisée. La compréhension humaine continuera à faire des progrès, affirme M. Johnson.

Le président communique la rectification suivante: "M. Valery Tarsis, du Centre des écrivains en exil, me prie de dire que par guerre chaude il entendait un guerre chaude idéologique. Je le remercie pour cette mise au point".

M. Anoma Kanie fait remarquer que la question que l'on est en train de discuter a été posée avec netteté par M. den Doolaard au cours de la séance du matin: "le fait pour un écrivain d'être engagé porte-t-il atteinte à son activité créatrice?" M. Miller a répondu qu'il s'agissait d'un faux problème, car l'écrivain, en tant qu'homme libre, préoccupé avant tout par le beau et le vrai, doit pouvoir s'exprimer sans se lier, pourvu qu'il soit fidèle à son idéal de servir la liberté. La vérité, critère ultime des démarches de l'écrivain, peut varier parce qu'elle n'est pas formelle. Dans la mesure où il croit l'avoir trouvée il doit s'engager à l'affirmer et la soutenir. On a dit ce matin qu'il ne fallait s'engager qu'en connaissance de cause; or l'écrivain, homme inquiet et à la recherche de la vérité, doit pouvoir s'informer. S'il remet constamment en question la cause dans laquelle il est engagé, il réaffirme son indépendance d'esprit. L'écrivain, membre de la famille humaine exprime les sentiments profonds de l'homme, sa tâche est de combattre la tyrannie et la haine pour le triomphe de la vérité et de la compréhension mutuelle.

Mme Ingeborg Drewitz (du P.E.N. de la République Fédérale d'Allemagne). Les impératifs de la publicité amènent l'écrivain à devenir une personnalité publique, parfois contre son gré. Nous connaissons tous le processus historique qui, détruisant la féodalité, a conduit à un "individualisme âpre" avec le résultat de faire perdre à l'individu son orgueil et son sens de la sécurité, et comme répercussion l'a incité à céder à l'aspiration socialiste d'une sorte d'utopie. D'une part nous avons la combinaison de rêves, de sentiments, de valeurs intellectuelles qui composent l'être humain—cet iceberg dont une faible partie seulement émerge. D'autre part nous avons la sécurité de la collectivité. Les deux existent, chacun a son système. Mme Drewitz croit que le rôle de l'écrivain dans la société devient de plus en plus celui d'un enseignant. Pour sa part elle préfère une société composée d'individus moraux à celle dont les maîtres sont ces "brutes infernales qui ont sept épidermes de plus que tous les autres".

M. Miller voudrait essayer de faire la synthèse de certaines idées qui ont été plus particulièrement évoquées pendant cette séance.

Il y a quelques jours, M. McLuhan, issu d'une société fortement technicisée, a déclaré que l'ère de la culture littéraire, l'ère de l'imprimé, était en train d'être supplantée par l'ère des circuits et de l'électronique. Le lendemain, un groupe d'écrivains latino-américains*, dont certains ne s'étaient encore jamais rencontrés, déclaraient spontanément à cette même tribune que le problème essentiel de leur pays—sauf erreur, sans exception—était d'apprendre à lire au peuple. Dans les deux cas ces hommes parlaient avec sincérité, et donnaient l'image de la réalité. Le problème de M. McLuhan est d'aller au-delà de la lecture, celui des latino-américains d'atteindre le niveau de la lecture. A chacun sa vérité. Il en est de même pour l'engagement; il n'y a pas de vérité une et absolue.

M. Miller peut se représenter que, vivant dans une société d'illettrés, il pourrait être attiré par le désir d'enseigner—parce que le peuple a envie de savoir. Il peut également s'imaginer qu'il pourrait être obsédé par l'idée d'être seul—une île de connaissance dans une mer d'ignorance. Mais, dans une telle situation, comment refuser l'engagement?

Il peut voir aussi un écrivain qui vit à Paris, Londres ou New York, dans un milieu littéraire envahissant, saturé par des messages commercialisés, par des conceptions artifielles qui n'ont aucun rapport avec la réalité quelle qu'elle soit—et qui se sentirait le devoir d'attirer l'attention de ses lecteurs sur les éléments de la nature humaine et de la société dans laquelle ils vivent, qui leur sont restés cachés.

L'intention de ceux qui ont parlé ici-même de l'écrivain en tant que personnalité publique a été de sauvegarder l'écrivain de toute contrainte, de l'aider à ne pas se laisser séduire par des opinions qui ne lui sont pas dictées par sa propre conscience. Qu'il s'engage ou non est, selon M. Miller, l'affaire d'un choix personnel.

Peu après la Révolution américaine de 1776–1783, des théâtres ouvraient leurs portes à Philadelphie et New York. M. Miller a lu des pièces qui avaient été jouées sur ces scènes. Les personnages étaient des Anglais avachis, pleins de partis pris et de condescendance—en un mot parfaitement détestables, et des Américains, braves types de paysans roublards, costauds, facilement roulés, mais dont l'honnêteté naturelle finissait toujours par triompher. Personne n'avait imposé ces types, mais les spectateurs n'auraient probablement pas toléré un Anglais aimable et vaillant. Il y a là une espèce d'engagement avant la lettre, qui a peut-être été imposé par l'opinion publique, par l'idée que l'Américain moyen se faisait de la réalité, ou par ses propres critères moraux.

"Je plaide", dit M. Miller, "en faveur d'une certaine tolérance fondée sur le fait que nous savons que la situation des hommes dans un certain pays est différente de celle des hommes dans un autre pays. Nous—

* Voir La situation de l'écrivain d'Amérique Latine, p. 273.

membres de P.E.N., plus que quiconque—devons tenir compte de ce fait, dans cette discussion, croire à la bonne foi de tout un chacun et au désir commun de rendre notre association universelle. Cela ne nous fera aucun bien si nous ne grandissons en sagesse".

M. Jyotirmoy Datta (Républ. de l'Inde, Calcutta), fait remarquer que des points de vue différents ont été exprimés au sujet de l'engagement. Des délégués du Kenya, de Corée et de la République nationale de Chine ont soutenu l'idée de l'écrivain engagé; M. Bell a proposé un état de doute perpétuel, Mlle Lehmann voudrait que l'écrivain soit réceptif et silencieux. M. Datta, lui, est d'avis qu'il faut écrire le plus beau poème possible, et espérer qu'il trouvera des lecteurs. Il répond à M. Bell que le droit de douter doit comprendre le droit de changer d'avis, car un homme qui ne croit rien n'est pas un homme du tout. Il lui semble qu'à l'Ouest les écrivains ont plus de peine à s'engager, et que dans les pays plus anciens l'engagement est devenu extrême.

M. Boldizsár demande la permission de revenir sur les discussions qui ont eu lieu au sujet des remarques "du plus noble d'entre nous", Ignazio Silone. Il est plein de respect pour Silone, et comme lui, respecte la vérité. Il aimerait faire une remarque sur une situation un peu délicate, mais tout d'abord une remarque personnelle. Il est Hongrois, la Hongrie a été mentionnée, certains pourraient penser: "Boldizsár est hongrois, est-ce qu'il se tait parce qu'il a peur qu'une fois de retour chez lui il soit persécuté au sujet de ce qu'il aurait dit?" Cela n'a pas de sens.

En fait, M. Boldizsár n'est pas, et n'a jamais été, un communiste. S'il parle maintenant, c'est parce que M. Silone a évoqué les événements qui se sont passés en Hongrie il y a dix ans. M. Boldizsár était un des intellectuels qui ont signé les "résolutions du Comité révolutionnaire". Silone est un des héros de sa jeunesse, son livre *Le pain et le vin* passait de main en main pendant la période du fascisme hongrois, car ce livre représentait pour eux la preuve de la dignité humaine, et était une source de confiance en l'avenir. Aujourd'hui il ne veut contredire M. Silone que sur un seul point, c'est d'avoir omis, dans son tour d'horizon, de tenir compte des changements qui se sont produits en Europe orientale. Spécialement en ce qui concerne la Hongrie il a commis une erreur en mettant toutes les formes de totalitarisme "dans le même panier". Quatre délégués hongrois sont présents à ce congrès, aucun n'a jamais été forcé d'entonner des hymnes de louange, aucun n'est un membre du Parti. Il y a dix ou vingt ans aucun d'eux n'aurait pu venir à New York.

Ceci est très important pour eux et pour leurs lecteurs en Hongrie. M. Gyula Illyés n'étant pas dans la salle, M. Boldizsár se permet de dire qu'il est "la plus grande personnalité vivante de la littérature hongroise", son autorisé s'étend au-delà des frontières de son pays. Pour lui et pour toute la Hongrie cultivée—c'est-à-dire 99% de la nation—la présence ici-même d'une délégation hongroise est un événement important, un symbole des modifications qui se sont produites et qu'aucun intellectuel ne saurait ignorer.

Le président est persuadé que la déclaration de M. Boldizsár est en étroit rapport avec la raison d'être du P.E.N. Personnellement, il a été témoin de cette évolution à Budapest. Il ajoute qu'ayant été l'hôte de l'Union des écrivains soviétiques il y a quelques années, il a pu constater que les Russes n'avaient pas "sept épidermes de plus", comme cela avait été prétendu ici-même. Ils ont le coeur chaud, et ne sont pas plus responsables de leur gouvernement que M. Young lui-même, Ecossais, ne l'est du gouvernement anglais à Londres.

Mme Mileva se sent obligée de poser à M. Miller une question personnelle concernant la résolution de paix proposée à la réunion de l'Exécutif international par M. Coutsoheras de Grèce. M. Miller avait proposé de ne pas aborder ce sujet—en quoi il avait raison—parce qu'il s'agissait d'une question politique. Elle désire demander à M. Miller s'il ne trouve pas que la remarque de M. Tarsis est également peu à sa place dans une réunion du P.E.N. En plus de cette question, elle désire protester contre la manière dont M. Tarsis a calomnié l'Union Soviétique et l'Union des écrivains soviétiques. Elle ne lui refuse pas le droit d'exprimer une opinion personnelle—que ce soit sur une personnalité soviétique, ou en disant: "j'ai honte du discours de M. Neruda". Quant aux opinions exprimées par M. Tarsis sur la Bulgarie—où il n'y a actuellement pas un seul écrivain en prison—les écrivains bulgares n'ont pas besoin que qui que ce soit prenne leur défense, et en tout cas pas M. Tarsis, mais, continue Mme Mileva, "je proteste contre le président de cette Table Ronde qui a toléré une déclaration purement politique qui est absolument contraire à la Charte du P.E.N.".

Le président rappelle au souvenir de Mme Mileva un épisode dramatique dans les 45 années d'existence du P.E.N., le Congrès de Dubrovnik en 1934, où des protestations analogues avaient été faites par les nazis délégués par le P.E.N. allemand. Ils avaient exigé que les antinazis allemands en exil soient expulsés du congrès Quand M. H. G. Wells, qui présidait, avait refusé de le faire, ils avaient bruyamment quitté la salle. M. Young rappelle à l'assistance que "celui qui craint la licence n'aime pas la liberté". Son opinion est qu'il préfère infiniment que les délégués disent exactement ce qu'ils pensent, et fassent part de leurs expériences, plutôt que de les voir suivre des procédures qui les empêchent de se comprendre. "Nous désirons une compréhension mutuelle sincère".

M. Miller relève, au sujet de l'intervention de M. Coutsoheras, qu'elle avait été faite à une réunion de l'Exécutif, et dans la forme d'une résolution qui devait être adoptée par cet organisme comme reflétant son point de vue officiel. Sous cette forme elle n'était pas à sa place. De plus, M. Miller pense que c'était une proposition qui n'avait pas de raison d'être. Les gens sont "contre la guerre" de la même manière qu'ils sont "contre le péché". Il va de soit que nous sommes tous contre la guerre. Mais qu'y peut le P.E.N? Le P.E.N. ne peut accomplir que des choses concrètes et spécifiques; la chose qu'il ne peut pas faire, c'est la paix. Comme président du P.E.N. International, il est persuadé que les membres ne tiennent pas à ce que le Comité exécutif passe son temps à prendre des résolutions stériles.

M. Nghiem Xuan Viet (du P.E.N. vietnamien) parlant français, présente quelques idées personnelles. L'artiste se doit tout d'abord de suivre ses tendance profondes en poursuivant le vrai et le beau avec le plus parfait désintéressement. S'il est né artiste, il doit se cantonner dans le domaine de son art, s'il est né lutteur il doit entrer dans l'arène. S'il suit sa propre nature le fait de s'engager ne peut nuire à son indépendance créatrice; en fait c'est dans ce climat de lutte convaincue et sincère qu'il trouvera l'épanouissement complet de sa personnalité.

Reste la question du critère d'après lequel on doit estimer un écrivain. L'artiste pur sera jugé suivant ce qu'il apporte à la recherche du beau et de la création. Pour l'écrivain combattant nous tiendrons compte de sa sincérité; un écrivain sincère peut se tromper de bonne foi. Quoique les moyens d'information actuels nous permettent d'être mieux renseignés, ils diffusent aussi de fausses nouvelles, il faut donc recommander aux écrivains de s'informer avec circonspection. En ce qui concerne le Vietnam, ils devraient visiter ce pays, étudier sa langue, et ne pas accorder leur appui à des mouvements qu'ils condamneraient s'ils étaient mieux informés—c'est ce qui est arrivé par exemple au sujet de Mao ou de Castro.

Quant à la guerre du Vietnam, il constate qu'il y a ici des auteurs connus qui condamnent cette guerre sans se demander où en est la cause, et quelle est la meilleure façon d'y mettre fin. Les compatriotes de M. Nghiem Xuan Viet demandent à ces auteurs de se renseigner sur place sur ce qu'est la véritable nature de ce mouvement soi-disant de "libération nationale". L'orateur pense qu'ils comprendraient alors que cela serait aussi catastrophique pour le Vietnam de s'arrêter à des demi-mesures, que cela avait été pour l'Europe avant la guerre quand Hitler annexait un pays après l'autre. La subversion est un grand danger. La bombe atomique vous tue, c'est tout. La subversion est pire, elle détruit notre âme, notre ordre social, notre liberté. En faisant face au danger avec résolution on aura la paix et la liberté qui doivent être le but final de l'écrivain, car c'est lui qui est responsable de la conscience publique.

M. *Nicanor Parra* (Républ. du Chili) parlant anglais, n'est ni membre d'un parti ni un écrivain engagé. Il fait toutefois remarquer à ceux qui croient que la littérature de propagande seule est autorisée dans les pays socialistes, que cela ne semble plus être le cas. Ses propres poèmes, que certains critiques occidentaux avaient qualifiés de "rien que du non-sens nihiliste", ont été traduits en russe et publiés par l'Union des écrivains soviétiques.

Mlle Shirland Quin (du P.E.N. anglais) croit que G. B. Shaw, qui était certainement une personnalité publique, n'aurait pas "toléré qu'on le nomme 'engagé' ". Son rôle de personnalité publique lui avait beaucoup apporté, car c'était un homme qui avait besoin de conflit pour aiguiser sa verve. Ayant un jour contredit une opinion éthique exprimée par la fondatrice du P.E.N., Mme Dawson Scott, il avait avoué après coup en riant qu'elle avait raison, et qu'il n'était intervenu que pour la stimuler à argumenter d'une manière plus percutante. Il y a eu des écrivains—par exemple D. H. Lawrence ou T. E. Lawrence—pour qui la vie publique représentait l'anéantissement de toute puissance créatrice. Pour elle, le silence, la tranquillité d'esprit préconisée par Mlle Lehmann, est de toute importance. Pour finir, Mlle Quin déclare qu'il n'est pas possible de parler de "l'écrivain", il y a "des écrivains" comme il y a des plantes dans le jardin, et chacun a besoin du sol et de la nourriture qui lui sont le plus favorables.

M. *Frank Doczy* (du P.E.N. australien de Melbourne) demande si un auteur peut être à la fois engagé et indépendant d'esprit, et ce qu'il faut penser de ceux qui "changent d'engagement".

M. *Bell* avoue qu'il est quelque peu perplexe devant la question: "la porte tournante a-t-elle été installée pour déterminer les positions politiques?" Il est difficile de répondre avec pertinence à des questions abstraites. Il se permet de rappeler—peut-être avec une certaine pédanterie—que la philosophie moderne essaye depuis quelques années de nous enseigner à éviter les termes abstraits. "Conscience" et "engagement" n'existent pas par eux-mêmes, ils n'ont de sens que pris relativement: conscience *de* quelque chose, engagement *à* quelque chose. Il veut se borner à attirer l'attention sur ce nouveau "principe d'activité" dans la manière de comprendre la connaissance.

M. *den Doolaard* conseille à l'écrivain d'être d'abord "engagé à son oeuvre". Ce n'est qu'après qu'il pourra soutenir des causes, à condition toutefois de ne pas y gaspiller ses forces.

M. Kamnitzer constatant que les membres du P.E.N. lui paraissent avoir la permission de parler politique en-dehors du Comité exécutif, fait remarquer, primo, qu'il était évident que l'écrivain en tant que personnalité publique ne pouvait être dissocié de la politique, l'opinion de M. Miller sur le Vietnam est largement partagée en Europe, et nous le remercions d'avoir pris position. Secundo, on a demandé à cette audience de soutenir un "régime dont le maréchal Ky est un imitateur d'Hitler" et M. Kamnitzer ne peut pas comprendre les applaudissements qui ont salué cette intervention. Tertio, il ne peut pas comprendre non plus comment cette "illustre assemblée" peut passer sous silence le bombardement du Vietnam au moyen de bombes au phosphore.

M. Georges Charaire (du P.E.N. français) pense que tous les écrivains sont engagés. Valéry disait d'ailleurs que l'acte créateur de l'écrivain engageait tout l'être. L'engagement implique la liberté, si l'on impose un engagement il n'existe plus.

Au temps où Debré était premier-ministre on racontait cette histoire: "De Gaulle téléphone à Debré et lui demande l'heure; Debré répond: 'l'heure que vous voudrez, mon général'." Eh bien, l'écrivain est une personne qui donne l'heure, et chacun donne l'heure de sa propre montre. La liberté est indispensable. Dès l'instant où il y a contrainte— qu'elle vienne du public ou de l'éditeur, qu'elle soit économique ou politique—il n'y a plus d'écrivain.

Au sujet de l'angoisse du monde devant la science, M. Charaire n'en a pas peur, car il pense que les époques scientifiques ont été des époques de grandes créations artistiques. Ce qui le préoccupe toutefois, c'est l'électronique, dont la diffusion énorme risque de tenter l'écrivain pour accéder au public le plus large, donc de descendre au niveau le plus bas et par conséquent de répondre: "l'heure que vous voudrez, mon général".

M. Nghiem Xuan Viet tient à rappeler au délégué de l'Allemagne de l'Est qu'il existe des machines à fabriquer les fausses nouvelles.

M. Wieland Herzfelde croit qu'un changement d'engagement peut être sincère ou pas sincère. Son propre engagement lui paraît correspondre avec la Charte du P.E.N. Tout dépend de qui on a comme adversaire—fasciste ou non-fasciste. "P.E.N. ne peut être qu'anti-fasciste".

M. Jacques Fiechter (du P.E.N. suisse de Genève) annonce aux auditeurs que le Centre genevois du P.E.N. suisse s'apprête à les recevoir dans un avenir proche avec affection et confiance.

Ce congrès a été sans doute une réussite. Premièrement, l'activité du Conseil exécutif. Deuxièment, en dépit des dangers de l'inflation verbale, un travail loyal et honnête a été fait, des hommes et des femmes, venus des quatre coins du monde, ont eu l'occasion de se rencontrer ici dans une atmosphère amicale, et d'apprendre à se comprendre mieux et à se respecter davantage.

Enfin, ce congrès est la démonstration que le P.E.N., dans le monde actuel, représente une grande espérance. Il y a six cents ans, dans trois petites vallées de la Suisse, des hommes libres ont élaboré une Charte où nous retrouvons les principes que le P.E.N. s'efforce d'implanter et de faire rayonner à nouveau et puisqu'en dépit des fautes, des luttes, des différences de races, de langues et de religions, l'expérience de cette communauté fraternelle a réussi, et puisque le P.E.N. représente actuellement cette bonne volonté, cet espoir, et cette affirmation de l'unité dans la diversité, on peut changer un mot au voeu de Victor Hugo et dire: "le P.E.N., dans l'histoire, aura le dernier mot".

M. Bell clôt la discussion à la demande du président. Il va essayer de faire ce que M. Miller avait fait à mi-chemin, voir si des thèmes communs ont émergé de la discussion.

Premièrement, l'écrivain engagé. Cela peut être utile de se demander ce que ces débats auraient été il y a 30 ans. A cette époque on s'engageait à une ligne, à une opinion politique spécifique. Aujourd'hui on parle d'engagement à la vocation d'écrivain. Cela semble impliquer que les passions politiques ne sont pas toujours une "situation religieuse". Il pense que c'est un progrès en ce sens qu'on n'exige plus un engagement total à une ligne politique. L'engagement à la vocation d'écrivain a remplacé l'engagement à une idéologie, à un dogme.

Deuxièmement, concernant la notion que l'écrivain a de la vérité. Il est bon de la comparer à celle des savants. On ne parle pas de science russe, de science américaine ou de science bulgare de la manière dont les nazis parlaient de science allemande, mais on parle de physique, de chimie ou de biologie. Les savants poursuivent des buts objectifs. L'écrivain a des desseins différents, il est un auteur bulgare, un auteur américain ou un auteur russe, parce qu'il s'exprime dans la langue et la culture particulière à son peuple. C'est son expérience qui lui fait connaître la vérité, tandis que le savant la cherche au-delà de l'expérience pour trouver des "normes communes". Ce fait confère une importance spéciale aux dires de M. Miller. Un écrivain doit se méfier de l'idée qu'il exprime une vérité totale, parce que son expérience n'est pas totale mais fragmentaire et expérimentale. Cela ne veut pas dire— et M. Bell n'avait pas, en recommandant une attitude de doute, eu l'intention de dire—que la foi n'existe pas, mais qu'elle doit être mise à l'épreuve, et c'est pourquoi le doute a "la priorité".

C'est dans cette perspective qu'il a apporté son opinion. Ce Congrès a essayé de faire ce que tous les intellectuels essayent de faire: créer une communauté ouverte. Par des discussions ouvertes nous avons cherché à nous comprendre les uns les autres.

La situation de l'écrivain
d'Amérique Latine

15 juin
SÉANCE HORS SÉRIE

Emir Rodriguez Monegal, PRÉSIDENT
Uruguay

Homero Aridjis
Mexique

Manuel Balbontin
Chili

Haroldo de Campos
Brésil

Carlos Fuentes
Mexique

Alberto Girri
Argentine

Juan Liscano
Vénézuéla

Carlos Martínez Moreno
Uruguay

M. A. Montes de Oca
Mexique

Pablo Neruda
Chili

Victoria Ocampo
Argentine

Juan Carlos Onetti
Uruguay

Nicanor Parra
Chili

J. Guimaraes Rosa
Brésil

Mario Vargas Llosa
Pérou

La situation de
l'écrivain d'Amérique Latine

M. Rodriguez Monegal, parlant anglais, déclare qu'il préside une séance *hors série* que ses collègues d'Amérique latine et lui-même ont proposée spontanément et que leurs hôtes d'Amérique du Nord se sont empressés d'organiser. Il présente ensuite au public les écrivains réunis sur l'estrade: MM. A. Montes de Oca (Mexique), Nicanor Parra (Chili), Victoria Ocampo (Argentine), C. Martínez Moreno (Uruguay), Carlos Fuentes (Mexique), M. Vargas Llosa (Pérou), Haroldo de Campos (Brésil), Manuel Balbontin (Chili), Homero Aridjis (Mexique). D'autres écrivains d'Amérique latine se trouvent dans la salle et ils se feront entendre de là. Le président annonce que les orateurs ne parleront ni espagnol ni portugais, mais français et anglais, les deux langues officielles du P.E.N., vu la présence d'une majorité de délégués venant d'autres pays.

M. Martínez Moreno, parlant français, fait remarquer que pour être à même de discuter la situation de l'écrivain latino-américain il est nécessaire d'utiliser le terme bien connu de "sous-développement". Il est significatif que l'espagnol ne soit pas l'une des langues officielles du P.E.N. En Amérique latine, le sous-développement a créé pour l'écrivain un problème de "non-communication". Ce dernier se trouve en effet gêné, freiné dans son rôle de témoin de son temps. Il vit à l'écart des grands centres culturels. Il n'existe que par des intermédiaires divers. Son anonymat l'empêche d'être reconnu par les siens comme homme de lettres professionnel. Seul un très petit nombre d'auteurs de ces pays parviennent à vivre de leur art. Il va de soi que ceci varie selon le pays, le marché littéraire, les maisons d'édition, le nombre d'habitants. Chaque écrivain ne peut rendre compte que des conditions qui existent dans son propre pays. L'unité latino-américaine que tous désirent si ardemment et cherchent à promouvoir dans leurs oeuvres est encore lointaine. Tous connaissent les obstacles, mais ce qui est difficile, c'est de savoir comment les surmonter. A certaines occasions les écrivains eux-mêmes ont exagéré leurs différends, les ont exacerbés et cultivés et pour finir se sont retrouvés seuls dans chacune de leurs républiques, désunis, s'ignorant les uns les autres et ignorés par le monde.

Ceci fait ressortir l'importance du congrès du P.E.N. M. Martínez Moreno est convaincu que chaque centre latino-américain du P.E.N. doit être raffermi tout d'abord en reconnaissant le fait que chacun a ses propres faiblesses qui lui sont particulières. Il ne pense pas offenser qui que ce soit en déclarant que le Centre d'Uruguay est extrêmement faible.

Il faut également mentionner l'anachronisme d'une culture officielle sans aucun rapport avec les cultures vivantes des pays d'Amérique latine. Il est possible que ce que Gide appelait "communion différée" en parlant des différences de classe, soit en partie responsable de cet état de chose. Les écrivains ne sont reconnus par les milieux officiels qu'avec grand retard. Ce n'est pas que les écrivains réclament des postes officiels . . . en tant qu'attachés culturels, par exemple. Ce qu'ils veulent c'est être reconnus comme étant les représentants vivants d'une culture vivante. Et c'est la triste vérité que dans toutes les républiques la culture officielle, est devenue une espèce de Panthéon—revues officielles, consécration officielle, obsèques officielles. Il faut qu'un écrivain soit mort, ou du moins réduit au silence pour qu'on lui accorde sa place au Panthéon. Il n'existe aucune simultanéité entre la culture vivante et créatrice d'une part et les valeurs culturelles exploitées et magnifiées officiellement de l'autre. C'est pour cette raison que les écrivains d'Amérique latine doivent apprendre à se connaître, se faire entendre, et écrire dans le but de mettre un terme à cette "non-communication".

M. Parra, parlant anglais, ne veut pas faire de généralités, mais donner un exemple concret des relations culturelles. En 1965 il a publié en Argentine un livre dont l'éditeur lui envoya 100 exemplaires à son adresse privée au Chili. A ce jour, les autorités postales chiliennes n'ont pas encore été légalement autorisées à lui remettre ces livres: "en d'autres termes, on ne permet pas aux livres d'entrer dans le pays, même si leur auteur est chilien".

M. Liscano, parlant français, fait remarquer que le marché des livres est très limité en Amérique latine, d'où il ressort que les occasions d'être publié sont très limitées, elles aussi. Les maisons d'édition se répartissent entre deux pôles. Dans le sud, il y en a à Buenos Aires, à Montevideo et au Chili. Au nord, à Mexico City. Entre les deux, de Panama à la Bolivie, il n'y a pratiquement pas une seule maison d'édition, et en tant que vénézuélien, M. Liscano peut parler en connaissance de cause lorsqu'il déclare qu'il est extrêmement difficile à un écrivain de se faire connaître parce que ce n'est pas chose facile que de trouver des arrangements pour se faire publier au Mexique ou dans les centres de la partie sud. Il n'existe qu'un seul écrivain vénézuélien qui jouisse d'une certaine réputation en-dehors de son propre pays—il s'agit de Romulo Gallegos, dont le roman *Doña Barbara* a été traduit en près de vingt langues, et cela en grande partie grâce à un prix que ce roman s'est vu attribuer en Espagne en 1928.

Une solution serait l'établissement d'une maison d'édition "Bolivarienne" unique qui pourrait subvenir aux besoins des marchés de Panama, Vénézuéla, Colombie, Equateur et Pérou. Une chose est certaine, les écrivains ne peuvent continuer à écrire sans éditeurs et maisons d'édition. A vingt ans, tout le monde écrit; mais continuer d'écrire sans être publié est un acte d'héroïsme. La raison principale pour laquelle tant d'écrivains émigrent en Europe ou à New York est le manque d'éditeurs dans les pays "Boliviens".

M. Vargas Llosa, parlant français, se trouve tant soit peu embarrassé de parler de la situation de l'écrivain au Pérou. Le congrès a entendu, le jour précédent, une discussion intéressante au sujet de l'écrivain à l'âge électronique. Les préoccupations des écrivains péruviens sont bien éloignées de ces problèmes. En fait, les leurs sont ceux de l'âge de la pierre. M. Vargas Llosa voudrait essayer de décrire la situation dans laquelle se trouvent les jeunes péruviens qui se sentent une vocation d'écrivain.

La carrière d'écrivain au Pérou est une carrière de frustration. Dans un pays qui a des conditions historiques, sociologiques et économiques telles qu'on les trouve au Pérou, l'importance sociale de la littérature est pratiquement nulle. La moitié de la population ne sait ni lire ni écrire. L'autre moitié vit dans des conditions asphyxiantes en marge de la vie culturelle—ouvriers des bidonvilles, paysans n'ont ni les moyens d'acheter des livres ni niveau scolaire suffisant pour pouvoir se consacrer à la littérature. La minorité qui a bénéficié d'une éducation et à qui le revenu permet d'acheter des livres et de financer une vie culturelle—la classe gouvernante du Pérou—ne s'est jamais intéressée aux choses culturelles, elle est même pleine de méfiance à l'égard de la culture, à l'opposé de ce qui se produit dans la plupart des autres pays latino-américains. Bref, le pays n'a pas de public qui lit, donc pas de maison d'édition; l'écrivain péruvien, par conséquent, est une sorte de phénomène, un personnage pittoresque mais anormal. Les jeunes qui se sentent un besoin d'écrire se voient en face d'une sorte de "machine à dissuader" morale et psychologique.

La plupart des poètes, dramaturges et romanciers péruviens sont des déserteurs, des gens qui ont publié un livre ou deux puis ont abandonné, déserté la vie littéraire. Et pourquoi? Parce que s'ils avaient persévéré, ils seraient devenus des proscrits de la société. Il va de soi que certains ont persévéré. Comment? En s'exilant: ils n'ont pas d'autre défense contre la "machine à dissuader". Il y a plusieurs variétés d'exils dont la plus traditionnelle est celle de se réfugier dans un pays étranger, parfois même un autre pays d'Amérique latine. La mort en exil des deux plus grands auteurs péruviens, El Inca Garcilaso de la Vega et le poète Vallejo est en fait presque symbolique.

Ceci est l'exil physique, mais il existe également un exil spirituel. On se retranche contre l'indifférence ou l'hostilité. Cela est inévitable là où un écrivain n'est pas soutenu par une culture nationale traditionnelle. Les écrivains qui ont besoin de nourritures spirituelles doivent lire des oeuvres étrangères, s'intégrer à des cultures étrangères—anglaise, française, "même américaine". Rejeter une telle intégration peut équivaloir à une sorte de patriotisme, mais cela correspond en même temps à se limiter à une culture étroite et appauvrie.

Un exemple d'exil spirituel au début de ce siècle est celui du poète péruvien José Marie Eguren, qui n'a jamais quitté Lima et qui avait pris comme sujet les gnomes et les fées nordiques, une flore et une faune étrangères au Pérou. Une autre sorte d'exilé, Cesar Moro, qui vécut en France et au Mexique, a choisi d'écrire en français, une langue étrangère—et dans sa poésie ce très grand poète n'a pas mentionné le Pérou une seule fois.

L'écrivain péruvien qui choisit de confronter la réalité chez lui doit vivre dans un état de tension insupportable et court les plus grands risques. Tout d'abord, celui de déserter la littérature. Ensuite, celui de devoir mener une double vie, une vie handicapée par le besoin de gagner sa vie en dehors de la littérature—celle-ci étant au Pérou une fonction non-sociale. Troisièmement, la politique. En Europe, on a souvent demandé à M. Vargas Llosa "pourquoi il existait tellement d'écrivains d'Amérique latine—et particulièrement de péruviens—qui sont engagés politiquement, de façon militante?" La réponse est qu'il est très difficile de se sentir membre d'une telle société. Un écrivain a tendance à se rebeller, à se laisser toucher par un sens de responsabilité politique et à indiquer aux autres hommes leurs responsabilités. Sa propre condition misérable en tant qu'écrivain en fait automatiquement un défenseur de ceux qui se trouvent dans la misère. Cela le pousse à voir que ceux qui tournent le dos à leur responsabilité vis-à-vis de cette misère font précisément partie de la classe gouvernante—qui pourrait acheter des livres mais qui ne le fait pas; qui aurait le pouvoir de faire du Pérou un pays digne mais qui n'en éprouve pas le besoin.

Et ce risque en contient un autre—l'assujétissement de la vocation littéraire à la volonté de changer la situation sociale. Un grand nombre d'écrivains pensent que ceci est une cause juste et honorable mais ceci est également une façon de déserter la littérature et de frustrer l'écrivain en tant que tel.

Bien que tout cela soit vrai, beaucoup d'écrivains péruviens protesteraient probablement s'ils entendaient ce panorama de la vie littéraire au Pérou et déclareraient que l'orateur a brossé un tableau infiniment plus pessimiste qu'il ne l'est véritablement; en effet ils ne sont pas du tout découragés par les conditions existantes. Grâce à eux, M. Vargas Llosa termine sur une note optimiste. La difficulté, le vide, la négligence et les déficiences de cette réalité sont pour ces écrivains un défi et un encouragement à l'action. Ceci est un fait heureux et pousse l'écrivain à poursuivre des buts ambitieux. Et M. Vargas Llosa termine en déclarant qu'en dépit de tout, la situation péruvienne est favorable, car dans l'histoire de la littérature nous avons un grand nombre d'exemples démontrant que dans des sociétés en voie de décomposition sont nées des littératures riches, ambitieuses et complètes.

M. Fuentes, parlant anglais, fait tout d'abord remarquer que le congrès semble discuter pour savoir si l'écrivain est en fait une sorte de dinosaure dont la position, la fonction et l'influence sont vouées à disparaître. En ce qui concerne l'Amérique latine, il est vrai qu'il n'existe aucune technique et que les media de masse constituent un obstacle plutôt qu'une aide à la communication. Il est vrai que dans des pays—et cela est valable pour la plupart des pays d'Amérique latine—où il n'existe ni législature, ni parti politique, ni syndicat d'ouvriers digne de ce nom, où les media de masse se trouvent entre les mains des "marchands les plus catastrophiques que l'on puisse imaginer", c'est à l'écrivain qu'il appartient de dire les choses que l'histoire et les media de masse ne mentionnent pas.

De l'avis de M. Fuentes, ceci représente un défi pour l'écrivain—et pour le langage, son instrument de travail dont on ne saurait exagérer l'importance. Dans son pays, le Mexique, la langue s'est trouvée pour ainsi dire kidnappée par le *statu quo* incarné par le parti paradoxalement intitulé Parti des Institutions révolutionnaires. Il est très courant au Mexique, de trouver un propriétaire parlant de "réforme agraire" un banquier parlant de "révolution prolétarienne", chacun se réfugiant sous la bannière de "la révolution", "la gauche", etc. Ce que l'écrivain peut y faire est problématique; nous savons comment Hitler a accaparé la langue et détruit tous les moyens de communication personnels et sociaux, forçant les écrivains de l'après-guerre à créer une nouvelle langue allemande. Aux Etats-Unis, les agissements de McCarthy ont correspondu en fait principalement à un accaparement du langage, attaquant les institutions au moyen d'adjectifs et d'épithètes.

Il fut un temps où les écrivains mexicains essayèrent de se retirer tranquillement pour cultiver leur jardin. Ils avaient oublié que la structure sociale tout entière était dominée par la puissance pyramidale résultant de la terrible conjonction de l'autocratie aztèque et du jésuitisme espagnol. L'intelligentsia inactive était restée l'unique secteur libéral du Mexique jusqu'à la période récente où les hommes au pouvoir ont exigé d'elle qu'elle rende publiquement hommage aux autorités. Tout d'abord il y eut la campagne publique dirigée contre le livre *Los hijos de Sanchez* (Les enfants de Sanchez), édité d'après des enregistrements réalisés dans les basses couches de la société par l'Américain du nord, Oscar Lewis. Ce livre fut qualifié de pornographique et condamné; la maison d'édition Fonda de Cultura Mexicana, bien connue pour sa politique libérale et créatrice, fut amputée de son directeur, Arnaldo Orfila Raynal, sous le prétexte chauvin qu'il était un Argentin, un étranger. Le livre fut condamné comme étant anti-social parce qu'il critiquait le gouvernement—"crime" dont la punition peut aller jusqu'à 25 ans de prison. Finalement, au printemps 1966, le gouvernement accusa l'Université de Mexico, de tradition libérale (mais dont la liberté académique était limitée), d'encourager des activités culturelles "antinationales"; pour avoir par exemple monté des pièces de Beckett et Ionesco, joué du Alban Berg et du Schoenberg, et avoir lu en public des oeuvres de poètes étrangers "décadants". En résumé, nous nous trouvons là en face d'une véritable corruption du langage qui a réduit la quasi totalité de l'intelligentsia mexicaine à se soumettre au *statu quo.*

M. Fuentes déduit de ces événements qu'en Amérique latine, la fidélité envers sa langue est la seule défense permanente. A cours du congrès on a parlé de l'écrivain "pur" opposé à l'écrivain "engagé", de Mallarmé opposé à Dickens. Il estime que les deux sont les défenseurs de l'écrivain en tant qu'esprit indépendant, qu'il le proclame dans ses livres ou d'une estrade. En Amérique latine, cette distinction n'a aucune signification. M. Fuentes croit qu'un Neruda ou un Borges, qu'un Carpentier ou un Asturias, un Octavio Paz ou un Cortázar, engagé ou non, ont tous contribué à la même défense.

Cependant, l'Amérique latine est soumise à une autre influence encore, un héritage de "schizophrénie historique". Par cela l'orateur veut dire que les différents pays ont été, à l'origine, créés sur la base de promesses utopiques qui ont rapidement été corrompues et reniées par les événements. (Les fondations de Vasco de Quiroga à Michoacán, par exemple, étaient inspirées par Sir Thomas More). La nature épique de l'histoire de notre continent (paradis perdu, noble sauvage, etc), se heurta aux prévisions eschatalogiques, et entre les deux, "notre vie personnelle concrète de tous les jours a pratiquement disparu". Ainsi, une des tâches de l'écrivain d'aujourd hui est de "créer un sens du présent".

Pour terminer, M. Fuentes voudrait souligner qu'en Amérique latine la littérature est "paralysée par le fait que dans la plupart de nos pays, la réalité est plus littéraire que la fiction". Peut-on imaginer des personnages littéraires plus totalement fictifs que les dictateurs Santa Anna, Rosas, Francia, Trujillo, Batista? La chose terrible dans cette vigueur historique est la "chronologie absolument fataliste et déterminée" qu'elle impose. Peut-être l'écrivain d'Amérique latine pourrait-il, grâce à son imagination, remplir la tâche modeste mais importante d'oblitérer cette fatalité en créant une "virtualité simultanée de l'espace".

M. de Campos, parlant anglais, voudrait parler de l'avant-garde de l'Amérique latine, dont il fait partie, de par son mouvement pour une poésie concrète, depuis le début des années cinquante. M. de Campos estime que l'avant-garde, et particulièrement ses relations avec les différents centres d'Amérique latine, n'est pas connue du tout. Au Brésil, par exemple, où l'on parle portugais, il n'existe que très peu de gens qui ont entendu parler d'un écrivain aussi important que Borges, encore moins connaissent Cortázar, et rares sont ceux qui ont entendu le nom de Vicente Huidobro. Lui-même voudrait apprendre à connaître les amis de ses collègues ici-présents.

Au Brésil, les auteurs de poésie concrète ont entrepris des expériences "de manière engagée", à la manière de Mayakovsky et Brecht. Ils croient, selon les termes mêmes de ces derniers, que "sans forme révolutionnaire il n'y a pas d'art révolutionnaire". Engagement moral et innovation technique vont de pair. En même temps, des Brésiliens plus âgés ont incorporé des techniques concrètes dans leurs oeuvres, comme par exemple Bandeira, Drummond de Andrade, Ricardo, Braga, Murilo Mendes et, jusqu'à un certain point, Cabral de Melo Nato. M. de Campos et ses amis ont republié un poème datant de 1870, *O Guesa Errante* de Sousa Andrade, qui rappelle *Canto general* de "notre Neruda," tout particulièrement dans la partie intitulée "O Inferno de Wall Street." Cette redécouverte est, de l'avis de l'orateur, aussi importante que "la redécouverte par T. S. Eliot des poètes métaphysiques anglais". Il s'agit là d'une attaque contre ce méli-mélo de capitalisme, de puritanisme et de progrès qui caractérise l'Amérique du Nord, écrite dans une sorte de vers polyglotte, elliptique, utilisant une technique de montage d'événements politiques, de rapports journalistiques et de références littéraires, qui donne un tableau ironique des débuts de l'Amérique du Nord "moderne".

Les poètes d'Amérique latine, ajoute M. de Campos, doivent tenir compte de la technique, élargir leurs vocabulaires et utiliser de nouvelles formes de communication—le poème-affiche, par exemple. Les vieilles formes livresques ne conviennent plus à la communication à grande échelle.

M. Montes de Oca, s'excusant de son anglais imparfait, est convaincu que les critiques exprimées par les écrivains latino-américains contre leur propre société sont plus efficaces que n'importe quel éloge. Neruda, Vallejo, Octavio Paz et d'autres grands talents ont fait des contributions importantes à la poésie universelle de notre époque. M. Montes de Oca croit en l'avenir d'une littérature latino-américaine.

M. Martínez Moreno dit qu'en Uruguay l'écrivain indépendant est depuis quelque temps un homme qui trouble ceux qui se trouvent au pouvoir parce qu'ils savent qu'il est plus facile de faire pression sur un petit fonctionnaire de parti que sur un artiste. Ceci explique ce que Vargas Llosa appelle leur "traditionnelle méfiance de la culture". Mais il existe un autre problème auquel on a fait allusion, celui des dimensions étroites du marché littéraire, et M. Moreno, en tant qu'écrivain uruguayen, se sent le devoir d'en parler.

L'orateur a souvent parlé de "la fatigue, la tension provoquées par le deuxième métier de l'écrivain créateur". Les media de masse ont créé une apparente similitude entre un écrivain—Graham Greene, par exemple—qui est libre d'écrire comme il le veut, et un autre qui, comme Juan Carlos Onetti, est un fonctionnaire. Les lecteurs achètent les livres sans rien savoir des conditions économiques et culturelles dans lesquelles ils ont été écrits. L'homme qui va au théâtre applique la même échelle de valeur à une pièce d'Arthur Miller qu'à celle d'un dramaturge solitaire de son propre pays, par exemple. Il va de soi que c'est inévitable, et en fait, les écrivains d'Amérique latine ne protestent pas; ils ne veulent pas la pitié, ils veulent qu'on les lise. Mais il est difficile d'imaginer comment redresser cette injustice.

Mme Ocampo, parlant français, voudrait dire un mot au sujet de la situation telle qu'elle se présente en Argentine, et est heureuse de penser que ce qu'elle a à dire est du côté optimiste. Un écrivain pour lequel elle a beaucoup d'admiration, M. Vargas Llosa, a parlé de la situation dramatique des écrivains péruviens. Mme Ocampo ayant consacré sa vie tout entière au monde des écrivains partage ses sentiments. Dans son pays, les livres d'auteurs argentins sont lus plus que jamais. Des jeunes écrivains, qui n'ont pas le nombre de disciples ou de lecteurs d'un Borges ou d'un Cortázar par exemple se tirent très bien d'affaire. Mme Ocampo estime qu'il est juste de mentionner ici la "Fonda nacional de las artes" qui existe en Argentine et qui aide les jeunes écrivains de talent à trouver des éditeurs—en fait, cette organisation aide les peintres également. La Fonda distribue des livres à travers les provinces—non pas avec le vague espoir de leur procurer des lecteurs, mais bien parce que ces lecteurs existent; Mme Ocampo a été impressionnée de voir quels livres sont les plus demandés, qu'il s'agisse de livres étrangers ou d'Amérique latine. Et elle est heureuse de faire partie de l'activité de la Fonda et de pouvoir la mentionner ici.

M. *Balbontin,* parlant anglais, déclare pour commencer que "l'indépendence de l'auteur est un fait que personne n'oserait contester". Ce droit est inaliénable et socialement indispensable. Mais il n'a pas été clairement défini. Les auteurs d'Amérique latine particulièrement, souffrent d'une "forme de coercition" qui a sérieusement limité leur indépendance. Elle provient de l'ignorance qu'Européens et Américains du nord ont de leurs oeuvres et ceci vaut d'ailleurs pour tous les écrivains issus de pays en voie de développement.

L'Amérique latine est un immense continent. Chronologiquement, elle est le troisième territoire dans lequel des formes de gouvernement démocratiques et républicaines furent établies. On y trouve un poète ayant reçu le prix Nobel, feue Gabriela Mistral, du Chili, et au moins quatre prix Nobel potentiels: Neruda, Carpentier, Borges et Asturias. Les niveaux sociaux et scolaires d'Amérique latine sont élevés en de nombreux endroits—bien qu'elle soit la "victime indirecte de la sombre légende qui s'est formée autour de l'Espagne au 16ème siècle". Et pourtant l'Espagne a eu plus de chance que l'Amérique latine, car cette dernière n'est que rarement mentionnée dans les manuels ou dans la presse du monde.

M. Balbontin estime que cette réunion internationale du P.E.N. doit songer au fait que l'indépendance de l'écrivain est en étroite relation avec le degré de connaissance que l'homme a de son monde. La "circulation confidentielle" de la littérature d'Amérique latine existe toujours; des éditions à tirage réduit et, "pour des raisons inconnues", la non-acceptation de l'espagnol parmi les langues officielles du P.E.N. Le Centre du P.E.N. chilien demande au P.E.N. International de donner une conclusion heureuse aux quatre aspirations fondamentales de l'Amérique latine, qui sont:

1. Inclure la littérature espagnole dans les programmes d'études de toutes les universités de pays dans lesquels il existe un centre du P.E.N.

2. Inclure des textes d'Amérique latine dans les programmes d'études des écoles secondaires.

3. Encourager des associations entre des maisons d'éditions d'Amérique latine et des autres continents dans le but de publier des traductions de la littérature latino-américaine classique et moderne.

4. Pour le P.E.N. International, nommer une commission composée d'Américains latins et d'autres chargée de choisir "une collection de base des 100 meilleurs ouvrages de la littérature d'Amérique latine, dont la traduction serait réalisée par des membres du P.E.N. spécialement choisis" que l'on proposerait ensuite à des éditeurs américains, français, anglais et allemands.

Le président demande la permission de répondre à trois constatations de M. Balbontin avant de donner la parole à M. Neruda. Langue: c'est parce que l'anglais et le français sont les seules langues officielles du P.E.N. que les orateurs de cette séance ont été obligés de faire usage "d'un anglais hésitant ou d'un français synthétique". Deuxièmement, Miss Carolyn Kizer, du *U. S. National Endowment for the Arts* a demandé de mentionner qu'un projet de contribuer à la traduction d'environ 100 ouvrages sélectionnés d'Amérique latine en anglais avait déjà été accepté par son président, M. Roger L. Stevens. Le troisième point du président est de suggérer que les propositions de M. Balbontin soient transformées en une motion qui serait présentée au P.E.N., si les auditeurs présents sont d'accord. [Ce qui fut accepté].

M. Neruda parle français. Secondant chaleureusement les propositions de M. Balbontin, il espère qu'une des réalisations de ce congrès— et non seulement de la séance latino-américaine—sera d'intensifier la vie de tous les centres du P.E.N. Nous avons vu à ce congrès la vitalité qui résulte de l'unité de nos divers esprits et expressions; nous avons été témoins d'une grande manifestation de vie créatrice. Pourquoi cet esprit ne serait-il pas stimulé dans chaque pays membre? Nous sommes sûrement tous persuadés que les écrivains devraient s'organiser, et certainement aucun de nous n'est disposé à encourager l'isolement ou la scission entre écrivains.

M. Neruda aimerait suggérer que M. Vargas Llosa—dont il rappelle les remarques intéressantes et pertinentes faites ici-même, et le magistral tableau de la vie péruvienne qu'il a brossé dans son dernier roman— prenne la tête d'un mouvement pour fonder un centre du P.E.N. au Pérou—désir qui a été exprimé à M. Neruda par d'autres écrivains péruviens. Quant à tous les autres centres du P.E.N., il voudrait qu'ils soient composés de vrais écrivains. Ce n'est pas qu'il soit contre les activités sociales dans le sein d'un centre du P.E.N., mais il lui semble que ce qui est important c'est la vie littéraire.

En attendant, le problème crucial en Amérique latine est d'obtenir que l'écrivain soit respecté. Il est affreux de devoir dire que son propre ami intime, le grand poète Vallejo qu'il voyait tous les jours du temps où ils étaient à Paris, est littéralement mort de faim, sans même que sa propre patrie lui ait offert une assistance quelconque. Et après sa mort on lui a fait des funérailles nationales fantastiques. Il y a bien des moyens de faire respecter l'écrivain. Leur illustre amie, Mme Ocampo, a depuis longtemps donné l'exemple avec sa revue, qui est une des grandes manifestations de la culture en Argentine. Dans la patrie de M. Neruda, leur plus grand poète, Gabriela Mistral, qui était née de parents pauvres, était toute sa vie restée fidèle à sa classe sociale sans jamais abandonner une grande dignité personnelle. Elle attribuait plus de valeur à ses poèmes traitant du martyre des pauvres au Chili— et les pauvres sont partout en Amérique latine—qu'à ceux qui avaient le plus de succès auprès des lecteurs.

Les écrivains latino-américains sont magnétisés par deux pôles: la culture universelle et la condition de leur peuple. La question qui se pose à eux est: pour qui est-ce que j'écris? Pour cette minorité qui connaît Mallarmé et Rimbaud, ou pour le peuple de mon continent? Les gens passent leur temps à dire à M. Neruda avec fureur ou approbation: "vous êtes un écrivain engagé!" En effet il est engagé; car il porte sur son dos le fardeau de soixante ou quatre-vingt millions de latino-américains illettrés. Son ambition s'exprime dans les termes de Gabriela Mistral "donner des souliers aux petits enfants dans l'hiver antarctique du Chili".

Ceci est une grande tradition qui remonte à la première grève des ouvriers chiliens en 1848. S'il en parle, c'est parce que presque tous les écrivains chiliens ont hérité de cette tradition. Comme l'ont relevé Fuentes et Vargas Llosa, la littérature ne peut s'abstenir de prendre une position qui tend à doter le monde de justice, de liberté, d'esprit créateur. En offrant de telles oeuvres à leur propre peuple, les écrivains d'Amérique latine les offrent à tous les hommes.

M. Rafael Tasis (du P.E.N. catalan), parlant français de la salle, désire rappeler aux auditeurs que sa ville natale, Barcelone, était la capitale de l'édition en langue espagnole, et que les éditeurs accueillaient les oeuvres latino-américaines avec enthousiasme. Il rend hommage à Mme Ocampo comme étant le plus grand éditeur de littérature moderne en Amérique du Sud et lui rappelle qu'après la guerre civile d'il y a trente ans, des éditeurs espagnols avaient émigré en Amérique latine et avaient fondé des maisons importantes, spécialement au Mexique et en Argentine. En Espagne, les éditeurs sont fiers de cette conséquence de la catastrophe espagnole.

Pour être à même de défendre leur langue et leur culture, il est nécessaire que des maisons d'édition soient établies partout où l'on parle espagnol. Et puisqu'il est difficile à des Chiliens, des Boliviens et des Péruviens d'être publiés chez eux, il faudrait qu'ils puissent l'être dans des pays voisins, partout où se trouvent des éditeurs.

M. Tasis ajoute un mot au sujet de la littérature catalane. Beaucoup de leurs écrivains vivent en exil en Amérique Centrale ou en Amérique du Sud. Lui-même a été publié au Mexique. Comme leurs collègues latino-américains, les Catalans luttent pour défendre leur langue, leur culture et leur littérature. C'est en leur nom qu'il désire appuyer les propositions de M. Balbontin.

Mme Aridjis (parlant anglais au nom de Homero Aridjis), relève que le tirage maximum pour un volume de poésie à Mexico est à peu près 2000 exemplaires, même qu'il soit destiné à toute l'Amérique latine. Il pourrait être plus grand si le système de distribution évoqué par M. Parra n'était pas si défectueux. Au Mexique les critiques ont tendance à juger la poésie en se basant principalement sur leurs sympathies ou antipathies personnelles dans les milieux littéraires. De plus, un poète qui ne parle pas de héros nationaux, et plus spécialement de ceux de l'époque d'avant la conquête, risque d'être stigmatisé comme étant un étranger, un non-patriote. D'autre part, la plupart des écrivains doivent assurer leur pain quotidien en travaillant à autre chose, beaucoup deviennent fonctionnaires, ce qui implique qu'ils doivent faire attention de ne pas offusquer le gouvernement par ce qu'ils écrivent. Le métier d'écrivain au Mexique est une sorte de martyre qui exige un grand courage.

Le Président Miller a appris plusieurs choses au cours de cette séance. Premièrement tout ce qui a été dit ici place le problème de "l'écrivain à l'âge électronique" dans une tout autre perspective, car cela nous rappelle que dans le monde entier on trouve la pauvreté et l'analphabétisme. Deuxièmement, le P.E.N. lui-même se trouve placé devant la tâche de rehausser le prestige de l'écrivain et de l'intellectuel dans les pays où il est si bas. Les écrivains d'Amérique latine eux-mêmes, et les correspondants étrangers dans les pays latino-américains, pourraient faire un commencement en faisant connaître l'admiration pour la littérature moderne latino-américaine qui s'est manifestée à ce congrès même, et dans la presse littéraire d'Europe et d'Amérique du Nord. Les centres du P.E.N. existants pourraient aussi contribuer à faire connaître cet état de choses et, comme l'a suggéré Pablo Neruda, de nouveaux centres du P.E.N. pourraient être fondés en Amérique latine afin d'assurer que là aussi on soit mis au courant. D'autres centres du P.E.N. pourraient trouver des moyens d'éveiller l'attention, et pas seulement à l'égard de la littérature latino-américaine.

M. Portella (représentant l'Agence de nouvelles de Cuba) se lève pour répondre à une question de M. Neruda, qui avait demandé pourquoi Alejo Carpentier, président du P.E.N. cubain, n'était pas présent. M. Portello s'est renseigné et a appris que l'invitation américaine était arrivée trop tard—à quoi l'orateur ajoute qu'il n'est "pas facile" pour les cubains de voyager vers "la civilisation occidentale".*

Le président clôt la séance en faisant remarquer que le résultat principal de cette réunion a été la révélation que l'écrivain latino-américain avait non seulement à lutter contre une situation professionnelle défavorable, mais qu'il se trouvait aussi au sein d'une transformation dynamique, à laquelle il pouvait contribuer au moyen de son travail créateur et par une prise de position critique face à "la réalité dure et cruelle". Déjà rien que le fait qu'ils aient été capables de réunir un groupe aussi important et aussi distingué, est une preuve de l'utilité du P.E.N. international. Il désire exprimer au P.E.N. américain leur reconnaissance aussi bien que la sienne de leur avoir accordé cette possibilité de décrire leur situation devant des écrivains des autres continents.

* M. Carpentier a été invité personnellement le 25 février 1966, et une invitation générale a été adressée au Secrétaire du P.E.N. cubain à la même date. Une seconde lettre a été envoyée au grand écrivain cubain le 28 avril. Toutes ces invitations sont restées sans réponse. En ce qui concerne l'entrée aux Etats-Unis, le chemin avait été préparé depuis longtemps par le P.E.N américain, dont le président avait reçu le 22 juin 1965 une communication du Coordinateur des Affaires cubaines au Département d'Etat disant ". . . Le Département n'a pas d'objection à ce qu'une délégation cubaine prenne part à la conférence de 1966". Des demandes de visas de la part de délégués cubains auraient été traitées de la même manière que les demandes provenant d'autres pays.—NOTE DU RAPPORTEUR.

Séance de Clôture

Samedi, 18 juin

M. Galantière, président du congrès, ouvre la séance en déclarant qu'il n'essaiera pas de résumer une semaine si pleine de variété, de nouveautés et d'incidents. Les thèmes présentés aux délégués ont été discutés avec une chaleur et un sérieux qui semblent confirmer que ces sujets sont bien d'actualité. L'ère électronique ne présente pas de problèmes pour les écrivains de partout, ou du moins pas encore. Le délégué philippin, M. Florentino, rappela aux auditeurs qu'il existe des régions où l'écrivain se trouve séparé de son peuple par le degré d'analphabétisme qui, puisqu'il n'encourage pas la fondation des maisons d'édition, limite sérieusement ses chances de se voir imprimer. Le président Miller fit la même remarque au cours de la brillante séance latino-américaine—rencontre que le Centre américain n'avait pas prévue et dont il est profondément reconnaissant envers les écrivains d'Amérique latine qui l'ont organisée spontanément. Le problème soulevé par M. Florentino et que le président Miller a si bien compris est un problème qui mérite peut-être d'être repris par un autre congrès ou colloque international du P.E.N., dans un proche avenir.

Au cours de ce congrès, des points de vue politiques se sont insinués avec un peu plus d'insistance qu'aux congrès passés. Le gouvernement d'une grande nation s'est vu, malheureusement, attaquer par un interlocuteur peu familier avec les traditions du P.E.N. au cours de la séance sur l'écrivain en tant que personnalité publique. A cette exception près, la discussion du thème se limita à son aspect littéraire et moral et fut remarquable par le respect accordé à une grande diversité d'opinions et de sentiments.

M. Caillois transmet les compliments de M. Maheu, directeur de l'UNESCO aux membres du P.E.N. international et au centre américain, pour le "succès magnifique de ce congrès". Il remercie le Secrétaire général Carver et son Comité de traduction pour avoir recommandé que des oeuvres écrites en certaines langues peu répandues, soient traduites et publiées sous le patronage de l'UNESCO. M. Caillois profite également de l'occasion pour exprimer sa satisfaction à constater l'esprit de coopération qui se développe entre le P.E.N. et COMES (Communauté européenne des écrivains), ce qui est d'un intérêt tout particulier pour l'UNESCO.

Il y a deux ans, au congrès d'Oslo, M. Caillos s'était permis de dire que P.E.N. ne serait complet qu'au jour où les héritiers de Cervantes et Quevedo, et ceux de Tolstoï et Dostoïevsky auraient pris place dans cette association. Il a suivi les efforts du P.E.N. pour amener les Soviets à siéger parmi nous, et il sait que ce n'est pas la faute du P.E.N. si ces espoirs ne sont pas encore réalisés. Il est heureux de rendre hommage à la bonne volonté et à la fermeté avec laquelle Arthur Miller a dirigé les négociations tendant à obtenir un résultat dans ce sens.

La présence de nombreux écrivains en provenance de continents qui jusqu'alors n'avaient été représentés dans les délibérations du P.E.N. que d'une manière inadéquate—l'Amérique latine, l'Asie, l'Afrique— lui a été une grande joie. Il sait bien que cela est dû aux efforts inlassables de Lewis Galantière, et à l'aide qu'il a reçue dans ce but de la part de fondations américaines à l'esprit éclairé. Cet "oecuménisme croissant" du P.E.N. fait très plaisir à l'UNESCO; la réception aux Nations Unies, qui avait été offerte aux délégués par la Mission américaine aussi bien que par le P.E.N. américain, a été la digne consécration et le symbole de cet oecuménisme.

Le congrès a été invité à se pencher sur le thème général "l'écrivain en tant qu'esprit indépendant" et à discuter les facteurs qui semblent aujourd'hui menacer l'indépendance de l'écrivain. L'un d'entre eux est l'affirmation que l'on entend de plus en plus, selon laquelle le fait d'écrire—et peut-être même la presse à imprimer elle-même—ne serait qu'une phase passagère de l'humanité qui devrait bientôt être fermée; qu'il est menacé par le son (radio) et par l'image (photographie), cette dernière dans les hebdomadaires illustrés, les films et à la télévision.

M. Caillois pense que cet argument néglige un besoin qui est plus ancien que l'imprimerie, plus ancien même que l'écriture. C'est le besoin de choisir, dans le flot continu de l'expression humaine, les paroles et les messages qui méritent qu'on se les rappelle, qu'on les utilise à nouveau et qu'on les garde éternellement en circulation. Cette . . . ambition, pourrait-on dire, qui caractérise la poésie, les dictons et les proverbes, même avant que l'homme ne sache écrire, est-ce trop d'espérer que, puisqu'elle a précédé la parole écrite, elle pourrait également survivre à l'écriture. C'est là que M. Caillois entrevoit l'essence même de la raison d'être de l'écrivain; l'essence de l'art des lettres et la démonstration du double sens du mot "lettre", c'est qu'il a le sens de "caractères", que ce soit l'acte de former des lettres ou d'écrire une oeuvre d'art.

A ce congrès, on a également exprimé une sorte de peur de la machine, cette création à laquelle on attribue maintenant les capacités de l'esprit humain et les sensibilités de la personne humaine. Quoique bien des participants à ce congrès aient admis qu'elle était plus grande en Amérique qu'en Europe, M. Caillois a constaté que cette peur s'était manifestée d'une manière encore plus prononcée à un colloque des Rencontres internationales de Genève l'automne dernier. Là elle avait été présentée presque comme mythologique; les orateurs accordaient à la machine toutes sortes de qualités, en commençant par la mémoire et l'intelligence. Comment une machine peut-elle avoir de la mémoire? Est-ce qu'un disque de phonographe a une mémoire? La ressemblance entre la machine et l'homme est que tout deux reçoivent une impression et la conservent, mais pour la première elle est "programmée", et la différence est que c'est l'homme qui la programme. L'homme prend une décision, en-dehors de la machine. Il choisit deux mots et les assemble; pas arbitrairement—ceci la machine peut le faire. Il les assemble de telle manière qu'ils reçoivent une nouvelle *valeur sémantique,* une manière qui prolonge et qui rehausse la signification que chaque mot avait séparément.

Le congrès a parlé d'un troisième sujet, qui paraissait troubler de nombreux participants à la discussion: l'appel à l'aide de l'humanité souffrante, et ses rapports avec l'engagement de l'artiste. On a posé la question: "qu'entendez-vous par "les masses"? Tous les dictionnaires donnent comme définition de "masse": un corps, un poids, une matière inerte. Et en parlant de la société nous devrions donc définir la masse comme étant, dans n'importe quelle société, ce qui agit et a de l'effet en vertu de son poids, et de son poids seulement, et qui, par conséquent, agit comme un frein, ralentissant chaque impulsion, chaque invention, chaque ferment.

Cela n'implique pas que la masse ne se trouve que dans les grands nombres. Elle est présente dans une foule, peut-être même dans une école, une clique, une avant-garde, autour d'une table de café—partout où il y a des préjugés, des partis pris; partout où ces préjugés pourraient paraître hardis ou osés, même s'ils sont le contraire—paralysants comme les règles d'une académie.

Voilà pourquoi l'indépendance est nécessaire à l'écrivain, et pour être indépendant, il doit être libre. Mais la liberté n'existe jamais dans le vide. La liberté de l'écrivain doit marcher de concert avec le libre choix d'une responsabilité. L'histoire fourmille d'exemples d'engagement: Démosthène en est un, Dante également, et aussi Agrippa d'Aubigné, ce poète huguenot des guerres de religion en France. Et quel en est le résultat? En lisant *Les Tragiques* d'Agrippa d'Aubigné, peut nous chaut qu'il ait été contre les catholiques, et qui se soucie de savoir si Dante était un Guelfe ou un Gibelin? Ce qui reste, c'est la beauté de leurs oeuvres, et selon les termes de Valéry, une fois que les choses qu'ils défendaient ont été oubliées, emportées par les flots de l'histoire, il est resté le monument, l'oeuvre est encore là.

Quant aux responsabilités qui devraient être asusmées avant que l'écrivain puisse être libre, M. Caillois place en premier lieu la responsabilité envers sa langue. Bien des écoles contemporaines cherchent à esquiver ces . . . servitudes; cherchent à échapper à la prosodie, à la logique, à la syntaxe, et même au langage articulé! Elles feraient mieux de se rappeler la colombe de Kant qui, trouvant la résistance de l'air difficile à surmonter, désirait voler dans le vide—dans lequel elle serait tombée à terre.

Puis il y a la responsabilité de l'homme vis-à-vis de ses prochains, qui exige de lui qu'il lutte contre ce qu'il y a de permanent en eux, et pour ce qu'il peut attendre de mieux de la plupart d'entre eux. Elargir la gamme de leurs émotions, approfondir leur conscience, leur connaissance d'eux-même, leur appréciation de la beauté des mystères de la vie. En un mot, à quelque domaine que s'adresse l'engagement de l'écrivain, il faut toujours qu'il garde un recul suffisant par rapport aux événements de tous les jours, particulièrement aux événements politiques.

Pour terminer, M. Caillois récite une parabole d'inspiration taoiste, qui raconte l'histoire d'un empereur qui avait décidé de construire un temple tel que le monde n'en avait jamais vu. Un architecte lui construisit ce temple, et l'empereur lui demanda comment il l'avait fait. "D'abord", lui répondit l'architecte, "je me suis rendu seul dans la forêt, et après avoir médité trois jours, j'ai vidé mon esprit de toute pensée de style, de mode, et d'approbation du public. Après trois autres jours, j'ai chassé de mes pensées les préceptes des maîtres, et les exemples historiques qui figurent dans nos manuels. Trois jours encore, et l'opinion de votre Majesté, vos blâmes ou vos louanges m'étaient indifférents, puis vinrent trois jours après lesquels le verdict de la postérité cessa de me concerner, et dans les derniers trois jours, je ne savais

plus ce que c'était qu'un temple; j'eus alors la vision d'un temple parfait, et me sentis libre de le construire".

Voilà, dit M. Caillois, du moins en théorie, une règle suprême, qui
pourra peut-être aider pratiquement quelque écrivain.

M. *Silone* qui lui succède, parle français, et dit qu'il a la tâche agréable d'exprimer, quoique dans une langue qui n'est pas la sienne, et
avec un vocabulaire de politesse mondaine plutôt limité—d'exprimer à
leurs hôtes américains, à David Carver et à Arthur Miller, toute sa
reconnaissance pour le style et la cordialité avec laquelle ils ont tous
été reçus à ce congrès. En y repensant, il a tout lieu d'être content. Il
est particulièrement heureux de rappeler que ce qu'il a dit lui-même
a provoqué des protestations, car s'il y a une chose qu'il déteste avant
tout, c'est la fausse unanimité, l'unanimité forcée, qui est souvent destinée à cacher de vraies divergences. Quant ses amis de la délégation
italienne et lui ont été interviewés il y a quelques jours par la radio
italienne, il s'est efforcé d'insister sur la pleine liberté de parole qui a
caractérisé ce congrès. M. Silone dit: "Ce congrès diffère des autres par
un détail: aucune personnalité politique, aucun ministre de l'éducation,
aucun maire, aucune autorité officielle n'a parlé de cette estrade", et
c'est l'impression la plus frappante qu'il en emporte.

Le Dr. Glanz-Leyeless, parlant anglais au nom du Centre du P.E.N.
yiddish, rappelle aux auditeurs les écrivains de renommée mondiale
qu'a fait naître "cette littérature entourée de dangers, qui chemine sur
une voie bordée de chausse-trapes"—un Shalom Aleichem, un Peretz,
et de nos jours, Isaac Bashevis Singer. Il remercie pour l'hospitalité qui
leur a été accordée, et exprime une reconnaissance spéciale au président
Miller pour avoir, dans son discours d'ouverture, fait allusion aux conditions de la littérature yiddish en Union Soviétique.

M. *Léon Dumas,* de la Guyane française, exprime sa satisfaction
d'avoir pu assister à ce congrès et évoque le nom des deux grands collègues qui ont avec lui fondé l'école poétique connue sous le nom de
Négritude, Aimé Césaire de la Martinique, et le Président Senghor, de la
République du Sénégal. Ils sont tous trois préoccupés de l'indépendance de l'écrivain, thème de ce congrès. Il aimerait dire à Rosamond
Lehmann, à Pearl Buck, à Arthur Miller et à Roger Caillois que leurs
messages lui sont parvenus ainsi qu'à ses amis, et les ont aidés à
remplir leur mission. C'est l'invitation de M. Galantière qui lui a
permis d'assister pour la première fois à un congrès du P.E.N. Il de-
mandera avec insistance, en Afrique aussi bien qu'à Paris, que l'Afrique
marche la main dans la main avec le P.E.N., et les auditeurs décou-
vriront l'année prochaine au congrès d'Abidjan combien le Président

de Côte d'Ivoire, Houphouët Boigny, est désireux que cela soit ainsi.

M. Michal Rusinek (du P.E.N. polonais) parlant français, dit que nous vivons un moment dramatique de l'histoire de l'humanité, un moment si rempli de grandes inventions et exerçant une telle pression, qu'il n'est pas étonnant que l'homme contemporain soit désorienté! Admiration et anxiété caractérisent notre attitude devant le monde qui nous entoure. D'une part nous ne sommes pas assez sûrs de nous, de l'autre nous le sommes trop. Quel peut être le rôle de la littérature sur cette planète agitée? En fait la littérature a dépassé la technique. Elle a découvert le mystère des émotions humaines "tout en continuant à célébrer les lumières du temps passé, de Homère à Mickiewicz, et au delà." Est-il vrai que la littérature soit devenue une source secondaire pour la connaissance humaine? Les observations de M. Rusinek l'ont persuadé du contraire.

Pour terminer, il remercie les hôtes américains et rappelle à tous ceux qui sont présents que si P.E.N. veut dire "poètes, essayistes, nouvellistes", cela veut aussi dire "Paix Entre Nous".

Le Dr. Hoffmeister a un court message à transmettre de la part de son Centre. Depuis six ans ils ont l'habitude, tout en se préparant à participer à un congrès du P.E.N., de compiler une bibliographie des oeuvres écrites dans le pays où le congrès a lieu, traduites en tchéque ou en slovaque et publiées en Tchécoslovaquie. Cette année c'est l'Amérique qui a été à l'honneur, et M. Hoffmeister est particulièrement heureux de transmettre ce message, et d'assurer les membres présents que tous les centres du P.E.N. recevront des exemplaires de cette bibliographie.

M. Galantière prie le Dr. Hoffmeister de transmettre les remerciements du P.E.N. américain au Centre tchécoslovaque pour cette touchante et généreuse marque d'amitié entre communautés littéraires. C'est une véritable surprise, et quand on pense aux préparatifs, à l'exactitude scrupuleuse, à la coopération de tant de personnes qu'une telle entreprise demande, cette surprise nous comble.

Le président Miller se lève pour faire son allocution finale que nous transcrivons à la première personne.

Le président Miller. Je vais vous parler de ce congrès d'une manière plus ou moins impressioniste, et je sais déjà que quand je m'assiérai, je regretterai de ne pas vous avoir dit certaines choses que j'aurai oubliées au moment même. Vous me pardonnerez peut-être de parler mal, mais du fond du coeur.

Je ne voudrais pas oublier de remercier nos interprètes vaillants et précis (applaudissements). Et j'exprime à M. Silone ma gratitude, car son esprit m'a encouragé à ne jamais perdre l'essentiel de vue (applaudissements).

Seul ce qui est déjà mort ne court plus aucun danger. Le P.E.N. international donne des signes de vie nouvelle, par conséquent les dangers augmentent. En écoutant les débats, j'ai pensé à M. U Thant; vous me permettrez de dire ici toute l'admiration que j'ai pour lui. Je veux dire aussi qu'il me semble que l'humanité a encore un très long chemin à parcourir avant qu'elle soit capable de se voir elle-même d'un point de vue réellement humain. Nous savons tous, par exemple, que les Nations Unies sont la plupart du temps paralysées parce que les intérêts des grandes puissances—beaucoup d'entre eux irréconciliables de jour en jour et d'année en année—sont tels, que toute la bonne volonté et toute la sagesse du monde ne servent à rien, et nous sommes là, impuissants, devant une succession de désastres et de catastrophes.

Il n'est pas forcé que ce soit le cas dans le cadre du P.E.N. Nous ne sommes pas ici pour représenter des armées, ou des révolutions, ou des contre-révolutions. Nous sommes ici parce que c'est important pour nous qu'il existe au moins un endroit où l'homme puisse parler avec une voix humaine. Je suis passionné dans mes idées et mes croyances comme le sont presque tous les hommes.

Je ne suit pas d'accord avec au moins les trois quarts de ce qui a été dit ici. Dix fois par jour j'ai eu envie de sauter en l'air et de contrer les arguments que j'entendais. Je l'ai fait de temps en temps, mais toujours dans le profond désir que rien ne se passe ici—rien—qui puisse faire du mal au P.E.N. Par exemple, je ne crois pas que cette estrade est celle d'où nous devons lancer un appel pour réchauffer la guerre froide (applaudissements).

Ceci ne veut en aucun cas dire que je serais partisan d'affaiblir, de délayer la charte du P.E.N. qui nous engage à défendre la liberté d'expression, mais cela implique que je suit opposé à ce qu'on associe notre Charte au renversement d'un gouvernement quelconque. Nous ne sommes pas une organisation politique, mais nous vivons à une époque qui vit sous une malédiction.

Pendant plus de vingt ans nous avons été endoctrinés par une méthode, une seule. C'est la destruction de chacun par l'autre. Le slogan est "nous ou eux", même au moment où la menace d'une destruction universelle qui n'épargnera aucun d'entre nous est suspendue sur nos têtes. Même si c'était la seule chose que P.E.N. arrive à faire, il doit apprendre—et ce sera dur—à chercher au-delà des clichés politiques du moment, les vérités humaines essentielles que ces clichés nous cachent, et qui, dans bien des cas, ont été créés dans ce but.

En tant que simple citoyen, j'ai souvent protesté contre l'injustice, la guerre, et d'autres actes que je considérais comme néfastes au bien-être des peuples. J'ai l'intention de continuer. Ici, au sein du P.E.N., nous devons tous de conserve chercher à mettre l'accent sur ce qui nous est commun, à isoler ce qui nous sépare, à regarder en face ce qui nous sépare et essayer de toutes nos forces d'aplanir nos différends. Il y en a qui ne peuvent être aplanis; reléguons-les au fin fond de nos esprits et occupons-nous de ceux qui peuvent l'être (applaudissements).

Maintenant, je tiens encore à dire quelquechose que j'ai remarqué pendant cette semaine, le rapport qui existe entre être un membre et être un chef. It est évident qu'il n'y a pas de magiciens dans les échelons supérieurs du P.E.N. Moi-même, je suis un président amateur. Je passe le plus clair de mon temps tout seul, à écrire. Je ne tiens absolument pas à devenir un chef de file, un président, ou quoi que ce soit de ce genre. Quand je vois des membres qui se comportent comme s'il y avait des solution gratuites de leurs problèmes, qui allaient leur tomber du ciel, cela me prouve que le P.E.N. international doit être vu dans une tout autre perspective.

Un exemple: mardi, j'ai dîné avec des membres latino-américains, six ou sept d'entre eux, et j'appris que plusieurs ne s'étaient jusqu'ici jamais rencontrés. Nous avons parlé, et parlé, la conversation était en train de devenir intéressante, quand on nous annonça à notre grand étonnement que le restaurant allait fermer—l'heure était tardive. Quelqu'un proposa de continuer le lendemain dans une chambre d'hôtel. Je suggérai aux latino-américains d'utiliser cette salle, et que leur discussion soit enregistrée. Ce qui fut fait, et j'ai appris beaucoup de choses sur leur compte, et il en fut de même entre eux. Rien de plus naturel que, s'étant réunis des quatre coins de leur immense continent pour la première fois, ils aient profité des possibilités que leur offrait le congrès du P.E.N. pour parler sérieusement de leurs problèmes.

C'est le hasard qui leur avait procuré cette occasion, après de longues années d'isolement réciproque.

Et il m'est venu à l'idée que je pourrais vous prier tous—quand vous serez chez vous, chacun dans votre pays—de rester tranquilles un moment et de vous demander: si j'étais président de mon centre du P.E.N., qu'est-ce que je ferais pour mon centre, avec mon centre, dans le sein de mon centre?

Il ressort qu'il y a des problèmes en Amérique latine qui peuvent être résolus sans argent, ou avec très peu. Ces écrivains désirent se revoir. Cela n'est pas ruineux pour un Péruvien de passer une semaine au Vénézuéla, à un Vénézuélien de rencontrer un Péruvien en Argentine. Puis j'ai appris que certains centres ont besoin de livres, de périodiques; eh bien, ce n'est pas un problème insurmontable. Nous avons appris, au P.E.N. à apprécier la valeur des rencontres personnelles; rien que ceci donne déjà au P.E.N. une raison d'être.

Je pense que la chose la plus importante qui soit dans les possibilités du P.E.N., c'est d'ouvrir ses portes aux jeunes. Cela devrait être le point numéro un des programmes d'activité de chaque centre. Si la jeunesse n'est pas représentée parmi vos membres, si P.E.N. n'arrive pas à représenter quelque chose pour les jeunes, il est en route vers la mort, pas vers la vie (applaudissements). Et ce n'est pas à moi de vous dire comment faire cela. Je ne connais pas la Belgique, ni la Bulgarie, ni le Chili. Ceci est votre tâche. Le P.E.N. n'est pas un club de retraités (applaudissements). Vous l'avez constaté vous-mêmes—et je puis le confirmer—que pour les américains, ce congrès a été une bonne chose; cela a attiré sur le P.E.N. l'attention de bien des écrivains américains qui l'ignoraient complètement, ou qui étaient indifférents ou cyniques. Mais cet intérêt réveillé ne durera pas si le P.E.N. américain n'arrive pas à représenter quelque chose pour la jeune génération d'auteurs américains. Et cela se répercutera sur le P.E.N. tout entier, car cela ne sert à rien de prétendre que ce qui se passe dans la littérature américaine n'a aucune influence au-delà de ses frontières.

J'aimerais encore vous dire qu'en ce qui me concerne, j'ai été très heureux d'apprendre que vous avez pour moi des sentiments chaleureux, et je regrette si j'ai parfois été abrupt avec l'un ou l'autre d'entre vous. C'était dans le dessein de faire avancer les choses. Je désire remercier M. Galantière et le juge Isaacs, et tout le groupe du P.E.N. américain qui a fait de ce congrès une chose formidable; et merci encore à tous ceux qui y ont participé (applaudissements).

M. Galantière est heureux de clore la séance comme elle avait débuté. sur une note fraternelle. Il va lire la traduction en anglais d'un message qu'il vient de recevoir de M. Giancarlo Vigorelli à Rome, Secrétaire général de COMES (Communauté des écrivains européens) qui télégraphie:

Aux écrivains du monde entier présents au congrès du P.E.N. à New York, COMES envoie ses meilleurs voeux pour un bon travail et des résultats meilleurs encore, et espère une défense accrue pour les droits et les devoirs, la dignité et la liberté d'expression pour tous les écrivains et toutes leurs oeuvres.

COMES est heureux et fier de notre collaboration. Il est particulièrement satisfait de notre action commune dans l'affaire Sinyavsky. Nous prétendons que cette mission honorable de nos deux secrétaires généraux à Moscou a été, en dépit des résultats négatifs escomptés, ni inutile, ni stérile. Je regrette profondément qu'il ne m'ait pas été possible de participer au congrès, et en mon nom et en celui de M. Giuseppe Ungaretti, président de COMES, je prie le président Miller, les vice-présidents internationaux du P.E.N. et le Secrétaire général Carver, ainsi que toutes les délégations, d'agréer mes salutations personnelles les plus cordiales.

L'ordre du jour étant épuisé, M. Galantière déclare clos le trente-quatrième congrès du P.E.N. international.

Program

XXXIV INTERNATIONAL P.E.N. CONGRESS

June 12–June 18, 1966

NEW YORK CITY

298

P.E.N. AMERICAN CENTER

PRESIDENT: Lewis Galantière

HONORARY SPONSORS

Pearl Buck

Frederick Burkhardt
President, American Council of Learned Societies

Alexander Calder

Aaron Copland

The Honorable Arthur J. Goldberg
Permanent Representative of the United States to the United Nations

Martha Graham

Raymond C. Harwood
President, American Book Publishers Council

Pendleton Herring
President, Social Science Research Council

James M. Hester
President, New York University

Kenneth Holland
President, Institute of International Education

Senator Jacob K. Javits

George F. Kennan

Senator Robert F. Kennedy

The Honorable John V. Lindsay
Mayor of the City of New York

Thomas F. Malone
Chairman, U.S. National Commission for UNESCO

Donald H. McGannon
Chairman, National Book Committee

Ludwig Mies van der Rohe

Henry Allen Moe
President, American Philosophical Society

Allan Nevins

The Honorable Nelson A. Rockefeller
Governor of the State of New York

The Honorable Dean Rusk
Secretary of State

John Steinbeck

The Honorable Roger L. Stevens
Chairman, National Council on the Arts

Rex Stout
President, The Authors League of America

Mark Tobey

Peggy Wood
Honorary Chairman, American National Theatre and Academy

DONORS

The congress was made possible by the sympathetic appreciation of its significance and the indispensable contributions of—

The Ford Foundation	Rockefeller Brothers Fund
The National Council on the Arts	The JDR 3rd Fund

to whom we here express our gratitude.

P.E.N. American Center acknowledges with warm thanks the generous support of—

The Aaron E. Norman Fund	Los Angeles P.E.N. Center
Carl M. Loeb, Rhoades & Co.	The Lucius N. Littauer Foundation
Corning Glass Works Foundation	The New Hope Foundation
The Deerfield Foundation	The Reader's Digest Foundation
Farfield Foundation	The Scherman Foundation
Fribourg Foundation	Mr. John Hay Whitney
The Janeway Foundation	The Xerox Corporation

The American Center expresses to the following its deep appreciation of hospitality, services and material contributions toward the organization of the congress:

The American Academy of Arts and Letters	Book-of-the-Month Club, Inc.
The Asia Foundation	R. R. Bowker Co.
The Asia Society	Harcourt, Brace & World, Inc.
The Institute of International Education	H. Wolff Book Manufacturing Company, Inc., Jesse Mines Press and Frederick W. Schmidt, Inc.
New York University	

The members of P.E.N. American Center are particularly happy to record here the warm support given them by their friends, the publishers named below:

Harcourt, Brace & World, Inc.

Book-of-the-Month Club, Inc.

Doubleday and Company, Inc.

E. P. Dutton and Company, Inc.

McGraw-Hill Book Company

Time Inc.

R. R. Bowker Co.

Harper & Row, Inc.

Grove Press, Inc.

American Heritage Publishing Co., Inc.

Follett Publishing Co.

Houghton Mifflin Co.

William Morrow & Co., Inc.

Charles Scribner's Sons

Viking Press, Inc.

Bantam Books, Inc.

The K. S. Giniger Co., Inc.

Little, Brown & Co.

St. Martin's Press, Inc.

A. S. Barnes & Co., Inc.

Chilton Trade Book Division

Cornell University Press

Dodd, Mead & Co.

Grosset & Dunlap, Inc.

Hastings House, Publishers, Inc.

The John Day Co., Inc.

Las Americas Publishing Co.

The Meredith Press

New American Library of World Literature, Inc.

W. W. Norton & Co., Inc.

Roy Publishers, Inc.

Vanguard Press, Inc.

Twayne Publishers, Inc.

Walker & Co.

Franklin Watts

Atheneum Publishers

Cambridge University Press

Farrar, Straus & Giroux, Inc.

New Directions

Oxford University Press, Inc.

Popular Library, Inc.

Taplinger Publishing Co., Inc.

University of Notre Dame Press

Alfred A. Knopf, Inc.

Pantheon Books

Random House, Inc.

The Writer, Inc.

Hill & Wang, Inc.

Frederick Ungar Publishing Co., Inc.

Yale University Press

Atherton Press

Pergamon Press, Inc.

Cornerstone Library, Inc.

Richard R. Smith Co., Inc.

Wayne State University Press

ORGANIZATION OF THE CONGRESS

CONGRESS HEADQUARTERS

Loeb Student Center
New York University
Washington Square, New York 10012

Arthur Miller, INTERNATIONAL PRESIDENT
David Carver, GENERAL SECRETARY
Lewis Galantière, CHAIRMAN OF THE CONGRESS

CONGRESS STAFF

Eleanor Kask Friede, COORDINATOR
Marion Bieber, DIRECTOR OF ROUND TABLES
Peter Franklin, PRESS OFFICER
Kathie Woods, ASSISTANT TO MR. GALANTIÈRE
Terry Lent, SECRETARY TO MR. GALANTIÈRE

INTERNATIONAL SECRETARIAT

Elizabeth Warner, ASSISTANT TO MR. CARVER
Helen Rogers, SECRETARY TO MR. CARVER

COMMITTEES OF THE CONGRESS

STEERING COMMITTEE

Lewis Galantière, CHAIRMAN

Edward Albee, John Brooks, B. J. Chute, Marchette Chute, William Cole, Leon Edel, John Farrar, Robert Halsband, Julius Isaacs, Elizabeth Janeway, Edgar Johnson, John Leggett, Harding Lemay, Lenore Marshall, Theodore Purdy, Roger H. Smith, Richard Taplinger

THEME COMMITTEE

B. J. Chute, CHAIRMAN

Edward Albee, Leon Edel, Ralph Ellison, John Hersey, Elizabeth Janeway, Lenore Marshall, Elmer Rice, Glenway Wescott

FINANCE COMMITTEE

Theodore M. Purdy, CHAIRMAN

Scott Bartlett, Marshall Best, John Brooks, John Farrar, Kenneth S. Giniger, Robert Halsband, Julius Isaacs, Truman Talley, Richard Taplinger

PUBLICITY COMMITTEE

Richard Taplinger, CHAIRMAN

William Cole, Roger H. Smith

EDITORIAL COMMITTEE

Marchette Chute, Roger H. Smith

CONGRESS EVENTS

Pique-Nique sur l'eau

Poppy Cannon, CHAIRMAN

Assisted by Caroline Kimball, The Jason Wyler Orchestra and entertainers from Hospital Tours, The Wine Institute of California, Restaurant Associates, Inc.

A Day in the Country

Eleanor Rawson, CHAIRMAN

Assisted by hosts of Setauket, Stony Brook and St. James, and the New York State University at Stony Brook

Home Hospitality

Dola de Jong, CHAIRMAN

Exhibits

Robert Halsband, CHAIRMAN

Program

8:30 P.M. **Poetry Reading by Pablo Neruda**
Archibald MacLeish presiding
(*English translations by Ben Belitt and others*)
Sponsored jointly by P.E.N. American Center and The
Poetry Center of the YM-YWHA.

SUNDAY, JUNE 12

10:00 A.M. **Meeting of the International Executive Committee**
Auditorium, Loeb Center

12:30 P.M. **Lunch**—Official delegates
Top-of-the-Park Restaurant, Loeb Center

2:15 P.M. **Executive Meeting resumes**

7:00 P.M. **Pique-nique sur l'eau**
A boat trip around Manhattan Island. Collation and music
on board.

MONDAY, JUNE 13

10:00 A.M. **Inaugural Session**
Auditorium, Loeb Center
Messages of welcome by Lewis Galantière, President, P.E.N.
American Center, Chancellor Russell D. Niles of New York
University, and the Honorable Roger L. Stevens, Chairman,
National Council on the Arts
Address by Arthur Miller, President, International P.E.N.
Address by Saul Bellow: "The Writer as Independent Spirit."

2:30 P.M. **Business Session**
Auditorium, Loeb Center
Members of delegations only

5:00 P.M. **Reception** offered by The American Academy and National
Institute of Arts and Letters.

TUESDAY, JUNE 14

9:30 A.M. **Round Table I**
Auditorium, Loeb Center
The Writer in the Electronic Age
Chairman: Marshall McLuhan, Director of the Center for Culture and Technology, University of Toronto.

12:30 P.M. **Luncheon** tendered by P.E.N. American Center.
The Commons, Loeb Center

2:00 P.M. **Round Table I resumes**
Auditorium, Loeb Center

5:30 P.M. **Reception** tendered jointly by the United States Permanent Representative to the United Nations and the P.E.N. American Center at United Nations Headquarters.

7:30 P.M. **Reception and Supper** offered by 22 members of American P.E.N. in their homes.

WEDNESDAY, JUNE 15

9:30 A.M. **Round Table II**
Gallery, Main Lobby Level
Literature and the Human Sciences on the Nature of Contemporary Man
Chairman: Louis Martin-Chauffier, member of the Académie des Sciences morales et politiques (France)

and simultaneously

9:30 A.M. **Round Table III**
Auditorium, Loeb Center
The Writer as Collaborator in Other Men's Purposes
Chairman: Robert Goffin, member of the Académie Royale de la Langue et de la Littérature Françaises (Belgium)

Afternoon free

7:00 P.M. **Reception and Collation** at The Museum of Modern Art.

THURSDAY, JUNE 16

9:30 A.M. **Round Table II** *(second session)*
Gallery, Main Lobby Level
Literature and the Human Sciences on the Nature of Contemporary Man
Chairman: Louis Martin-Chauffier

and simultaneously

9:30 A.M.   **Round Table III** (*second session*)
             Auditorium, Loeb Center
             The Writer as Collaborator in Other Men's Purposes
             Chairman: Robert Goffin

             Afternoon free

8:30 P.M.   **Performance** of "Annie Get Your Gun" at The New York State
             Theater of Lincoln Center.
             Alternatively, Arthur Miller's "View from the Bridge" at
             the Sheridan Square Playhouse, 77 Seventh Avenue.

FRIDAY, JUNE 17

9:30 A.M.   **Round Table IV**
             Auditorium, Loeb Center
             The Writer as Public Figure
             Chairman: Douglas Young, Professor in the University of
             St. Andrews (Scotland)

2:00 P.M.   **Round Table IV resumes**
             Auditorium, Loeb Center

7:00 P.M.   **Reception and Dinner** in honor of the guest delegations offered
             by the members of the American Center. Grand Ballroom,
             The Plaza Hotel, Fifth Avenue at 59th Street.

SATURDAY, JUNE 18

10:00 A.M.   **Closing Session**
             Auditorium, Loeb Center

SUNDAY, JUNE 19

10:30 A.M.   **A Day in the Country**
             P.E.N. members and friends in three small neighboring com-
             munities of Long Island—Stony Brook, Setauket and St.
             James—and the staff of the State University at Stony Brook
             invite the delegates to their homes for lunch and lawn
             parties.

Guests, Delegates, Observers

P. E. N. GUESTS OF HONOR

Matej Bor, *President of the Bled Congress, 1965*
David Carver, *General Secretary, International P.E.N.*
Franz Theodor Csokor, *President, Austrian P.E.N. Center*
Yves Gandon, *President, French P.E.N. Center*
Robert Goffin, *International Vice-President*
Gyula Illyés, *Hungarian P.E.N. Center*
Anoma Kanie, *Ivory Coast P.E.N. Center*
Rosamond Lehmann, *President, English P.E.N. Center*
Mira Mihelić, *Vice-President of the Bled Congress, 1965*
Arthur Miller, *International President*
Victoria Ocampo, *International Vice-President*
Elmer Rice, *International Vice-President*
Ignazio Silone, *International Vice-President*
Sophia Wadia, *Founder, All-India P.E.N. Center*

INVITED PARTICIPANTS

Joseph W. Abruquah, *Ghana*
Saul Bellow, *United States*
Jean Bloch-Michel, *France*
Roger Caillois, *France*
Léon Damas, *French Guiana*
Haroldo de Campos, *Brazil*
Alberto S. Florentino, *Philippines*
Carlos Fuentes, *Mexico*
R. Buckminster Fuller, *United States*
Alberto Girri, *Argentina*
John Hearne, *Jamaica*
Ismaïl Hussein, *Malaysia*
Chang Nancy Ing, *National Republic of China (Taiwan)*
Cheik Hamidou Kané, *Senegal*

P. Lal, *India*
Melvin Lasky, *England*
Juan Liscano, *Venezuela*
Horia Lovinescu, *Roumania*
Louis Martin-Chauffier, *France*
Marshall McLuhan, *Canada*
Czeslaw Milosz, *United States*
Marco Antonio Montes de Oca, *Mexico*
Carlos Martínez Moreno, *Uruguay*
H. A. Murena, *Argentina*
Maurice Nadeau, *France*
Pablo Neruda, *Chile*
James Ngugi, *Kenya*
Kathleen C. Nott, *England*
Gabriel Okara, *Nigeria*

Juan Carlos Onetti, *Uruguay*

Masaru Otake, *Japan*

Nicanor Parra, *Chile*

Ramon Parres, *Mexico*

A. K. Ramanujan, *India*

Emir Rodriguez Monegal, *Uruguay*

J. Guimaraes Rosa, *Brazil*

Ernesto Sábato, *Argentina*

Ediriweera Sarachchandra, *Ceylon*

Sulaksana Sivaraksa, *Thailand*

Roger L. Stevens, *United States*

Mario Vargas Llosa, *Peru*

Sandor Weöres, *Hungary*

Okogbule Wonodi, *Nigeria*

Douglas Young, *Scotland*

Yu Hsu, *Hong Kong*

REPRESENTING UNESCO

Roger Caillois, *Director of the Literature Section,* UNESCO
Rosamond Gilder, *President, International Theatre Institute*
Paul Tabori, *International Film Center*

DELEGATES AND OBSERVERS

Afghanistan
Saduddin Shpoon, *observer*

Argentina—Argentine P.E.N. Center
Alicia Jurado, *official delegate*
Victoria Ocampo, *official delegate, guest of honor*
H. A. Murena, *guest*
Ernesto Sábato, *guest*
Alberto Girri, *guest*

Australia—Melbourne P.E.N. Center
Hesba F. Brinsmead, *official delegate*
Frank A. Doczy, *official delegate*
Elizabeth D. Clancy
Henrietta Drake-Brockman
Gerald Glaskin

Australia—Sydney P.E.N. Center
Maysie C. Greig, *official delegate*

Austria—Austrian P.E.N. Center
Siegfried Freiberg, *official delegate*
Hilde Spiel, *official delegate*
Friedrich Bergammer
Franz Theodor Csokor, *guest of honor*
Martha Hofmann
Ernst Waldinger
Friderike M. Zweig

Belgium—Belgian P.E.N. Center
(French expression)
Mme. Louis Dubrau, *official delegate*
Carlos de Radzitzky, *official delegate*
Andrée De Croix
Robert Goffin, *guest of honor*
Fernand Jacquet
Edmond Kinds
Guy C. Van Valle

Belgium—Belgian P.E.N. Center
(Flemish expression)
Willem Roggeman, *official delegate*

Brazil—Rio de Janeiro P.E.N. Center
Faustino Nascimento, *official delegate*
Haroldo de Campos, *guest*
J. Guimaraes Rosa, *guest*
Leonard Anthony Casso, *observer*

Bulgaria—Bulgarian P.E.N. Center
Anna Kamenova, *official delegate*
Leda Mileva, *official delegate*

Canada—Canadian P.E.N. Center
Lawrence Lande, *official delegate*
Katherine Roy, *official delegate*
Robert Charbonneau
Clayton Gray
Jean-Jacques Lefebvre
Fernand Ouellette
Gilbert Picard
Jean-Guy Pilon
Pierre Villon

Marshall McLuhan, *guest*

Ceylon—Ceylon P.E.N. Center
Ediriweera Sarachchandra, *official delegate, guest*
Ariyasena J. Gunawardana

Chile—Chilean P.E.N. Center
Virginia Cox Balmaceda, *official delegate*
Maria Elvira Piwonka, *official delegate*
Manuel Balbontin

Pablo Neruda, *guest*
Nicanor Parra, *guest*

China—Hong Kong P.E.N. Center
M. William Hsu, *official delegate*
Winston W. Lo, *official delegate*
Virginia C. T. Chau
Yau-woon Ma
Larry N. Shyu

Yu Hsu, *guest*
Benedict C. Wong, *observer*

DELEGATES AND OBSERVERS (CONTINUED)

China (National Republic of)—Taipei
P.E.N. Center
Jan-tze Shieh, *official delegate*
Hsu-pai Tseng, *official delegate*
Stanway Cheng
Chang Nancy Ing, *guest*
Hua-ling (Leslie) Nieh
Lan Wang

Wai-lim Yip, *observer*

Czechoslovakia—Czechoslovak P.E.N.
Center
Adolf Hoffmeister, *official delegate*

England—English P.E.N. Center
Philip A. Hope-Wallace, *official delegate*
Mary Treadgold, *official delegate*
Boyd Alexander
Geoffrey Bainbridge
Kate Barlay
Gaston Bart-Williams
Alvin Bennett
Theodore Besterman
Vera Blackwell
Ivy Crowther
Heather Dickson-Wright
Peter Elstob
Dorothy Fellows
Anthony L. Glyn
Celia Goller
Hugh Harris
Mary Harvey
Margery Hinds
James A. Joyce
Fredoon Kabraji
Leopold Labedz
Robert Lantz
Egon Larsen
Rosamond Lehmann, *guest of honor*
Edward Lucie-Smith
Mercedes I. Mackay
Doreen Marston
M. Hughes Miller
Katharine Morris
Reginald Nettell
James Ngugi, *guest*
Kathleen C. Nott, *guest*
Theodora Olembert
Sydney Primost
Josephine Pullein-Thompson
Shirland Quin
Celia Ramsey
Rona Randall
Alastair Reid

Helen Rosenau
Annie E. Salmon
Renée Shann
Joan Murray Simpson
Robin Skelton
Ruth Speirs
Paul Tabori
Arthur B. Thompson
Grace E. Thompson
Emma Tollemache
Alfred H. Unger
Wilhelm Unger
Peter Vansittart
Marjorie Watts
Francis Ferenc Weiss
Herbert Ziman

Melvin Lasky, *guest*

Estonia—Estonian P.E.N. Center
Ants Oras, *official delegate*
Aleksis Rannit, *official delegate*
Harri Asi
Aleksander Aspel
Salme Ekbaum
Henno Jänes
Hanno Kompus
Viktor Koressaar
Asta Linnolt
Karl Rumor
Edgar V. Saks
Victor Terras
Arved Viirlaid

France—French P.E.N. Center
Jean de Beer, *official delegate*
Jean Follain, *official delegate*
Claire Sainte-Soline, *official delegate* of
the Maison Internationale
Anne Auger
Elisabeth Renée Barbier
Henri-Jean Barraud
Pierre Béarn
Roger Belluc
Jean Bloch-Michel, *guest*
Roger Paul Boiry
Ginette Bonvalet
Marthe Brodmann
Roger Caillois, *guest*
Georges Michel Charaire
Ladislas Dormandi
Pierre Duret
Mme. Jean Durtal
Regina Fransès
Yves Gandon, *guest of honor*

DELEGATES AND OBSERVERS (CONTINUED)

France—French P.E.N. Center
(*continued*)
Henri Gardet
Caroline Glyn
Anne Guillaumet
Ionel Jianou
Suzanne Lion
Paulette Loewel
Anne Marie Lunière
Louis Martin-Chauffier, *guest*
Gerda Montier-Caspary
Maurice Nadeau, *guest*
Paul Nöel
Emmanuel Roblès
Sandor Torday

French Guiana
Léon Damas, *guest*

Germany—P.E.N. Center East and West
Wieland Herzfelde, *official delegate*
Heinz Kamnitzer, *official delegate*
Wilhelm Girnus
Günther Weisenborn

Germany—Federal Republic P.E.N.
Center
Hermann Kesten, *official delegate*
Dolf Sternberger, *official delegate*
Hilde Domin
Ingeborg Alice Drewitz
Gottfried Fischer
Adolf Frisé
Emil Gumbel
Geno Hartlaub
Janheinz Jahn
Ernst Johann
Rudolf Krämer-Badoni
Ernst Heinrich Kreuder
Horst Friedrich Krüger
Kurt W. Marek
Hans Sahl
Rosemarie Schöffler
Wolf Jobst Siedler
Werner E. Stichnote

Germany—German-Writers-Abroad
P.E.N. Center
Egon Larsen, *official delegate*
Gabriele Tergit-Reifenberg, *official delegate*
Arthur Apfel
Moritz Goldstein
Kurt Grossman
Hans Habe

David Luschnat
Paul Nettl
Karl O. Paetel
Arno Reinfrank
Hans Sahl
Kurt Stein
Alfred H. Unger
Ernst Waldinger

Ghana
Joseph W. Abruquah, *guest*

Greece—Greek P.E.N. Center
John P. Coutsoheras, *official delegate*

Holland—Dutch P.E.N. Center
Simon Koster, *official delegate*
A. den Doolaard
Fem Rutke

Hungary—Hungarian P.E.N. Center
Iván Boldizsár, *official delegate*
Gyula Illyés, *official delegate, guest of honor*
Amy Weöres
Sandor Weöres

Iceland—Iceland P.E.N. Center
Kristjan Karlsson, *official delegate*
Matthias Johannessen

India—All-India P.E.N. Center
Leela Harishwar Dayal, *official delegate*
Mansukhlal Jhaveri, *official delegate*
Zeenuth Futehally
K. Bhaskra Rao
Soma Vira
Sophia Wadia, *guest of honor*
K. B. Vaid

Jyotirmoy Datta, *observer*
Balwant Gargi, *guest*
P. Lal, *guest*
A. K. Ramanujan, *guest*

Indonesia—Indonesian P.E.N. Center
Sutan Takdir Alisjahbana

W. S. Rendra, *observer*
Subagio Sastrowardojo, *observer*

Iran
F. M. Esfandiary, *observer*

DELEGATES AND OBSERVERS (CONTINUED)

Ireland—Belfast P.E.N. Center
Judith B. Rosenfield, *official delegate*
Rachel B. Rosenfield, *official delegate*

Ireland—Dublin P.E.N. Center
Charles E. Kelly, *official delegate*
Arthur Rae, *official delegate*
Hubert M. Butler
Edward J. Carroll
Austin Clarke
Hilda D. Lamb
Petronella E. O'Flanagan
James J. Scott
Patrick G. Spillane

Israel—Israeli P.E.N. Center
Simon Halkin, *official delegate*
Yehuda Yaari, *official delegate*
Haim Brandwein
Gabriel Preil

Italy—Italian P.E.N. Center
Paolo Milano, *official delegate*
Umberto Morra di Lavriano, *official delegate*
Antonio Barolini
Mauro Calamandrei
Glauco Cambon
Piero Chiara
Goffredo Parise
P. M. Pasinetti
Ignazio Silone, *guest of honor*
Ugo Stille

Ivory Coast—Ivory Coast P.E.N. Center
Christophe Assamoi, *official delegate*
Anoma Kanie, *guest of honor*
Amon Daby

Jamaica—Jamaica P.E.N. Center
Martin William Blake, *official delegate*

John Hearne, *guest*

Japan—Japan P.E.N. Center
Sei Ito, *official delegate*
Nobuyuki Tateno, *official delegate*
Yoko Matsuoka
Masuru Otake

Takako Uchino, *observer*

Kenya
James Ngugi, *guest*

Korea—Korean P.E.N. Center
Chang Ho Choi, *official delegate*
Yong Ho Kim, *official delegate*
Bum Suck Cha
Byung Hwa Cho
Kyung Hee Cho
Sook Hi Chun
Tou-Shik Kang
Won Ko, *guest*
Hwa Sung Park
Moon Chun Ro

Young-ha Choo, *observer*

Latvia—Latvian P.E.N. Center
Helmars Rudzitis, *official delegate*
Gunars Salins, *official delegate*

Ilze Skipsna, *observer*

Malaysia
Ismaïl Hussein, *guest*

Mexico
Homero Aridjis, *observer*
Carlos Fuentes, *guest*
M. A. Montes de Oca, *guest*
Ramon Parres, *guest*

New Zealand—New Zealand P.E.N. Center
Malcolm John Mason, *official delegate*

Nigeria
Gabriel Okara, *guest*
Okogbule Wonodi, *guest*

Norway—Norwegian P.E.N. Center
Karna Dannevig, *official delegate*

Pakistan—East Pakistan P.E.N. Center
Yusuf Jamal Husain

Noon Meem Rashed, *observer*

Peru
Mario Vargas Llosa, *guest*

DELEGATES AND OBSERVERS (CONTINUED)

Philippine Republic—Philippine P.E.N. Center
Alberto S. Florentino, *official delegate, guest*
F. Sionil Jose, *official delegate*
Josefina Constantino
Amante Paredes

Poland—Polish P.E.N. Center
Julian Przybos, *official delegate*
Michal Rusinek, *official delegate*
Leopold Tyrmand
Maria Waserman-Wislowska

Roumania—Roumanian P.E.N. Center
Alexandru Balaci, *official delegate*
Horia Lovinescu, *official delegate*
Mihail Petroveanu
Zaharia Stancu
Romulus Vulpescu

Scotland—Scottish P.E.N. Center
Lavinia Derwent, *official delegate*
Alistair Mair, *official delegate*
Andrew S. Cairncross
May C. Jenkins
Ruth Ratcliff
Douglas Young, *guest*

Senegal—Senegal P.E.N. Center
Ousmane Socé Diop

Cheik Hamidou Kané, *guest*

Spain—Catalan P.E.N. Center
J. M. Batista i Roca, *official delegate*
Rafael Tasis, *official delegate*

Sweden—Swedish P.E.N. Center
Sven A. Delblanc, *official delegate*
Tore O. Tallroth, *official delegate*
Ingrid H. Arvidsson
Per Olov Enquist

Switzerland—Basel P.E.N. Center
Gertrud Isolani, *official delegate*
Ursula von Wiese, *official delegate*

Switzerland—Geneva P.E.N. Center
Claude Arsac, *official delegate*
Jacques Fiechter, *official delegate*

France Igly

Thailand—Thai P.E.N. Center
Sulaksana Sivaraksa, *official delegate, guest*

Trinidad—Wilfred Cartey, *observer*

Uruguay—Uruguayan P.E.N. Center
Carlos Martinez Moreno, *guest*
Juan Carlos Onetti, *guest*
Emir Rodriguez Monegal, *guest*

Venezuela
Juan Liscano, *guest*

Vietnam (South)—Vietnam P.E.N. Center
Pham Viet Tuyen, *official delegate*
Nghiem Xuan Viet, *official delegate*

Virgin Islands
Tram Combs, *guest*

Writers-in-Exile P.E.N. Center (American branch)
Algirdas Landsbergis, *official delegate*
Dragomir Nenoff, *official delegate*
Mikhail K. Argus
István Csicsery-Rónay
Boris Filipoff
Tibor Florian
Emery E. George
Gyula Gömbös
Roman B. Goul
George Ivask
Leslie Konnyu
Hryhory Kostiuk
Imre Kovacs
Gregory Kozak
Wadym Lesytch-Kirshak
Pawel Mayewski
Czeslaw Milosz, *guest*
Aleksis Rannit
Leonid Rzhevsky
Vladimir Samarin
Stasys Santvaras
Henryk Szancer
Imre Szekely-Molnar
Ostap Tarnawsky
Valery Tarsis (London branch)
Zoya Yurieff

DELEGATES AND OBSERVERS (CONTINUED)

Yiddish P.E.N. Center

Leib Feinberg, *official delegate*
Aaron Glanz-Leyeless, *official delegate*
Samson Apter
Ephraim Auerbach
Rachmil Bryks
Benjamin Demblin
Chaim Fox
Israel Knox
Samuel Margoshes
Wolf Pasmanik
Melech Ravitch
Elias Schulman
Boruch Shefner
Morris Steingart

Yugoslavia—Ljubljana P.E.N. Center

Matej Bor, *official delegate, guest of honor*
Mira Mihelić, *official delegate, guest of honor*
Bogdan Pogačnik

Yugoslavia—Skopje P.E.N. Center

Tome Momirovski, *official delegate*

Yugoslavia—Zagreb P.E.N. Center

Jure Kastelan, *official delegate*
Svetozar Petrović, *official delegate*
Darko Suvin

United States—P.E.N. American Center

Leon Edel, *official delegate*
Julius Isaacs, *official delegate*
David Abrahamsen
Renata Adler
Edward Albee
Ruth Aley
Julia C. Altrocchi
Cleveland Amory
Charles Angoff
Ruth Nanda Anshen
Emanie Arling
Ernest B. Ashton
Ralph Backlund
Anna Balakian
Nona Balakian
Ian Ballantine
Antonio Barolini
Richard W. Baron
Donald Barthelme
W. Scott Bartlett
Harry Behn
Sally Belfrage

Daniel Bell
Saul Bellow, *guest*
Simon Michael Bessie
Marshall A. Best
Ann Birstein
Robert Bly
James Boatwright
Carl Bode
Arna Bontemps
Philip Booth
Warren E. Bower
Faubion Bowers
Micheline L. Braun
George Britt
John Brooks
Francis Brown
Pearl Buck
Peter Burchard
Edward L. Burlingame
Ben Lucien Burman
Hallie Southgate Burnett
Melville Cane
Poppy Cannon
Ernestine Gilbreth Carey
John Cheever
B. J. Chute
Marchette Chute
Robert M. Coates
Carolyn Coggins
Morton N. Cohen
Elizabeth Boatwright Coker
William Cole
Saul Colin
Stefan Congrat-Butlar
Marc Connelly
Margaret Cousins
Norman Cousins
Malcolm Cowley
Nona Coxhead
Jean Dalrymple
Anita Daniel
Guy Daniels
Peter Davison
Storm De Hirsch
Dola de Jong
David Dempsey
Babette Deutsch
Edward L. Doctorow
Maurice Dolbier
Roger B. Dooley
Barrows Dunham
Ralph Ellison
Monroe Engel
Kurt Enoch
Eleanor Estes

DELEGATES AND OBSERVERS (CONTINUED)

United States—P.E.N. American Center
(continued)
Nancy W. Faber
Ladislas Farago
Peter Farb
Walter Farley
John Farrar
Edward Field
Harold Flender
James Thomas Flexner
Charles B. Flood
Helene Fraenkel
Frederick Franck
Gerold Frank
Anne Fremantle
Frances Frenaye
Erik J. Friis
Lewis Galantière
Rosamond Gilder
Kenneth S. Giniger
Mirra Ginsburg
Rochelle Girson
Bernard Glemser
Virginia Kirkus Glick
Julian Gloag
Alexander Gode-von Aesch
Jean Gould
William Goyen
Antoni Gronowicz
Gerald J. Gross
Hans Habe
James B. Hall
Robert Halsband
Margaret Halsey
Zoltan Haraszti
Alan Harrington
H. R. Hays
Anthony Hecht
August Heckscher
Laura Z. Hobson
Edward Newman Horn
Nancy Lenkeith Horneffer
Fannie Hurst
Moritz Jagendorf
Elizabeth Janeway
Alexander Janta
Peter S. Jennison
Edgar Johnson
William Jovanovich
Bel Kaufman
Alfred Kazin
Donald Keene
Frances Keene
Mary Kennedy
Claire Kenneth

Hermann Kesten
John Oliver Killens
Robert H. Kimber
Hanna Kister
Carolyn Kizer
Rita Halle Kleeman
John Knowles
Jerzy N. Kosinski
Frederick Laing
Felicia Lamport
Richmond Lattimore
Henry Goddard Leach
John Leggett
Harding Lemay
Emil Lengyel
William E. Leuchtenburg
Louis P. Lochner
Harold Loeb
Stefan Lorant
Robert Lowell
Robie Macauley
Elliott B. Macrae
Nora Magid
Tom Mahoney
William Maier
Irving Malin
Alida Malkus
Saul Maloff
Frederick Manfred
Marya Mannes
Kurt W. Marek
James Marshall
Lenore G. Marshall
Madeline Mason
James R. McConkey
Kenneth McCormick
Elizabeth Heppner McIntosh
Joost A. M. Meerloo
Daniel Melcher
Arthur Miller, *guest of honor*
Edwin Haviland Miller
John L. Mish
Ann Moray
Hans J. Morgenthau
Ivan Morris
Frederic Morton
Stanley Moss
Donald Myrus
Victor S. Navasky
Edna Deu Pree Nelson
Anaïs Nin
Joseph North
Sidney Offit
Irene Patai
Hertha Pauli

DELEGATES AND OBSERVERS (CONTINUED)

United States—P.E.N. American Center
(continued)
Catherine Owens Peare
Kathrin Perutz
Virgilia Peterson
Kenneth Pitchford
Bentz Plagemann
Richard R. Plant
Jenö Platthy
Norman Podhoretz
Thomas Clark Pollock
Arabel J. Porter
Margaret Leech Pulitzer
Theodore M. Purdy
Aleksis Rannit
Eleanor S. Rawson
George Reavey
Franklin D. Reeve
Claire R. Reis
Elmer Rice, *guest of honor*
M. L. Rosenthal
Ishbel Ross
Blair Rouse
E. N. Sargent
Kyrill Schabert
Franz Schoenberner
Wilfrid Sheed
Vifvan Shellabarger
William L. Shirer
Evelyn Shrifte
John Simon
Isaac Bashevis Singer
Chard Powers Smith
Datus C. Smith, Jr.
Roger H. Smith
Eugenie Soderberg
Theodore H. Solotaroff
Peter Sourian
Donald E. Stanford
John Steinbeck
Ruth Stephan
A. M. Sullivan
Truman M. Talley
Richard Taplinger
Arthur Thornhill, Jr.
Newton F. Tolman

Willard R. Trask
Barbara W. Tuchman
John R. Tunis
Tomi Ungerer
Jean Starr Untermeyer
John Updike
Lilla Van Saher
Louise Varèse
Elizabeth Gray Vining
Richard Walsh, Jr.
Lynd Ward
May McNeer Ward
Franklin Watts
Helen Hoke Watts
Theodore Weiss
René Wellek
Anna Mary Wells
Erik Wensberg
Lael Tucker Wertenbaker
Glenway Wescott
Victor Weybright
Elie Wiesel
Kenneth Wilson
Thaddeus A. Wittlin
Peggy Wood
Martin Yoseloff
Friderike M. Zweig

Bonnie R. Crown, *guest*
Paul Engle, *guest*
R. Buckminster Fuller, *guest*
Adrian Larkin, *guest*
Nan Martin, *guest*
Roger L. Stevens, *guest*

Wilfred Cartey, *observer*
Ernest Howell, *observer*
Bogdan Raditsa, *observer*
Piroska Szenes, *observer*
Martha Wadsworth, *observer*

United States—Los Angeles P.E.N. Center
Louis Mertins, *official delegate*
Oliver Carlson
Mildred McNeilly

LIST OF SPEAKERS

Abrahamsen, David
Abruquah, Joseph W.
Alisjahbana, Sutan Takdir
Aridjis, Homero
Arsac, Claude (Mme.)

Balaci, Alexandru
Balbontin, Manuel
Barraud, Henri-Jean
Bell, Daniel
Bellow, Saul
Blackwell, Vera
Bloch-Michel, Jean
Boldizsár, Iván
Bor, Matej

Callois, Roger
Cartey, Wilfred
Charaire, Georges Michel
Chiara, Piero
Choi, Chang Ho
Chute, Marchette
Combs, Tram
Coutsoheras, John P.
Csokor, Franz Theodor

Damas, Léon
Datta, Jyotirmoy
De Campos, Haroldo
den Doolaard, A.
Doczy, Frank A.
Domin, Hilde
Drake-Brockman, Henrietta
Drewitz, Ingeborg A.
Durtal, Jean (Mme.)

Edel, Leon
Ellison, Ralph

Fiechter, Jacques

Florentino, Alberto S.
Follain, Jean
Fuentes, Carlos
Fuller, R. Buckminster

Galantière, Lewis
Gandon, Yves
George, Emery
Girnus, Wilhelm
Glanz-Leyeless, Aaron
Goffin, Robert

Herzfelde, Wieland
Hoffmeister, Adolf
Hope-Wallace, Philip A.

Illyés, Gyula
Ito, Sei

Janeway, Elizabeth
Jhaveri, Mansukhlal
Johnson, Edgar
Jovanovich, William

Kamenova, Anna
Kamnitzer, Heinz
Kané, Cheik Hamidou
Kanie, Anoma
Keene, Donald
Konnyu, Leslie
Ko, Won
Krämer-Badoni, Rudolf

Lande, Lawrence
Lasky, Melvin
Lattimore, Richmond
Lehmann, Rosamond
Liscano, Juan
Lovinescu, Horia
Lucie-Smith, Edward

Martin-Chauffier, Louis
McLuhan, Marshall
Meerloo, Joost A. M.
Milano, Paolo
Mileva, Leda
Miller, Arthur
Milosz, Czeslaw
Momirovski, Tome
Montes de Oca, M. A.
Martínez Moreno, Carlos

Nadeau, Maurice
Nenoff, Dragomir
Neruda, Pablo
Ngugi, James
Niles, Russell D.
Nott, Kathleen C.

Ocampo, Victoria

Parra, Nicanor
Parres, Ramon
Petroveanu, Mihail
Podhoretz, Norman
Pogačnik, Bogdan

Quin, Shirland

Rannit, Aleksis

Rice, Elmer
Rodriguez Monegal, Emir
Rosenau, Helen
Rusinek, Michal

Sainte-Soline, Claire
Silone, Ignazio
Simon, John
Sivaraksa, Sulaksana
Spiel, Hilde
Sternberger, Dolf
Stevens, Roger L.
Suvin, Darko

Tabori, Paul
Tarsis, Valery
Tasis, Rafael
Tseng, Hsu-pai
Tuchman, Barbara
Tuyen, Pham Viet

Vargas Llosa, Mario
Viet, Nghiem Xuan

Wadia, Sophia
Weöres, Sandor

Young, Douglas